Interaction in Families

Wiley Series in Psychology for Practicing Clinicians

IRVING B. WEINER, Editor

MISHLER and WAXLER · Interaction in Families
An Experimental Study of Family
Processes and Schizophrenia

INTERACTION IN FAMILIES

An Experimental Study of Family
Processes and Schizophrenia

ELLIOT G. MISHLER AND NANCY E. WAXLER

Department of Psychiatry
Harvard Medical School

John Wiley & Sons, Inc.
New York · London · Sydney · Toronto

Series Preface

This series of books in psychology is addressed to clinicians and their students in psychology, psychiatry, and social work. Its scope should also prove pertinent to pediatricians, neurologists, and other clinicians who deal with problems of human behavior. Although many aspects of psychology are relevant to the activities and interests of the practicing clinician, the series concentrates on the three core clinical areas of psychopathology, personality assessment, and psychotherapy.

Each of these clinical areas can be discussed in terms of theoretical foundations that identify directions for further development, empirical data that summarize current knowledge, and practical applications that guide the clinician in his work with patients. The books in this series present scholarly integrations of such theoretical, empirical, and practical approaches to clinical concerns. Some pursue the implications of research findings for the validity of alternative theoretical frameworks or for the utility of various modes of clinical practice; others consider the implications of certain conceptual models for lines of research or for the elaboration of clinical methods; and others encompass a wide range of theoretical, research, and practical issues as they pertain to a specific psychological disturbance, assessment technique, or treatment modality.

Irving B. Weiner

Preface

The study of clinical problems and the use of patients and their families as study populations relies heavily for its success on the support and cooperation of the clinical staff and administration of the treatment institution. This study was carried out at the Massachusetts Mental Health Center. Here we were able to draw on a strong research tradition, which had been established over many years and reflected the work of previous investigators and administrators, and on the continuation and strong affirmation of this tradition by the present Superintendent and Professor of Psychiatry, Jack R. Ewalt, M.D. Although they were aware that participation in the study by patients and their families might create additional difficulties in their work, the psychiatric residents and chiefs of service with direct responsibilities for clinical management and treatment were helpful and responsive to research needs.

The study owes most to the patients and their families and to the families who composed the control sample. All cooperated as unpaid volunteers in a study that demanded time and involvement and which they knew would be of no immediate benefit to themselves; their motivation for participating was that they were being asked to contribute to the scientific study of families. In the nature of things we cannot acknowledge them individually but it seemed to us that on the whole they found the study interesting and learned that scientific research on human behavior could be a nonthreatening experience. We hope that, if they read this book they will feel that their participation was worthwhile.

The day-to-day work was carried out by a group of research assistants who worked with us for periods of time that varied from one summer to three years. Individually and collectively, they were alert, sensitive, intelligent, and responsible. The high quality of the coding and the clarity of the code manual reflect, in particular, the seriousness with which they approached their work. Working as research assistants with responsibility for a multitude of administrative and statistical tasks, library research, and copy editing were Elaine Faunce, Polly French, Sharon Garner, Nancy

Howell Lee, Carol Petkun, Priscilla Roth and Donna Shockley. The Misses Faunce and French also formed part of the coding group along with Dorothy Altman, Paulette Cooper, Miriam Dushman, Karen Fernekees, Carol Grossnickel, Ann-Marie Keenan, Julie Kemble-Smith, Julie Moody, Sally Schreiber, and Theresa Spiegel. Betty Grossman, Elaine Faunce, Ann-Marie Keenan, and Harriet Robinson did the arduous typing that was required to produce typescripts for analysis from the tape recordings of family discussions.

Many colleagues and investigators engaged in the study of families and concerned with the relationship of family processes to schizophrenia have been generous with their comments at various points in the development of the study; our debt to them has been recorded in other contexts. During the data collection phase, Alan Blum contributed to the study through his interest and criticism. We are particularly grateful to Kenneth Kenniston, Loren Mosher, and David Reiss for their careful reading of the manuscript and for their critical and constructive comments. The manuscript was also given a close and critical reading by the members of a research seminar directed by one of the authors, with the result that some parts of the presentation and argument were modified; we are grateful for the help and interest of Yasin Balbaky, Bertram Cohler, Roderick Durkin, Arthur Elstein, Harold Garfinkel, Henry Grunebaum, Robert Liberman, Donald Light, David Pavy, Eng-Seong Tan, and Josef Vana.

In addition to the support of the Massachusetts Department of Mental Health and the Department of Psychiatry of the Harvard Medical School, the research reported here was funded by research grant MH-06276 from the National Institute of Mental Health for the period 1962–1966 and grant GS-1225 from the National Science Foundation for 1966–1968. We are pleased to acknowledge their support, for without it this study could not have been undertaken.

The development of suitable and efficient computer programs for processing and analyzing the mass of quantitative data generated in the study was accomplished by Robert Greenes and Stephen Lorch. Their interest in and concern with the substantive issues of the research resulted in our being able to carry out a complex and difficult operation with a minimum of problems.

Finally, Mrs. Alice D. Beal has served as secretary to the project for almost its entire history and has been responsible for typing applications, grant proposals, revision after revision of coding instructions, and revision after revision of the present volume. Her care and efficiency made our task an easier one.

Elliot G. Mishler
Nancy E. Waxler

Boston, Massachusetts
July 18, 1968

Contents

Interaction in Families

Chapter 1

Background and Aims
of the Study

This volume reports a study of families and schizophrenia. Inasmuch as an extensive literature on this topic exists, this introductory chapter outlines several distinctive features of the present study in order to alert the reader to what he may expect to find and what he may not expect to find in the chapters that follow.

A central aim of the research is to determine whether there are distinctive patterns of interaction in families of schizophrenic patients. Our interest in this problem derived in part from the observations of clinical investigators who had in recent years become particularly concerned with the social, interpersonal, and interactional features of their patients' families. Based on these observations, a number of theories have been proposed regarding the possible etiological role of the family in the development of schizophrenia. (For a critical review of some of the leading formulations, see Mishler and Waxler, 1965). Although these theories differ from each other in many important respects, the qualities of family style and structure to which each refers are observable behaviors. For example, pathological functioning in the child has been hypothesized as related to whether the affect and content of parental communication are congruent with each other; to whether parental roles are complementary and consistent with cultural prescriptions; and to the degree of flexibility or rigidity of family patterns of role relationships.

Our objective has been the application of more systematic methods of research to the study of these aspects of families and their relationship to schizophrenia. This has involved the use of a control group research design and of concepts and methods derived from the experimental study of small groups for the observation, measurement, and analysis of family interaction. An experimental procedure was used to generate discussions among family members, a number of code-category systems were developed to systematically code these samples of interaction, and the resultant scores were then subjected to intensive statistical analysis. The complex research design included controls for the premorbid social adjustment and sex of patients; in addition to normal control families, the well siblings of patients served as an intrafamilial control, we followed a strategy for data analysis that permits us to specify whether differences found in interaction patterns are general characteristics of the family or are specific to particular members or to situations in which the patient is present.

The book is relatively long on methods and empirical findings and relatively short on theoretical speculation and on implications for clinical practice. This reverses the balance usually found in discussions of schizophrenic patients and their families; it is a literature that tends to be disproportionately speculative and assertive. Our emphasis on methods and data actually reflects the high value we place on theory. We view theory building as a serious activity. It requires rigor and precision in thought, and detailed attention to questions of the logical consistency of propositions and the empirical relevance of concepts. These requirements have been neglected in favor of quick-and-easy generalizations that frequently have turned out, on closer inspection and continued study, to be empty and unproductive. Often one "grand idea" becomes the fountainhead to which all observations and empirical findings are related while discrepant data is dismissed or overlooked; or observations from a few limited and special cases are used as the basis for universal propositions with little concern for differences between the original situation and the situations to which the propositions are applied. Our own approach to problems of theorizing emphasizes: (a) a distinction among different levels of analysis, particularly between the properties of individuals and groups; (b) a specification of legitimate relationships between conceptual and empirical units of analysis; (c) a clarification of assumptions that enter into alternative conceptual models for interpreting empirical findings.

This approach has an unfortunate consequence. The reality of family relationships and of their significance for personality development is too complex to be captured by a single metaphor or aphorism. To the extent that our data begin to approximate this reality and our concepts to correspond with the data, the results resist summary in neat and simple phrases. Throughout the book we have attempted, nevertheless, to summarize major trends in the findings and at the same time to make explicit the relationships of findings both to the methods that generate them and to the alternative models of interpretation. Because appreciation of the meaning and significance of the findings depends on an understanding of the methods and the interpretive assumptions, both of which are described in detail in succeeding chapters, no attempt will be made in this introduction to summarize findings. Rather, we intend only to outline important stages and general characteristics of the study.

Several distinct yet interdependent stages may be distinguished in an empirical study. There is, first, the stage of gathering observations; second, the processing of observations, that is, reducing and assembling them in a form that allows for the next step of statistical analysis; and, finally, the interpretation of the analyses. In brief, a study is a series of transformations of information—from observations into data, and from data into findings. At each of these points we make use of techniques and methods developed in other areas of sociological and social psychological research, particularly in the experimental study of small groups and the study of social organization. Among the outstanding methods adapted from the small group research laboratory for investigation of interaction in families are the following: control group research designs, standard stimulus situations, direct observation and tape recording of discussions, the application of standard code-category systems to score interaction, and the statistical analysis of quantified data. From research on social organizations we borrowed and adapted a multilevel approach to the analysis of data on families as social systems. Each of these aspects of the study will be discussed briefly.

The need for control group designs is self-evident; without suitable controls there is no way to determine the degree of specificity of the findings, that is, whether the behaviors found in families of schizophrenic patients are to be found only in such families. The choice of control variables, however, depends on the investigator's judgment of the theoretical importance of different variables and on practical considerations. From our examination of current theory and research in this area we believed it necessary to observe both parents in interaction with their child and that the following comparisons would be critical: between the families of male and female patients; between the families of patients with different levels of premorbid social adjustment as well as between patient and normal families; and between family interaction in the presence of the patient and one of his/her well siblings. For these reasons the research design included controls for the sex of the patient, premorbid social adjustment, normality, and sibling status. Applying these and several other criteria reduced markedly the number of families that were eligible for inclusion in the study. For example, of all schizophrenic patients admitted to the source hospital during the sampling period, only 13% met all criteria of eligibility. Much of this reduction was a function of three criteria of eligibility: residence in the Boston area, parents alive and living together, and presence in the household of a well sibling of the same sex and approximate age as the patient.

The method of revealed differences was used as the basic experimental procedure. In our work parents and one of their children—on one occasion, the patient, and on a second occasion, his/her sibling—responded individually and privately to a questionnaire that resembles a standard value or attitude inventory; the family members then came together and were asked to discuss a number of items on which they privately disagreed, and to try to reach agreement on an answer that would best represent the family decision. This procedure, first introduced by Strodtbeck (1951), has been used in a number of family studies. Two of its advantages are the use of standard items that may be constructed and tailored to the purposes of the study and the fact that family members find it both reasonable and nonthreatening to talk together about their opinions. In our study the experimenter first reported back to the family an item on which they disagreed and then left them alone for their discussion. We were particularly concerned about problems of experimenter effects on family behavior. The two experimenters, each of whom conducted experimental sessions for each of the types of family included in the study, took pains to follow a standard set of instructions so as to minimize the impact of differential relationships with and associated differential expectancies of families. The family discussions were tape recorded and transcribed; these typescripts are the basic protocols used for analysis and interpretation. This report is based on a total of 88 experimental sessions contributed by 49 families.

A number of different code-category systems were used, some of them adapted from other research and others developed specifically for this study. They vary in the number and complexity of categories from dichotomous presence-absence codes for such behavioral events as interruptions and fragments to multicategory codes requiring, as in the Acknowledgment code, complex inferences as to the intent of the previous speaker. Each category set is exhaustive and each was applied independently to the discussion typescripts. This approach is indebted to procedures developed in research on interaction in small experimental groups. It is essentially an exercise in the microanalysis of behavior. The codes were each indepenently applied to the smallest meaningful segments into which the discussion could be divided; we refer to this as a unitizing procedure. We hoped through the use of several different codes to secure information on a number of different dimensions of interaction rather than to be restricted to the study of one or two.

Problems of coding reliability were matters of high priority. All coders received intensive training and codes were used only when high levels of reliability were achieved; usually we required a minimum level of 85% agreement between coders on act-by-act comparisons. (cf. Waxler and Mishler, 1966). The coding process was monitored and a one-ninth sample of typescripts was selected randomly for a continuing check to ensure that reliabilities did not drop below acceptable levels.

From the coded typescripts a large number of scores were computed, each code providing the basis for several of these "interaction indices." These scores, for individual family members and for the families as collective social units, were then subjected to a number of statistical analyses. The aim was to locate those variables on which there were statistically significant differences among the three types of family in the study— normal controls, and the families of patients with either good or poor histories of premorbid social adjustment. The results of these analyses are presented in the five core chapters of this report.

Interaction indices were grouped into five domains or variable clusters, each representing an important aspect of group functioning. These are: expressiveness, strategies of attention control and person control, disruptions in communication style, and responsiveness. In each area significant and theoretically meaningful differences were found between the different types of family. A multilevel approach to data analysis was developed that allowed us to pinpoint whether families differed from each other as collective units or whether differences were specific to individual members or to one or the other experimental situation.

As we noted earlier, the findings are too complex and detailed for brief summary. However, two general points may be made. First, the rationale underlying the choice of particular control variables—sex, premorbidity, and a sibling of the patient—receives considerable support. Each of these variables makes a difference and the detailed comparisons they permit result in a more differentiated and precise description of family functioning than would otherwise be possible. Second, significant differences between normal parents and the parents of schizophrenic patients occur even more frequently than between the patients themselves and either their well siblings or the normal controls. This is strong evidence in favor of the assumption that has stimulated and guided much of the recent work on schizophrenia: that the family should be the focus of theoretical and empirical attention.

Like most investigators in this area, we had hoped to learn something about the etiological significance for schizophrenia of certain types of family behavior. Many of our codes, and the interaction indices derived from them, had their source in theories that were explicitly etiological (cf. Mishler and Waxler, 1965). Like other investigators, however, we were faced with the problem that this was an ex post facto study, that is, the observations were collected after the event in question had already occurred. Schizophrenia in a son or daughter had already been recognized, diagnosed, and had provided the grounds for hospitalization before the family entered our laboratory. How to account for an event on the basis of information ascertained only after the event is a problem that is common to all ex post facto investigations. The solution requires a determination of the time order of variables, but this solution can only be approximated by the introduction of statistical controls for selected variables. In the end the attribution of causality in such studies rests on a variety of inferences and assumptions about both independent and dependent variables.

We have argued that there are three alternative frameworks of interpretation, each equally plausible on a priori grounds, that could be used to make theoretical sense of the empirical findings. The three frameworks or models, differing from each other in the assumed time-ordering of variables, are as follows: (a) an etiological framework in which it is assumed that the behaviors found to be characteristic of families of patients existed before the illness and were implicated in its development; (b) an adaptive or responsive framework in which the patterns of behavior are viewed as having developed along with or in response to problems posed by illness in a member of the family; (c) a situational interpretation in which behavior is viewed as reflecting the fact of hospitalization with consequent differences in expectations and orientations to the experiment.

For findings within each cluster of variables we asked whether a reasonable and meaningful interpretation could be provided by each of the alternative frameworks. In assessing their relative credibility we found that at times we relied on certain specific patterns of findings and at other times we introduced into the line of argument assumptions about the stability of certain variables, about normal family life, and about the nature of schizophrenia. We concluded that a definitive choice among the three explanations could not be made on the basis of one ex post facto study. However, we believe that the clarification of the problem that resulted from our analysis will help to focus future research more sharply on this question of alternative explanations; as this happens there will be a reduction in the amount of ambiguity and uncertainty that exists.

Finally, two other considerations entered into and strongly affected our work. First, we have been as much concerned with normality as with pathology. Normal families were included in the research design not only as research controls, but also because of a specific interest in patterns of normal family functioning. Although there is as yet little observational data on the families of schizophrenics, there is even less on the families of normals. A number of assumptions about normal family life and the behavior of normal parents form the background against which theories have developed about pathogenic family processes. On the whole, there is a lack of empirical data to support these assumptions. Before pathogenesis is ascribed to behaviors observed in the families of patients under clinical treatment, it is necessary to determine the range of normal variation. For these reasons, although the primary focus of our analysis and interpretation has been on schizophrenia and its relationship to specific patterns of family interaction, we have also been concerned with the implications of the findings for our understanding of normal families and normal personality development.

Second, in seeing our work as a bridge between clinical-psychiatric and academic social science traditions, we hoped there would be some traffic in both directions. In describing some of the general features of the study we have been emphasizing one direction, that is, the application of methods and concepts drawn from sociology and social psychology to the study of a clinical problem. It is probably evident from this, and it will become increasingly clear in succeeding chapters, that our research is not an example of a clinical investigation. Among other important features of the study that distinguish it from the latter are the facts that neither the patients nor their families were in a treatment relationship with the researchers, the research was defined for them as independent of their clinical association with the hospital, families were assured that the research data would remain confidential and would not become part of the clinical record, and no evaluation was made of modes of intervention or treatment. In this connection one further point should be noted. The sources of all the data in the study are observations and recordings of family interaction; no information is used that derives from interviews, psychological tests, or psychiatric assessments of family functioning. In part because the study more closely resembles the model of traditional theoretical research on small groups than it does the clinical model, we believe that its findings may be as relevant to research and theory on general problems of social relationships as to the understanding of schizophrenia. The methods developed in the study, particularly some of the new codes and the strategy for data analysis, are widely applicable. Perhaps more importantly, some of the variables that proved of particular interest and appear to be critical to the functioning of relatively permanent groups such as families have heretofore been neglected in traditional small group studies. We would hope that on the basis of the present work dimensions of interaction like responsiveness and disruptions in communication style will receive more general attention.

The aim of this brief introduction has been to acquaint the reader with our general orientation to research on families and schizophrenia. A detailed presentation of our methods and findings is found in succeeding chapters, and in the concluding chapter we discuss some of the implications of the study for theory and future research.

Chapter 2

Research Design, Sample, and Experimental Procedure

Research Design

The design of the study (see Table 2.1) includes families who have schizophrenic children with either good or poor premorbid social adjustment histories as well as families who have normal children. These families are further subdivided depending on whether the children participating are male or female. A distinctive intrafamilial control is the inclusion of a well sibling of the same sex as the schizophrenic patient in a separate experimental session with the parents. Parents of normal children also participate twice, once with one child and again with another child of the same sex. Thus in each experimental session three family members —father, mother and one child—are present and are asked to interact with each other on a set of discussion items; usually, the second experimental session has been scheduled one week after the first. The tape recordings of these three-person discussions provide the basic data for the study.

The need for control groups in studies of clinical populations is obvious, yet the lack of adequate control group designs has been an equally obvious failing in psychiatric research. (See, for example, the Group for Advancement of Psychiatry (G.A.P.) Report, "Some Observations on Controls in Psychiatric Research," 1959). Ideally, control groups should be chosen to

Table 2.1   Research Design: Numbers of Experimental Sessions for Each
Family Type [a]

Type of Family	Family of Male Child Session		Family of Female Child Session	
	Patient	Sibling	Patient	Sibling
Schizophrenic				
Good premorbid history	5	5	7	3
Poor premorbid history	15	14	3	3
	Sibling	Sibling	Sibling	Sibling
Normal	10	10	6	7
				N = 88

[a] The total of 88 sessions consists of 39 families who participated twice and 10 families who participated once. Among the nine schizophrenic families that participated once seven came only with the patient child and two only with the well child. One normal family session was unusable because of a recording failure.

maximize the precision with which the extent and limits of generalizations drawn from findings can be stated. In the study of family interaction processes and schizophrenia we would want, again ideally, to be able to state which factors are present in all families having schizophrenic children but only in such families. Clearly a design of the necessary strength and elegance is not possible at this time; we do not know the critical variables nor would it be possible within the scope of a single study to control all that we now believe to be important. Therefore we have used a strategy in designing the study that allows us to make comparisons with previous empirical work and at the same time adds independent variables that appear, in the clinical and theoretical literature, to be especially significant. Another equally important consideration in the selection of control variables is the availability of control groups and the ease with which control variables can be measured prior to the family's participation. With these considerations in mind, four control variables were selected: presence of schizophrenia in the family, type of illness history, sex of the patient, and presence of a well sibling of the same sex and close in age to the patient.

Clinical observations and theory, until very recently, did not make explicit distinctions between families of schizophrenic patients and families of patients with other psychiatric illness. Also, largely because of the context in which they gather information, clinicians have not usually observed normal families, or those in which no child has been diagnosed as having psychiatric symptoms. Reading the clinical descriptions of interaction patterns in schizophrenic families, families of neurotic patients, families of children with school phobias, and families of children with reading disabilities leaves us with two important questions. First, are we seeing a "family with a disturbed child" syndrome, not specific to schizophrenia, and is the family pattern therefore a response to disturbance rather than a cause of disturbance? Second, are the patterns described found in normal families just as often and with the same intensity as in the schizophrenic families? To answer these questions would naturally require different control groups: a set of families with a nonschizophrenic but disturbed child as well as a set of normal families.

Recent empirical studies have used different families as controls to help answer these and related questions. A comparison of families of schizophrenic children and families of delinquents is directed to the first question: are different disturbance patterns in the children, in this instance withdrawal and acting out, related to different styles of interaction in families? (Stabenau et al, 1965). Morris and Wynne (1965) have compared families of schizophrenic children with families of neurotic children to investigate a similar question. The effect of relatively long periods of disturbance and hospitalization is controlled by Farina (1960) in his selection of parents of tuberculosis patients to compare with parents of schizophrenics. This latter control group sheds light on the question whether the patterns of interaction observed after the fact of the illness are general responses to any chronic illness or are related to the specific illness pattern.

In this study we have selected the "normal family" as the control that is particularly relevant to the most general question in which we are interested: Are families of schizophrenic children different from families in which children have no illness of any kind? If no important differences are found in this comparison, we would argue that, for the purpose of understanding schizophrenia, further comparisons with families representing other illnesses, such as neuroses, would not be useful. If, on the other hand, we began with another illness type as a control for schizophrenia, and found differences between families of that type and the schizophrenic families, a comparison with a set of normal families would still be required in order to understand the significance of these differences for schizophrenia. In an ideal design we would include as controls both normal families and "other illness" families. Our resources did not permit so complete a design but we have attempted to approximate it by including two types of schizophrenia along with the normal controls.

Within the sample of schizophrenic families we have introduced a second control variable—the premorbid adjustment of the schizophrenic patient. In the contemporary literature on schizophrenia there is general agreement that schizophrenia is not a unitary illness; whether it is composed of a subset of single and clearly defined illnesses or is a "continuum of social behavior encompassing a wide range of malignancy" along which any one schizophrenic patient can be placed, is not so clear (Kantor and Herron, 1966, p. 12). But strong empirical evidence from psychological, sociological, and biological research requires that we subdivide the set of schizophrenic patients along one or another of the sorting dimensions. Differences in prognosis, responses to treatment, personality characteristics, physical performance, and physiological response have been shown between schizophrenic patients classified as acute versus chronic; as process versus reactive; paranoid versus nonparanoid; hebephrenic versus catatonic versus paranoid; and as having good versus poor premorbid social adjustments. (See Maher, 1966, for a review and discussion of these findings.)

Theories of family interaction and schizophrenia have also pointed to possible differences between the family patterns of certain subtypes of schizophrenia. Wynne and Singer (1963) suggest that amorphous and fragmented family communication styles may be related to the process and reactive dimension in schizophrenia. Further, empirical evidence from Farina's study (1960) has shown that the parents of schizophrenic sons with good premorbid histories and those with poor premorbid histories differ in their use of selected interaction patterns. This evidence, along with the availability of a sample of young, newly admitted patients having schizophrenia, and an easily applied instrument for rating their case histories (Phillips, 1953), led us to select the dimension of premorbid social history for subdividing the schizophrenic sample. There is probably considerable overlap in the classification of schizophrenic patients along the social adjustment dimension, the acute-chronic dimension, and the reactive-process dimension. (See Kantor and Herron, 1966, for a discussion of this problem.)

The third independent variable in the study design is the sex of the children who participate in the experiment. There has been insufficient attention paid in research and theorizing to whether the patient is male or female, and to the relationship between the sex of the child and family patterns. Lidz and his co-workers (1965) are a notable exception; they predict different parental roles in families producing schizophrenia in male children from those producing schizophrenia in female children. The importance of the schizophrenic patient's sex in explaining family differences cannot be determined from earlier studies of family interaction since at first only male patients were used (Farina, 1960). More recently, although both male and female patients and their families have been included, with one exception (Cheek, 1964b) the male and female families have not been separately analyzed (Stabenau et al., 1965; Sheldon Singer, 1965). If, however, as many of the psychologically and sociologically oriented clinicians and theorists assume, schizophrenia is in some sense an identity problem, and further, if the process of identity development is different for male and female children, then we would expect that the parental role models for male and female children would be different. The control for the sex of the child in the design of the study allows for this comparison.

The final control variable in the design is the presence of a well child of the same sex from the same family. Many clinicians, after having observed parents and their schizophrenic patient child, have asked why the other children in the family are not also schizophrenic if the parental influence is so harmful. This question is dealt with by some theorists who suggest that family contexts differ for each of the children in the schizophrenic families. Wynne and Singer (1963) propose that changes through time in the parental relationships and the family situation provide differing contexts for children born at different times; one of the children may be "selected" as the deviant child to help resolve the family conflict. Thus we may expect that parents will have a different relationship with their schizophrenic child than with a normal child in the family. Several experimental investigations include the well siblings of patients. However, comparisons of differential parental behavior toward the sick and well child are hampered either because the design did not match the sex of patient and sibling (Sheldon Singer, 1965), or both children were present in the same interaction situation with their parents (Stabenau et al., 1965 and Reiss, 1967).

We have chosen in the design of this study to look at the parents' interaction with two of their children of the same sex. This design allows us to control for the fact that parents are expected to and probably do behave differently with their male and female children; if we find differences in family interaction with the schizophrenic and nonschizophrenic child these differences can be attributed to the fact of the illness and not to the sex of the child. Furthermore, by examining the interaction of parents with two normal children, in the control group of normal families, we can provide some evidence for differences in family interaction that one would "normally" expect between parents and two children of the same sex in the same family.

This combination of control variables in the experimental design allows us to shed light on a wide range of interesting questions about family structure and interaction patterns in schizophrenic and normal families. We can specify in great detail the differences in structure between schizophrenic and normal families after the schizophrenia has been formally diagnosed. At this point in time we can also describe differences and similarities between two types of schizophrenic families, those in which the patient's illness is recently developed and those in which the illness has developed over a long period of time. Each of these comparisons can be made for families with male and female children. We can also answer the question, Do parents interact differently with their schizophrenic and well children? Finally, we can compare the role and interaction style of the schizophrenic child himself with his own well sibling.

This is perhaps the point at which to introduce an important question of interpretation that will occupy us at some length in our discussion of findings. The problem arises from the ex post facto nature of the study. Regardless of the findings, whether we find similarities or differences between control and patient families, we cannot provide a definitive answer to the etiological question, Is the behavior of the parents a cause of the child's illness? This is a limitation of all ex post facto and cross-sectional designs and not a fault that is peculiar to our study. Our approach to the problem is to make explicit three alternative frameworks of interpretation: etiological, responsive, and situational. These differ in the assumed time ordering of relationships between family interaction patterns and the child's illness. We then examine the patterns of findings in each of the variable domains in order to determine the relative degree of credibility of each interpretation and to clarify the additional assumptions that must be introduced. This procedure, of contrasting the three types of explanations with each other, is followed in our discussions of findings and a more specific statement of how they differ from each other will be found there.

These limitations, however, need not reflect on the utility of the data collected. It seems reasonable to assume that if there are no differences in styles and patterns of interaction between families with schizophrenic children, after the fact of the illness, and normal families, then moving to a longitudinal study, in which the above etiological questions should legitimately be asked, would not be especially useful. For this reason the cross-sectional design appears to be the strategic first step.

Criteria or Classifying Families on the Independent Variables

Every family or patient must be classified along each of the independent variables before its participation in the study. In this section we outline briefly the specific measurement techniques; detailed measures are provided in Appendix A.

Presence of Schizophrenia

Records of all admissions to one hospital were examined for all patients who had been given any one or a combination of the following diagnoses (see the section on sampling for details of this technique):

1. Schizophrenic reaction
2. Schizophrenia: hebrephrenic
3. Schizophrenia: catatonic
4. Schizophrenia: paranoid
5. Schizophrenia: acute undifferentiated
6. Schizophrenia: chronic undifferentiated
7. Schizophrenia: schizo-affective

No patients with diagnoses of borderline schizophrenia were included in the sample; no patients with organic brain damage, alcoholism, addiction, or mental retardation as secondary diagnoses were included. Finally, no patient whose diagnosis changed to a nonschizophrenic one at the time of discharge was included in the sample.

These diagnoses were taken from the formal anamnesis written by the psychiatrist in charge of each patient and thus were based on an average of three to five weeks of intensive interviewing with the patient with the addition of psychological tests and laboratory tests. The patients thus selected are our index cases and together with their parents and well siblings constitute our sample of "families with schizophrenic children."

Criteria for Normality

Normal children were selected from church and school lists. The formal criterion for normality in the child is the absence of a history of hospitalization for schizophrenia or any other psychiatric illness. No direct measures of this criterion were made; instead, we assumed that neither child had been diagnosed as schizophrenic and hospitalized for this illness.[1] Informal evidence based on observations of and conversations with the families suggests that our assumption was a correct one; for example, most normal families seemed, from their questions and comments, to be generally uninformed about the local psychiatric hospitals. The normal children selected in this way are our control cases and, together with their siblings and parents, comprise the sample of "normal families."

Premorbid Social Adjustment of the Schizophrenic patient

Each patient diagnosed as having schizophrenia and otherwise meeting the sampling criteria was classified as having had a Good or a Poor premorbid social adjustment by his score on the Phillips Scale of Premorbid Adjustment (Phillips, 1953). This instrument is composed of five subscales each

[1] A subsample of five of these normal families was used in another study (Reiss, 1967) in which a question about previous hospitalization for treatment of a psychiatric illness was asked of each family member. None of the 20 family members reported having had treatment.

of which is applied to the patient's past social history as reported in case records by the staff psychiatrist and social worker. The scales include ratings for recent sexual adjustment, social aspects of sexual life during adolescence, social aspects of recent sexual life, history of personal relations, and recent adjustment in personal relations. Scale scores range from 0 through 30, with 0 standing for a Good pre-morbid history. The cutting point selected for this study, between 18 and 19, differs from the standard cutting point partly as a result of the skewing of the sample toward the Poor premorbid history end of the scale. This is largely a result of the fact that married patients were not included in the sample. (See Appendix A for scoring details and the distribution of scores.)

Using this scale to discriminate between types of schizophrenic patients allows us to sort out schizophrenic patients whose premorbid social history has been essentially "normal" from those in whom there has been a long course of withdrawal or isolation. A typical Good premorbid schizophrenic patient in our sample is a young man of 19 who had many friends through adolescence, was captain of his high school football team, and was, until six months before his hospital admission, engaged to a girl from his home town. At the end of his sophomore year in college, where he had prospects of being an exceptional football player and a good student, he suddenly experienced delusions and uncontrolled outbreaks of aggression against himself and others. After a short hospitalization he returned home and then to college.

This benign social history is in contrast to that of a typical Poor premorbid schizophrenic patient also included in the sample who, at the time of his participation, was 24 years old but had been treated as a psychiatric outpatient since age 6. He had never had a close friend, male or female, had managed to finish high school only with exceptional support from the school, and since graduating had held a series of menial jobs. His hospitalization occurred as a result of continued deterioration in his ability to care for himself and to concentrate on his work. After his discharge he returned home but was unable to begin working.

Criteria for Selecting the Nonpatient Children

Each schizophrenic patient selected for the study had a sibling of the same sex also unmarried and living at home. When there was more than one sibling meeting the criteria the one closest in age to the patient was selected, whether he was younger or older than the patient; in instances where there were two siblings close in age other factors such as which one could most easily participate led to the selection of one of them. The second major criterion for selection was that the sibling had never been hospitalized for a psychiatric illness; information was obtained from the family history section of the patient's hospital record.

Normal control families were selected from church and school lists; the selection of each family was contingent on its having two siblings of the same sex living at home. If several children were close in age the parents were given some choice in selecting which children could most easily participate.

The order in which the two children participated with the parents was left partly to the parents and circumstances of the family's schedule; however, concern with finishing the study with approximately equal numbers of patient-first and well-sibling-first sessions in the schizophrenic families led to some effort to balance the ordering. In instances where both children participated, the patient child was first in 15 families and the well child first in 8. The order of participation of the children in normal families was left to the family.

Sex of the Children Participating

Both schizophrenic and normal families are classified as either "male" or "female" families depending on the sex of the children participating. While the interaction patterns of the parents are treated as indicators of their behavior with their male or female children this does not mean that the parents may not also have children of the other sex who did not participate in the study. Twenty-seven of the 49 families had children of both sexes.

Sampling and Recruitment

The experimental design specifies the characteristics of patient and control families required in the sample. Other sampling and recruitment policies also entered into the selection of families. First, we were concerned with being able to generalize and relate our findings to a larger population of cases that was clearly, if perhaps narrowly, defined. This concern led to sampling from lists of patient and normal children rather than simply collecting families as they became available or as they volunteered. We will present data below on the relationship between the sample of patient families who participated in the study to the population of schizophrenic patients from which the sample was drawn as an indicator of the degree to which generalization is possible.

Second, we were interested in selecting a set of families having characteristics in common beyond the control variables described above that were required by the experimental design. These additional controls provide a clear and specific definition of the families sampled and thus permit a more accurate generalization to the larger population of families. Furthermore, additional limits set on sample selection allow for the control of variables that we have reason to believe may affect the dependent variables, family interaction patterns. Length of the patient's hospitalization as well as such variables as race, marital status, and age were selected as additional controls for sampling purposes. This approach to sampling provides a carefully but narrowly defined set of cases.

Finally, the technique for recruitment of families from the sample was designed to control, to the extent that this is possible, for the family's motivation for participation in the study and thus the family's perception of what was being asked of it. Some previous studies of family interaction, especially of families with hospital or clinic affiliations, have been explicitly or implicitly presented to the families as part of the treatment program, or as required for further participation in treatment. In some instances hospital authorities such as the treating physician or the family's social worker were used as recruiters for the study (Lerner, 1965; Lidz et al., 1965). Our recruiting technique was designed to separate the experimental study from the treatment program of the source hospital in order to maximize the possibility that all families, those with schizophrenic children and those with normal children, perceived their participation in the same way—as part of a scientific research project.

Sampling Procedure

With these general policy considerations in mind, the populations of schizophrenic patients and normal children were listed and samples drawn from each.

Sample of Schizophrenic Patients. The source of all schizophrenic patients in the study was the list of all inpatient and day hospital admissions to the Massachusetts Mental Health Center during the period January 1, 1963 to February 1, 1965. (Patients admitted to the outpatient clinic were not included in the population.) This hospital is a small teaching hospital in which one major focus is on the psychotherapeutic treatment of schizophrenic patients. The admissions to the hospital represent this focus in that many patients are likely to be young, acute schizophrenics who have not had previous hospital admissions. Therefore the use of this hospital as the source population from which the sample was drawn successfully controlled for length of the patient's hospitalization.

From the list of all admissions during this time period, every patient who met all of the following criteria was included in the sample of the study.

1. Diagnosis: schizophrenia of any type, without organic brain damage, alcoholism, addiction, or mental retardation
2. Race: white
3. Age: 16 or over
4. Marital status: unmarried, divorced, or separated
5. Residence: living with parents (or in college dormitory) in the Boston metropolitan area
6. Parents: both alive and living together
7. Language: English spoken by all family members
8. Sibling: sibling of same sex as patient, living at home (or in college dormitory), and unmarried, divorced, or separated
9. Adoption: patient and sibling not adopted children, or adopted, before age 5

Of the 971 admissions to the hospital from January 1, 1963 through December 31, 1963, 28% or 272 were diagnosed as schizophrenic. The addition of schizophrenic patients admitted after that time period gave us a population of 373 schizophrenic patients from which to draw those fitting the other criteria listed. When these criteria were applied, 50 (or 13.4%) of the schizophrenic patients were retained in the sample. A loss of cases due to stringent sampling rules was in large part a result of the fact that parents of the patient lived outside the Boston area, that siblings were married and living away from home, or that one or both parents were dead. (See Appendix A for detailed tables showing sources of loss of cases due to sampling criteria.) The final sample of families of patients contains fewer families of females than of males because fewer female schizophrenic patients meeting all sampling criteria were available in the source hospital. This is probably a result of the fact that female schizophrenic patients are more likely to be married and thus not eligible for the sample.

Sample of Normal Children. The sample of normal children was drawn from a population of names obtained from three sources: a Catholic University for men, a Catholic women's college, and three Protestant churches. Each of the schools included in its college records the necessary information about family composition, age, and residence; thus we sampled directly from the records. Church lists, on the other hand, were obtained by asking a church official for the names of families who had adolescent and young-adult children. Colleges and churches were used as sources in order to match the normal sample with the schizophrenic sample on social class, religion, and ethnicity.

The criteria used for selecting normal control families were the same as for the index families except, of course, for the presence of schizophrenia. No formal comparison between the sample of normal children and the full population from which it was drawn could be made. This sampling procedure provided 41 normal families meeting all of the sampling criteria.

Recruitment Technique

The 50 schizophrenic families and the 41 normal families were asked, by letter, to participate in research studying "the ideas and opinions of different members of the same family." They were told, "We need to have families come to the hospital together so that they have a chance to tell their ideas and to talk them over." Although the letters were slightly different for the schizophrenic and the normal families, because the patient families had had extensive contact with the hospital where the experiment was held, each form attempted to stress the scientific, research goal of the study, and the fact that we were interested in the family's opinions but would treat these as confidential data. (Copies of these letters are included in Appendix A.) Naturally "research" is more clearly understood by some families than by others but in the follow-up phone call, again, the separation of the study from the treatment program was made explicit.

Each letter was followed by a telephone call to arrange an appointment. It is at this point that further attrition in each sample occurred, owing to refusals to participate. Of the 50 schizophrenic families meeting all criteria, 18 (or 36%) refused and 32 participated. Of the 41 normal families, 24 (or 58%) refused and 17 agreed to participate. Refusals came in many forms. Generally, families indicated lack of interest, inability to schedule a meeting involving three people, or suspicion about what they were being asked to do. One family repeatedly failed to appear after making an appointment and a few could not be contacted because they had moved or had no telephone.

A comparison of the participating schizophrenic patient families with those that refused, using data obtained from the patient's case record, shows that the families of male patients, those with younger patient children, and those with a higher educational level were more likely to take part in the study. There are, however, no statistically significant differences between the refusers and the participants (see Appendix A). Too little data is available to make the comparison for the normal families.

Final loss of cases from the original sample occurred at the time of the second family session when the parents were asked to reappear with a different child. As indicated in Table 2.1, 10 families participated only once; only four of these refused to participate in the second session. One of these refusers was a patient; three were patients' well siblings. In the remaining patient families one patient had been admitted to another hospital and thus was unable to participate, and in four families there was no eligible well sibling; these latter families were all families of female schizophrenics added at the end of the study to enlarge the female sample. In one instance—a normal family—a second session was lost because of a recording failure.

Relationship of the Schizophrenic to the Normal Sample

Normal families were obtained from sources that would provide families matching the schizophrenic sample on certain background characteristics. Although families were not matched case by case, there was an attempt to balance each sample so that the total sample distributions did not differ. When the participating sample of schizophrenic families is compared with the normal families, there are no significant differences between them on total family income, father's occupation, father's education, mother's education, family religion, parents' birthplace, and grandparents' birthplace (see Appendix A for detailed tables). While not differing significantly the group of normal families tends to have somewhat higher social status and a greater percentage of Catholics while the schizophrenic family sample has a larger proportion of Southern and Eastern European ethnic group members.

Degree of Generalization Possible from the Two Samples

Both the schizophrenic and the normal family samples are highly selected and clearly defined. The former represent a population of families with young, unmarried schizophrenic children. Although the schizophrenic patients include those with both good and poor premorbid social adjustments, none could be considered "chronic" in the sense of having had long or frequent periods of hospitalization. All patient families are intact, with parents and children living together, and have enough organization and control within the family to bring four members together for research purposes. Normal families too, are highly selected in that they are all intact families with unmarried, young adult children.

Paradoxically, the aim of selecting carefully defined samples (with the consequent restriction of the populations represented) is to increase the generality of findings. It is true that the great majority of schizophrenic patients come from families that are ineligible for participation in the study—the families are not intact, the patient does not live at home, other siblings are married. Thus the study sample does not represent the population of all schizophrenic families and it would not be valid to estimate a population parameter on the basis of a sample characteristic. For example, if we find that 25% of the statements made by members of our sample of schizophrenic families begin with the pronoun "I," we could not then go on to assert that this percentage was a characteristic of all schizophrenic families; we would have to qualify the generalization carefully by pointing to all the special defining features of our sample. This is a trivial problem in the present instance, however, because this study is not directed toward such descriptive statements about schizophrenic and normal families. We wish to make inferences about the associations between interaction patterns and the normality-schizophrenia distinction. We want to know whether there are nonrandom differences between normal and schizophrenic families that can be attributed to the presence or absence of schizophrenia in one of the children. The extent to which such a finding can be generalized is a function of how well other variables have been controlled that would "contaminate" or confound the relationship. Such confounding effects occur when variables that are not the focus of investigation are correlated with either the independent or dependent variables (see Kish, 1959; and Blalock, 1961, for discussion of these problems). For example, differential durations of hospitalization would be likely to affect family interaction resulting in differences between patient and well sibling sessions and between normal and patient families; these effects could not easily be separated from the effects in which we are really interested, namely, the differences between interaction with schizophrenic and nonschizophrenic children.

In general this problem is dealt with in the design of studies by controlling and randomizing the potentially confounding variables. With the small sample used in the present study, statistical controls for such variables as race or presence of siblings were not possible and the samples were selected to be homogeneous in these respects. Other variables such as premorbidity and sex of patient are used as major controls in the statistical analysis. Finally, some variables such as ethnicity, social class, and religion were permitted to vary within each sample with the restriction that the normal and schizophrenic samples be matched on these variables.

On the whole the scope and validity of generalizations drawn from a study are a function of the degree of success achieved in "purifying" the sample of confounding variables. In addition to the caution against overgeneralizing from a small sample, however, there is an additional qualification of this study's findings. Certain types of family have been eliminated from the research design—for example, families in which only one parent is present, or Negro families; thus a direct extrapolation from the findings requires additional assumptions that these families are like those actually included. With due recognition of these qualifications, there remains the paradox that restrictions on the sample that make it "unrepresentative" of the population of schizophrenics serve to increase the generality of the findings about differences in interaction between normal and schizophrenic families.

Experimental Procedure

The experimental procedure makes use of Strodtbeck's (1951) method of revealed differences to generate discussions among the three family members present at each session. The tape recordings of the family's interaction provide the basic data source.

Three general research policies guided the development of the experimental procedure. First, we needed to construct an experimental situation that would provide the kind of data relevant to the theories of interaction in families having schizophrenic children. Because these theories are mainly focused on styles of communication and specific aspects of role-taking, it was necessary to elicit from the family a sample of communication that would allow for the occurrence of these predicted patterns. Second, we were concerned with observing the family's modes of communication in a well controlled, clearly defined situation in which, ideally, all families perceived and experienced the situation in the same way. We particularly wanted to rule out aspects of the situation that the schizophrenic and normal families might interpret differently. Our third general concern, which also set limits on the experimental procedure, was with providing for the family a situation inherently interesting and involving, that seemed "real" and sensible from their point of view. Each of these concerns led to certain more specific decisions about experimental procedures.

The revealed-difference technique was selected in order to encourage a fairly free and involving family discussion that could, in turn, be productive of the kinds of interaction pattern theorists have predicted for such families. Free discussion rather than such alternatives as doing concrete work (puzzle solving, for example) or discussing family conflicts in a therapy context provides data at the relevant theoretical level and thus calls for less inference from the experimental situation to the family's usual style of interaction.

In order to provide a standard, defined situation, experienced in the same way by the schizophrenic and normal families, all aspects of the experiment were treated as "research" rather than linked with treatment. The experimenter left the room while the family members discussed the items among themselves; this removed the effect of the presence of a stranger and authority figure and, at the same time, differentiated the experimental situation from family therapy or group therapy sessions in which many members of patient families participated. Other aspects of the situation were controlled so that extraneous variables would not affect the family's discussion. These controls, borrowed from research methods for the study of small groups, consist of the use of standard experimental instructions, a small group laboratory room especially set up for recording and observation, a limited set of topics for the family's discussion, the selection of discussion items in a standard way, and the rotation of experimenters. The details of these procedures are described below.

The interest in creating an experimental procedure that would be both sensible and engaging to the family was not, as might be expected, a result of hypothesis that putting a family in an unrealistic or unfamiliar situation provides invalid information about the family's mode of interaction. (See Reiss, 1967, for evidence that family members asked to participate in a relatively unfamiliar task interact in ways that are theoretically sensible.) Instead, the policy resulted from concern with maintaining the family's motivation to participate through the second experimental session and an interest in providing some feeling of satisfaction with its own performance to the family, especially to those families having a relatively close and long relationship with the hospital in which the experiment was conducted.

The Revealed-Difference Questionnaire

Each experimental session began with standard instructions for the three members to complete privately the 38-item Revealed-Difference Questionnaire. This consists of a set of questions about everyday interpersonal situations and general values, many of them having to do with parents and children and each having two possible answers. A selected set of items on which the three family members disagreed (where one member chose one answer and the other two members chose the second answer) were then given back—or "revealed"—to the three-person family group for discussion and possible resolution of their disagreement.

The revealed-difference technique was first developed by Strodtbeck (1951) to generate discussions between husbands and wives. Recently the same technique has been used to investigate families having a disturbed or deviant member (Caputo, 1963; Cheek, 1964a; Farina, 1960; Stabeneau et al., 1965), although in each of these studies somewhat different stimulus materials provide the content for the disagreements. The use of this method to provide a stimulus for the family's discussion has the advantages that the pool items is the same for all families and a standard rule for selection can be applied.

The Revealed-Difference Questionnaire used in this study was developed by combining items previously used by Strodtbeck and others with new items (See Appendix A for Revealed-Difference Questionnaire). After pretesting on several large groups of subjects we selected the final 38 items on the basis that each of the two answer categories was relatively equally chosen and the item wordings were clear. No attempt was made to develop items having content covering a systematically defined set of conflicts or family issues since the content of family discussions is not of major interest in the experiment. However concern with providing relatively nonthreatening topics for discussion led us to omit some items that we felt families might have difficulty discussing. Instead items were selected on which family members would readily disagree, in which they would be interested, and about which they would have opinions. An example of two items, along with their answer categories, is the following.

6. A foreman sees one of his crew taking some company materials home from work. Should he report him or should he just ignore it?

Report him   ———

Just ignore it   ———

7. Theresa, who is 23 years old, lives with her mother and father who are honest, hard-working people but who have never learned to speak English very well. Theresa feels uncomfortable about inviting young men into the house and is afraid this will spoil her chances of finding a good husband. She wonders if she shouldn't move to her own apartment with a friend. What should she do?

Move in to her own apartment   ———

Stay with parents   ———

In the first experimental session the Revealed-Difference Questionnaire was administered individually to both parents and the child. In the second session the questionnaire was administered to the second child while the parents filled out a Background Questionnaire (see Appendix A). Instructions for the Revealed-Difference Questionnaire are as follows.

As we mentioned in our letter to you we are interested in learning about the ideas and opinions of many families and that is why we asked your family to come in.

First, we would like to have your opinion about a number of problems that come up for most people at one time or another. As you fill out this questionnaire, remember that there are no right or wrong answers; just put down your own opinion. If you find it difficult to choose between answers just select the one that comes closest to your own opinion. Make sure that you answer each question and work as quickly as you can.

You'll see that the questionnaire is in two sections; when you finish the first part will you hand it to me and then go right on with the next part.

Will you fill in the things on the first page, too.

To facilitate scoring and selection of items to be discussed by the family the questionnaire was divided into halves. As soon as the family members finished the first half of the items these were removed for scoring and the family members continued filling out the second half. At the end of this time a partial set of "disagreement" items had been selected and the family could move immediately to the small group laboratory for the three-person discussions.

Experimental Instructions

The experimental instructions given to the family provided a standard definition of the situation for all families. All families were told the following.

> Now I'm going to ask you to discuss some of the situations that you read about on the questionnaire.
>
> (*Second session*: What we're going to do now is similar to what the two of you did last week. I'm going to ask you to discuss some of the situations on the questionnaire that your (son/daughter) filled out tonight and that you (parents) filled out last time.)
>
> But first let me explain about this room. The reason we came down here was so we could get an accurate record of your opinions and ideas as you talk about them. This room is set up for that kind of special recording. These microphones are connected to a tape recorder in the next room.
>
> Now, as you might have expected there were some situations on which you were all in agreement, and some on which you had different opinions. Sometimes the mother and father might disagree, sometimes the mother and son/daughter might disagree, and sometimes the father and son/daughter might disagree. We've picked out some of the items on which there was a disagreement and now we'll give each of you a chance to defend your own point of view and to explain why you selected the answer you did. You can take about ten minutes to talk it over and see if, during that time, you can reach a family decision, that is, come to an agreement on the answer that best represents the thinking of the whole family:
>
> When you've reached an agreement, someone can signal me through the one-way mirror by holding up his hand. Then I'll come back into the room and give you another one to talk about.
>
> This is the first one.

Thus relatively equal stress was put on giving ideas and opinions about the issue and coming to a family agreement; the latter was not required, however, by the instructions or the nature of the experimental procedure.

Following the experimenter's reading of the instructions, he continued by reading the first randomly selected Revealed-Difference Questionnaire item, identifying the answers that father, mother, and son/daughter had given to that item. The experimenter then took the written item with him when he left the room. An optimum time of 10 minutes per item was suggested in the experimental instructions, as pretesting had shown that families needed some encouragement to go beyond the first few minutes of fairly superficial discussion. The average time taken to discuss nine items was approximately 50 minutes.

The manner in which the experimenter presents the experimental instructions and interacts informally with the family before the experiment has a subtle effect on the family's interpretation of what it is being asked to do. In order to maintain control over these effects each experimental session was run by one of the two investigators with the second experimenter ordinarily observing this interaction in order to maintain standard procedures. Within the limits of scheduling, there was also an attempt to distribute experimenters across different types of families so that differential experimenter effects, if they occurred, would be canceled out. (See Appendix A for the distribution of experimenters.)

Recording Procedures and Physical Setting

All family sessions were tape-recorded using a four-channel recorder. A separate microphone was placed on the table in front of each of the three family members and the fourth microphone was used by an observer sitting behind the one-way mirror to record onto the same tape the sequences of "who speaks to whom." This recording procedure was adopted after comparing, in pilot work, a typescript made from a multiple-channel recorder and a typescript of the same discussion from a single-channel recording. About 25% of the codable acts were lost with the single-channel procedure. More important, the loss was not random but differential; quieter participants suffered the greatest loss and certain types of act such as fragments and simultaneous statements were lost disproportionately. Because many hypotheses about interaction in families having schizophrenic children refer to attempts to control or withdraw from interaction—phenomena that may be reflected in such verbal behavior as interruptions, lowering of voice volume, incomplete remarks, and asides—separate microphones were essential.

The laboratory room in which the family interacted was also designed specifically to allow for accurate and clear recordings of communication. This small, soundproof room contained only a round table and three chairs, set so that the faces of the three members could be seen through the one-way mirror. Family members were allowed to choose their own seating arrangement.

Selection and Sequence of Discussion Items

The Revealed-Difference Questionnaire provides a pool of 38 items for possible discussion by the families. From this pool, any one family is asked to discuss only those items on which there is a disagreement among the three members present. The rules for selection of nine "disagreement" items from the family's pool of disagreement were designed to systematically rotate agreement, or coalition, patterns in the same way in all families. These items were selected so that the first one presented to the family represented an agreement between mother and child, both of whom disagreed with the father; on the second item the mother was the isolate and on the third item, the child. This pattern of father–mother–child isolate sequences was repeated three times, resulting in nine items altogether. Within each of the isolate patterns items were selected randomly. In the few instances when there were not three items for each isolate pattern, that pattern was skipped in the sequence. When the family spent little time on the first items, additional items beyond the first nine were added; when discussion of the first six items took longer than an hour the family was stopped at that point. The number of items was manipulated in order to obtain approximately 50 minutes of tape-recorded interaction per family. (Appendix A provides the full distribution of family sessions by number of items discussed.)

Since the pool of "disagreement" items differed from first to second session (because different children had filled out the Revealed-Difference Questionnaire at each session) the family generally discussed new items in the second session. However in 15 of the 88 sessions it was necessary to repeat one item and, in seven sessions, two or three items. The systematic effect of this repetition has not been investigated although observation of the families suggested that some parents had forgotten that they had discussed the item before; others remembered but had further opinions about it, and only a few families simply decided not to discuss it extensively for the second time.

Observations of On-going Interaction in Families

In contrast to many small-group experiments, this study used ongoing observation of the interaction as a source of only one interaction variable, "who speaks to whom." Other interaction codes were applied to typescripts made from the tape recordings; the rationale for this technique will be presented in the following chapter.

One observer sat behind the one-way mirror in such a position that he could see the faces of all three people in the family. As members spoke he recorded into a microphone, and thus onto the fourth track of the tape, who was speaking and at whom he was looking as he spoke. Eye movements of the speaker rather than his probable intent were taken as the indicator of the person, or persons, to whom his speech was directed. This recorded information was coordinated with the speaker's content at the time the tape recording was transcribed.

Chapter 3

Measurement Techniques

In chapter 2 we outlined the design of the experiment and described the methods, both selective and procedural, that were used to insure control over possible contaminating variables. These steps led to the point at which a tape recording of a three-person family group discussion was available as the basic data source. In this chapter we present the rationale for selecting particular dependent variables to be derived from the recordings as well as the details of the measurement techniques used to transform the tape recorded interaction into usable numerical scores for the appropriate comparisons.

Because theories and clinical descriptions of interaction in families with a schizophrenic child tend to have multiple foci and tend to cut across many conceptual levels it is not useful at this stage of empirical work to derive a single interaction measure that covers the breadth of theoretical concerns. Furthermore previous empirical work on both *ad hoc* and natural groups suggested that reliable and valid measures of interaction could be obtained by the application of coding systems to small units of interaction in contrast to ratings or observers' judgments. These two factors led us to rely on a relatively large set of independent coding systems, each applied to every simple sentence in the family's discussion; these codes serve as indicators for specific dimensions of the general dependent variable, "family interaction."

The sequence of procedures through which the tape recording of a family discussion is transformed into codable units that can be converted to scores for statistical analysis is outlined in Chart 3.1.

Chart 3.1   Steps in Processing Family Discussion to Obtain Interaction Scores

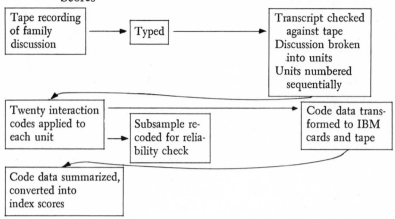

The Interaction Codes

In any empirical study decisions about the conceptual level and content of the dependent variables as well as the procedures used to measure them have a profound effect on all later stages of the study, particularly on the findings it is possible to report and thus on the inferences made from the findings back to the original theories. For this reason we attempted, in developing dependent variable measures, to make the rationale for measurement decisions as clear and as explicit as possible at each stage.

The major goal of the measurement procedures was to provide reliable and objective indicators of family interaction related to theory and clinical observations and allowing for enough flexibility in the analysis for new and unpredicted patterns to occur. To meet this goal within the limits set by the experimental situation we decided to work solely with small units of interaction that could be coded objectively and examined in a variety of ways. Interaction codes, characteristic of much small-group research, contrast with observers' ratings, more often used in psychiatric research (see, for example, Lerner, 1965, and Baxter, 1962). First, because observer ratings are generally applied to large units of interaction—sometimes a whole group session—the flexibility of later analysis is reduced and studies of change across time are difficult. Further, since the units used in interaction coding are normally quite small (perhaps a simple sentence or a statement of a few sentences in length), categorization is more likely to be reliably done than when a single judgment about a large body of material is required. Besides their flexibility and reliability, interaction codes applied to small units of speech have the further advantage of allowing us to measure qualities of interaction or communication. Fragments, incomplete sentences, and repetitions may be clearly related to other qualities of family interaction; yet these subtle and varied styles of communication cannot be reliably judged by an observer. Complex sequences of actions may also be important in distinguishing between types of interaction but these can only be obtained by combining discrete units, separately coded; an observer is unable to make these complex combinations quickly enough to provide the same degree of reliability.

No single interaction code meets the requirement of providing data appropriate to the examination of hypotheses from several different theories. For example, Lidz's (1957) hypotheses about parental role taking and Bateson's (1956) stress on the strategy of metacommunication call for quite different levels of measurement. Concern with being able to shed light on several of these conceptual levels, then, pushed toward the development of several independent codes. In addition to assuring theoretical relevance the use of multiple-coding systems allows for the examination of empirical relationships between codes. A combination of variables—for example a "style" variable such as the frequency of interruptions, compared with a "content" variable such as quality of the affect—provides a complex picture of the quality of family interaction that would be unattainable if a single, all-inclusive code system were used.

Decisions about the type of instrument (interaction code systems) and the number of instruments (many independent codes) were followed by the selection of code content. Guiding this selection were theories about schizophrenic families as well as previous empirical findings. Although none of the theories provides one or a few concepts that are defined with enough clarity to allow for direct quantification, all of the theories afford definitions and descriptions suggesting aspects of interaction that can be objectively measured. For example, to measure Wynne's concept of pseudomutuality (Wynne, et al., 1958) in its simplest form we may code expressions of positive and negative affect, or the amount of overt hostility or conflict in the family.

Previous empirical findings also suggest content areas that may be fruitful in describing the structure of schizophrenic and normal families. Farina (1960), in his study of parents of schizophrenic and tubercular patients, showed that the total number of interruptions, indicating "family conflict," differentiated between schizophrenic and the normal parents and, within the schizophrenic group, between those with good and poor premorbid social adjustments. Gottschalk's work on verbal behavior of psychotic patients suggested that it would be useful to examine the use of certain pronouns such as "I" and "we" as indicators of identification with the family and with one's own role in it (Gottschalk et al., 1957).

In addition to studies of psychiatric patients and their families, research on small *ad hoc* groups was also a source of concepts and specific interaction codes. For example, the distinction between expressive and instrumental leadership described by Parsons and Bales (1955) and measured by Slater (1955) in *ad hoc* groups is similar to role differences in families described by Lidz (1965). The content code, Interaction Process Analysis, used by Slater was thus an obvious choice for use in this study. Measures for the expression of affect (Mills, 1964) and indicators for psychological mechanisms of defense (Weintraub and Aronson, 1962) were also suggested by the small group studies.

The interaction codes developed for the study were therefore selected for their theoretical and clinical relevance, for their objectivity and reliability, and for the flexibility in analysis that they would provide. Each code is designed to measure some specific aspect of family interaction. Each code is independent of all other codes and is applied to each unit of interaction, the "act" or simple sentence. We will describe here the purpose of the code and its source, and will list and briefly define the code categories. Finally, we will show how the code is used to describe a family's style of interaction. (Full coding definitions are found in Appendix B, the *Interaction Code Book*.)

Summary Descriptions of Interaction Codes [1]

Acknowledgment Stimulus and Acknowledgment Response. These are two independent codes that together measure the degree to which the intent and content of a particular statement are acknowledged, or taken into account, by the following speaker. Each statement is viewed as a stimulus that calls for a specific response from the following speaker; for example, a stimulus statement in the form of a question calls for an answer, and an answer having narrowly defined content. Each statement is also viewed as a response to the previous stimulus and is coded on the basis of the degree to which the stimulus expectation is fulfilled. In the above example, if the question is fully and completely answered then the response is coded as being completely acknowledging.

The sources for the development of these codes came from Ruesch's discussion of modes of acknowledgment and devious acknowledgment in

---

[1] The codes listed here are the sources of interaction data reported in this book. A number of other codes (Metacommunications, Subjects, Objects, Negations and Retractions) were also applied to the family typescripts; these are described in detail in the coding manual, Appendix B. In the types of aggregate score analyses reported in this book differences between families on these codes were scattered and infrequent. Some work with these codes is continuing in the correlational and sequential analyses now under way.

his book *Disturbed Communication* (1957), as well as from a number of examples of family interaction provided by Wynne and Singer (1963), all of which exemplify their concept of "fragmented communication." In contrast to the other interaction codes listed, these codes are applied to the speaker's full statement (sometimes composed of several acts) rather than to each act taken singly.

The stimulus quality of a statement is coded according to the kind of expectation the speaker has for the person who responds. Brief definitions of each of the code categories are listed below.

ACKNOWLEDGMENT: STIMULUS

1. Inductions or direct commands: statements requesting or demanding certain behaviors or opinions of others in the family
2. Questions: statements having the grammatical form of a question
3. Affirmative statements: complete statements not in the form of a question or induction
4. Elliptical affirmative statements: one-word statements implying a complete sentence and having a clear meaning out of context
5. Fragments: a word or group of words with unclear content
0. Not ascertainable

The response quality of a statement is coded according to the degree to which it acknowledges the preceding stimulus statement. The code categories are the following (specific definitions of the response categories are keyed to the quality of the stimulus to which the statement is a response).

ACKNOWLEDGMENT: RESPONSE

1. Complete acknowledgment: the response explicitly recognizes both the content and the intent of the previous speaker's statement
2. Partial acknowledgment: the response explicitly recognizes either the content *or* the intent of the previous speaker's statement
3. Recognition: the response recognizes that the previous speaker has spoken but responds neither to his content nor his intent
4. Nonacknowledgment: the response clearly does not recognize the fact that the previous speaker has spoken
5. Fragment: the response has unclear content
6,7,8. Fragment: the stimulus is a fragment; therefore the degree of acknowledgment of the stimulus cannot be judged
0. Not ascertainable

These codes permit measurement of several phenomena hypothesized as critical features of interaction in families of schizophrenics. For example, the quality of "imperviousness" in the parents of schizophrenic children may be measured by the degree to which parents fail to acknowledge other family members (Bowen, 1959). The failure to acknowledge that anyone in the family is setting rules, when rulesetting actually occurs, is suggested by Haley (1959) as a characteristic schizophrenic family maneuver; this is also measurable with the Acknowledgment code. General lack of responsiveness to a family member as a separate person who has unique motives and expectations is a descriptive quality that is found in several family theories and that may be indicated by the degree to which family members acknowledge each other.

Affect. The affect code classifies each act according to the affective quality of the words used, from the point of view of their meaning in the common culture. No cues other than the commonly understood, literal meaning of the words are used; thus the speaker's intonation and the context of the speech are not taken into account in judging whether an act has positive or negative affective quality. The assumption behind this code is similar to assumptions made for projective tests, namely that the words a speaker chooses to use, particularly the words with affective connotations, are indicators of his own affective state or needs. For example, if a family member uses the verb "to like" his sentence is coded in the positive affect category regardless of the context in which it occurs or the tone of voice used to express it, and this is used to indicate his feeling of positive affect.

This code is an expanded form of Sign Process Analysis, an interaction measure originally developed by Mills (1964) and used to measure the sequence of affect orientations in an *ad hoc* group. It has been revised here to include two explicit dimensions, one having to do with the quality of the feeling expressed (positive, negative, or neutral), and the other with the interpersonal relationship implied (whether this is explicit or implicit).

Categories in the affect code are the following.

1. Positive affect expressed about an interpersonal relationship: acts with words describing closeness to another person
2. Positive states of people: acts with words describing one person's state of gratification or pleasure
3. Positive qualities: acts with words referring to valued or pleasureable situations
4. Neutral: all acts having no implication of a state or relationship of pleasure or displeasure
5. Negative qualities: acts with words referring to situations that are not valued or pleasureable

6. Negative states of people: acts with words describing a person's state of displeasure or dissatisfaction
7. Negative affect expressed about an interpersonal relationship: acts with words describing aggression against or distance from another person
0. Not ascertainable

Measurement of the manifest affective quality of interaction with the use of this code provides data relevant, for example, to Wynne's hypothesis about "pseudomutuality" (Wynne, et al., 1958) in schizophrenic families; the avoidance of negative affect words and the expression of positive affect words by a family may indicate the extent to which the family is following rigid and narrowly confining rules about disagreements or hostility. In combination with a second code for expressiveness (Interaction Process Analysis), the affect measures provide evidence for discrepancies between the affective meaning of the words used and the affective meaning implied by intonation and context; this kind of discrepancy is one form of "double-bind" (Bateson, 1956).

Focus. The categories of the Focus code refer to aspects of the immediate situation mentioned by the family members. They are based on the assumption that there are general problems that all small groups must handle, such as the adaptation or "task" problem and the integration or "socio-emotional" problems described by Bales (1949), as well as specific problems required by the experimental procedure. Acts may be classified according to their reference to the state of agreement or disagreement in the family, since the situation in which the family finds itself is one of disagreement. Acts may also refer to the procedures or rules of the experimental situation. Reference may also be made to interpersonal relationships, or "expressive" problems, and to the discussion item itself, the "adaptive" problem.

Focus code categories are as follows.

1. State of agreement: acts explicitly recognizing agreement or disagreement between family members
2. Rules, procedures and context: acts questioning, commenting on, or suggesting procedures for the family to follow in its discussion
3. Persons' states: acts referring to attributes or qualities of family members in the experimental situation
4. Other persons' opinions: acts commenting on, questioning, or referring to opinions of other members or the family as a whole
5. One's own opinions: acts explicitly referring to one's own opinions
6. Content of the discussion item: acts that accurately repeat discussion item content without any added evaluation
7. Personal experience: acts referring to real and hypothetical experiences of oneself or other family members

8. Opinion and evaluation of discussion item: acts referring to content of discussion item with an added evaluation or interpretation
9. Not ascertainable

The degree to which different families choose to focus on certain aspects of the group situation is useful in understanding their possible organizational problems. For example, the family that makes a large number of references to personal opinions of members may be said to be "responsive" to each other in a sense similar to the responsiveness measured by the Acknowledgment code. A family that makes no reference to the state of agreement or the procedure for discussion may be assumed to be poorly organized or, perhaps, aware of the rules to the extent that no explicit mentions are necessary.

Fragments. These are five independent codes, each of which refers to one kind of deviation from a smooth and continuous flow of speech. The modes of speech fragmentation measured by the codes are incomplete sentences, repeated words and phrases, words or phrases with unclear content, and laughter. The fifth code is a summary measure of the number of different fragment indicators in any one act.

Fragmented and broken speech patterns have been measured in a number of previous studies that served as a source for the development of these codes. Mahl (1956) showed that in certain special situations some patterns of discontinuous speech were associated with the speaker's anxiety. Gottschalk's work (Gottschalk et al., 1957) points to differences in the use of "filler" words between psychiatric patients and normal subjects. Zuk (1963) suggests that laughter has an important function in the interaction of the schizophrenic family.

Despite the fact that these styles of communication have been measured in a number of studies there is no general agreement among investigators about their conceptual meaning. They are used here as indicators of a kind of speech fragmentation that, if it occurs at moderate rates, is highly functional for group interaction. For example, fragmentation in the form of hesitations in speech have been shown to occur at points of uncertainty, where new information is introduced (Goldman-Eisler, 1958). Speech disruptions allow for the kind of adaptation and change in the course of interaction that are not possible when communication is rigid, formal, and uninterrupted.

The five Fragment codes and their categories, are as follows.

INCOMPLETE SENTENCES
1. Presence of an incomplete sentence: all uninterrupted sentences having an incomplete idea
0. No incomplete sentence

REPETITIONS

1. Presence of a repetition: all acts in which a word or phrase is exactly repeated
0. No repetition

INCOMPLETE PHRASE

1. Presence of an incomplete phrase: all acts containing a word or words having unclear meaning
0. No fragment

LAUGHTER

1. Presence of laughter: all acts containing the symbol "L" provided in the typescript at the point that laughter occurs
0. No laughter

NUMBER OF FRAGMENTS IN ONE ACT

1. One fragment indicator
2. Two fragment indicators
3. Three fragment indicators
4. Four fragment indicators
0. No fragment indicators

Interaction Process Analysis. This code is one that has been widely used in studies of small group processes as well as in family studies (see Caputo, 1963; Sharan, 1966; Strodtbeck, 1951). It is used in this study in a form similar to the original one developed by Bales (1951) with certain changes in coding procedures necessary to ensure higher reliability. Composed of 12 categories, the code takes into account the content of the speech, the assumed intent of the speaker, and the context in which the speech occurs and provides two major areas, expressive and instrumental, into which each act may be classified.

The method used for application of the code differs from that advised by Bales and from that used in many *ad hoc* small group studies (see Slater, 1955, for example). Instead of having an observer coding as the interaction proceeds, coding is done from the typescript while the observer listens to the taped interaction. The purpose of this method is to allow for accurate coding of each act (whose boundaries are clearly defined on the typescript) while, at the same time, providing the data on intonation necessary for making a reliable coding judgment. (See Waxler and Mishler, 1966, for an empirical study of the relationships between the two techniques for scoring Interaction Process Analysis.) The unit for IPA coding is the complete sentence, or complete idea; this may include more than one act.

Among the concepts found in theories about schizophrenic families that may be examined with Interaction Process Analysis codes are those having to do with role-taking. For example, Lidz's formulation (1957), suggesting a reversal of normal role-taking patterns between the parents in schizophrenic families, may be indicated by the proportion of mothers' and fathers' acts classified in the "expressive" and "instrumental" segments of the code. The distinction in the code between positive and negative affect or expressiveness also provides a direct measure of affect that complements the one provided by the Affect code; together they are useful as an indicator of one type of "double-bind."

The Interaction Process Analysis categories are summarized below.

1. Shows solidarity: acts that function to give status, help, or reward to another family member
2. Tension release: spontaneous expressions of affect, functioning to release tension
3. Agreement: acts that state agreement, acceptance or understanding, generally around an issue rather than a person
4. Gives suggestion: acts making a suggestion about procedures
5. Gives opinion: acts that include opinions or suppositions, usually about the discussion item
6. Gives orientation: acts giving nonevaluative information
7. Asks for orientation: questions asking for nonevaluative information
8. Asks for opinion: acts in the form of questions about opinions, usually about the discussion item
9. Asks for suggestion: acts in the form of questions about procedures or direction of the group
10. Disagreement: acts showing as disagreement, passive rejection, or having a mildly negative tone
11. Shows tension: acts indicating personal tension
12. Antagonism: acts that have a hostile or aggressive tone or that function to dare, attack, or insult
0. Not ascertainable

Interruptions. The code for interruptions includes both successful and unsuccessful interruptions. In the first instance the first speaker stops when interrupted, leaving his idea incomplete; in other words, he is "talked down." In the second instance the interrupted person continues to talk so that the two persons are speaking simultaneously. Since making a judgment about the presence of an interruption depends on hearing the spoken interaction, the typist and the person checking the typescript follow a set of rules defining interruptions and, when these occur, insert appropriate symbols in the written script. The final coding operation is applied to these symbols. Because of questions to be asked in the analysis, this information is coded with two separate and independent codes, once to indicate who is interrupted and the second to indicate who interrupts.

Farina's findings (1960) for two types of schizophrenic parents compared with parents of tuberculosis patients suggested that total interruption rates may stand as indicators of family conflict. Interruptions have also been used by Stabenau et al. (1965) as a measure of family disorganization. The rate of interruptions and simultaneous speech is viewed here as an indicator of fragmented or disrupted communication similar in function to repetitions, incomplete sentences, fragments, and laughter. Examination of the source of interrupting speeches may also lead to conclusions about strategies of control or modes of exercising power.

Code categories for the two measures of interruptions are as follows.

INTERRUPTING OTHERS
 1. Interrupting acts: all acts in which the speaker succeeds in stopping the preceding speaker from completing his idea
 2. Simultaneous acts: all acts in which the speaker breaks into the preceding statement but does not succeed in stopping the first speaker before his idea is completed
 0. All other acts

BEING INTERRUPTED
 1. Speaker unsuccessfully interrupted by father
 2. Speaker unsuccessfully interrupted by mother
 3. Speaker unsuccessfully interrupted by child
 4. Speaker successfully interrupted by father
 5. Speaker successfully interrupted by mother
 6. Speaker successfully interrupted by child
 0. All other acts

Pauses. This code measures the occurrence of silences in the family interaction. A pause is coded for each period of silence judged by the listener to be one in which someone should be speaking. In other words, pauses include only longer, "uncomfortable" silences.

Goldman-Eisler (1958) has shown that pauses in speech function to introduce new and less predictable information; thus the incidence of silent periods in group interaction may be an indicator of flexibility or ability to adapt to new situations. Zuk (1965) has interpreted the use of silences in family therapy sessions as strategies of power and control.

The Pause code categories are the following.

 1. Presence of a pause: the act contains a silence judged to be "uncomfortable" by the listener
 0. All other acts

Statement Length. This code is used as a source for derivation of a measure of average length of statements. All acts that are the first acts in a new speaker's statement are coded. The proportion of "first" acts to all acts for any one speaker provides a measure of the average number of acts in that speaker's statements.

The Statement Length code is as follows.

1. First act in a statement
0. All other acts

Speaker. This code is applied to each act.

1. Father: all acts spoken by father
2. Mother: all acts spoken by mother
3. Child: all acts spoken by child
0. Not ascertainable: all acts in which the speaker is not clear

To Whom. This code is applied to each act on the basis of who is the target of that act. The basic data for coding is supplied by the observer who watches the family through a one-way mirror and records on the fourth track of the tape the eye-movements of each person as he speaks. The code makes the assumption that the person one looks at while speaking is the target of one's speech. If, within his speech, the speaker looks at a second person in the family then the target of the act is changed accordingly. Information about the target of each action is coordinated with the speech and recorded on the typescript; it is then ready to be classified into the code categories listed below.

The targets of family members' statements are important in understanding coalition patterns; for example, if there is no consistent pattern of giving and receiving acts between two members of a schizophrenic family, this is evidence for Haley's prediction (1959) that these families have unstable coalitions. Also, information about targets of control strategies—which member of the family is most often interrupted, for example —provides valuable information about family interrelationships and thus family structure.

The categories of the To Whom code are as follows.

1. To father: all acts directed to the father
2. To mother: all acts directed to the mother
3. To child: all acts directed to the child
4. To neither: all acts directed to no one, or spoken when the speaker is looking away from other family members
5. To both: all acts directed to two members at one time
0. Not ascertainable: all other acts

Coding Procedures

The above interaction codes are theoretically relevant, are applicable to family interactions, and, on pretest, were shown to provide different distributions of scores across a number of families and other groups. To use them it was necessary to transform the tape recording, through a set of steps, to the point at which the codes could be applied, and from there, to reduce the set of raw codes to a small number of numerical scores on which statistical comparisons could be made.

This set of transformations will be described below. (Detailed methods for each transformation are described in Appendix B.) Each step is designed to minimize processing errors and thus to provide measures that accurately represent the family's interaction. A second goal is to retain data in the form that will allow for the greatest flexibility in later analysis; flexibility here refers to the possibility of making both multiple comparisons across families and family members and comparisons within the sequence of interaction for any one family.

Transcription of the Tape

Once the family's interaction had been recorded on the four-track tape it was then typed, following a set of transcription rules (see sample typescript below). These rules oriented the typist against "making sense" out of the interaction by directing her to retain all of the content of interaction and to retain the sequence of events as they actually occurred. Content such as ungrammatical constructions, slips of the tongue, meaningless fragments, and repetitions were recorded as the typist heard them. Symbols standing for certain incidents that were later to be coded —laughter, interruptions, simultaneous speech, and pauses—were inserted, following specific rules established in the codes. The typist was thus oriented toward providing a completely accurate recording of the family's interaction without adding her own interpretation through rewording, editing, or providing unnecessary punctuation.

An average of 18 hours was required for typing a 50-minute taped discussion using the four-channel transcribing equipment; typescripts ranged in length from 30 to 100 pages, with an average of 60 pages. Typescripts were recorded on dittomasters so that many copies of the same family session could be available for the most efficient coding operation.

Checking of the Transcript

Because of our concern with measures of style of speech and sequences of specific actions, a completely accurate typescript was required. For this reason each typescript was systematically checked against the tape recording by a second person who corrected all content, checked the two new sets of information to the typescript, the To whom data re- insertions of symbols for laughter, interruptions, and pauses, and added corded on the fourth channel of the tape, and the indications of simul- taneous speech. The latter information was noted by underlining and linking the statements that were spoken concurrently. This checking operation took an average of 15 hours per family session.

Breaking Interaction into Codable Units

All codes were applied to the same small units of interaction, similar in size and form to a simple sentence with one subject and one predicate. Family sessions had an average of 1800 of these units. Boundaries of units were marked directly on the typescript.

Although the rules for unitizing are complex and detailed they have one major objective, that of dividing the flow of interaction into small, standard units that are large enough to have meaningful and codable content and yet are not so large as to be ambiguous. The ideal unit is a simple English sentence; however, because conversation is not carried on in simple, complete sentences a set of rules for exceptions was developed. These rules take into account such grammatical forms as compound sentences, dependent clauses, sentences that have incomplete predicates or subjects, and sentences we have labeled "elliptical" sen- tences, that is, those phrases that have clear meaning but are not gram- matically complete. Since the unitizing operation was closely connected with the coding operation, care was taken to develop rules for unitizing that would allow for a single application of every interaction code to the unit. For example, because the Affect code generally uses the verb of the sentence as its major indicator (e.g., "to like" indicates positive affect) it is important to apply the code to a unit that is likely to have a verb and to have only *one* verb.

The sample typescript included here provides concrete examples of units that result from application of the unitizing rules. Any speaker's full statement or speech may be composed of only one or of many units; this is in contrast to interaction units used in other studies, where the full uninterrupted speech is coded as one whole (Cheek, 1964a). Parts of speeches that have too little content to be coded by most of the inter- action codes—defined as "fragments" in the unitizing rules—are included within a complete, codable unit. For example, "The these people ahh some people can take it," is one unit that includes the fragment, "the these people."

Sequential Numbering of Units

To provide for the analysis of specific sequences of acts, each unit was serially numbered from the beginning of the family session to the end. When the interaction is orderly and unbroken, acts are numbered in the order in which they occur; however, when simultaneous speeches occur a set of rules is applied to determine sequence. Generally these concurrent statements are ordered to retain in one sequence the complete "idea" of one speaker before the second speaker's acts are allowed to continue.

The unitizing and numbering of one family session took approximately 10 hours. In order to provide a check on the accuracy of the previous unitizing step, the sequential numbering of any typescript was usually done by a second person.

The processing steps, from transcribing through sequential ordering of acts, were the operations necessary to transform the raw data of family discussions into a codable form. Each step was directed toward maintaining the accuracy of the original taped interaction.

SAMPLE TYPESCRIPT [2]

Experimenter: Mrs. Burns' husband died two weeks ago and since then she has spent most of her time sitting at home and feeling sad. Her daughter insists that it would be much better right now for her to find things to do and keep busy so that she won't think about her husband's death. Which do you think is better?

On this one, Mother and Father said, "Keep busy and not think about him." Son said, "Take time to get over his death."

Who-to-Whom
                    63   64
F-S   Fa   Well you can't/you can't (S) <u>forget about it by staying</u> at
                                                                        66
             <u>home or anything like that (S)</u> <u>and (NA)/(S)</u> <u>but by going</u>
                    67
             to work/just the same like you should do/

---

[2] Notes to Typescript: F-O in Who-to-Whom column means the speaker was not looking directly at either of the others; slant marks (/) are boundaries of coding units; long pauses are (P); interruptions are (I); and simultaneous speeches are (S). Simultaneous speeches are underscored and linked together with lines. (NA) means that the content of the speech was not ascertainable.

		65
M-S	Mo	(S) Actually you never forget about it/
		68 69
	Mo	(S) But by keeping busy/ you're trying not to brood/
		70 71
F-O	Fa	Ahh I mean/maybe not may maybe you shouldn't do it,/I
		72
		don't know./
F-S		73 74
		But ahh while you're at work/or while you're at work/or
		75 76
		while (S) you're with somebody else/you're you bound to
		forget her about it./
		77 78
	Son	(S) I can see umm/ Yeah/
		79 80 81
F-S	Fa	But if you don't forget about it/you kin get sick/(S) you know/
		83 84 85
		I'mm mmm mean/yyyyyou you're/you're staying in the
		86 87 88
		house/ and broodin over it/that's no good/(S) You've got
		to ahh get out./
		82
	Son	(S) (L)/
		89 90 91
M-S	Mo	(S) You can make yourself sick/ brooding./ Even a doctor'd
		tell you that/
		92
	Son	O.K./
		93 94
M-S	Mo	They told Helen./ Get out/
		95
	Fa	Yes/
		96 97
M-S	Mo	She used to dress in black all the time/(S) Take the black off./
		98
	Fa	(S) It's it/
		99 1700 01
	Mo	Wear bright colors./ Get out./ Mix in with people./ Good
		02 03 04
		thing she had to/ She was getting sick./ All right?/
		05
	Fa	Yeah./
		06

Mo   Agreed?
        07   08
Son   O.K. (P) / You got me on that one. /

Coding Methods

Each of the interaction codes was applied to every act or unit in the family session that was marked on the typescript. With the exception of the Interaction Process Analysis code and the code for pauses, for which the coder used both typescript and tape recording, all coding was done directly from the typescript. The specific coding methods, to be described below, were developed to insure that data from coding would be reliable and unbiased and in a form that would allow for efficient computer analysis.

An important aspect of coding methods involves the training of coders, where there is special concern with their understanding and use of the codes and the resulting reliability of the code data. All coders were women college graduates, who were selected on the basis of their general intelligence and interest in research rather than for their knowledge and training in social sciences. Each coder was trained to use three to five different codes. Each code required a separate training period with a group of two or more coders, beginning with practice coding on pretest materials. In the course of training, code problems were reviewed act by act, the code was reclarified, and further pretest material was coded, reviewed, and clarified, to the point at which intercoder agreement on an act-by-act basis reached a stable position above 85%. Ongoing reliability checks continued throughout the actual coding operation on a one-ninth sample of all interaction.

To provide for further control over possible halo effects and other biases in coding, additional controls were built into the procedure. Coders worked with typescripts that were unlabeled as to family type; thus coding was "blind" to the major independent variables of the study. In some cases it was possible to discern that the family had a schizophrenic child from the content of the discussion; however, whether the patient was present, and what type of adjustment history the patient had, would have been extremely difficult to detect. Further, halo effects resulting from the contamination of later coding of the same family were partially controlled by giving coders only the even-numbered or only the odd-numbered discussion items for any one family; no coder worked with a full family session. Also each person coded a large number of families applying a few codes, in contrast to applying all codes to a small number of families, when sterotypes of or hypotheses about family members could easily develop and affect later coding.

Finally, to increase coding efficiency, several independent codes were applied to the data in one reading of the typescript. Each code is included in one of nine separate coding operations on the basis of degree of complexity and level of inference required. For example, all of the following codes are easily and reliably applied in one operation: Incomplete Sentences, Repetitions, Incomplete Phrases, Laughter, Total Fragments, Negation, and Retraction.

Preparation of Code Data for Data Processing

Code numbers applied to each act in a family's discussion were recorded by the coder directly on mimeographed code sheets having IBM column numbers recorded horizontally across the top and sequential act numbers recorded vertically down the left margin. Thus any row on the code sheet referred to one act in the discussion; within that row were recorded code numbers for each of the codes applied to that act.

To allow for the greatest flexibility in data analysis, all of the code data referring to any one act was punched into a separate IBM card along with identifying material and sequence number. Thus for each family session there were approximately 1800 IBM cards. This format allowed for innumerable types of aggregation of acts, for within-act correlations, and for the analysis of act sequences. Finally, greater efficiency in analysis came from the direct transfer of card data to tape for use on high-speed computers.

Coding Reliability

The reliability of the measurement techniques has an important bearing on the confidence that may be placed in findings from the study, particularly in the case of interaction codes that have not been validated by previous research. However, in the study of group interaction there are no standard techniques for obtaining reliability data or for computing reliability indices, and no minimum levels of agreement that are generally accepted. Instead, techniques and levels of agreement are more often determined by the specific problem, the type of code, level of data analysis planned and the time and money available. (See Waxler and Mishler, 1966, for a discussion of these reliability problems.)

The approach used here for determining coding reliability was selected largely on the basis of plans for analysis of the data. Not only are we concerned with comparing agregated distributions from any of the codes—for example, comparing the proportion of one mother's total acts coded into the Complete Acknowledgment category of the Acknowledgment code with the same proportion for another mother—but we are also interested in examining sequences of single acts within any family session. This latter mode of analysis demands that the reliability of code judgments be acceptable for every act taken singly rather than simply for the total proportion of acts aggregated into a code category at the end of a session. (See

Heinicke and Bales, 1953, for an example of reliability obtained by comparison of marginal totals.) For this reason, all reliability measures were obtained from act-by-act comparisons between two coders. That is, each act, or unit, in the reliability sample was coded independently by two coders and their judgments compared; if they placed the unit in the same category that judgment was said to be consistent, or reliable.

A second concern, having relevance to the technique for collecting reliability data, has to do with maintaining the level of reliability over the long period of time required to code 88 family sessions. Because it is quite possible that coders, who use the code consistently at the time immediately following their training, unconsciously change the coding rules and thus introduce inconsistency into their judgments, a method for collecting ongoing reliability measures was used. One-ninth of each family session (one discussion task) was routinely coded by two independent coders and their level of agreement computed. If at any time the agreement level dropped below the cutoff point, coding was then stopped and the coders retrained.

There are no standard rules stating the level of agreement necessary in order for a code to be considered reliable. The level required for act-by-act agreement in this study is 85% and with the exception of two codes, Interaction Process Analysis and Acknowledgment Response, this level of agreement was met by all codes, both at the time of coder training and throughout the coding process. Act-by-act percent agreements for all codes on which reliability measures were collected are shown in Table 3.1. A second method useful for evaluating coding reliability is the use of the statistic k (Cohen, 1960), which removes from the percent agreement value the amount of agreement that would be expected by chance due to marginal distributions. Mean k values obtained from a random sample of 10 discussion items are also shown in Table 3.1. As is apparent from the table, reliability measured by k (on a much smaller sample) is somewhat lower than the simpler per cent measure.

A number of codes used in the study are not included in Table 3.1. The codes for Negations, Retractions, Repetitions, Incomplete Phrases, Laughter, Incomplete Sentences, and Total Fragments involve judgments about the presence or absence of certain words, symbols, or grammatical constructions that are so objective and simple to make that unreliability results only from clerical errors. Unreliability in the use of notations for Interruptions, Pauses, and Who-to-Whom, if it occurs, would be present at the earlier stages of typescript preparation rather than at the coding stage; the degree of unreliability at these earlier stages was not directly measured although the typescript-checking operation provided correction of errors. Reliability measures for the targets of speeches—the To whom data—were not computed because at no time was a second independent observer used to record these

Table 3.1 Reliability of Selected Interaction Codes: Mean and Range of Act-by-Act Per cent Agreement Between Two Coders; k Values for Act-by-act Agreement [a]

| Code | % Agreement | | | k Value |
	Number of Discussion Tasks	Mean	Range	Mean [b]
Acknowledgment, Stimulus	88	92	81–100	.84
Acknowledgment, Response	87	67	54–84	.59
Affect	87	87	65–99	.74
Focus	88	88	70–98	.80
Interaction Process Analysis	87	64	34–89	.62
Metacommunications	85	97	88–100	—
Objects	84	85	65–100	.76
Subjects	87	88	75–100	.87

[a] One discussion task in each experimental session was randomly selected for the reliability check; each task contains an average of 200 acts.
[b] Ten discussion tasks from the sample of families were selected for computation of k values.

data. However, all of the above codes not included in Table 3.1 were coded by two persons on a sample of from 25 to 30 discussion tasks (in contrast to the total 88 discussion tasks used for other codes) and each of these codes reached a per cent agreement level above 95%. The exception, Total Fragments, had 90% reliability.

The reliability levels reported in Table 3.1 refer to the act-by-act consistency for the interaction codes in the form in which they are applied by the coders; that is, no categories were combined or omitted. However, we are also concerned with the reliability of the interaction data in the form in which they are to be analyzed statistically. For purposes of analysis the raw code data are transformed into interaction indices (to be described in detail in the following pages) that involve combinations of code categories and conversion to percentage scores. The mean per cent agreement between two coders on a randomly selected sample of 10 family discussion tasks for each of these interaction indices is shown in Table 3.2.[3] Reliability of the index scores derived from the Metacommunication code is not presented because the frequencies of acts in the code categories are very low. No reliability of the index scores is reported for Incomplete Phrases, Incomplete Sentences, Repetitions, Laughter, Negation, Retraction, Interruptions and Simultaneous Speech because each has the same reliability level as the full code.

[3] The specific method used to compute the reliability of interaction index scores is described in Appendix A. 10.

As is apparent from the table the combination of code categories and their standardization into interaction indices result in higher reliability levels, particularly for those codes—Interaction Process Analysis and Ac-

Table 3.2   Reliability of Interaction Indices: Mean and Range of Per cent Act-by-Act Agreement Between Two Coders [a]

Code	% Act-by-Act Agreement	
	Mean	Range
Acknowledgment (Stimulus)		
1/total	99	98–100
2/total	98	96–100
3/total	92	88–98
4/total	95	90–98
5/total	96	93–98
Acknowledgment (Response)		
$1 + 2 + 3 + 4$/total	91	86–96
$1 + 2 + 3/1 + 2 + 3 + 4$	97	88–100
$1/1 + 2 + 3$	87	72–94
$2/1 + 2 + 3$	73	56–91
$3/1 + 2 + 3$	81	70–92
Affect		
$1 + 2 + 3$/total	92	86–97
$5 + 6 + 7$/total	95	92–99
4/total	91	85–99
$1/1 + 2 + 3$	97	83–100
$7/5 + 6 + 7$	97	88–100
$1 + 7/1 + 2 + 3 + 5 + 6 + 7$	97	84–100
$1 + 2 + 3/1 + 2 + 3 + 5 + 6 + 7$	98	94–100
Interaction Process Analysis		
$1 + 2 + 3 + 10 + 11 + 12$/total	84	69–97
$4 + 5 + 6/4 + 5 + 6 + 7 + 8 + 9$	97	91–100
$1 + 2 + 3/1 + 2 + 3 + 10 + 11 + 12$	90	51–100
$1/1 + 2 + 3$	96	75–100
$12/10 + 11 + 12$	99	90–100
$1 + 12/1 + 2 + 3 + 10 + 11 + 12$	96	76–100
$2 + 11$/total	94	83–100
Focus		
1/total	99	93–100
2/total	95	85–100
4/total	95	83–100
5/total	97	91–100
7/total	97	88–100
8/total	95	88–99

Table 3.2   Reliability of Interaction Indices: Mean and Range of Per cent Act-by-Act Agreement Between Two Coders [a] (Continued)

Code	% Act-by-Act Agreement	
	Mean	Range
Subject		
0/total	97	95–100
$1 + 2 + 3 + 4 + 5/1 + 2 + 3 + 4 + 5 + 6 + 7$ $+ 8 + 9 + 11$	96	91–100
$1/1 + 2 + 3 + 4 + 5$	99	98–100
$2 + 3/1 + 2 + 3 + 4 + 5$	100	98–100
$4/1 + 2 + 3 + 4 + 5$	100	99–100
$5/1 + 2 + 3 + 4 + 5$	100	98–100
$11/6 + 7 + 8 + 9 + 11$	98	94–100
Object		
0/total	94	88–97
$1 + 2 + 3 + 4 + 5/1 + 2 + 3 + 4 + 5 + 6 + 7$ $+ 8 + 9 + 11$	93	88–99
$1/1 + 2 + 3 + 4 + 5$	100	——
$2 + 3/1 + 2 + 3 + 4 + 5$	100	——
$4/1 + 2 + 3 + 4 + 5$	100	——
$5/1 + 2 + 3 + 4 + 5$	100	——
$11/6 + 7 + 8 + 9 + 11$	94	85–100

[a] The mean reliability level for each index score was derived from a randomly selected sample of 10 discussion tasks, each of which contains approximately 200 acts. The technique for computing the percent agreement for an interaction index is described in Appendix A.10.

knowledgment, Response—on which the overall code reliability was lower than 85%. Thus for all of the codes reliabilities are adequate, both for use in the form of aggregate scores and for sequential analyses.

Interaction Index Scores

The essential question being asked in the study is whether families having schizophrenic children interact differently from families having normal children, when interaction is measured by the application of the set of interaction codes. We are interested, however, in moving beyond simple profile analyses of the frequency distribution of acts within any one interaction code. It is not enough to be able simply to say that one family's acts cluster at the "positive affect" end of the code while another family gives more "negative affect," nor to say that mothers of normal children ask more questions than other mothers. Instead, we need aggregate measures in the form of quantitative scores that can be compared across families and to which statistical tests can legitimately be applied. Further, we need to reduce the number of different variables to a manageable set rather than handling each of the approximately 100 code categories as a separate variable. In order to meet these requirements—comparable quantitative scores and reduction of variables—the raw data in the form of frequencies in each code category are reduced to 79 interaction index scores, each of which is stated in the form of a percentage.

The reduction in number of variables is handled by combining the frequencies in several categories within a code. For example, a measure of "expressiveness" is obtained by combining categories, 1, 2, 3, 10, 11, 12 in the Interaction Process Analysis code, all of which require some evidence of affective expression in the act. This summation of code categories effectively reduces the numbers of separate variables and at the same time provides a summary measure that is theoretically interesting. Although theoretical interest is the major rule for combining code categories, empirical distributions of frequencies are also taken into account and thus a category with exceptionally low frequencies is ordinarily combined with another.

Frequencies of certain kinds of actions, however, are difficult to interpret when comparisons are made across a set of families. How can we understand a finding that shows one family with 250 interruptions in a session having 1000 acts and another family with 250 interruptions in a session having 2000 acts? Because the total number of acts differs for every family and for every family member, frequencies are converted to an index score in the form of a percentage that provides a standard score allowing for meaningful comparisons across families and across members. The baseline for the percentage is most often the total number of acts for the family, or the member, in the session, although it may also be the total frequency in a certain subgroup of categories, depending on theoretical interest.

Thus each interaction index score is a percentage obtained by combining frequencies in certain code categories and dividing this summed score by the total number of acts in the session. This interaction index is obtained for each family member in each session, for the whole family in each session, and for each member and the whole family in the two sessions combined. Interaction indices for individuals have as their baselines the total number of acts of that individual.[4]

The use of scores in the form of percentages is not necessarily a standard method for analysis of interaction data. Examples of analyses of un-

---

[4] A complete list of Interaction Index scores, their formulas and definitions, is in Appendix A. 11.

standardized frequencies in code categories can be found in Cheek (1964) and Reiss (1967). The decision to use interaction frequencies converted to percentage form follows from two arguments. First, we assume that it is the proportion of a certain type of act occurring within the total context of interaction that has a specific effect; thus one positive affect act in the context of 100 acts has, for us, the same effect or importance as 10 positive affect acts in the context of 1000 acts. (Each of these speakers would receive an index score with the value 1%). The alternative argument, that the one positive affect act is so unusual that it may have an effect on other people far beyond that of other single acts, is interesting but seems to have less general validity. The second argument for conversion of act frequencies into percentage scores is an empirical one. Because each family member and each family as a whole has a different rate of participation, the failure to standardize code frequencies allows the differential rate of participation to have an effect on the value of each interaction code; all category frequencies are contaminated by rates of speaking. For example, the family that talks for a relatively long period of time, with all members talking simultaneously, and thus produces a large number of acts, will necessarily have the highest frequency of complete acknowledgment acts, positive acts, incomplete sentences, etc., of all families. In order to treat the interaction code as a measure of the defined content it is necessary to remove the effect of participation rate; participation rate can then be treated as a variable in itself.

In addition to controlling for participation rate by converting code frequencies into percentages, a second form of control is built into the index scores. Baselines for some index scores, that is the value used for the denominator of the proportion, consist of the frequencies of acts in a small number of categories rather than the total numbers of acts in the whole session. This method is used to provide a set of index scores from the same code that are independent of each other. An example is the following: the index score for Positive Affect consists of frequencies of acts in categories 1+2+3 divided by the total number of acts in the session, thus giving a measure of the proportion of a person's total action that has any positive affective quality. The next question we might ask is, How are these positive actions distributed? Do some family members use the "positive acts referring to interpersonal relations," coded in category 1, at a higher rate than others? Thus the next index score to consider consists of all acts in category 1 divided by the total number of acts in categories 1+2+3. In this second index score the effect of differing proportions of positive affect acts for different speakers is controlled for; thus, even though, on the first index score, the two speakers may differ significantly, this difference does not affect their scores on the second index. The technique has the same effect as does controlling for successive variables in survey data; each new variable is examined with the effect of the previous one controlled. The majority of the multiple-category interaction codes provide index scores in this form.

The measurement techniques described in this chapter are complex and detailed, yet each has as its major goal the conversion of the tape-recorded family discussion to a form in which statistical comparisons can be made between families. At the same time, safeguards are provided at each step against altering the style and content of family interaction in the process of measurement. The steps in the process of data reduction consist of converting the tape to an accurate typescript and dividing interaction into small units, to which a large number of interaction codes are applied. Codes combine theoretical relevance with reliability and flexibility. In order to allow statistical analyses of frequencies in code categories, the frequencies are aggregated and converted to interaction indices. The following chapter will present the mode of analysis and the statistical methods used to compare the structure and style of interaction of schizophrenic and normal families.

Chapter 4

Strategy for Data Analysis
and Interpretation

Introduction to the Problem

The basic question of the study may be restated briefly and simply: What are the differences and similarities in interaction between normal families and families of schizophrenic patients? Problems of data analysis arise because the research design and the types of data collected permit this question to be asked in a large number of specific ways. Many different units and foci of analysis are possible, and each is a legitimate and interesting specification of the general question about differences between normal and patient families. Thus we may ask whether mothers in these different types of families differ from each other, or whether it is the fathers who differ, or whether the families qua families differ. Since there are two experimental sessions for each family—one with the patient and the other with his well sibling present—we may also ask whether differences between families appear in either or both sessions, and whether family behavior varies from session to session. At this stage in our understanding of and knowledge about family behavior and its relationship to schizophrenia, it seemed worthwhile to try to deal with as many of these questions as possible, provided that we could be clear about how the questions and the consequent findings were related to each other.

A strategy for data analysis was required that would (a) take advantage of the special features of the research design; (b) provide an orderly and systematic way of dealing with a large number of variables; and (c) permit us to distinguish between family, role, and situational (or session) effects. Each of these particular requirements will be described briefly in turn, in order to indicate the nature and range of problems for which our approach to data analysis was designed.

The research design includes several different control variables; this means that multiple comparisons enter into the first step in the examination of a variable. Controlling for premorbidity of the patient has the direct consequence that all subsequent comparisons are among three rather than between two types of family; that is, we are always comparing normals, good premorbids, and poor premorbids rather than schizophrenic with nonschizophrenic families. An indication of the increased complexity that accompanies the introduction of this third family type may be suggested by the fact that whereas there are only three possible rank order relationships between two types of family—either may be higher than the other or they may be equal—there are 13 possible relationships among three types of family. The intrafamily control of the well sibling also has the consequence of multiplying analyses because it produces two separate discussions for each family; interaction in each session may be examined separately or the two sessions may be pooled. Finally, in controlling for the sex of the patient (and concomitantly for the sex of the well sibling) we emerge with two different types of family: families of male and female schizophrenic patients; these are treated in our analyses as two separate samples, and all analyses are conducted separately within each of the two types.

Second, there is the large number of separate dependent variables—the 79 Interaction Index scores. In reporting and interpreting findings these have been clustered into five conceptual domains; each of the data chapters focuses on one of them and the variables that have been grouped together will be described in those chapters.[1] There is another set of problems associated with the inclusion of many dependent variables, namely, the relationships among them. Broadly speaking, there are three modes of analysis that might be undertaken: marginal, correlational, and sequential. This report is concerned only with marginal analyses; summary scores based on the overall frequency of an individual's (or family's) participation during an experimental session are computed separately for each interaction index. These 79 index scores are treated as independent of each other, and relationships between them and the control and independent variables

[1] Whereas 79 index scores were analyzed and examined, only 34 of these are reported in this book.

are explored separately for each one. In a sense the same question is asked 79 times: Is there a difference between these families on variable X? on Y? and so forth. In a correlational analysis one uses correlation between variables—either within-act or marginal correlations—as the dependent variable; here, the question is whether the magnitude of the correlation varies among the different families included in the study. Finally, in sequential analyses one focuses on the temporal relationships between variables rather than on the aggregate scores that average out fluctuations and patterning over time. Both correlational and sequential analyses are complex, and their efficiency and usefulness depend on knowledge gained from first-order marginal analyses. The results of second-order analyses of the data in this study will be reported in future publications.

The third complicating factor reflects our conceptual concern with separating the effects of family, session, and family member on the dependent variables. In more general terms these are group, situational, and role effects. Our data permit each of these types of analysis, and we believe that each of them is important and relevant to the central questions of the study. It is therefore imperative to clarify the meaning of each of these analyses, the differences among them, and their relationships to each other. This requires a set of principles for the organization and interpretation of the several types of analysis. The rest of this chapter describes the paradigm for analysis developed for this purpose; results are reported in succeeding chapters.

Paradigm for Analysis

The idea of "experimental designs" is taken for granted in branches of experimental psychology and social psychology and the relationships between the design of the experiment and the statistical analysis of different effects on the dependent variable—of the experimental and control variables and of interaction—have been elaborated in precise and elegant detail. Less attention has been paid to an equally important problem in the study of social systems, namely, the problem of the design of the analysis.

The objectives are essentially the same as in the design of experiments, namely, to separate the effects of various factors on the dependent variable. The problem, however, is considerably more complicated because in the analysis of social systems those factors in which we are interested are often not independent of each other. For example, one of the main concerns in the study of relationships between individual performance and social organization is to separate the effects on an individual's behavior of three analytically distinct factors: his membership in the organization, his specific role position within the organization, and his particular personality characteristics. In an experimental setting where the independent variables may be manipulated directly it is theoretically possible to examine the effect on any one variable insulated from the effects of others by techniques of experimental control and randomization. In the real world of families the several independent variables are entangled with each other and the effects of particular variables can be examined only through statistical procedures that control for or partial out the effects of other variables.

The solution to the general problem of distinguishing both conceptually and empirically among these different types of factor, essentially on different levels of social-psychological analysis, requires a formalization of the procedural rules that are followed in moving from basic observations on individuals to final scores that characterize either groups, roles, or persons. In addition, the use in combination of these different levels of analysis requires a set of "rules of inference" for interpreting consistencies and inconsistencies across levels. The paradigm for analysis described below that is followed in the presentation and interpretation of findings contains an explicit formulation of both the rules of procedure through which scores are assembled to denote features of groups, roles, and persons, and rules of inference that form the basis of interpretation of findings from the several analyses.

The most serious and sustained effort to come to grips with and work out systematic solutions to this problem is found in the work of Paul Lazarsfeld and his students and co-workers (Kendall and Lazarsfeld, 1950; Lazarsfeld and Rosenberg, 1955; Lazarsfeld and Menzel, 1961; Blau, 1960; Coleman, 1961). Our approach draws on their efforts. In particular we use the scheme proposed by Riley because it provides a comprehensive framework that includes the special types of analysis and rules developed by earlier investigators (Riley, 1963). In developing a set of rules of inference, we have followed the model outlined by Davis for the analysis of "compositional effects" (Davis et al., 1961). The particular requirements of our study have led us to adapt and modify in some respects the rules set forth by Riley and Davis, but in essential respects the design for data analysis used here is an application of their approach.

These investigators have been particularly sensitive to several types of fallacies in the interpretation of data about social behavior, and the approach is designed in part to clarify the problems involved when hypotheses and data refer to different units of analysis. For example, an ecological or aggregative fallacy arises when motivations are imputed to individuals to interpret or account for their behavior on the basis of comparisons across groups. In other words, the data refer to groups—one level of analysis—while the hypotheses refer to individuals—another level of analysis. This fallacy appears in one form when differences between mean scores for groups of persons are used as if these aggregate scores provide a valid basis for interpreting individual behavior. A more common illustration of the fallacy in sociological writings has been the interpretation of correlations between population indices, that is, ecological correlations, as if they were individual correlations (Robinson, 1950). Thus, to cite a famous example, we might take the positive correlation between the proportion of Negroes in census tracts and differential rates of mental hospital admissions to mean that Negroes are more likely to be admitted to mental hospitals; as it turns out, it is the whites living in the Negro areas who contribute disproportionately to the admission rate. Similarly, a study of family interaction might show that total amounts of participation are lower in families of schizophrenic patients than in normal families. If this were interpreted to mean that schizophrenics are low participators this would be another example of the ecological fallacy, because the differential rates could be reflecting differences in the behavior solely of mothers and fathers and not of children (as is true for many of our findings).

A psychologistic fallacy—more common among psychologists, as its label implies—arises when data gathered on individuals are used as the basis for interpretation without regard to the social contexts within which the individuals are behaving. Thus if one found higher levels of verbal participation by sons in normal families than by schizophrenic sons this might be interpreted as further evidence of the schizophrenic process. However, the interpretation would have to be qualified if we discovered that the normal parents also had higher levels of such behavior than the patient's parents, and that the proportion of the family's total participation contributed by schizophrenic and normal sons was relatively equal. Thus the psychologistic fallacy involves an overinterpretation or overemphasis of individual psychological factors when fuller understanding requires knowledge of the group or social context of the individual's behavior.

In Riley's framework a "social system analysis" is a complete and comprehensive analysis that is constituted by a set of distinct though related "partial analyses." This approach to the analysis of social systems makes explicit and clarifies the types of data and comparisons appropriate to each of several distinct levels of theory and analysis: the group and the individual and their combinations. We shall be using only two of Riley's types of partial analysis, but a brief outline of the full framework is necessary to indicate how the different analyses are related to each other.

The basic distinction is between "group" and "individual" analyses. The former is focused on differences between groups (families, in our study), without reference to the individuals composing the groups, and the latter is concerned with differences between individuals, (in this case, family member roles), without reference to their group membership. The differ-

Chart 4.1 Sources of Scores for Group, Individual, and Structural Analyses of Families [a]

		Type of Family								
					Schizophrenic					
		Normal			Good Premorbid			Poor Premorbid		
		001 002 . . . *n*			101 102 . . . *n*			201 202 . . . *n*		
Patient Session $_{(Pt)}$	Fa									
	Mo									
	Pt									
	Fam									
Sibling Session $_{(sib)}$	Fa									
	Mo									
	Sib									
	Fam									
Combined Sessions $_{(c)}$	Fa									
	Mo									
	Ch									
	Fam									

[a] Each cell in each of the matrices represents a different score on a variable. Each family—001, 002, 201, and so forth—has 12 scores listed in the column, a separate score for each family member and for the family as a whole in each session and for the sessions taken together. In each case the index score is based only on the acts contributed by the family member to whom the score applies. Thus an index score for the father of case 001 in the patient session (Fa_{pt}) is the percentage of *his* total participation in that session in the relevant code category; the score for the family across both sessions (Fam_{c}) is the percentage of the total participation of *all members* in both sessions coded into the particular category. In the main group and structural analyses the basic comparison is between the three types of family with the scores represented by each row

ences between them can be seen in the different sources of scores for comparisons between family roles versus comparisons between families as groups, shown in Chart 4.1.

In a purely individual analysis we might compare fathers with mothers irrespective of family type and experimental session. The cells for combined session scores for fathers in normal and schizophrenic families would be summed and averaged, as would those for mothers. The comparison would be: $\overline{X}_{Fa_c}$: $\overline{X}_{Mo_c}$ on variable "Z". An illustrative hypothesis for which this form of analysis is appropriate would be: fathers interrupt more than mothers. Because the effect of membership in different types of families is one of the basic concerns of the study, this level of individual analysis is not relevant to our aims and interests and it will not be pursued further.

In a group analysis, the percentage index score for each family as a whole is computed; these are then summed, averaged, and compared. Thus if the hypothesis to be tested is that the rates of interruption vary among these types of families, then the comparison is: normal $(\overline{X}_{Fam_c})$: good premorbid $(\overline{X}_{Fam_c})$: poor premorbid $(\overline{X}_{Fam_c})$.[2] Many of our comparisons will be of this type; in addition, as will be seen below, the significance and meaning of other partial analyses is in large part a function of their relationship to findings at the group level of analysis. This level of analysis is concerned with properties of families that cannot be reduced to individual levels of explanation despite the fact that the original source of data is the behavior of individuals.

The irreducibility of findings at the group level to explanations in terms of individual behavior is a direct function of how the scores for families as groups are constructed, as may be seen by reference to Chart 4.1. A family's interruption score, Fam_{pt} for example, is calculated by taking the frequency of all interruption acts contributed by all family members and

---

treated separately; thus there are 12 separate analyses of each Index score: $N_{Fa_{pt}}$: $G_{Fa_{pt}}$: $P_{Fa_{pt}}$, $N_{Mo_{pt}}$: $G_{Mo_{pt}}$: $P_{Mo_{pt}}$, . . . , N_{Ch_c} : G_{Ch_c} : P_{Ch_c}, N_{Fam_c} : G_{Fam_c} : P_{Fam_c}. Other analyses involve comparisons between rows within each family type. For example, Intersession comparisons: $N_{Fa_{pt}}$: $N_{Fa_{sib}}$ or $G_{Pt_{pt}}$: $G_{Sib_{sib}}$; and Intrafamily comparisons: $P_{Fa_{pt}}$: $P_{Mo_{pt}}$: $P_{Pt_{pt}}$ or $G_{Fa_{sib}}$: $G_{Mo_{sib}}$: $G_{Sib_{sib}}$.

Here, as in other data tables, the standard designation for family sessions, as shown by the second subscript, is as follows: "pt" refers to the session when the patient was present; "sib" refers to the session when the patient's well sibling was present; "c" refers to scores obtained from the two sessions combined.

[2] The statistical tests used in the analysis are described in pages 73-76. Nonparametric tests were used and most of them involve a comparison of mean ranks rather than mean scores. In this exposition of the design of the analysis it is simpler to state the comparisons as between mean scores; the argument is the same but the reader should bear in mind that the findings will be somewhat different in form.

dividing this by the total number of acts contributed by all members of the family in that session. Variations among family members in either total acts or frequency of interruptions are not taken into account in computing family scores; each act and each interruption is counted equally regardless of its source. It is evident that this type of family score, used in the group analyses, is very different from the unweighted average of family member scores.

As Riley points out, an understanding of the distinction between group and individual analyses is necessary to avoid both "ecological" and "atomistic" fallacies, the former being interpretation of individuals on the basis of group comparisons, and the latter an interpretation of group differences on the basis of individual comparisons. Although each is a legitimate but "partial" approach to the analysis of social systems; they are relatively independent of each other and must be used together if the aim is to make statements about both individuals and groups.

Two more complex forms of analysis are related to this basic pair: contextual analysis, in which the focus is on the individual but with explicit reference to the group context; and structural analysis, in which the focus is on the group but with reference to internal role differentiation.

In a contextual analysis the aim is to separate group from individual effects on a dependent variable by the direct comparison of types of individuals within types of groups; typically, the same independent variable is used to classify both individuals and groups. Thus in our study we might ask if high and low interrupters (persons) differ from each other in the same way on negative affect in high and low interrupting families (group scores). Here the procedure would be to rank all families on the basis of their overall interruption rate ($\overline{X}_{Fam_c}$) and to classify families as high or low; then all individuals would be ranked on their interruption rate ($\overline{X}_{Fa_c}$, $\overline{X}_{Mo_c}$, $\overline{X}_{Ch_c}$) and classified as high or low. Finally, high and low interrupters would be compared on their rates of negative affect within high interrupting families *and* within low interrupting families to see if the differences between them were the same or different in these two contexts. Contextual analyses that keep the individual as the focus of attention will occupy us at later stages in the work. They will be helpful in clarifying the ways in which family and role patterns interact to affect an individual's behavior. At this point, the family as a group is our primary concern; structural analyses are of more immediate interest since they keep the group as the central focus. (For examples of contextual analyses, see Davis et al., 1961 and Blau, 1960.)

Riley describes two types of structural analysis—within-group and segmental analyses. In both the aim is to determine whether relationships found at the group level are the same as or different from relationships within separate group components, that is, within the structural elements of the group. The definition of structural elements of a group will vary, of course, with the theory and the specific problem under study. We shall treat family-member roles, that is, father, mother, and child, as such structural elements. We shall also treat the two experimental sessions as separate segments for these analyses although here we are not dealing with substructures of the family but with two different situations or stimulus environments, in one of which the schizophrenic patient is present and in the other his well sibling.

In a within-group structural analysis we compare differences between elements across groups. Typically the variable used to classify groups is related to or similar to that used for classifying substructures; this is analogous to what is done in a contextual analysis. One example is a comparison of the schizophrenic member of the family (the patient) with a nonschizophrenic member (the well sibling) in families differing in their degree of schizophrenia (good vs. poor premorbid families). However, these analyses involve restrictions (such as the exclusion in this example of normal families that do not contain schizophrenic children) that make this analysis less appropriate and useful for our purposes than the other form of structural analysis.

In a segmental structural analysis, each element or segment of the group is compared across the different types of group. In this study this involves a comparison of fathers with fathers, of mothers with mothers, and of children with children in the three different types of family. Thus, having found a difference in rates of interruption among families at the level of a group analysis, this form of structural analysis then asks whether the same pattern is present in each of the role segments of the family, namely, for fathers, mothers, and children. Here we would compare normal ($\overline{X}_{Fa_c}$) : good premorbid ($\overline{X}_{Fa_c}$) : poor premorbid ($\overline{X}_{Fa_c}$); similar comparisons would be made for mothers and children. As noted above, we shall also use the two experimental sessions as segments for this form of analysis. In these comparisons we shall be asking whether the pattern found for the family across both sessions ($\overline{X}_{Fam_c}$), that is, when the presence or absence of the schizophrenic child is not taken into account, is the same or different in each of the two segments—in one of which the schizophrenic child is present and in the other his/her well sibling.

In addition to these forms of group and segmental structural analysis, described by Riley, we also report what may be considered a second-order structural analysis. The first-order analyses treat the family-member roles and experimental sessions as two different types of group segments. The second-order analysis brings them together for a role-within-session set of comparisons. For example, we shall compare fathers in different family types with each other in the patient session and again separately within the well sibling session. In terms of the scores in Chart 4.1 this comparison is (normal)$\overline{X}_{Fa_{pt}}$: (good)$\overline{X}_{Fa_{pt}}$: (poor)$\overline{X}_{Fa_{pt}}$ and (normal)$\overline{X}_{Fa_{sib}}$: (good)$\overline{X}_{Fa_{sib}}$: (poor)$\overline{X}_{Fa_{sib}}$.

The several different types of analysis are outlined in Chart 4.2; this format will be followed in the presentation of findings.

Riley's framework for a complete social system analysis includes group, individual, contextual, and structural partial analyses. Our data are most appropriate for and our theoretical interests most compatible with and relevant to the group and segmental structural analyses. Together these will constitute the first analytic step. The group analyses allow us to answer such questions as whether the normal, good, and poor premorbid families differ as collectives, or in their general cultures, without regard to the internal role structure of the families. The segmental structural analyses

Chart 4.2   Framework for Group and Segmental Structural Analyses [a]

| Group Analysis | | | Segmental Structural Analyses | | | | | |
| | | | Roles | | | Roles within Sessions | | |
N	G	P	N	G	P	N	G	P
$\overline{X}Fam_c$	$\overline{X}Fam_c$	$\overline{X}Fam_c$	$\overline{X}Fa_c$	$\overline{X}Fa_c$	$\overline{X}Fa_c$	$\overline{X}Fa_{pt}$	$\overline{X}Fa_{pt}$	$\overline{X}Fa_{pt}$
			$\overline{X}Mo_c$	$\overline{X}Mo_c$	$\overline{X}Mo_c$	$\overline{X}Fa_{sib}$	$\overline{X}Fa_{sib}$	$\overline{X}Fa_{sib}$
			$\overline{X}Ch_c$	$\overline{X}Ch_c$	$\overline{X}Ch_c$			
				Sessions		$\overline{X}Mo_{pt}$	$\overline{X}Mo_{pt}$	$\overline{X}Mo_{pt}$
			$\overline{X}Fam_{pt}$	$\overline{X}Fam_{pt}$	$\overline{X}Fam_{pt}$	$\overline{X}Mo_{sib}$	$\overline{X}Mo_{sib}$	$\overline{X}Mo_{sib}$
			$\overline{X}Fam_{sib}$	$\overline{X}Fam_{sib}$	$\overline{X}Fam_{sib}$	$\overline{X}Ch_{pt}$	$\overline{X}Ch_{pt}$	$\overline{X}Ch_{pt}$
						$\overline{X}Ch_{sib}$	$\overline{X}Ch_{sib}$	$\overline{X}Ch_{sib}$

[a] In the analysis nonparametric statistical tests are used that are based on comparisons of mean ranks. The scores in the chart should therefore be understood as mean ranks rather than as scores. The basic comparison is of the three family types with each other on each score. Tables reporting findings include the level of statistical significance and whether a family's mean rank is high (H), middle (M), or low (L).

allow us to investigate the roles of particular family members within each of the family cultures. These analyses also permit an examination of the degree to which family cultures and roles change in the presence or absence of the schizophrenic child. Within this general framework of group and structural analyses we have also carried out across-session and within-family comparisons. The former directly compares the behavior of family members in the two experimental sessions and asks if the amount of change between sessions is statistically significant in any of the family types; the latter asks if there are significant patterns of role differentiation in any family type in either session. These across-session and within-family analyses are subordinate to the main across-family analyses; the particular statistical tests employed will be described in a later section of this chapter and findings are incorporated in the data chapters.

Guides for Interpreting Relationships Between Group and Structural Analyses [3]

The group analysis provides answers to our most general question, namely, do the families of normal, good and poor premorbid schizophrenic patients differ from each other as collective social units? In this analysis no account is taken of the internal composition of the family in terms of member roles or of differences between the family's behavior in situations when either their schizophrenic or their nonschizophrenic child is present. In segmental structural analyses, this collective unit is partitioned in two independent ways: (a) into three segments or structures of family roles, that is, father, mother, and child; (b) into the two segments representing the two experimental sessions. This permits us to ask about each of these segments the same question asked at the group level. In developing this approach, in which several "partial" analyses are used in combination, we have argued that this will permit a more comprehensive picture of and a fuller understanding of the functioning of these families as social systems. There is however, the problem that the analyses may not agree with each other. That is, differences found between families in the group analysis may be present for all, some, or none of the family roles; they may be present or not in either experimental situation; differences for the mother, father, or child may be present in either or both of the experimental situations. In anticipation of

[3] As indicated at an earlier point, we will also pursue second-order structural analyses that combine roles and sessions, asking, for example, whether overall differences between fathers are present in the patient and/or sibling session (see Chart 4.2). Interpretations of relationships between these findings and those from the first-order role and session structural analyses follow the same interpretive guides described here for group and structural analyses.

these possibilities we have constructed a set of guides to interpretation based on the similarity in direction and strength between levels of analysis.

Findings at both group and structural levels of analysis may be characterized in terms of their direction and strength; relationships between the two analyses may be defined by the degree of similarity in direction and strength between these findings. The following definitions of these aspects will be used.

1. Direction: This is the rank order of family types as high, middle, and low on scores on a dependent variable, that is, an Interaction Index. The statistical test of significance used to evaluate differences among the three types of family is the Kruskal-Wallis "H" test; this nonparametric statistic is based on a comparison of the mean ranks of the groups being examined. (Details of the several statistical tests used in the full range of analyses are presented in a later section of this chapter.) Thus the H, M, and L designations refer to the relative mean ranks of the three family types in the study. When rank orders of family types on Group and structural analyses are identical, this is counted as the "same"; if the rank orders differ in any away, the patterns are "different."

2. Strength: For present purposes, a relationship is "strong" or present if the difference is statistically significant with a p value of .20 or less; the relationship is "weak" or not present if the p value is greater than .20. This liberal criterion was adopted because the study was not designed to test one or two hypotheses but to explore trends and patterns across different variables and different levels of analysis.

A large number of relationships between findings from group and structural analyses could be specified by taking into account differences in degrees of strength or particular variants of the rank order patterns. We have reduced the full range of possibilities by using strength and similarity of direction as dichotomies to classify findings: findings are significant or not significant; they are the same or different in rank order pattern. The result is the set of types of relationships outlined in Chart 4.3.

Each of the six types of relationships listed in Chart 4.3 between group and segmental structural analyses implies something different about the nature and meaning both of interaction patterns within each type of family and of the differences between families. Each type will be illustrated with a concrete example using data from the study. In identifying and distinguishing these types from each other we have been concerned particularly with locating and clarifying the "source" of the effect on the dependent variable. In other words we are interested in whether a sig-

Chart 4.3 Relationships Between Findings of Group and Structural Analyses

Group Analysis	Segmental Structural Analysis	Relationship Type
Significant differences	No Significant Differences	I. Collective Effect
	All significant: same patterns as group analysis	Collective and Role Effects: II. Replicated pattern
	Some significant: of same pattern as group analysis	III. Congruent pattern
	Some significant: but pattern(s) differ from group analysis	IV. Incongruent pattern
No significant differences	Some significant differences	V. Role effect
	No significant differences	VI. No group or role effect

nificant difference between normal and patient families represents a group (that is, family as collective), or role (that is, family member), or situation (that is, experimental session), or interaction effect. In its logic this approach is similar to that of the analysis of variance, in which the variance in a set of scores is partitioned into its separate sources in order to determine the effects of different variables. In procedure, it resembles the application of successive control variables in social research. The clarification of group, role, situational, and interaction effects seems to us essential to the understanding of families as social systems. Two of the types listed in Chart 4.3 are "pure" effects of the group or of roles (types I and V); three are "interaction" effects (II, III, IV), and one is the "no effect" case. Each type will be illustrated below with a concrete example using data from the study.[4]

It will be evident in the following illustrative discussion, and in the later interpretation of findings, that there is an assumption that differences in interaction scores between types of families represent differential family "norms" for the display or expression of the particular behavior under examination. The quotation marks are to indicate that our use of the term is loose and heuristic; it serves as an organizing idea rather than a systematic concept. We do not have any information, beyond the behavioral uniformities themselves, to demonstrate that there are shared

---

[4] Our distinctions among these types and our approach to their interpretation derives from the analysis of "compositional effects" by Davis and his colleagues (Davis et al., 1961). Similarities between our types and analyses and theirs will be noted when relevant.

expectancies within families (either within or outside their immediate awareness) regarding these behaviors, or that behaving in a particular way is required in order to avoid sanctions. On the other hand, it seems to us reasonable to assume that systematic differences in behavior between types of family, and the uniformities within each that such differences depend on, reflect different constraints operating on the members of these families. Whether these constraints are pervasive and apply to all members in all situations is the central question to which this multilevel analysis is directed. We shall use the term "norm" both descriptively to refer to behavioral uniformities that differentiate families from each other and, depending on the pattern of findings of the different levels of analysis, as a basis for inferring the types of constraints that may be operating. (Our usage is more consistent with traditions in social psychology than sociology; compare, for example, Sherif, 1958, with Gibbs' recent discussion of the problem of defining types of norm, 1965.)

Type I. Collective. Differences among families are significant in the group analysis, but no significant differences are found in the structural analysis. In our study this states that the normal, good and poor premorbid families are different as collective units, but that there are no differences in the role behavior of different members of the family. That is, fathers do not differ from fathers, mothers from mothers, nor children from children among the three types of family. An example of a Type I pattern is found in our measure of question-asking from the Acknowledgment-Stimulus code (frequency of questions divided by total number of acts).

	Family (Patient Session)				Role Segments (Patient Session)			
	Normal	Good	Poor	p		N	G	P	p
% Questions	Low	Middle	High	.20	Father	L	M	H	n.s.
					Mother	L	H	M	n.s.
					Child	L	M	H	n.s.

Because the measure of the family as a collective unit does show significant differences between types of family, but these relationships disappear at the level of roles, then we may infer that the differential effect of group climates in these families on the quality of interaction does not operate through the different roles. Davis et al. refers to this as a "pure" group effect. This may also be thought of as a family norm effect. The pattern might, for example, occur in the following way. Each type of family follows an implicit norm prescribing that a certain proportion of their acts be questions. The preferred level of questioning varies across families—the normal families having a lower level than the schizophrenic families—but the norms do not prescribe that each member of the family contribute questions at a rate that is proportional to the overall norm. Depending on the course of the discussion, there will be differences among families in the proportions of question-asking acts contributed by different family members. For example, in one family on one occasion, the mother may question at a disproportionately high rate to counterbalance low rates by the father and child, thus bringing the overall rate to the proper normative level; in another family, the members may be relatively equal in their rates of question asking. If this were the case we would find significant differences in the group analysis, but would not find these differences in the structural role analysis. This would be the collective effect illustrated above.

Type II. Replicated Pattern. The pattern consists of a statistically significant relationship at the family collectivity level along with a replication of this relationship in each of the segments in the structural analysis. Our measure of "acknowledgment of others" provides an example of this type. (Acknowledgment-Response code).

	Family (Combined Sessions)				Role Segments (Combined Sessions)				
	Normal	Good	Poor	*p*		N	G	P	*p*
% Acknowledgment	High	Middle	Low	.01	Father	H	M	L	.05
					Mother	H	M	L	.02
					Child	H	M	L	.05

There appear to be several ways to interpret this kind of relationship. Davis et al. call it a "bandwagon" effect because the original group effect is intensified for each role player. Blau calls it "structural" effect, that is, one that does not change when each individual is examined. It tells us that the role each person plays in the family is consistent with the general norms of the family. In our example we might interpret the finding as indicating that all of the role players conform to the differential family norms about "acknowledging."

TYPE III. Congruent Pattern. This type differs from replication in that one or two of the segmental analyses drop to nonsignificance; however the patterns that remain significant are identical in rank order with the group level comparison. The interaction effect here has the following meaning: there is conformity to family norms for particular roles (or in particular situations) but not in others. Our measure of "rate of being interrupted by others" exemplifies this effect.

	Family (Combined Sessions)				Role Segments (Combined Sessions)				
	Normal	Good	Poor	*p*		N	G	P	*p*
% Interruptions	High	Low	Middle	.20	Father	H	L	M	.20
					Mother	H	L	M	.20
					Child	H	M	L	n.s.

In the example the family cultures differ significantly in their general rates of being interrupted by others but these differences seem to operate only in the roles of father and mother. The children in all three types of family have patterns of being interrupted that do not differ significantly from each other. Thus the patterns of interruption of parents are consistent with the family norm although the pattern of interruption of children is not.

Type IV. Incongruent Pattern. This differs from the other two collective-role interaction types in that one or more of the segmental comparisons is both statistically significant and different in pattern from the statistically significant finding in the group analysis. As in all of the interaction types, where findings of both group and structural analyses are significant, interpretations must take explicit account of both group and structural levels. An example from our "degree of acknowledgment" (Acknowledgment-Response code) shows this relationship.

	Family (Patient Session)				Role Segments (Patient Session)				
	Normal	Good	Poor	p		N	G	P	p
% Acknowledg-ment	High	Middle	Low	.01	Father	H	M	L	.20
					Mother	M	H	L	.10
					Child	H	M	L	.02

Here the combined effect of family norms and roles differs for different role players in the family. Fathers and children in normal families have relatively high rates of acknowledgment, as does the normal family as a whole. However, mothers in normal, highly acknowledging families do not acknowledge as much, while mothers in good premorbid, medium acknowledging families are highest among mothers in acknowledgment. Thus in this type of pattern there are both the effects of "role" and of "group" that serve to specify more clearly the functioning of each of the family types. In this example there is evidence that mothers in normal and good families deviate in terms of acknowledgment, whereas fathers and children conform to the family norm.

Type V. Role Effect. The opposite of the Type I collective effect is found when there is a random (or nonsignificant) pattern at the group level but one or more significant patterns at the level of roles.

An example of this pattern of findings, which Davis et al. call a "pure role effect," is found in an analysis of questions (Acknowledgment-Stimulus code).

	Family (Well Sibling Sessions)				Role Segments (Sibling Session)				
	Normal	Good	Poor	p		N	G	P	p
% Questions	Middle	High	Low	n.s.	Father	M	H	L	n.s.
					Mother	L	H	M	.20
					Child	H	M	L	n.s.

Here a significant difference among families occurs only for one of the role players and not for the family as a whole. Thus one can say that a differential relationship between question asking and family type is specific to one role in the family, that of the mother. It is empirically possible for other kinds of role effect to occur as well as the one in the example, two role players may have statistically significant patterns in the absence of a group pattern. If this occurs it would be seen as a specification of each of the roles. It is possible for these two patterns to have different directions. For example, if the father role in the example were statistically significant rather than "random," we could state something about role differentiation with regard to question asking in the different families.

Type VI. No Group or Structural Effect. This is the case of no significant differences among family types at either the group level of analysis or in the several segmental comparisons. It is a multiple confirmation of the null hypothesis that tells us that there are no differences among normal, good, and poor premorbid families in their general norms, or among different family members, or in their behavior in different situations. Thus this approach, by providing a specification of the variety of ways in which the families are not different, permits, even in the null case a more meaningful interpretation of their similarity to each other than is possible with the usual nonsignificant finding.

As has been suggested through the use of concrete examples, each of the six types of relationship between group and structural analyses is found in our data. In the following chapters this classification of patterns of findings will be used as a guide to interpretation.

Across-session and Within-family Analyses

The group and segmental structural analyses, derived from Riley's scheme, provide a set of detailed answers to the major question of the study: how and in what situations are schizophrenic families and their members different from normal families? All these analyses involve comparisons across the three types of family, or across role players in the three types of family. There are, however, other theoretically relevant aspects of family structure that may be related to the structural analyses but are not explicitly provided for in the Riley paradigm. These are the patterns of role differentiation within these types of family and the degree of stability or change in behavior from situation to situation for families and their members. The internal structure of role relationships within the family and the degree to which family members alter their behavior when in different situations with different children may be examined with our data. Combined with the findings from the structural analyses, these analyses will provide an even more complex and explicit picture of family relationships.

Across-session Comparisons. The first question asks whether any family member, or a family as a whole, changes its behavior, as measured by our interaction index scores, from one session to the next. This might be thought of as a measure of reliability except for the fact that the two situations are qualitatively different; in one the schizophrenic child is present, and in the other his well sibling is present. Thus we are asking whether any one role player consistently alters his behavior in the presence of the patient, or whether the whole family's style or quality of interaction is different when the sick child is present.

Comparisons across the two sessions also allow us to ask a second question, that cannot be asked in the segmental structural analyses: is the behavior of the patient child significantly different from the behavior of his own well sibling? Does the patient, labeled as the "deviant," take a role different from another child in his own family? Knowledge about these differences adds to the validity of inferences from the structural analyses about the parents' responses to the patient child.

Within-family Comparisons. A major aspect of theories about normal and schizophrenic family structure has to do with role differentiation within the family. For example, Lidz (Lidz et al., 1957b) suggests that in some schizophrenic families normal parental roles are reversed, with the mother taking the instrumental role and the father the expressive role. A direct test of hypotheses about role differentiation requires a form of analysis wherein the three members of each family are compared with each other. We would assume that roles are differentiated within a family, or that a role specialist exists, if, for example, the father is always highest on a particular type of behavior, the mother always medium, and the child always lowest within one or another of the family types.

The presence or absence of specialization within a type of family can then be combined with findings from the structural comparisons, adding further evidence for the existence of certain structural patterns. For example, if one type of family is consistently different, and higher, than other members on Positive Affect, but there is no role differentiation within the families, we would argue that norms for the expression of positive affect are different in each type of family, yet these norms apply in the same way to every family member. If role specialization were present instead, it would be more reasonable to assume that the rules for behavior differ from those in other families but apply differentially to role players within the family.

The statistical tests used in these across-session and within-family analyses, as well as in the structural analyses, are described in the following section.

Statistical Tests. We have already indicated that this report focuses on marginal analyses, that is, comparison of different family types using aggregate scores in the form of Interaction Indices each examined separately. The small sample size, the large number of comparisons required by our analysis paradigm, the likelihood that many of the score distributions are not normal, and the properties of a marginal analysis were all considerations that entered into our selection of nonparametric statistical tests. These tests, described briefly below, may all be found in standard texts that include nonparametric approaches (for example, Siegel, 1956). Because many different statistical comparisons are made using the same basic data (Interaction Indices) reference may be made to Chart 4.4, in which each type of comparison and its data source is described. Each of the tests listed in the chart is described in more detail in the following sections.

Across-family Comparisons. Testing for the significance of differences between normal, good, and poor families is the basic comparison in the group and structural analyses outlined above. The unit of analysis is either the family score on an index—in the group and session comparisons—or a family member's score in the role and role-within-session comparisons. Two different but related tests are used: The Kruskal-Wallis "H" test and the Mann-Whitney "U" test.

Both tests are based on comparisons of mean ranks for the different samples, that is, family types. The procedure is to take the scores from all families and to rank them in a single series; the ranks for each family type are then summed and averaged separately. The "H" test (sometimes called a one-way analysis of variance by ranks) may be used with three or more samples, while the "U" test is restricted to the two-sample case. Both tests tell us whether the differences in mean ranks are significantly different from the chance variation that might be expected if the samples were drawn from the same population. A significant difference is likely to appear only when families of the different types cluster at different points along the full series of ranks. We have used the "H" test to evaluate the significance of differences among all three types of family and the "U" test for comparisons between each of the pairs of families. Inasmuch as we are concerned with patterns and trends in the findings rather than with testing one particular hypothesis, we have taken a probability value of .20 on the "H" test as an indication that the differences across families deserve attention; on the "U" test a probability value of .10 is required. These are all two-tailed tests.

Across-session Comparisons. One of the across-family analyses described above involves comparisons between normal, good, and poor family members within each of the two experimental sessions. We might

Chart 4.4   Statistical Comparisons and Their Data Source

Group Analysis			Roles	N	P	G		Roles Within Sessions N	P	G
	N P G		Fa_c	d	e	f	Fa_{pt}	s	t	u
			Mo_c	g	h	i	Fa_{sib}	v	w	x
Fam_c	a[a] b c		Ch_c	j	k	l				
							Mo_{pt}	y	z	aa
			Sessions	N	P	G	Mo_{sib}	bb	cc	dd
			Fam_{pt}	m	n	o	Ch_{pt}	ee	ff	gg
			Fam_{sib}	p	q	r	Ch_{sib}	hh	ii	jj

I.   Across-family Comparisions: within each row, comparisons are made across family types

     "H" test: Three types of family (or role player) are compared across a row; for example, a with b with c, or bb with cc with dd

     "U" test: Any two of the three types of family (or role player) are compared across a row; for example, j with k, or cc with dd

II.   Across-session Comparisions: all comparisons are made down the columns

     "rho":   Within a column, correlations across sessions for families (or role players) are made; for example, t with w or o with r

     "T" test: Within a column, differences across sessions for families (or role players) are computed; for example, $(gg - jj)$, or, $(m - p)$

III.   Across-session Variability: amounts of change between sessions are compared

     "H" test: Differences across sessions for three role players from different families are compared with each other; for example, $(s \text{-} v)$ with $(t \text{-} w)$ with $(u \text{-} x)$

     "W" test: Differences across session for three members within a family are compared with each other; for example, $(s \text{-} v)$ with $(y \text{-} bb)$ with $(ee \text{-} hh)$

IV.   Within-family Comparisions:

     "W" test: Three role players within a family are compared; for example, u with aa with gg or w with cc with ii

---

[a] Letters are used to identify the cell from which data are drawn. The data within each cell are a set of Interaction Index scores, described in detail in Chapter 3. N, P, and G stand for normal and poor premorbid schizophrenic and good premorbid schizophrenic families.

find significant differences between fathers, for example, in either the patient or the sibling session or in both sessions. However these separate sessions analyses do not tell us whether an individual's behavior has changed markedly or remained stable from session to session. We want a more direct measure of the degree and direction of change from one interaction situation to another, and we want to be able to evaluate the relative degree of change among the members of different family types; that is, are normal fathers more or less stable from situation to situation than the fathers of schizophrenic patients? The several statistical tests described below are designed to answer these questions.

Even among families of any one type, that is, normals, goods, or poors, there is considerable variation on interaction scores. One question about intersession consistency is whether the families maintain the same rank order relative to each other in both sessions; that is, do the families who are high in the patient session remain high in the well sibling session? This type of consistency is evaluated through the use of a rank order correlation, the Spearman rho. This statistic is not affected by intersession shifts in the mean level of scores, nor by absolute score differences between ranks. A significant rho will occur if the units being compared— either families or family members—retain the same positions in the rank orders of the two sessions.

Whereas the rank-order correlation tells us about the consistency of a group of families relative to each other across the two sessions, the Wilcoxin matched pairs signed-ranks test, or "T," tells us whether a set of families consistently changes in both direction and level of its interaction scores from one session to another. The "T" test is based on difference scores, that is, the difference between a family's (or family member's) scores in the two sessions. For any one family type, the difference scores, taking direction into account, are ranked in a single series. A significant "T" results if the sum of the ranks for differences in one direction (for example, when scores for the patient session are higher than scores in the sibling session) are significantly higher than the sum of ranks for differences in the other direction. When these two sums of ranks are relatively equal this indicates that whether a score is higher or lower in one or the other session is a matter of chance. The test is applied separately to each family type.

It is evident from these brief descriptions of the sources of these two statistics, both of which focus on intersession consistency, that they are relatively independent of each other; either the rho or the "T" may be statistically significant, or both may be, or neither may be. A combination of a significant rho and a nonsignificant "T" indicates a high order of stability, because not only does the rank ordering across families remain stable but levels of behavior remain the same from session to session. A significant rho and "T" combination indicates that the two sessions produce different levels of behavior but that all families alter their rates in a proportionately equal way.

There are two other types of across-session analysis that are carried out, both involving the computation of intersession difference scores and the comparison of different roles with each other. The first focuses on differences across family types in amounts of session-to-session change (or intersession variability) for each member role. Thus we ask whether normal fathers show more or less change from one session to another (or more or less variability since direction of change is not taken into account) than the fathers of schizophrenics; the same question is asked for mothers, and for differences in the behavior of the two children. The Kruskal-Wallis "H" test is used to evaluate the significance of the differences across families in these change scores. The second analysis focuses on within-family comparisons of the intersession differences. For example, within normal families are the fathers more variable from situation to situation than the mothers and children? The same question is asked about each of the schizophrenic family types. Kendall's coefficient of concordance, "W," is used to evaluate the consistency of the rank ordering of father, mother, and child roles in the amount of change between sessions.

Within-family Comparisons. Finally, we are interested in whether there are consistent and systematic patterns of role differentiation within any of the family types. Among normal families on, for example, an index of expressiveness, are mothers consistently higher than fathers? Does this pattern reverse in the patient families, as is hypothesized in some theories of schizogenic families? Are there differences between sessions in these rank-orderings? The index scores of the three members of a family are ranked relative to each other. Kendall's coefficient of concordance, "W," is used to evaluate whether there is consistency in the rank positions for families of the same type; that is, are mothers consistently found in rank position 1, and so forth. This statistic does not take score levels or the magnitude of the differences into account; a significant "W" would simply indicate that there is consistency in the rank ordering of roles within families.

Alternative Frameworks for Interpretation

The previous sections of this chapter may be thought of as instructions for reading tables. In describing how the statistical analyses were carried out and organized for presentation and discussion, we have at the same time also shown the reader how to "read back" from the compressed and summarized information in the tables to the arrays of scores that were used to characterize interaction. These instructions are general in that they apply to all variables under study. In themselves they provide no guides for the substantive interpretation of patterns of statistical findings. The basic question of interpretation remains, that is, what does it mean for our understanding of relationships between schizophrenia and family interaction to find, for example, that normal families are significantly higher than poor premorbid families on an acknowledgement index and that the findings are "replicated," that is, present in each of the role as well as the group analyses?

In our approach to interpretation, as with our approach to measurement and statistical analysis, we have tried to be attentive to the special features of the study, particularly its research design and experimental procedures. We noted in the introduction that the results of an ex post facto study are open to three alternative types of interpretation: etiological, responsive, and situational. These differ in the assumed time-ordering of the variables of schizophrenia in a child and the interaction of family members as displayed and measured in our experimental situation. An etiological model assumes the temporal priority in the real history of the family of the specific patterns of family interaction. This is the minimal assumption. A strong etiological interpretation assumes further that the family patterns were causal and that they persisted over time and could be found in the samples of behavior we collected. A responsive interpretation reverses this temporal ordering; distinctive patterns of family interaction developed after, and perhaps even in response to, the onset of schizophrenia in the child. In other words, the members of the family have adapted to the special demands and requirements of a person who behaves in deviant and atypical ways. Finally in a situtional interpretation the focus shifts to the facts of patienthood and hospitalization; the child not only shows behavior that might theoretically be described as schizophrenic, but has been diagnosed as such and treated as a patient. Having a child who is a patient, rather than simply a child who behaves differently, establishes a special relationship of the parents with the hospital and may in turn influence orientations toward and behavior in the research situation.

These three alternatives are abstract and hypothetical. Reality, presumably, involves some combination of them. Another theoretical position, the transactional theory of behavior, attempts to bypass these distinctions and the problems they pose by suggesting that causality should be approached in terms of complex feedback models or sets of interdependent forces; attempts to isolate one factor such as prior family relationships as an etiological agent in schizophrenia are viewed as naive and unlikely to be productive. This approach marks a different strategy for research and theory building from our own. We believe that problems of causal analysis are not solved by simply asserting a transactional point of view. Distinctions among variables must still be made; the direction, form, and strength of their relationships must still be determined. The limitations of the simpler causal models that we compare with each other can be understood only after detailed analysis of their relevance and applicability to various empirical findings. The results of such analyses will help clarify the requirements of the more complex models that may be necessary, and these may turn out to be transactional ones.[5]

Therefore we believe that an attempt to interpret findings in terms of each of these frameworks—etiological, responsive, and situational—will permit us to clarify the requirements for a more realistic and comprehensive theory that links schizophrenia to family interaction. To this end the findings within each domain of variables are examined with the following question: can we understand or make sense out of the findings if the underlying relationship is etiological, responsive, or situational? How this is done will become clear in the discussions of specific findings. It will also become clear that reliance on factors external to the data themselves is necessary in these interpretive discussions. For example, findings from other studies, current theories about normal and pathological development, assumptions about the stability of the variables measured, and the severity of the patient's illness are taken into account in supporting one or another of the explanatory frameworks.

An illustration drawn from our data and our later discussion may help to clarify this procedure of comparing etiological, responsive, and situational models with each other. Findings from the group analysis of an index of acknowledgment, reported in Chapter 9, show a rank ordering from high to low acknowledgment of normal, good premorbid, and poor premorbid families. However in the detailed role-within-session analyses, a congruent pattern is found only in the patient session for mothers and daughters; that is, schizophrenic daughters and their mothers interacting together show this pattern but it does not appear in the other comparisons. As we argue in more detail in Chapter 9, this pattern appears to us to be most consistent with an etiological model: it is specific to particular members of the family interacting with each other, the degree of nonresponsiveness is directly related to the severity of the patient's illness, and the differences between mothers of normal and schizophrenic daughters are consistent with other observations about the imperviousness of the "schizophrenogenic" mother.

It is possible to argue that these data could also fit a responsive model of interpretation. For example, the differentials between the goods and the poors might reflect the length of time that parents have had to interact with and manage a schizophrenic child. Parents in the poor group, with a

---

[5] Blalock has provided a formal and elegant analysis of the problems of making causal inferences from nonexperimental research. We believe that our approach shares the spirit of his analysis although our detailed procedures differ (Blalock, 1961). Also, see Bell for a discussion that parallels ours in many particulars (1959-60, 1967).

chronic and long-standing problem, may have learned to ignore, and therefore fail to acknowledge, their child's potentially disturbing and disruptive behavior. Good parents, with a problem of more recent origin, would not yet have attained this level and would fall closer to the normals in our data. Because of the specificity of some of the findings, the responsive interpretation in this instance seemed to us less plausible than the etiological one.

This concludes our discussion of the methods and procedures used in the study. The following chapters report the findings.

Chapter 5

Expressiveness

The vocabularies of everyday life and the theories of social science both attest to the importance of expressive quality of behavior and experience. We speak routinely and naturally of some persons, some gestures, some performances as more expressive than others. Webster defines expressive acts as "vividly representing the meaning or feeling to be conveyed," and this seems, intuitively, to be the core meaning of expressiveness in typical usage.

Theory and research require a more precise definition with explicit distinctions. In the technical literature of psychology and the social sciences, expressiveness is often restricted to (and sometimes identified with) marked manifestations of feeling, affect, emotion. This is then contrasted with nonexpressive or cognitive aspects of behavior, for example, with the functional significance or substantive reference of the act. A related distinction, found frequently in sociological writings about relationships in families and small groups, is between socioemotional and instrumental behavior, that is, between acts focused on interpersonal feelings as compared to those directed to the solution of tasks or problems. Further, feelings may be pleasant or unpleasant, and this distinction also has had an important place in the study of psychological and social processes.

In addition to this general interest in levels of expressiveness and the affective quality of acts, these dimensions of behavior have also been a focus of attention in discussions of family relationships and schizophrenia. Interest in the modes of expression and levels of feeling or emotion in schizophrenia is evident in some of the earliest attempts to define and formulate the properties of schizophrenia as a clinical entity. For example, among Bleuler's basic criteria, special significance is attached to the bluntness or flattening of affect; the schizophrenic is less expressively responsive than either normals or other psychiatric cases. "In the outspoken forms of schizophrenia, the 'emotional deterioration' stands in the forefront of the clinical picture. . . . Many schizophrenics in the later stages cease to show any affect for years and even decades at a time. . . . Even in the less severe forms of the illness, indifference seems to be the external sign of their state; an indifference to everything—to friends and relations, to vocation or enjoyment, to duties or rights, to good fortune or to bad" (Bleuler, 1950, p. 40). Many reports, including clinical observations and questionnaire studies, refer to mothers of schizophrenics as cold, impervious to the needs of others, and impersonal in their relationships; this cluster of attributes helped earn her a pejorative title—the schizophrenogenic mother. Studies of families of schizophrenic patients have revealed an absence of genuine warmth and expressiveness in interpersonal relationships; for example, the pattern of relationships has been described as one of pseudomutuality (Wynne et al. 1958).

In each of these formulations—referring to the schizophrenic, to his mother, and to his family—there seems to be an implicit model in which nonexpressiveness is viewed as a mechanism of defense, a defense against real-but-denied feelings. Thus, for the patient, the lack of expressed feelings signifies to others a lack of interest and concern; this is likely to dampen their efforts to engage him in a meaningful but potentially threatening relationship. The mother's distance guards her from the dangers of intimacy that would follow a more openly expressive relationship. In the family there is a mutual protection pact in which feelings are collectively denied.

Theorists concerned with the affective quality of family life have emphasized the negative, hostile, and unpleasant features of relationships among members of families of schizophrenics. Thus Lidz points to a "schismatic" type of marital relationship torn by chronic and overt conflict in which hostile attacks of one parent on the other are the order of the day. (Lidz et al., 1957b). Similarly, on the basis of her study of parents of schizophrenic patients, Lu also reports high levels of overt parental conflict (Lu, 1962).

Analyses of the family as a social system, with the socialization of the young as its basic function, have focused on the instrumental-expressive dimension as one of the central axes for parental role differentiation (Parsons and Bales, 1955). Findings from a cross-cultural study show a pervasive normative pattern in which fathers are instrumental leaders and mothers expressive leaders; the definition of these patterns is markedly similar to the variables and indices that will be used in our analysis: ". . . instrumental leadership focused on the achievement of tasks and expressive leadership focused on emotionally supportive behaviors . . ." (Zelditch, 1955, p. 340). Lidz has suggested that some schizophrenic families show a reversal of this general pattern, with fathers being the expressive and mothers the instrumental leaders. (Lidz et al., 1957b).

The observations and formulations summarized above suggest two general hypotheses that will serve to guide our analyses and our interpretation of findings. We expect levels of expressiveness to be higher in normal families than in the families of schizophrenic patients and the affective quality of behavior to be more positive in normal families. These differences should appear in comparisons of families as collective units as well as in comparisons of normal fathers, mothers, sons, and daughters with their counterparts in the families of patients. Although we will compare good and poor premorbid families having either male and female patients we have made no differential predictions for these subtypes because the literature on expressiveness and affect does not distinguish systematically between them. We also expected to find a differentiation between parental roles in normal families with mothers more expressive than fathers.

There are several reasons for stating these ideas as expectations and guides rather than as formal hypotheses to be confirmed or disconfirmed by our data. First, as will be seen below, we have several different indices of expressiveness and affect. Although we expected a degree of consistency across the measures, we also expected them to show some differences; current knowledge did not seem to provide reasonable grounds for a detailed specification of the pattern of similarities and differences that might be expected. Second, the validity of our measures was unknown. We did not know, for example, whether our codes for positive feeling included expressions of pseudomutuality as well as genuine warmth. Although questions of validity are present in the interpretation of any findings, they require particular consideration if findings are not consistent with other evidence or with the general expectations based on previous work. Finally, the form of analysis followed produces such a large number of specific comparisons that, except for the general expectation of consistency across levels of analysis, it did not make sense to attempt to develop an elaborate set of discrete hypotheses.

We shall report findings on both direct and indirect indices of expressiveness and affective quality. We refer to indices derived from the Bales IPA code as direct since the coder attempts to classify acts on the basis of their functional significance for the members of the family as they are interacting. In our procedure for the use of the Bales IPA the coder listens to the tape recording while reading the typescript, which permits taking tone of voice into account, and uses the preceding statement as a context for understanding the function and meaning of the statement. By providing the coder with more information, that is, tone of voice and an enlarged context, than is available when the Affect code is used, we assume that the code more closely represents and is therefore a more direct measure of what is intended and understood by participants in the discussion. In contrast, the Affect code is designed to classify each act according to the literal affective content of the words used. The point of view used to make a judgment about affect is the point of view of the meaning of the words in the common culture, not the affective meaning that would be understood in the context of the interaction or conveyed by the tone of voice used. For this reason each act is coded as if it were an isolated element and the generally accepted affective meaning of the words is given to the act (Appendix B). When using the Affect code the coder works only with the typescript. The affect indices of expressiveness and affective quality are referred to as indirect since the overt intention of the participants, as marked by their tone of voice and the contexts within which they respond, are ignored and only the literal definition of the words they use enters into the coding decision.

Here, as elsewhere in the study, the research strategy is to use multiple measures of the same concept with the aim of defining more precisely, through a comparison of findings from these different measures, the meaning and significance of the concept for the relationship between family interaction and schizophrenia. It was expected that differences across family types would be in the same direction for both direct and indirect measures. The consistency between measures, may be reduced, however, if the affect expressed overtly is discrepant with the affect expressed covertly; this has been suggested as one type of "double bind" used by families of schizophrenic patients (Bateson et al., 1956).

The Bales IPA code contains 12 categories; the coding unit is usually a speaker's full sentence unless there is a clear change in content. The first three and the last three categories include acts that, respectively, are positively or negatively toned in feeling, that is, are expressive acts; the middle six categories are task directed or nonexpressive and include acts that give or ask for information, suggestions, or opinions. The indices we shall use denote levels of expressiveness (or nontask behavior) and the negative or positive affective quality of expressive acts. Some examples of statements coded into IPA positive and negative expressive categories are listed below. It will be recalled that both tone of voice and context are also used in IPA coding so that these illustrations are partial and incomplete but may still serve to provide a picture of the types of acts that enter into the indices.

Following these illustrations, the categories of the Affect code will be described and illustrated. The examples are selected from the Code Book and from acts that were actually coded into the different categories.

IPA Code Categories and Examples: Expressive Acts

Positive Affect

01   *Shows Solidarity:* Focus is on the relationship to the other person; acts that raise other's status, give help, reward, show affection or approval.

/and the boy has a perfect right to ah talk back/
/We all get fed up Robert./
/Good, I'm with you on that/

02   *Tension Release:* Spontaneous expressions of affect; many acts are nonverbal.

/(L) You get?/
/but Ma doesn't let me (L)/
/So you've got a black sheep this time/
/(L)/

03   *Agreement:* Focus is on the content of the discussion; included are statements of agreement on an issue, or passive acceptance and compliance, and supportive statements not strong enough to go into category 01.

/I would agree/
/Yeah/
/and I guess/ Mommy looks at it the same way/

Negative Affect

10   *Disagree:* Mild expressions of negative affect, including actual disagreement, passive rejection, or the withholding of resources.

/(I) that's beside the point/
/all our disagreeing/
/Yeah/ but she's only/(S) she's only four and a half/

11   *Shows Tension:* Both verbal and nonverbal evidence of tension that is largely personal.

/Let me finish/
/now wait a minute/
/(S) it doesn't say this, Margaret/

12   *Antagonism:* The more extreme manifestations of negative affect shown in both content and tone of voice.

/Well for your information, dear, last summer we had a lawn party/
/(I) Really cut him huh?/
/(I) You still disagree/ what did you put up your hand for?/

The IPA categories focus on the distinction between the expressive and the instrumental functions of a statement. Each act is coded in terms of the primary meaning of the statement in which it is included. As is apparent in the list of categories, positive or negative feeling tone as well as the intensity of expressed feeling are also coded. In contrast, the Affect code developed in this study is concerned with the positive, negative, or neutral affective quality of each act. As we noted earlier, in coding affect only the semantic meaning of the words in the common culture is used; further, each act is coded as if it were an isolated segment and attention is not paid to the full statement or to the discussion context. The assumption underlying the Affect code is similar to that of projective personality measures; the relative use of positive, negative, and neutral words to express one's self is assumed to reflect the individual's affective orientation, though not necessarily his overt communicative intention, in the situation. Affect code categories and some illustrations are listed below.

Affect Code Categories and Examples

01 *Positive Affect—Moving Toward:* Acts that involve coming closer to another person or persons by giving or receiving, liking or becoming like, or being with other persons.

/all would have to work together/
/the child should have its mother/
/You have to tell someone/
/My mother didn't want to live alone any more/

02 *Positive Affect—Positive States of People:* Acts in which people are described in states of gratification or pleasure that have no explicit interpersonal components.

/as though Jack enjoys his house and his home so much/
/she wants to play for amusement/
/whether he was happy playing/
/Kenny brings out a good point/

03 *Positive Affect—Positive Qualities:* Acts that include words that refer to positively valued states, judgments, or situations in the absence of explicit reference to interpersonal relationships or states of persons.

/Yes/
/All right/
/That's true/

04 *Neutral Affect:* All acts that have no implication of a state or relationship of pleasure or displeasure; these tend to be descriptive statements without qualifying and evaluative adjectives or adverbs.

/You know/
/how old is the guy/
/Now there was an incident about a week ago there/
/I think/

05   *Negative Affect—Negative Qualities:* Acts that refer to states and situations that are generally seen as bad, dissatisfying, or unpleasurable.

/and it lowers your authority/
/and it's not right at all/
/no/
/That's a different stinking story/

06   *Negative Affect—Negative States of People:* Acts that describe people as being in a state of displeasure or dissatisfaction are included here.

/but she's too inexperienced herself to know good from bad sometimes/
/he was upset at the time/
/what are you frowning for?/
/and then when she got scared/

07   *Negative Affect—Moving Against/Away from People:* Acts that refer to attacking someone, punishing someone, leaving someone, or being attacked, punished, or deserted.

/if a fellow doesn't have the regard for his mother/
/They could argue with me/
/So you would tell little white lies/
/How can you spend so much time away from the house/

Families of Sons: Findings

Levels of Expressiveness

The paradigm for a social system analysis presented in Chapter 4 is followed in reporting findings. Group and structural analyses, focused on comparisons across family types, are described first. The flow of interpretation moves from findings at the level of families as groups, to the two types of segmental structural analyses—role and session differences between families—to the second-order structural analyses of roles-within-sessions. Intersession comparisons are then presented that focus on differences between sessions for the families and for each family member. Finally, the members of a family are compared with each other, using within-family analyses, to determine whether there are systematic differences between fathers, mothers, and children in their interaction roles and whether the patterns in the different family types are similar to or different from each other. Findings for families of male patients on the several indices of expressiveness and affective quality will be reported and discussed before proceeding to the analyses of female patient families.

Findings for direct and indirect measures of levels of expressiveness are presented in Table 5.1. The direct measure, the index of IPA expressiveness, is the proportion of all acts that are coded into any of the first three or the last three of the IPA code systems (these are the expressive categories defined and illustrated above). The reciprocal of this index might be thought of as the level of instrumental activity or task directedness. The indirect index of expressiveness derived from the Affect code is referred to in the table as an index of affectivity. It is based on the proportion of all acts coded into the three positive and three negative affect categories defined above. The reciprocal of this index may be thought of as affective neutrality.

It will be recalled that our general hypothesis regarding family type differences in levels of expressiveness was that normal families would be higher than patient families. This hypothesis is confirmed fairly strongly in the analyses of the direct index, but the evidence on the indirect measure is ambiguous at best.

The major finding on levels of IPA expressiveness is that normal families are highest and good families lowest. The rank order position of normals was part of the initial hypothesis; the consistently low rank position of members of good premorbid families was unexpected. Significant differences between the families are found at the group level of analysis; as collectives, these families are different from each other. When the families discuss their differences one would expect to observe more expressions of feeling in normal families, including positive and negative comments about each other as well as expressions of pleasure and of irritation, than in either of the patient families but particularly more than would be observed within the families of good premorbid patients. The median percentages for expressiveness bear out this expectation.[1] In the patient and well-sibling sessions respectively, the overall rate of expressiveness for normal families is 33% and 28%, for poor premorbid families they are 30% and 27%, and for good premorbids, it is 21% and 28%. Differences across families are more marked in the patient session, as is shown also in Table 5.1, where significant differences are found only for that session although the rank ordering of families remains the same in the well-sibling session.

In the structural analysis by roles significant differences appear for fathers and mothers but not for children. This pattern reappears in the more detailed analyses of roles-within-sessions where the rank order patterns for all

[1] Median percentages for all index scores for patient and well-sibling sessions separately, are reported in Appendix A. 12.

Table 5.1   Levels of Expressiveness: Direct and Indirect Measures[a]
(families of sons: group and structural analyses)

Variable	Group Analysis	Roles and Sessions		Roles within Sessions	
	$H\,M\,L\;\;p$		$H\,M\,L\;\;p$		$H\,M\,L\;\;p$
		Fa_c	N P G .20	Fa_{pt}	N P G .05
		Mo_c	N P G .05	Fa_{sib}	N P G —
		Ch_c	N P G —		
Direct:				Mo_{pt}	N P G .20
IPA expressiveness	Fam_c N P G .05	Fam_{pt}	N P G .05	Mo_{sib}	N P G .10
		Fam_{sib}	N P G —		
				Ch_{pt}	N P G —
				Ch_{sib}	N P G —
		Fa_c	P N G —	Fa_{pt}	P N G —
		Mo_c	N P G —	Fa_{sib}	P N G —
Indirect:		Ch_c	P N G —		
Affectivity	Fam_c N P G —			Mo_{pt}	N G P —
		Fam_{pt}	P N G —	Mo_{sib}	N G P —
		Fam_{sib}	N P G —		
				Ch_{pt}	G P N —
				Ch_{sib}	G P N —

[a] Notes to Table 5.1 and other tables reporting group and structural analyses: The number of families varies for different comparisons. The following chart shows N for types of family by session and sex of patient; the letters N, G, P, refer, respectively, to normal, good premorbid and poor premorbid families.

	Male			Female		
	N	G	P	N	G	P
Combined sessions	10	13	5	6	2	3
Patient session	10	15	5	7	3	7
Sibling session	10	14	5	6	3	3

Two nonparametric tests are used to evaluate the significance of differences across family types. The Kruskal-Wallis "H" assesses the significance of differences in mean ranks across all three family types—normal, good premorbid, and poor premorbid. The mean rank of the family type in each comparison is shown as H (high), M (middle), members of the family remain the same but significant overall differences are found only for fathers in the patient session and for mothers in each session. Although the rank order patterns for children are identical with those of the parents in both structural analyses, this should not obscure the remarkable fact that the children do not differ significantly from each other. This is remarkable since in the patient session two of the children are diagnosed schizophrenic patients who are being compared with a normal son from the control families. Despite the fact that patients' parents are markedly different from normal parents in levels of IPA expressiveness, the patients and normal sons do not differ significantly from each other.

There are no significant differences on the indirect index of affectivity but one trend is worth noting. Good premorbid families are lowest in rank in the group, role, and session analyses, as they were in the analyses of IPA expressiveness. Thus, although they are clearly more instrumental and less expressive than the other families, there is also a tendency for them to be more affectively neutral. There is no clear pattern in the ordering of normal and poor premorbid families. On this indirect index, differences in median percentages across families are trivial; about 50% of the total number of acts in each session are coded in the affectively neutral category for the typical family of each type.

From the analyses reported above, we have learned that the members of normal male families are relatively high and the members of good premorbid families are relatively low with respect to each other on their rates of expressiveness. This is most apparent on a direct measure of this behavior and the differences are strongest for parents, particularly in the patient session. There is a further important question of whether family members differ significantly in the two sessions, that is, whether the two interaction situations—one with the schizophrenic son and the other with his sibling (in the case of normal parents, with two different children)—produce differences in the behavior of parents on these indices; and whether there will be differences in levels of expressiveness between the two sons in each family type.

Two types of statistical analysis were undertaken to answer these questions (the same analyses are used on other variables that will be discussed in succeeding sections and chapters).[2] The first makes use of the Wilcoxin

---

(Notes to Table 5.1 Continued)

and L (low); significance levels of "H" of .20 or less are listed in column p. The Mann-Whitney "U" test is used to evaluate significance of differences between separate pairs of family types; levels of significance are shown by brackets between family types, that is, .10 by - - - - - - and .05 by ———.

[2] To avoid further complicating the tables, the results of these statistical tests will not be presented in full in them but will be reported in the discussions of specific findings.

Signed-Ranks Test (T) and involves a comparison of matched cases. For example, each normal father's score in the patient session is compared with his score in the well sibling session; both the direction and amount of difference are taken into account in the calculation of the statistic. A statistically significant difference will occur only when most of the fathers are higher in the same type of session and when any reversals involve small magnitudes. Thus, for example, this test will tell us whether fathers in poor premorbid families are systematically higher (or lower) in the patient or well-sibling session; the same test is then applied for all members of all family types.

The second statistical analysis combines across-session with across-family comparisons. The average change in expressiveness from session to session is computed separately for fathers, mothers, and sons in each family type; since the direction of change is not taken into account, this score may be thought of as a measure of intersession variability. Family roles are then compared across family types to determine whether there are significant differences, for example, between normal, good, and poor premorbid fathers or between scores for mothers or scores for sons. This analysis will tell us, for example, whether the differences in behavior on the part of poor premorbid mothers between a situation in which they interact with their schizophrenic sons and one in which they interact with his well sibling are any greater than the differences in behavior for normal mothers interacting with their two different, but both normal, sons.

Findings from the Wilcoxin matched-cases analyses of intersession differences for family members are easily summarized. In only one instance are there systematic differences between sessions in rates of expressiveness for either the direct or indirect measures—normal fathers are consistently higher in the patient session than they are in the sibling session. The median percentage for normal fathers in the patient session on expressiveness is 41%, which is considerably higher than the median for any other family member of any type of family in either session. This finding is difficult to interpret since the assignment of Normal family sessions as "patient" or "sibling" was done randomly.[3] At this point, we shall therefore treat this finding as a chance occurrence.

The lack of significant intersession differences for any member of either

---

[3] The designation of one of the normal family's experimental sessions as the "patient" session and the other as the "sibling" session was done in such a way as to eliminate order effects, that is, any systematic bias that might result from all of one kind of session having occurred first or second in time. The procedure involved randomly selecting one of each pair of normal sessions and labeling it as the "patient" control session; the other session became the "sibling" control session. These designations were then used in all analyses.

the Good or Poor premorbid schizophrenic families suggests a high level of stability in their rates of expressiveness. Further evidence for stability in this type of behavior is found in rank order correlations computed for each role in each family type. There are significant Spearman rhos for all members of normal and poor premorbid families; that is, for example, the fathers in normal families maintain the same rank relative to each other in both sessions, and the same is true for other members of these and the poor premorbid families. The fact that a similarly high rank correlation is found for children in these families (where two different individuals are compared) suggests that there is a family norm that applies across situations which regulates appropriate levels of expressiveness for fathers, mothers, and sons. Findings for good premorbid families are less consistent, but the number of cases is so small for intersession comparisons that the lack of significant correlations may simply be a reflection of sample size.

Analyses of intersession variability, in which amount but not direction of difference is taken into account, produce scattered and inconsistent findings. On the direct index of IPA expressiveness, normal fathers are more variable than the fathers of either good or poor premorbid patients, but normal mothers and sons are less variable than their counterparts in patient families. There is only one significant difference on affectivity; the good premorbid patient and his well sibling are most different from each other and the poor premorbid patient and his well sibling most like each other, with the two normal sons falling between on their extent of difference.

The findings from the across-family comparisons presented in Table 5.1 showed normal parents high and good premorbid parents consistently low on IPA expressiveness with a tendency for the latter to be low on affectivity; the differences appeared to be stronger in the patient session. The findings on intersession differences are neither strong nor consistent and serve neither to clarify nor to explicate the across-family differences. As negative findings, they caution against the "obvious" interpretation that the stronger differences in the patient session reflect marked and systematic changes in parental behavior toward their patient son as compared to their well son; the strongest intersession difference—for normal fathers—was a chance finding.

Turning to the intrafamily analyses, we may ask whether there are systematic patterns of role differentiation within any of these family types. For example, are normal mothers consistently more expressive than normal fathers, and is there a role reversal within schizophrenic families—as might be expected on the basis of past research?

Our findings are essentially negative. Kendall's Coefficient of Concordance, W, is used to determine whether the rank order pattern within a family for father, mother, and son is similar for the families of any type;

the two experimental sessions are examined separately, providing six analyses for each variable, that is, role patterns for normal families in the patient session and the sibling session and similarly for good and poor premorbid families. There is only one significant finding: for normal families in the well-sibling session we find mothers high on affectivity, fathers low, and children in the middle. Although this is consistent with expectations, it is too weak a reed on which to rely for interpretations of within-family role differentiation on expressiveness or the relationship of intrafamily patterns to across-family differences. Again, there is no support for the obvious explanation that intrafamily differences between parents and sons would account for the stronger differences found for parents than for sons in the across-family analyses in Table 5.1.

Levels of Expressiveness: Summary of Findings for Families of Sons. The major finding is that the parents of normal sons tend to be relatively high and the parents of Good premorbid schizophrenic sons tend to be low on behaviors that are directly expressive; the differences are particularly strong in the patient session. These differences do not appear to be a function of marked changes in parental behavior when in the presence of their schizophrenic son in comparison to their behavior when with their well son; on the whole, there is marked stability in rates from session to session. Two other negative findings deserve emphasis. First, there are no significant differences in expressiveness between schizophrenic sons and their well siblings, nor between normal sons and either of the sons in the schizophrenic families; second, there is no consistent pattern of role differentiation within any of the types of families. The absence of clear role differentiation within either normal or patient families is surprising in view of previous research and theory, which had suggested that normal mothers would be more expressive than fathers and that this pattern would reverse for parents of patients.

We tentatively propose that the findings reflect the operation of a general family norm regarding appropriate levels of expressive behavior. Members of normal families—whether father, mother, or son—are expected to be more expressive when interacting with each other than are the members of patient families; members of good premorbid families, including the schizophrenic son and his well sibling, are expected to be low in expressive behavior. The rates in good premorbid families are sufficiently low to suggest the possibility that this is defensive; that is, their high levels of instrumental and affectively neutral activity are consistent with an interpretation that they are defending themselves against expressions of affect and feeling. The indirect Affect measure is less sensitive to these differences than the direct IPA measure of expressiveness; however, the findings on both measures, particularly with reference to the low rank position of good premorbid families, tend to reinforce each other. The stability across sessions of family members in all types of families is noticeable. This high degree of stability supports the interpretation offered above that a general family norm is operating and that the presence of different members of the family—in this instance one son or the other—has only small effect on this area of behavior.

Affective Quality of Expressiveness

The measures of levels of expressiveness analyzed in the previous section do not distinguish between the positive and negative qualities of expressed feelings but refer only to whether or not acts reflect feelings as well as substance. Table 5.2 includes findings on the affective quality of these acts, that is, whether the feelings expressed are positive or negative, pleasant or unpleasant. Again, direct and indirect measures are used, derived respectively from the IPA and Affect codes. The Indices are ratio scores that refer to the relative amounts of positive to negative affect within all expressive acts; this procedure controls for level of expressiveness. A high rank means that the family is relatively higher on the ratio of positive to negative affect than other families.

Findings for both measures are consistent with each other. Normal families as a whole and normal mothers and fathers are uniformly more positive in the quality of their expressive behavior. Good premorbid families and the parents within them are almost as consistently negative in the affective quality of their expressiveness; however, fathers appear to be relatively more positive in the patient session. Again, it is striking that the patterns for sons not only are not significant but are not the same as the rank-ordering for parents.

Thus the higher level of expressiveness in Normal families is associated with disproportionately more positive feeling; the lower level of expressiveness in Good premorbid families is associated with disproportionately more negative feeling. Poor premorbid families are in between on both levels and affective quality of expressiveness. We proposed above that the consistently low level of expressiveness in good premorbid families represents a collective defense against the expression of feelings; these findings suggest that positive feelings are at least as threatening as negative feelings. We would expect, when observing good premorbid families, to see an emotionally flat discussion marked by occasional expressions of irritation, annoyance, and criticism of each other. Relative to them, normal families should appear to be enjoying themselves and the situation. Both of these expectations are consistent with our observations of these families during the experimental sessions.

In comparison to the findings on levels of expressiveness (Table 5.1),

Table 5.2 Affective Quality of Expressive Behavior: Direct and Indirect
Measures
(families of sons: group and structural analyses)

Variable	Group Analysis				Roles and Sessions				Roles within Sessions			
	H	M	L	p	H	M	L	p	H	M	L	p
					Fa$_c$ N P G —				Fa$_{pt}$ N G P .20			
					Mo$_c$ N P G .20				Fa$_{sib}$ N P G .20			
					Ch$_c$ P N G —							
Direct:												
Ratio IPA	Fam$_c$ N P G .20								Mo$_{pt}$ N P G .20			
Positive: Negative					Fam$_{pt}$ N G P .20				Mo$_{sib}$ N P G —			
					Fam$_{sib}$ N P G —							
									Ch$_{pt}$ G N P —			
									Ch$_{sib}$ P N G —			
					Fa$_c$ N P G .20				Fa$_{pt}$ N P G .05			
					Mo$_c$ N P G .20				Fa$_{sib}$ N P G —			
					Ch$_c$ P N G —							
Indirect:												
Ratio Positive:	Fam$_c$ N P G .20								Mo$_{pt}$ N P G .05			
Negative affectivity					Fam$_{pt}$ N P G —				Mo$_{sib}$ N P G —			
					Fam$_{sib}$ N P G —							
									Ch$_{pt}$ P G N —			
									Ch$_{sib}$ P N G —			

there are significant differences across families on the indirect index of
affective quality derived from the Affect code and these differences are
consistent with those found for the IPA direct measure. Thus, although
only the amount of feeling expressed in a direct and manifest way (IPA
expressiveness) discriminates between normal and patient families, the
quality of the affect expressed distinguishes the families, whether it is
expressed directly or indirectly. Because the differences across families
on these two measures are in the same direction and of roughly the same

degree of strength, there is no evidence in these analyses of summary scores for the hypothesis that there would be a discrepancy for schizophrenic families between affect expressed at these two levels.

Turning to the intersession comparisons, there are no significant differences between sessions for any family member in any type of family on the direct IPA index of affective quality. On the indirect affect index, normal fathers are significantly more positive in the patient session. This is consistent with the general finding for normal families that high levels of expressiveness are associated with positive feelings; however, as with the earlier findings for normal fathers on higher levels of expressiveness in this experimental session, this difference is difficult to attribute to anything but chance.

A finding that perhaps merits more serious consideration is that poor mothers are significantly higher, that is, more positive, on the affect index in the session with their schizophrenic son than in the session with their well son. They appear to change more than mothers in other families in the types of feeling expressed. Thus in the analysis of intersession differences on the IPA index of positive-to-negative feelings poor mothers show most variability, normals next, and goods least. Another striking finding for poor premorbid families is that on both indices the intersession rank order correlations are significant for all members of these families; that is, within poor families fathers have the same rank standing relative to each other in both sessions and the same is true for mothers and sons. This last finding argues for the strength and pervasiveness in poor premorbid families of a family rule regarding the affective quality of expressed feeling. Even when one family member, the mother, radically shifts her balance of positive to negative feelings from one session to another, the shift is an orderly one since the rank order correlation across mothers remains significant despite the significant change in the relative rates of positive to negative affect.

Analyses of role differentiation within families on the indices of affective quality are essentially negative. One significant pattern appears: for normal families in the patient session, fathers are high on the affect index and mothers low, with children in between. This finding simply reflects the disproportionately high rate of positive affect for normal fathers in this session.

The findings do not support previous research and theory on the specific patterns of role differentiation that would be accepted in these types of family. That is, there is no evidence here that in normal families mothers are either more expressive or more positive in feeling than fathers, nor is there any indication that the reverse pattern is present in families of schizophrenic sons.

Affective Quality: Summary of Findings. The general pattern of findings is one of congruence between group and structural analyses. Differences across families at the group level of analysis on both indices where normals are high, good premorbids low, and poor premorbids in-between tend to be repeated for mothers and fathers and in the patient session. Although the rank order patterns remain the same in the sibling session comparisons the differences are no longer statistically significant, and the rank orders for the children show no consistent patterns, nor do any of them reach significance. No evidence of role differentiation was found for any of the family types. Only the mothers in poor premorbid families showed marked intersession differences with more positive affect in the patient session, but this was against a background of high intersession stability for members of these families.

There is evidence, we believe, in the interfamily differences and the lack of intrafamilial differences, for the presence of differential family norms or standards for expressing feelings. The parents are the prime "carriers" of the norm and the differences between them are most clearly seen in comparisons that involve interaction with the patient son. Changes in behavior for any parent are relatively slight and when with his nonpatient son, although the rank ordering across families remains the same, the differences are no longer significant.

Interpersonal Affective Orientations

Against this background of findings on levels of expressiveness and their positive and negative quality, we turn to questions about the interpersonal focus of this behavior. There are specific categories within both the IPA and the Affect codes where other persons are the focus of the behavior. In the IPA code the two extreme categories—showing solidarity and antagonism—refer respectively to positive and negative interpersonal orientations; in the Affect code the two extreme categories denote moving toward and moving against other persons. It is consistent with the distinction we have been making between these codes as direct and indirect measures that in the IPA categories an affective interpersonal act would be directed toward a person present in the situation while the Affect interpersonal categories include any affective act that refers to relationships between persons.

The following excerpts from family discussions illustrate the differences between these two codes and will provide concrete reference points for our interpretation of findings.

Coded as positive interpersonal, or showing solidarity, by the IPA code are comments like those italicized.

Fa   In the beginning is/when you need some break with it.

Mo   Yeah/and you need somebody to say/do things./ *All right/I'm with you on that.*

Fa   No./ But I'll bet/ sometimes he did.

Mo   ' *I I see your point./*

Dau Y-Yeah/ I agree there/ but I like I say/ I- She should find out the other faults/ and yeah/

Fa   (I) No/ it that's right./ *You just read the question differently/* than we did/ that's all.

Coded as negative interpersonal acts, or showing antagonism, by the IPA code were the following underlined segments.

Mo   You're thinking to yourself/ it must be a frightened child./ Some children aren't that frightened./ They just don't know what to do.

Fa   *Well for your information, dear, last summer we had a lawn party/* and you got two little nephews./ They belong to your sister.

Son (S) I'm still ahh/ I still disagree with you two./ I feel that/

Fa   (I) *You still disagree./* What did you put up your hand for.

Positive interpersonal acts under the rules of the Affect code include the following.

Son One man can't do the job./ No./ I don't believe that at all./ *All would have to work together.*

Fa   . . . but if it's not necessary to work/ *the child should have its mother.*

Mo   If I didn't care for their company/ but I think/ *that when you're working with a group of people/* I mean/ you try to get along.

Fa   Now we had a home of our own there/ All you little boys were small./ My father passed away./ *My mother didn't want to live alone any more.*

Coded as negative interpersonal affect were the following.

Fa   Well I always told them/ *they could argue with me/* if they wanted to.

Mo   . . ./ Naturally I'd ask you/ where were you all day?/ *How can you spend so much time away from the house?/* . . .

Mo   . . ./ or take away someone something they like./ They might
       want to watch television/ *and you restrict them*/saying you can-
       not watch television tonight/ . . .

Table 5.3 presents findings from the analyses of the IPA indices of interpersonal affective orientations: total, positive, and negative interpersonal
expressiveness. Since we are primarily concerned with the extent to which
expressive acts have an interpersonal focus, each of these scores is standardized: the index of interpersonal expressiveness is the proportion of all
expressive acts that are coded in the two extreme IPA categories (all instrumental acts are excluded from the base). The indices of solidarity and antagonism are based respectively on the proportions of positive expressive
and negative expressive acts coded into positive and negative interpersonal
categories. It should be noted that interpersonal acts are highly infrequent,
by either IPA or Affect code definitions, and typically account for less than
5% of a family's or an individual's total participation. In view of this relatively low rate of occurrence, the consistent and fairly strong findings reported below are all the more striking; they suggest a high degree of stability
in the differential patterns of interpersonal orientation in these families.

In the group level of analyses there is a significant difference among
families on each index and the patterns are identical although varying somewhat in strength. Poor premorbid male families are highest in their overall
level of IPA interpersonal expressiveness and in their rates for both solidarity and antagonism. Normal families are lowest in each instance and good
premorbids are in-between. Thus, in the cultures of these families, poor
premorbids direct a higher proportion of their expressive acts than either
good premorbids or normals toward persons, and a higher proportion of
both their negatively and positively toned expressive acts are also directed
toward persons. The families of poor premorbid male patients are more
likely to direct their feelings toward persons regardless of the general level
or quality of feeling. Normal families, in contrast, put relatively more of
their feelings into noninterpersonal content. The focus of feeling for poors
is not only more interpersonal but is also more concrete in being directed
toward persons present in the situation. This is not simply a function of a
more positive interpersonal orientation since the same pattern is present
for antagonistic as well as for solidarity behavior.

In two important respects these findings stand in contrast to those on
levels of expressiveness and affective quality presented earlier. First, normal
families were high on those variables but are low on these interpersonal
indices. Second, in the previous analyses good premorbid families were
most distinct when compared to the other two types, but on interpersonal
orientations the poor premorbid families are most different from the
normals and goods.

Table 5.3 Interpersonal Affective Orientations: Direct (IPA) Measures
(families of sons: group and structural analyses)

Variable	Group Analysis		Roles and Sessions		Roles Within Sessions	
		$H\,M\,L\ \ p$		$H\,M\,L\ \ p$		$H\,M\,L\ \ p$
			Fa_c	P G N .10	Fa_{pt}	P G N —
			Mo_c	P G N .10	Fa_{sib}	P G N .01
			Ch_c	P N G .10		
Interpersonal expressiveness	Fam_c	P G N .05			Mo_{pt}	P N G .20
			Fam_{pt}	P N G .20	Mo_{sib}	P G N —
			Fam_{sib}	P G N .05		
					Ch_{pt}	P N G .10
					Ch_{sib}	P N G .20
			Fa_c	P G N —	Fa_{pt}	G P N —
			Mo_c	P G N .20	Fa_{sib}	P N G .20
			Ch_c	P N G .20		
Positive interpersonal expressiveness	Fam_c	P G N .20			Mo_{pt}	P G N —
			Fam_{pt}	P G N —	Mo_{sib}	G P N —
			Fam_{sib}	P G N .20		
					Ch_{pt}	P N G —
					Ch_{sib}	P G/N .20
			Fa_c	P N G .05	Fa_{pt}	P N Q .05
			Mo_c	P N G —	Fa_{sib}	P G N .10
			Ch_c	N P G —		
Negative interpersonal expressiveness	Fam_c	P G N .20			Mo_{pt}	P N G .20
					Mo_{sib}	P G N —
			Fam_{pt}	P N G .01		
			Fam_{sib}	P G N —	Ch_{pt}	N P G —
					Ch_{sib}	G P N —

[a] Instances of tied mean ranks, for example the good and normal well siblings on positive interpersonal expressiveness, are shown in the tables by a slash mark, as in G/N.

When we turn to the structural analyses of roles and sessions, a striking consistency with the group pattern is found in the high rank for poor families on each of the three indices in both sessions and for each of the family member roles (with the one exception of a nonsignificant pattern for children on antagonism). On 14 of the 15 segmental structural comparisons, on 10 of which the differences across family types are significant, the poor premorbids are highest, as they are in the group analysis. Good and normal families vary in their rank relative to each other; for example, on the index of IPA interpersonal expressiveness, normals are lowest in the well-sibling session and good premorbids are lowest in the session with the schizophrenic patient. On the other hand, on solidarity the group pattern is repeated in both sessions with normals lowest and goods in the middle. Only on the index of antagonism do we find significant differences between good and normal families. It appears that when the schizophrenic son is present in good premorbid families there is a particularly marked lack of direct hostile confrontation of other persons. Our interpretation of the high level of instrumental behavior in good families in the patient session as a defense against the expression of feelings would fit with this pattern; direct hostility expressed toward others in the situation would seem to be subject to more restraint and suppression than in other families.

With regard to the high rank of the poor families there is a replication of the significant group differences on the overall interpersonal index in each of the separate role and session analyses. Although they retain their high rank in these analyses of the solidarity and antagonism indices, some of the differences are no longer significant and these findings suggest a pattern of congruence. There are some interesting incongruent patterns in the relative ranking of good and normal in the structural analyses. The low rank for goods on antagonism in the patient session has already been noted; each member of the good family is also lowest in rank on this index although only differences between fathers are significant. Further incongruencies appear in the role-within-session analyses. For example, whereas good premorbid families tend to hold the middle rank in these comparisons, good premorbid mothers are lowest in their rate of interpersonal expressive behavior in the patient session and good premorbid fathers are low in their rate of positive interpersonal activity in sessions with their nonschizophrenic sons; both parents are lowest in antagonism when with their patient sons. Further, good premorbid sons, whether schizophrenic or not, tend to be lowest in their rates of both interpersonal and positive interpersonal behavior. Thus, although the general family culture of the good premorbids seems to locate them between normals and poor premorbids on each of these dimensions of behavior, there are specific situations for specific family members on which their rates of interpersonal activity are particularly low.

One difference between the findings for positive and negative interpersonal expressive behavior is of particular interest. Differences among families on solidarity are present only in the well-sibling session; on the index of antagonism, family differences are present primarily in the session with the patient son. Underlying norms for the direct expression of positive feelings toward others appear to be differential for these families in situations when the well son is present, with the poor premorbids being high in their rates of such behavior. Norms for the direct expression of negative feelings toward others, however, appear to be differential in situations when the schizophrenic son is present, with the poors again being high in their rates of behavior in this index. Thus, although the rank order patterns among the families do not vary markedly across the different indices, the relative strength of the differences among families does vary. In sessions with their schizophrenic son we would expect on the basis of these findings to see relatively more supportive and interpersonally positive behavior among poor premorbids than among the other families.

The special sensitivity of members of good premorbid families to this interpersonal dimension of interaction, and in particular to its negative component, is shown in the structural analyses of antagonism. Although the good families fall between normals and poors in the group comparison, each of the role analyses and the patient session analysis is incongruent with this family pattern in the specific sense that the good premorbids are now found at the lowest rank. Thus for fathers, mothers, and their sons, and for the family in the patient session, good premorbids are lowest in their rates of antagonism. This finding is clarified by the role-within-session analyses; there are significant differences for each member of the family in the patient session between the goods, who are at the lowest rank, and the highest ranking family type in each comparison. The rank orders are different in the well-sibling session and less significant with only the fathers in this session showing significant differences that are consistent with the overall family culture differences.

In summary, these findings suggest that members of good premorbid male families tend to avoid directly supporting or attacking other persons in the situation; they are especially likely to reduce their rates of antagonistic behavior when the schizophrenic son is present. The members of poor premorbid male families are consistently high in their rates of interpersonal expressive behavior, both positive and negative in quality. We would propose a tentative interpretation stating that this reflects a tendency among poor premorbids toward concrete, personal, and particular forms of expression since the noninterpersonal categories of expressive behavior include acts that are either more general or less directly personal, for example, brief interjections like "Yeah" or "But" and laughter. Normal family cultures are low on each of these indices of interpersonal expressive behavior. In the context of their generally high rate of total expressive behavior we suggest that this indicates a wider dispersal of affect among a variety of types of acts and therefore the proportion of such acts that are interpersonal tends to be relatively low in comparison to the other two families.

Findings for Affect interpersonal indices corresponding to the IPA scores discussed above are presented in Table 5.4. On the whole, the Affect indices are less discriminating. There were statistically significant differences on 22 of the 36 comparisons across all three family types (using the Kruskal-Wallis "H" test) on the three IPA interpersonal indices; only 9 of the 36 differences are significant on the three Affect interpersonal measures. However the findings serve to clarify and specify the meaning of interpersonal and expressive behavior in these families.

In rates for interpersonal affect and positive interpersonal affect, normal families are consistent with their rates of IPA interpersonal expressive behavior; they are lowest in rank (except for sons among whom this pattern has also varied on the IPA scores.) Not many of these differences are significant but both the significant and nonsignificant patterns are consistent with each other. Thus parents in normal families tend to be relatively low in the degree to which their affective behavior and their positive affect is directed toward other persons, whether these persons are present in the situation or are abstract representations of persons. Their differences from parents in other families are strongest in the well-sibling session, and on the positive index somewhat more marked for mothers than fathers. Patterns for sons vary from session to session and are generally not significant.

When the relative ranks of good and poor premorbid families are examined, we find a striking and remarkable reversal on the Affect interpersonal indices as compared to the IPA interpersonal measures. On the latter (Table 5.3) poor premorbids were consistently high; on 33 of the 36 possible comparisons, poor premorbids were higher than goods, and on 22 of these comparisons the overall differences across family types were statistically significant using the Kruskal-Wallis test. On the Affect measures, this order is reversed; on 24 of the 36 possible comparisons the good premorbids are higher than the poors, and on 8 of these comparisons the overall differences are significant.

Intersession and intrafamilial analyses have been relatively unproductive to this point, but some interesting patterns emerge on these interpersonal indices. Normal families appear to be relatively homogenous and stable in their rates of interpersonal affective behavior; there are no significant within-family differences and on several of the measures there are significant rank-order correlations between sessions for one or more of the family members. The strongest degree of intersession consistency is in the IPA interpersonal

Table 5.4 Interpersonal Affective Orientation: Indirect Affect Measures
(families of sons: group and structural analyses)

Variable	Group Analysis				Roles and Sessions				Roles within Sessions			
		H	M	L p		H	M	L p		H	M	L p
Interpersonal affect	Fam$_c$	G P N		—	Fa$_c$	G P N		—	Fa$_{pt}$	G P N		—
					Mo$_c$	P G N		—	Fa$_{sib}$	G P N		.10
					Ch$_c$	G P N		—				
									Mo$_{pt}$	G P N		—
					Fam$_{pt}$	G P N		—	Mo$_{sib}$	P G N		.20
					Fam$_{sib}$	G P N		.10				
									Ch$_{pt}$	N P G		—
									Ch$_{sib}$	G P N		—
Positive interpersonal affect	Fam$_c$	G P N		.20	Fa$_c$	G P N		—	Fa$_{pt}$	G P N		—
					Mo$_c$	G P N		.20	Fa$_{sib}$	G P N		—
					Ch$_c$	P N G		—				
									Mo$_{pt}$	G P N		—
					Fam$_{pt}$	G P N		—	Mo$_{sib}$	G P N		.20
					Fam$_{sib}$	G P N		.10				
									Ch$_{pt}$	N P G		—
									Ch$_{sib}$	P G N		—
Negative interpersonal affect	Fam$_c$	G P N		—	Fa$_c$	G P N		—	Fa$_{pt}$	G N P		—
					Mo$_c$	N P G		—	Fa$_{sib}$	P G N		—
					Ch$_c$	G N P		—				
									Mo$_{pt}$	N P G		—
					Fam$_{pt}$	N P G		—	Mo$_{sib}$	P G N		—
					Fam$_{sib}$	G P N		.20				
									Ch$_{pt}$	N P G		.20
									Ch$_{sib}$	G N P		.20

and positive interpersonal scores. With respect to internal homogeneity and situational stability, poor premorbid families stand in sharp contrast to normals. For example, there is a rare significant intrafamily difference: in the patient session poor mothers are highest, the patients lowest, and the father in-between on rates of IPA positive interpersonal behavior. In addition, on intersession comparisons, one or more members of poor families are significantly more different, or more variable, from one session to the next than the members of other families. This higher degree of variability for poors occurs on both direct and indirect indices and for each type of interpersonal orientation. For example, poor fathers are most variable on the overall IPA index and the positive Affect indices, mothers on the IPA positive and the negative affect scores, sons on the overall and positive IPA measures, and the poor family as a whole on the negative IPA index. For goods the differences among members and between sessions are more focused and specific: there is a higher rate of negative interpersonal affect expressed in the sibling session and the sibling tends to express more negative affect than either of his parents or his brother, the patient. Thus on the IPA negative interpersonal antagonism index each member of the good family and the family as a whole expresses more antagonism in the sibling than the patient session. On the Affect negative interpersonal measure, the sibling has a significantly higher rate than his brother and within the sibling session is higher than either his mother or father.

Affective Interpersonal Orientations: Summary of Findings. These findings on affective interpersonal orientations serve to specify the interpretation offered earlier on differences among these types of families in ways in which affect is expressed. Normal families, who were shown to be relatively more expressive and more positive, distribute their feelings among a variety of targets and their rates of interpersonal affect tend to be relatively low. In a sense they are undiscriminating in how their feelings are expressed; there is little discrepancy between the direct and indirect modes of expression, the family members do not differ from each other, and their rates in the two sessions are similar. Poor premorbid families, who were moderately expressive and positive, show high rates of interpersonal expressive behavior on the direct IPA index. We have suggested that this reflects a mode or style of behavior oriented to the immediate situation since this rate indicates a disproportionately high allocation of feelings directly expressed toward other persons. Their decline to a middle rank on the indirect affect interpersonal scores would fit with this hypothesis since the latter includes more abstract personal references. They are, in addition, highly variable from session to session but their differential rates are not systematically related to whether it is the patient or his sibling that is present. Finally good premorbids, who were least expressive but most negative in those feelings expressed, show high rates of indirect interpersonal behavior in the context of lower rates of direct interpersonal behavior; feelings are not expressed toward each other but reappear indirectly in abstract personal references. Negative interpersonal feelings are more evident in the well-sibling session, being higher in this session for each member of the family even on the direct IPA index, and the sibling seems to have a special and distinctive role since he is particularly high on indirect expressions of negative interpersonal feeling.

Families of Daughters: Findings

Levels of Expressiveness

There are fewer families of female patients included in the study than of male patients. The small sample size is likely to reduce the number of statistically significant findings and also demands more than the usual caution in interpreting those that appear. For this reason, as well as for our general interest in differences and similarities between the two types of family, we shall use the findings on male patients and their families as an explicit framework for interpreting analyses of female patient families putting particular stress on parallels and contrasts in the findings.

Findings for families of female patients on direct and indirect measures of levels of expressiveness are presented in Table 5.5. There is only one significant difference on the direct IPA measure, for the daughter in the patient session, when poor patients are highest and good patients are lowest. There is somewhat more consistency in the indirect Affect measure; good premorbid parents tend to be lowest in rank. In comparison to the findings for males on these index scores, these findings were weak. The one consistent trend—the low rank position for good parents on affectivity— repeats the finding in the analysis of male families.

With the small number of cases in our sample of female families, only one across-session comparison is statistically meaningful—the comparison of intersession variability for each family role. Is the difference in their behavior from one session to the next greater for fathers of normal, good, or poor families? For mothers? For daughters?

On the IPA direct index we find poor mothers and daughters more variable than those of good families, who are more variable than those of normal families. Within the sample of male families, normal mothers and sons were also found to be less variable than mothers and sons in patient families.

Table 5.5   *Levels of Expressiveness: Direct and Indirect Measures*
(families of daughters: group and structural analyses)

Variable	Group Analysis	Roles and Sessions		Roles within Sessions	
	$H\ M\ L\ \ p$	$H\ M\ L\ \ p$		$H\ M\ L\ \ p$	
Direct: IPA expressiveness		Fa_c	N G P —	Fa_{pt}	N P G —
		Mo_c	P G N —	Fa_{sib}	N P/G —
		Ch_c	G N P —		
	Fam_c G N P —			Mo_{pt}	N/G P —
		Fam_{pt}	N G P —	Mo_{sib}	P/G N —
		Fam_{sib}	G N P —		
				Ch_{pt}	P N G .20
				Ch_{sib}	G N P —
Indirect: affectivity		Fa_c	N/P G —	Fa_{pt}	N P G —
		Mo_c	P N G .10	Fa_{sib}	N P G —
		Ch_c	N G P —		
	Fam_c P N G —			Mo_{pt}	P N G —
		Fam_{pt}	P N G —	Mo_{sib}	P N G .20
		Fam_{sib}	N P G —		
				Ch_{pt}	G P N —
				Ch_{sib}	N G P —

Affective Quality of Expressiveness

Findings for female families on the positive-to-negative affective quality of expressive bahavior are in Table 5.6. On the indirect Affective index, the findings at the group level of analysis are significant and congruent with the session and role analyses; poor premorbid families are high in their relative balance of positive to negative affect and good premorbids are low, with normals in between. This pattern at the group level is found in the patient session and for both parents, but the rank order shifts and the pattern drops to nonsignificance for daughters and for the well-sibling session. In the group, role, and session analyses, there are no significant differences on the direct IPA index but the rank order patterns are the same—poors, normals, goods—except in the patient session comparisons (where, nevertheless, the goods remain low).

These findings are similar in one important respect and different in another from those for male families (see Table 5.2). The similarity lies in the low-rank position for good premorbid families: the difference lies in the rank ordering of poors and normals. Among male families, poor premorbids tended to fall in the middle (on several of the variables) and normals and goods were therefore most different from each other. In these analyses of female patient families the normals are in-between and the two

Table 5.6 Affective Quality of Expressive Behavior: Direct and Indirect Measures

(families of daughters: group and structural analyses)

Variable	Group Analysis				Roles and Sessions					Roles within Sessions				
	H	M	L	p		H	M	L	p		H	M	L	p
					Fa$_c$	P	N	G	—	Fa$_{pt}$	P	N	G	—
					Mo$_c$	P	N	G	—	Fa$_{sib}$	P	N	G	—
Direct: ratio IPA					Ch$_c$	P	G	N	—					
Positive: negative	Fam$_c$	P	N	G	—					Mo$_{pt}$	P	N	G	—
					Fam$_{pt}$	N	P	G	—	Mo$_{sib}$	P	N	G	—
					Fam$_{sib}$	P	N	G	—					
										Ch$_{pt}$	N	G	P	.20
										Ch$_{sib}$	P	G	N	—
					Fa$_c$	P	G/N		.10	Fa$_{pt}$	N	P	G	—
					Mo$_c$	P	N	G	.20	Fa$_{sib}$	P	G	N	—
					Ch$_c$	G	N	P	—					
Indirect: Ratio positive:	Fam$_c$	P	N	G	.20					Mo$_{pt}$	P	N	G	.20
Negative affectivity					Fam$_{pt}$	P	N	G	.20	Mo$_{sib}$	P	N	G	—
					Fam$_{sib}$	P	G	N	—					
										Ch$_{pt}$	N	G	P	—
										Ch$_{sib}$	G	P	N	.05

types of schizophrenic families tend to be most different from each other. As will be seen, this pattern occurs on many other variables.

In the detailed role-within-session analyses the findings for mothers are congruent with the group and role analyses. Fathers show a more variable pattern, particularly on the Affect index.

Findings for daughters in the role-within-session analyses show an incongruent pattern that is sufficiently strong to merit attention. Differences between the rank order patterns in the two sessions are particularly striking, and consistent for the two different measures. In patient-session comparisons, normal daughters are high with poor premorbid patients low and the good patients in the middle; in well-sibling comparisons, normal daughters are lowest and the well siblings of patients are higher. The good siblings are notably incongruent in being significantly high on their balance of positive-to-negative affectivity. There is a hint in these findings of role differences in the behavior of schizophrenic and nonschizophrenic daughters with the former tending to be relatively more negative in their affect while their well sisters tend to be more positive.

There are no significant or consistent across-session differences for any family role.

Interpersonal Affective Orientations

Table 5.7 contains findings for the analyses of the direct IPA measures of interpersonal affective orientations. In the group analyses for total and positive indices the differences across families are significant and the rank order patterns are identical to those found for families of male patients (see Table 5.3). Poor families are highest, normal families lowest, and goods in-between on the extent to which their expressive behavior and their positive affect are directed toward persons present in the situation. On the index of negative interpersonal expressiveness (where the pattern for male families was the same as on the other indices), the poor premorbid female families shift to the lowest rank and the goods are highest; poor premorbids apparently direct a high proportion of their positive acts toward persons, but a relatively low proportion of their negative acts toward them.

Role and session analyses for the IPA interpersonal measure are generally congruent with the group analysis in that normal parents and normal families remain low in both sessions. There is some shifting in relative rank between poors and goods. Children are incongruent, with poor daughters (both patients and siblings, as demonstrated in the role-within-session analyses) shifting to the lowest position. In a family culture that emphasizes interpersonal expressiveness, the poor premorbid daughters and their sisters are deviant in displaying a relatively low rate of this behavior. In the structural analyses of the positive IPA index, poor parents and poor families in

Table 5.7 Interpersonal Affective Orientations: Direct (IPA) Measures
(families of daughters: group and structural analyses)

Variable	Group Analysis H M L p	Roles and Sessions H M L p	Roles within Sessions H M L p
Interpersonal expressiveness	Fam$_c$ P G N .05	Fa$_c$ P G N .10 Mo$_c$ G P N .10 Ch$_c$ G N P .20 Fam$_{pt}$ P G N — Fam$_{sib}$ G P N —	Fa$_{pt}$ P G N — Fa$_{sib}$ P G N — Mo$_{pt}$ G P N .20 Mo$_{sib}$ G N P .20 Ch$_{pt}$ G N P — Ch$_{sib}$ G N P .20
Positive interpersonal expressiveness	Fam$_c$ P G N .10	Fa$_c$ P N G .10 Mo$_c$ P N G — Ch$_c$ G P N — Fam$_{pt}$ P G N — Fam$_{sib}$ P N G —	Fa$_{pt}$ P N G — Fa$_{sib}$ P N G — Mo$_{pt}$ P G N — Mo$_{sib}$ N P G — Ch$_{pt}$ G N P .10 Ch$_{sib}$ G P N —
Negative interpersonal expressiveness	Fam$_c$ G N P .20	Fa$_c$ G N P — Mo$_c$ G N P .05 Ch$_c$ G N P .20 Fam$_{pt}$ G/N P — Fam$_{sib}$ G N P —	Fa$_{pt}$ G N P — Fa$_{sib}$ G P N — Mo$_{pt}$ G P N — Mo$_{sib}$ G N P — Ch$_{pt}$ N G P — Ch$_{sib}$ G N P .10

both sessions remain high but not significantly so; this same tendency is evident in the role-within-session analyses.

The pattern of findings for the index of negative interpersonal expressiveness is significant and differs from the pattern found for the other two indices and from the findings on male families. On this index the poors drop to the lowest rank and this position is maintained in the role and session analyses; in the role-within-session analyses, the patterns become more variable except those for daughters, and, significantly, for the siblings the poors remain consistently low. Here it is the daughters in poor premorbid families who tend to be particularly low in their rates of negative feeling expressed toward persons in the situation.

The position of the good premorbid female patient families on this negative interpersonal index is of particular interest. First, their high rank position is at variance with the findings for male patients, whose consistently low rank on this and related indices led us to interpret their behavior as a defense against the direct expression of personal feelings. Such an interpretation would clearly not fit the findings for female families. The congruence of the structural analyses where all members retain the high rank position on negative interpersonal behavior except the patients themselves, recalls the findings of Lidz and his collaborators. These investigators found that female schizophrenics were more likely to come from schismatic families in which there was more open conflict, and male patients from skewed families in which patterns of conflict and disturbance were less manifest (Lidz et al., 1957b). Although the pattern is present only for one subgroup of schizophrenic patients, the good premorbids, our findings are consistent with theirs in that more antagonism is expressed in the families of female patients than those of males. It is important to note that good patient daughters and their well siblings are generally more interpersonally expressive—being higher on the positive as well as the negative index—and that the well daughter is significantly more positive in her affect than other daughters (see Table 5.6).

Findings on the Affect interpersonal measures are in Table 5.8. Only one difference approaches significance. No consistent patterns are evident, and the findings do not permit any useful comparisons with the findings on the IPA indices or with the findings for male patients.

There are no significant across-session analyses for either the direct or indirect measures of interpersonal expressiveness.

Families of Daughters: Summary of Findings

In comparison to the findings for families of sons, significant differences are sparse and scattered for families of daughters. Some of the findings parallel those of the male families; for example, good premorbids tend to

Table 5.8 Interpersonal Affective Orientation: Indirect Affect Measures
(families of daughters: group and structural analyses)

Variable	Group Analysis		Roles and Sessions		Roles within Sessions	
		$H\ M\ L\quad p$		$H\ M\ L\quad p$		$H\ M\ L\quad p$
			Fa_c	P N G —	Fa_{pt}	G P N —
			Mo_c	P G N —	Fa_{sib}	N G=P —
			Ch_c	P G N —		
Interpersonal affect	Fam_c	N=G=P —			Mo_{pt}	G P N —
			Fam_{pt}	G P N .20	Mo_{sib}	G N P —
			Fam_{sib}	N G P —		
					Ch_{pt}	P G N —
					Ch_{sib}	G N P —
			Fa_c	N G P —	Fa_{pt}	G P N —
			Mo_c	N G P —	Fa_{sib}	G P N —
			Ch_c	P G N —		
Positive interpersonal affect	Fam_c	G P N —			Mo_{pt}	N G P —
			Fam_{pt}	G P N —	Mo_{sib}	G N P —
			Fam_{sib}	G N P —		
					Ch_{pt}	P G N —
					Ch_{sib}	N P G —
			Fa_c	N P G —	Fa_{pt}	G P N —
			Mo_c	P N G —	Fa_{sib}	N P G —
			Ch_c	N P G —		
Negative interpersonal affect	Fam_c	P N G —			Mo_{pt}	G P N —
			Fam_{pt}	G P N —	Mo_{sib}	N P G —
			Fam_{sib}	N P G —		
					Ch_{pt}	P G N —
					Ch_{sib}	N G P —

be low in expressiveness and in the positive quality of their affective behavior, and poor premorbids tend to be high in their rates of total and positive interpersonal activity. In contrast to the findings for male families, in which the overt expression of negative affect was consistently low for good premorbid families, among female families we find the goods high on this dimension, particularly the well daughter. We suggested that the families of schizophrenic daughters that had good premorbid histories seemed to fit the schismatic family model first described by Lidz et al. (1957b).

One general trend is that among female families the two types of schizophrenic family are most different from each other; the normal families fall between them on many analyses. Among male families the normals tend to fall on one or another end of a dimension with the two schizophrenic types of family holding adjacent ranks. This is a difference in the rank ordering among female and male families that also appears in the analyses of several other variables; this finding will be discussed in Chapter 11.

Discussion

To this point our emphasis has been descriptive. We turn now to the question of interpretation. Specifically, how can we understand the relationship between differential family patterns of expressiveness and schizophrenia? Summaries of findings were presented in reporting statistical analyses of the level, affective quality, and interpersonal focus of expressiveness; another general summary would be redundant. Instead, findings will be reviewed and commented on at relevant points in the discussion.

In Chapter 4 we stated that findings from the study could be interpreted in terms of three alternative frameworks—etiological, responsive, and situational. In the first it is assumed that family interaction plays an etiological role in the development of schizophrenia; in the strictest sense the theory asserts that the way parents behave toward each other and toward their child has led to schizophrenia. A responsive model of interpretation reverses the causal sequence; interaction is viewed as a response to schizophrenia in the child. Finally, hospitalization may have led to different orientations to the experimental situation and thus to different patterns of family interaction. The statistical findings of the present study in and of themselves do not permit us to distinguish among these interpretations for, in addition to the extra-empirical assumptions that are always involved in interpreting data, this study is cross-sectional rather than longitudinal in design and uses only one standard experimental situation. (See Bell, 1967, for a discussion of problems in interpreting the direction of effects in child development studies.)

We cannot hope, therefore, to decide between these alternate interpretive frameworks in any definitive sense. Rather we shall proceed by asking how each of these frameworks "makes sense" of the data, and, in the course of this, will attempt to be explicit about the assumptions that must be introduced if the data are to be understood as etiological, responsive, or situational. There is a fourth, more inclusive model, namely, some variant of a field, or transactional, or interactional framework. From such a perspective the behavior of the family would be viewed as a complex function of those factors that have been separated out from each other in constructing the etiological, responsive, and situational models. Unless the functional relationships among its component variables are defined in a systematic and precise way, an inclusive model tends to degrade into a statement that "everything affects everything else." In the end all models of human behavior may well be transactional, but at this stage in our understanding of families and schizophrenia it seems more useful to explore the limits and possibilities of simpler approaches. The particular requirements for a more complex model will be clearer after such an exploration and we will be in a better position to construct a more viable and useful model than what at present would at best be only a vague generalization about the essential unity and interdependence of factors affecting behavior.

Our procedure is as follows. Take a set of findings for a particular variable, for example, the several indices of expressive behavior in this chapter, and interpret them as evidence for each model—etiological, responsive, and situational—of family interaction and schizophrenia. Many types of finding will fit equally comfortably within any of these frameworks. Other findings, particularly certain intersession and intrafamilial differences and similarities, may demand more complicated chains of inferences and assumptions if they are to be accounted for in terms of one model than of another; in these latter instances we would argue that the more parsimonious model provides a better fit. The aim of this series of interpretive discussions, examining each variable in turn, is to clarify the strengths, weaknesses, and implications of each alternative. As we have indicated, a definitive choice between them will not be possible, and is perhaps not desirable now, but the requirements for and the consequences of a choice of interpretive models will hopefully be clarified by the approach undertaken here.

Ideally an adequate model should account for the full range and specificity of findings, for similarities as well as for differences. The study design and the mode of analysis used have allowed for many comparisons: between normal and schizophrenic families, between two types of schizophrenic family, among members of the same family, between situations where the patient of his/her sibling is present, and between families of male and female patients. It is more likely that each model will fit some subset of findings better than others. Keeping in mind the full range of findings, however, will permit us to determine the particular problems faced by each approach.

In approaching the data from an etiological viewpoint it is convenient to take normal families as a standard and then to compare how the schizophrenic families differ from them and to ask in what ways these differences might enter into the development of schizophrenia. The typical normal family, abstracting a general picture from the detailed findings, would show the following pattern: it would be relatively more expressive and more positive in affect that the typical schizophrenic family, stable from situation to situation in level and style of expressive behavior, undifferentiated in terms of member roles, similar in the direct and indirect expression of affect, and unselective in the target toward which feelings are expressed. Norms for expressing feelings in the normal family thus appear to be pervasive and family organization is relatively loose with little discrimination between who expresses the feelings or toward what they are directed. Although on the whole schizophrenic families also display a high degree of stability from situation to situation, it is also apparent that situational differences appear more often than in normal families, that there is some evidence of differentiated roles, and that distinctions are made between direct and indirect levels for expressive feelings. These differences are more evident and more consistent among the families of male patients.

Even within an etiological perspective there are differences between specific theories in the variables that are seen as pathogenic. For example, Lidz and his collaborators have stressed the pathogenic implications of deviations from normal role relationships. They have argued that the blurring of generational boundaries between parents and children, the presence of marital discord, and substitution of a parent-child alliance for the normal parental coalition, and the reversal of culturally-prescribed expressive and instrumental roles for wives and husbands, respectively, are all conducive to schizophrenia (1965). Although there is some evidence of more strain and conflict in the schizophrenic families, particularly the good premorbids, on the whole our findings suggest much more symmetry in expressive behavior between wife and husband and between parents and children than this model assumes. The general thrust of the findings would be more compatible with a model that stresses the quality of relationships rather than their content (for example, Wynne et al., 1958). The data would be consistent with an interpretation that schizogenic families are relatively more rigid in structure than normals with specific asymmetrical relationships. The higher levels of instrumental and lower levels of expressive behavior found in the families of schizophrenic patients are assumed to reflect a collective defense against the expression of feelings; this, in turn, may be viewed as resulting in a more rigid structure of interpersonal and role relationships. Following the line of reasoning of Wynn et al., it might be argued that it is the rigidity and inflexibility of the demands placed on the child that increase his vulnerability to schizophrenia. The defensive function of this pattern of family organization would hinder the exploration of alternative modes of behavior that is necessary for normal personality development.

Two findings on particular roles deserve mention. First, the mother of the schizophrenic son is more supportive when with her sick son than when with his well brother. The data do not tell us "whom" she is supporting but are consistent with the characteristics of overprotectiveness that have been noted frequently in the literature; it depends apparently on the presence of the patient. Second, sick and well daughters contrast with each other in that the former are antagonistic and the latter positive in feelings expressed toward their parents. This bad girl–good girl division has also been remarked in other reports of pathogenic families.

Differences between good and poor premorbid families are somewhat more difficult to interpret etiologically than differences between normal and schizophrenic families. What we have been saying above about the rigidity and defensiveness of schizogenic families applies particularly to the goods; they are least expressive in both male and female family comparisons. The paradox is that the families of patients who would be thought of as less sick, that is, those with good premorbid histories, are most different from the normal families. Within an etiological framework we might argue either that levels of premorbidity indicate different types of schizophrenia, each of which develops in a different type of family, or that the premorbidity index reflects neither different types nor different stages of the illness but reflects instead the relative capacities of families to contain disturbed and disturbing behavior. Wynne and Singer's observations of the families of fragmented and amorphous schizophrenics would be one variant of the first line of reasoning (1963). The argument would be as follows. Good premorbid patients are acute or reactive schizophrenics, are likely to show fragmentation as a primary feature of their thought disorder, and come from families that are rigid and overorganized. Poor premorbid patients are process schizophrenics who are amorphous in the quality of their thinking, and come from families that are somewhat disorganized. The alternate etiological interpretation, which focuses on differential capacities of families to contain the illness, would posit that the high level of control and organization in the good families either helped the patient to maintain adequate control or permitted the family to contain the disturbance, so that the illness did not come to or require the attention of outsiders until later in the child's developmental history than was the case with poor premorbid patients.

Clearly these data cannot settle the question. Further, since a family organization that functions to contain disturbance can as easily be thought of as a response or adaptation to it, this last argument borders closely on a responsive interpretation. Simply reverse the direction of causality: under the impact of illness in a child, one group of families has become disorganized (or underorganized) and the other has responded by rigid control and overorganization. A responsive interpretation is also compatible with a view of premorbidity as a valid index of the onset of the illness: the more recent the onset, that is, the better the premorbid history, the stronger the current stress being experienced by the family and the more likely that they will appear rigid, defensive, and overcontrolled in comparison to families where the onset was earlier, that is, the poor premorbids.

The credibility of a responsive interpretation is further strengthened when one finds differences between parents but similarities between children. Since some of the children in the comparisons are schizophrenic, and therefore clearly different from both their siblings and normal controls on many criteria, their relatively normal behavior in these situations suggests that the parents may be behaving so as to "normalize" their sick child's behavior, and doing so successfully. The more "abnormal" picture of the good premorbid parents would, in this view, be a sign of the greater difficulty and the increased effort required for parents to bring an acutely ill patient's behavior within the normal range. The stronger differences between parents found in the patient session than in the well sibling session add support to this responsive interpretation since this suggests that the parents modify their behavior to become more like normal parents when the child can behave appropriately.

It is as unsatisfying for the authors as for the readers to conclude this chapter on a note of indecision. The data would not justify discarding one or another of the models. Although no clear support for the situational model was found, both the etiological and responsive models have been shown to be compatible with the findings, and this compatability was not achieved by the introduction of unreasonable assumptions. Other findings will be reviewed in the same manner and in the same spirit.

Chapter 6

Power:
The Strategy of Attention-Control

All theories about family structure assume that normal families have a particular pattern of internal differentiation based on power and status. They state that the parents in the family are expected to play the high power roles and the children to have less power and lower status. Among a number of theorists relationships are assumed between the power structure associated with generational differences and the socialization function of the family. These theories state that parents are normatively required to exercise control over the environment and control over the child in order to protect and to teach him. Their roles require them to make the child do things he would not ordinarily do. This ability to influence or control other persons' behaviors is what we mean by "power."

However, the power structure of normal families, from the point of view of family theories, is not stable and fixed. Instead parents relinquish power as the child is able, in the course of his development, to take over more and more control of his own life. In the normal family a child's dependency is temporary rather than permanent. The fact that power gets redistributed within the family as the child matures suggests that older children can be expected to attempt to influence other family members, to be deferred to in certain situations, and to have a real effect on family decisions. At the same time, these theories point to the fact that status differences associated

Interaction in Families

with generations are not completely erased. Even during adolescence and young adulthood parents are expected to retain a certain level of power and control over their child, although as Parsons and Bales suggest (1955, p. 117) parental sanctions may have a somewhat different quality than at earlier stages of the child's development. "They sanction more and more as members of the community rather than as parents of this particular child."

Descriptions of families having schizophrenic children provide striking evidence for the hypothesis that there are major differences between the normative family pattern and these pathological families in terms of power structure. Schizophrenic families seem to have highly distorted or unclear distributions of power or maintain early patterns far beyond their original usefulness. For example, Lidz et al. (1965), in their discussion of schismatic and skewed marital role patterns, point to the failure to maintain the generational role pattern normally expected in families. In schizophrenic families the mother and her son may maintain a powerful alliance over the father, who relinquishes his generational role, or the mother and daughter may switch power positions, with the mother playing the less powerful "child" role.

Lu (1962) describes a somewhat different set of power relationships in families having schizophrenic children, also discrepant from the normative pattern. Parents make contradictory demands on the maturing child. They press toward continuing their child's dependence on them; yet, at the same time, they demand that the child take major steps toward independence. Thus the power relationship that might be seen in these families is a constant fluctuation between parental attempts to control the child and parental attempts to give the child a great deal of freedom. The difference between power relationships in schizophrenic and normal families, from Lu's point of view, is in the degree to which parents allow the child to raise his status and accumulate power as he matures.

Haley (1959) also suggests that schizophrenic and normal families differ in their exercise of power. In his formulation the difference does not lie in distribution of control over different family members but instead in the ways that this control is carried out. The schizophrenic family member characteristically attempts to influence others but, at the same time, explicitly refuses to acknowledge that he is doing so. Thus the power differences that actually exist in the family are not confirmed by the behavior of the members. Haley writes, "These families tend to become incapacitated by necessary decisions because each member will avoid affirming what he does and therefore is unable to acknowledge responsibility for his actions, and each will disqualify the attempts of any other to announce a decision.

Both the act of taking leadership and the refusal to take leadership by any one family member is condemned by others" (Haley, 1959, p. 366).

The general tenor of these theories is clear. The power structure in schizophrenic families does not follow the culturally prescribed normative pattern. Generational differences may disappear; ambiguous influence strategies may be used; rigid role patterns may be maintained beyond the period of their usefulness. All of these hypotheses suggest the potential usefulness of empirical investigation of power structure in schizophrenic and normal families.

The concept of "power," however, is complex and multidimensional. One dimension is the "resource" on which an individual's power is based; in Blau's exchange theory an individual's power rests on a set of scarce resources with which he may bargain (Blau, 1964). In a family the power resources of parents may range from special training, knowledge, or experience, to physical size; the power resources of a child are such qualities as a reserve of emotional responsiveness that may be freely given or withheld.

Depending on the number and type of resources that a family member holds, each member will have a certain "amount" of power relative to other members of the family. The ways in which types and numbers of resources are combined into the total "amount of power" are probably quite different for different families; in some families physical size may make the greatest contribution to the relative power differences while in others it is verbal manipulation that is most important. Thus it does not seem reasonable to measure relative "amount" of power by simply summing a member's available resources or by assigning weights to resources since in either instance we make assumptions that may not be valid ones for a particular family.

For example, some small group experimenters select one variable—often rate of participation—as the indicator of "amount" of power. It is assumed that the person who talks most is most powerful. However, when we investigate natural groups having a long history and presumably having a set of norms for influence attempts, it seems reasonable to assume that power may be exercised in many different and subtle ways, with talking being only one of these. Blau suggests (1964) for example, that in a group with highly developed norms a person who is truly most powerful may need only say a few words to maintain control over the discussion.

Therefore we do not attempt here to infer the nature of a person's power "resources" from his observed behavior. Neither do we select one behavior variable, or weight and sum a set of variables, to draw conclusions about "amount" of power. Instead, we have measured a set of observable behaviors that indicate different "strategies" of exercising influence.

Naturally, an influence strategy that a family member chooses to use is in some way related to his resources. For example, the resource of "expertise" is most likely to lead to influence through verbal information-giving activity. However, the social context in which interaction takes place also sets certain limits on the influence strategies, defining some strategies as appropriate and others as inappropriate. Our experimental situation calls for verbal interaction and this implicity rules out such behaviors as a strategy of physical force. In contrast, since the amount of time for talking is limited by the experimenter's rules, control of time becomes an important and acceptable influence strategy.

Our focus on control strategies, that is, on the behavioral techniques that group members use to influence other members, has not until recently been a common approach to the problem of power in groups. Sociologists and social psychologists have traditionally been more concerned with power structure and thus with relative amounts of power held by different role players and with the relative task effectiveness of certain power structures over others. The investigators who became interested in group processes are the ones who began looking at the ways in which individuals attempt to obtain what they want from other group members. This focus on strategies of influence is particularly evident in the writing of group therapists who observe subtle and yet clearly understood interpersonal techniques that effectively influence others.

Two strategies for the exercise of power are evident in the families we observed. First, family members attempt to influence other members and to control the course of interaction by using behavioral devices that maintain the focus of attention on the speaker. We have selected several interaction measures that, in combination, tell us something about how this "attention control" strategy is used, by whom, and in what contexts. Indicators include rate of participation, the target of speeches, and length of statements.

The second power strategy is one in which direct attempts at confronting and controlling other family members are most prominent; these are the "person-control" strategies. Included are measures of attempted and successful interruptions of others and question asking. Each of these interaction techniques is assumed to act on another family member directly by forcing that person to stop talking or to respond in a content area limited by the controller.

Each of these power strategies is examined in a limited and clearly defined situation that allows certain strategies to be used and prevents the use of others. One major expectation in the experimental situation is that influence attempts will be verbal rather than behavioral, that family members will talk to each other and comment on opinions and ideas but that no one will use physical force or threaten to leave the room in order to influence others. Second, the amount of time to talk and to come to an agreement is limited by the nature of the experimental situation; for this reason, talking time is a scarce commodity that may be controlled in order to exert other power strategies and to prevent others from doing the same thing. Thus the interaction context and related expectations about "appropriate" behavior put some limits on the control strategies families are likely to use.

As is the case with all of the interaction indices, the indicators standing for strategies of control are examined within the structural format that allows specification and location of the family and role difference. Further, we compare the use of control strategies in the two family situations, when the schizophrenic patient is present and when his well sibling is present, and we ask whether the power strategies are used differentially by members within each family.

Attention-Control Strategies: Families of Sons

The strategy of attention control is one that we commonly recognize and use in many interaction situations. We notice and comment on a child who "is the center of attention" or an adult who puts himself "in the spotlight." It is also clear that so long as a child, for example, remains the center of attention he succeeds in maintaining control over the content and flow of interaction in the whole group, preventing others from talking freely to each other and focusing discussion on his behavior.

Maintaining control over the attention of other group members is a power strategy in itself in the sense that it prevents other members from attracting attention to themselves or to what they have to say. Thus while one person is the "center of attention" others cannot use other power strategies. Second, use of the attention-control strategy opens up the possibility for the use of more direct control devices such as giving verbal orders or attempts to influence through the content of an argument. The attention control strategy is an interaction device preliminary to and generally necessary for other power techniques.

The three indicators selected to stand for attention-control strategies are measures of participation rate, who speaks to whom, and statement length. Each of these is a measure of communication structure in that none takes into account the content of interaction. These aspects of "talking time" are an especially important control device for these families because the task requires verbal interaction and there is a limited amount of time available to the whole family to complete the task. Therefore the allocation of talking time to each member should be an indicator of the relative use of a scarce commodity and the relative opportunity available to exercise other strategies of control. Each of the three indicators, however, taps a slightly different mode of control over attention.

The first indicator is the measure of participation rate. It provides an indication of the proportion of the family's total interaction monopolized by each of the three members.[1] The assumption we make here is that while one person is speaking he is controlling the attention of the other two members and therefore is preventing others from exercising power.

Comparisons across the three kinds of families on the use of this attention-control strategy are shown in Table 6.1. There are no general role effects; that is, none of the role players uses this strategy at a different rate in the three kinds of families. However, there is a role effect specific to the son in each of the family sessions. Normal sons talk relatively less than either patients or their siblings in both good and poor premorbid families. The median percentages of the families' total participation for normal sons are 26% and 28%, for good patients and their siblings, respectively, 32% and 30%, and for poor patients and their siblings, 28% and 30%.[2]

Table 6.1   Attention-control Strategies
(families of sons: group and structural analyses)

Variable	Group Analysis	Roles and Sessions		Roles within Sessions	
	H M L p	*H M L p*		*H M L p*	
		Fa$_c$	G P N —	Fa$_{pt}$	G P/N —
		Mo$_c$	N P G —	Fa$_{sib}$	G P N —
Participation rate		Ch$_c$	G P N —		
	Fam$_c$			Mo$_{pt}$	N P G —
				Mo$_{sib}$	N P G —
				Ch$_{pt}$	P G N .10
				Ch$_{sib}$	P G N .20

[1] Participation rate is measured by computing the proportion of all coded acts of the family spoken by each of the three members. Therefore participation rate comparisons at the group level cannot be made since each family's score is equal to 100%.

[2] The nonparametric statistical tests used in our analysis involve a comparison of mean ranks of percentage scores; they do not take into account absolute percentage scores. If the distributions are markedly skewed, it is possible that the rank order across family types of median percentages may be different from the ordering of mean ranks. This is an instance of such an anomaly; the poor premorbid patient has the highest mean rank, but the good premorbid patient has the highest median percentage.

Both parents in all situations participate at approximately the same rates. Thus the control of attention seems to be a power strategy particularly useful to the poor schizophrenic patient and his well sibling; in contrast, normal sons participate at a consistently lower rate. None of the role players consistently changes his participation rate across the two interaction situations. Even the two children in the schizophrenic families talk at similar rates, thus providing evidence for the stability of the schizophrenic sons' attention-control role. Further, the measure of variability within types of family points to the stability of rates of participation for sons in these families; in both normal and good families sons are significantly less variable across situations than are parents. Thus normal sons show rates of participation that are stable and low, and good sons show stable medium rates.

Finally, when we examine the use of this attention-control strategy within each of the family types the differentiation between role players in the normal families is further supported. Not only do normal sons participate less in comparison to sons in schizophrenic families but they also participate consistently less than their own fathers. However, although the schizophrenic sons use attention-control devices more than other sons, they are not consistently the high participators within their own families.

On participation rate, and on several other strategy-of-control indices reported in this and the following chapter, analyses of intersession and within-family differences are often more revealing of the different patterns of role differentiation and of the distinctive functions of these control strategies in the different types of families than are the across-session analyses presented in the tables. For this reason somewhat more attention will be given in our discussion to the findings of these other analyses. As an example, an examination of intersession differences serves to reinforce the impression that emerges from Table 6.1 of the stability of participation rates.

The use of this attention-control device seems, therefore, to be a strategy especially useful to both the sons in the poor schizophrenic families and, to a lesser extent, to good sons. The use of attention-control in normal families, a somewhat stronger and more consistent finding, follows the theoretical expectation about normal families. Normal sons make fewer attempts to control the family's attention than do their parents, and especially fewer than their fathers. On this variable, therefore, the theories about family role differentiation and schizophrenia find some support in that there are clear generational differences in the normal families, whereas in the schizophrenic families parental roles are less clear and generational roles may be reversed.

Questions about the relationship between this set of findings and that aspect of family theory having to do with the parents' relinquishment of power as the child matures may be raised here. As the theories suggest, even though the normative pattern is for the parents to allow the child greater independence over time, theory would predict that there remains a status difference and accompanying power difference in families throughout adolescence and early adulthood. As we see in our data the normal son who is an adolescent or young adult retains the low power position in comparison to his father and mother. The schizophrenic sons' high participation rate may indicate that parents in these families give their children even more independence than in the normal families, or that the power structure is simply more ambiguous. The latter interpretation is more reasonable in the face of the finding that there are no participation differences within the schizophrenic families, that is, the patient son does not consistently participate at a higher rate than his own mother or father.

The second indicator for the "attention-control" strategy is a measure of targets of actions, or who speaks to whom. Any one person's acts may be distributed to two other family members or to no one in particular.[3] The way in which a family member chooses to distribute his actions is here assumed to be an indicator of his understanding of the relative importance or relative power of the other members. If he directs a large proportion of his speeches to one member we assume that he feels this member has potential power; his paying little attention to another member indicates he feels that member has little potential power or importance in the situation.

This strategy of "paying attention" is therefore assumed to function as an act of deference to a person in a higher power position. Therefore, in conjunction with the participation rate findings, we may further specify the power strategy patterns in these families. Not only do we know who attempts control over attention but, from the point of view of family members, who is relatively more important as well. The assumption that speaking to a person implies deference or respect rather than control is based largely on empirical relationships between variables. In our data it is generally the family members who participate at the highest rate who also receive most attention from other members and the lowest participators who receive fewest acts.[4]

---

[3] Our measure of targets of actions is based on whom the speaker is looking at as he talks. Thus it is possible for a speaker to respond to another's speech and yet avoid looking at anyone. This latter instance is an example of speaking "to no one."

[4] The empirical relationship between a member's participation rate and receipt of acts from others is a common finding in small group studies (See Bales et al., 1951, for example.) It should be pointed out that in the present study this relationship is not an artifactual one; it would be possible for a member to be the source of a large proportion of the family's statements and, at the same time, to receive a very small proportion of another member's attention. The base for the participation rate percentage is the sum of the whole family's acts; the base for the "to whom" percentage is the sum of the speaker's acts.

Data for the relative distribution of acts to the father are shown in Table 6.2. When comparisons are made across family types there are interesting and significant differences in the degree to which family members pay attention to fathers. At the family culture level normal fathers receive proportionately more acts than do poor fathers, who receive more than good fathers. This pattern is congruent with session level, where differences in acts directed to father occur only when the patient son is present; here normal fathers receive more attention than poor fathers, who receive more than good fathers.

The source of the differences in attention rates is apparent on examination of role differences. It is sons in the three families who contribute most clearly to the "attention to father" pattern, and this is significantly evident in the session when the patient son is present. Normal sons talk to their fathers more than do the poor and good patient sons; 33% of the normal sons' acts are directed to fathers whereas the median percentage scores for poor and good sons are 16% and 15%, respectively. In the well-sibling session differences in acts directed to the father disappear. There are no significant differences in proportions of mothers' acts directed to fathers.

Before continuing with a discussion of acts directed toward mothers and sons, we shall examine further evidence for differences in fathers' power in families, supplied by comparisons made across the two sessions. The patient son in the good premorbid schizophrenic families consistently directs fewer acts to his father in comparison with his own well siblings. The same difference occurs for the good family as a whole, with significantly fewer acts directed to the father when the patient child is present than when the well child is present. It is only in the good family, however, that we find differences between the two interaction situations in amounts of attention paid to the father. In none of the families is there role specialization between mother and son in who speaks most often to the father.

We have noted that types of father, when compared with each other, do not differ significantly in their own rates of participation. However, we found here that, even though all fathers talk at similar rates, sons pay them varying amounts of attention. Normal sons pay more attention to fathers than do the schizophrenic sons, especially patients in good families. This finding is similar to that reported by Lennard et al. (1965); of all six possible who-to-whom patterns in the male family triad he found that only the son-to-father interaction provided significant differences across types of family, with normal sons speaking much more to their fathers than schizophrenic sons. From the point of view of our interpretive framework, therefore, normal sons must see their fathers as having relatively more importance, whereas good schizophrenic sons see their fathers as having less potential power. This is in the context of the previous finding showing that schizo-

Table 6.2   Attention-control Strategies
(families of sons: group and structural analyses)

Variable	Group Analysis		Roles and Sessions		Roles within Sessions	
	$H\,M\,L$	p	$H\,M\,L$	p	$H\,M\,L$	p
Acts directed to father	Fam_c N P G	.05	Fa_c		Fa_{pt}	
			Mo_c N G P	—	Fa_{sib}	
			Ch_c N G P	—	Mo_{pt} N P G	—
			Fam_{pt} N P G	.01	Mo_{sib} N G P	—
			Fam_{sib} N P G	—	Ch_{pt} N P G	.10
					Ch_{sib} G P N	—
Acts directed to mother	Fam_c G P N	—	Fa_c N G P	.20	Fa_{pt} N G P	—
			Mo_c		Fa_{sib} N G P	—
			Ch_c G P N	—	Mo_{pt}	
			Fam_{pt} G P N	—	Mo_{sib}	
			Fam_{sib} N P G	—	Ch_{pt} P G N	.20
					Ch_{sib} N G P	—
Acts directed to child	Fam_c P G N	.10	Fa_c G P N	—	Fa_{pt} P G N	.20
			Mo_c G P N	.05	Fa_{sib} G P N	—
			Ch_c		Mo_{pt} G P N	.05
			Fam_{pt} P G N	.01	Mo_{sib} G P N	—
			Fam_{sib} P G N	—	Ch_{pt}	
					Ch_{sib}	

phrenic sons use the strategy of high participation to a greater extent than do other sons.

The allocation of acts to the mother in each of the families is shown in Table 6.2. In comparisons made across family types there are no family culture or session effects; all families direct acts to mothers at approximately equal rates. However, fathers' roles differ depending on the type of family, with normal fathers paying more attention to their wives than good fathers, who pay more attention than poor fathers. This attention paying by father to mother is not specifically associated with the presence of either child.

One difference in amount of attention paid to the mother is associated with the presence of the patient son. In this instance the schizophrenic patients, and especially the poor premorbid patients, pay more attention to their mothers than do the normal sons. If talking to the mother indicates recognition of her relative importance, then, from the point of view of the fathers in schizophrenic families, mothers have a weak power role; from the point of view of the schizophrenic patient son, mothers have a relatively strong power role. This finding is most evident in the poor families. The patient son-to-mother attention pattern is especially interesting when we recall that these same patient sons pay relatively little attention to their fathers. It is important to note that the normal son, who pays most attention to his father, pays least attention to his mother in contrast to other sons.

A comparison of acts directed to mothers across the two interaction situations shows that no role player in any family consistently alters his rates of attention to the mother in the two sessions. However, when comparisons are made between the three members of the same family we find that in the poor premorbid families there is a consistently different allocation of acts directed to the mother by other family members; when the poor patient son is present he always talks to his mother more than his father does. Addition of these findings to those already presented provides a clearer picture of the attention-control patterns in the poor premorbid schizophrenic families. The poor schizophrenic patient speaks more than other sons do in their families. However, he speaks less often to his father and more often to his mother than do other sons, and more often to his mother than does his father. His use of the attention-control strategy and his recognition of the importance or power of his mother suggests, along with the large proportion of attention received from his mother (to be discussed below) that a mother–patient son power coalition exists in the poor premorbid families. In contrast, in normal families we have seen that the father generally speaks more than others in his own family; he also speaks to the mother more than other fathers do, and the son and mother (although the latter not significantly so) speak more to the father. Thus normal fathers use the strategy of attention control and their status is recognized by mothers and sons.

Table 6.2 shows the proportion of the family's acts directed to the sons. Comparisons made across types of family indicate that there is a family culture difference in the attention paid to the son. Chidren in schizophrenic families receive more attention than do normal children, with sons in the poor premorbid families receiving most. This family culture effect is further specified in the two sessions; the group differences are stronger and in the same direction in the patient session and disappear in the well-sibling session. Thus when the schizophrenic patient is present he receives more attention than the comparable normal son; the greatest attention is paid to the poor son and somewhat less attention to the good son.

The disproportionate attention paid to sons has its source most strongly in mothers rather than fathers in these families. Although there is a reversal in ordering between mothers in good and poor premorbid families, schizophrenic mothers in general speak more often to their sons than normal mothers do. This difference is specified further by examination of the mothers' roles in the two sessions: when with their patient sons the mothers, good more than poor, pay more attention to their sons than do normal mothers to their sons. This difference disappears when the well son is present. A comparable difference between fathers' roles occurs when the patient son is present; fathers of schizophrenic sons speak more often to their sons than do normal fathers, specifically, poor fathers are high, good fathers are medium, and normal fathers are low.

Differences in attention paid to the schizophrenic son are further emphasized in comparisons made across the two sessions, in which it is clear that parents of poor premorbid patients alter their behavior toward their two sons by speaking significantly more often to the patient than to the comparable well child. There are, however, no within-family role differences in the allocation of the "speaking to son" role.

In comparison with normal sons, sons in the schizophrenic families are seen by both parents as important targets of the parents' attention. Furthermore, the differences in attention paid to sons by parents are clearest when the patient son is present and are especially apparent in families of poor premorbid schizophrenic sons who receive more attention from both parents than do their siblings. The relative high status of the patient son in contrast to the normal son is therefore given further support.

Data from the final measure of targets of acts is shown in Table 6.3. These are statements that the speaker makes while avoiding eye contact with other family members. This strategy of interaction is interesting as a technique in which attention is diverted from family members to a general audience; it thus succeeds in avoiding recognition of another person's im-

Table 6.3 Attention-control Strategies
(families of sons: group and structural analyses)

Variable	Group Analysis				Roles and Sessions				Roles within Sessions			
	H	M	L	p	H	M	L	p	H	M	L	p
					Fa$_c$ G P N			—	Fa$_{pt}$ G N P			—
					Mo$_c$ G/N P			—	Fa$_{sib}$ G P N			—
					Ch$_c$ N G P			—				
Acts directed to no one	Fam$_c$ G P N			—					Mo$_{pt}$ N G P			—
					Fam$_{pt}$ G P/N			—	Mo$_{sib}$ G N P			—
					Fam$_{sib}$ G N P			—				
									Ch$_{pt}$ N G P			—
									Ch$_{sib}$ N P G			—
					Fa$_c$ G P N			—	Fa$_{pt}$ G P N			.20
					Mo$_c$ P N G			—	Fa$_{sib}$ P G N			—
					Ch$_c$ P N G			—				
Length of statement	Fam$_c$ P G N			—					Mo$_{pt}$ P G N			—
					Fam$_{pt}$ G P N			—	Mo$_{sib}$ P N G			—
					Fam$_{sib}$ P N G			—				
									Ch$_{pt}$ P G N			—
									Ch$_{sib}$ P G N			—

portance while at the same time successfully monopolizing the time and attention of the whole family. Speaking "to no one" allows a family member to exercise his own attention-control strategies, yet avoids any weakening of this position from giving attention to other members. Comparisons made across types of family and types of role player show only one significant difference in the use of this strategy: the father in the patient session. However, even though families do not differ in the proportions of acts directed "to no one" this strategy is an important phenomenon to the extent that it comprises from 22 to 28% of all acts in a family session. There are no systematic changes in its use across the two sessions. However, an interesting pattern of role differentiation within families is shown in the poor premorbid schizophrenic families. Here, in each of the family sessions, the poor father consistently talks "to no one" more than does the mother in the same family. We already have evidence for the relatively low power position of the poor father; he talks at about the same rate as other fathers but he receives relatively few acts, especially from his son and he pays more attention to his patient son than other fathers pay to their sons. Thus his use of the "talking to no one" strategy, along with his tendency to talk to his son rather than his wife, may be his way of safely maintaining a rather precarious, minimal level of control in his family. He can talk to a general audience and to a low-status member, yet he does not attempt to talk to his wife, perhaps for fear of a response that might further reduce his status.

To this point we have dealt with two aspects of the total rate of participation in families, allocation of talking time among the three family members and allocation of a member's acts to the possible targets in the family. Each of these has served as an indicator of the strategy of "attention control." A different attention-control strategy is one in which the speaker monopolizes time, and thus attention, by speaking in long, uninterrupted statements. A longer and usually more organized speech focuses the attention of the family member on the speaker and also allows the speaker to use other control strategies such as providing information or giving orders.

Data for our measure of length of statements are presented in Table 6.3. There are no family culture or session effects in the use of this attention-control strategy. However, one role effect is significant: fathers when with their patient sons use significantly different statement lengths. Good premorbid fathers give the longest, poor fathers medium, and normal fathers short speeches. This role difference for fathers is further specified by comparisons made across two sessions. Not only do good premorbid fathers differ in comparison with other fathers, they also consistently change their attention-control strategy across sessions, lengthening their speeches when their patient son is present. Finally, when we examine role differentiation within families, good premorbid fathers' mode of control is further emphasized. When good parents are with their patient sons, the father consistently uses this time-monopolizing strategy more often than other members in his own family.

All of this evidence is consistent and strong and points to the role that the good father takes. He does not participate at a rate different from the other fathers. Yet when he does speak he makes long speeches, longer than other fathers' and longer than those of other members of his own family. Further, this strategy is specifically associated with the presence of his patient son. Monopolizing long segments of time may be the good father's chosen control technique, selected for use with the schizophrenic patient because it is direct, not subtle, and because it clearly limits the number of possibilities of response by the other family members.

Investigation of strategies of attention-control in male families points to consistent and patterned differences in the use of these strategies by normal and schizophrenic families and by role players within each of the families. In particular, attention-control strategies are used differentially by fathers and by sons, but not by mothers. Furthermore, differences are largely confined to the session when the patient son is present.

Thus when findings on all measures of attention-control are compiled the power structures of the three kinds of families stand out as empirically different and theoretically interesting. Families of normal sons tend to follow the theoretically expected pattern for normal families with the father using attention-control devices more than others in his family, especially more than his son; furthermore, he is treated as an important person by his son, who talks to him more often than do other sons. Normal mothers do not differ from other mothers in rate of participation, yet they receive more attention from their husbands than do other mothers. These patterns, in combination with the fact that the normal son receives little attention from either parent, suggest a power coalition between normal parents, with the father playing the strongest power role. The normal son is distinctly the least powerful person, at least in his use of these direct strategies of attention-control.

In contrast to the normal family, families of good premorbid schizophrenic sons show a power structure centered around the patient son rather than around the father. Both sons in good families use attention-control strategies more often than other sons. However, it is the patient son who is seen as important by the mother, and, less significantly so, by the father. The mother is paid a medium level of attention by both father and son. It is the father who is paid the least attention, particularly by his patient son. The use of attention-control strategies thus suggests a structure in which the good premorbid patient son is clearly the greatest user and recipient of attention in the family, with the father at the bottom. A patient son-mother coalition is suggested by the patient's medium rate of attention paid to his mother and the high rate given back by the mother. This is contrasted to the low rate of attention paid to the father by both mother and son that leaves the father in the low-power, isolate position, at least in terms of attention control. However, the good premorbid father has selected the alternative strategy of monopolizing long segments of time as his special strategy of control especially for use when his patient son is present.

Finally, poor premorbid schizophrenic families have structured themselves around attention-control strategies in a way different both from normal and good families. Here both sons use the strategy of high participation to maintain attention on themselves; however, it is only the patient son who is recognized and paid attention to by the two parents. Fathers pay more attention to their patient sons than do other fathers; mothers follow this pattern to a less strong degree. The attention-control position of the patient son is complemented by his paying attention to mother. Thus the poor family seems to have a patient son-mother power coalition in which the father recognizes the son's position but is largely isolated. However, the poor premorbid father uses one attention-control strategy particular to his role; he consistently avoids recognizing the importance of other family members by directing his attention to the group in general.

Attention-Control Strategies: Families of Daughters

We will look at attention-control strategies in families of daughters in somewhat less detail because the smaller sample size precludes making the within-family and across-session comparisons possible in the male families.

The first measure of attention control is participation rate, or the extent to which a member maintains control of interaction time and thus focuses the family's attention on his own behavior. These data, for the families of females, are shown in Table 6.4. Here there is one general role effect, for the daughter, that is further specified in the two sessions;

Table 6.4   Attention-control Strategies
(families of daughters: group and structural analyses)

Variable	Group Analysis	Roles and Sessions		Roles within Sessions	
	H M L p		H M L p		H M L p
		Fa_c	P N G —	Fa_{pt}	P G N —
		Mo_c	N P G —	Fa_{sib}	P N G —
Participation rate	Fam_c	Ch_c	N G P .20		
				Mo_{pt}	G P N —
		Fam_{pt}		Mo_{sib}	N G P —
		Fam_{sib}			
				Ch_{pt}	N G P .05
				Ch_{sib}	P G N —

the role effect disappears in the well-sibling session and is congruent and strengthened when the patient daughter is present. Normal daughters are significantly higher in participation than either patient daughter and participate at a median rate of 37%. Good schizophrenic patients are next highest, with a median of 29%, and poor schizophrenic daughters are lowest, with a median of 14%. Although differences in the use of attention-control strategies are limited to daughters, as in the analysis of male families they were limited to sons, the ordering of differences is reversed. We shall return to this point in a later discussion.

We have assumed that the degree to which a person is paid attention is an indicator of that person's importance or power; the member who is spoken to most often is the recipient of deference and respect and is therefore a high-power member. In Table 6:5 are data showing the proportion of a family's acts directed toward the father. There are no family culture, session, or general role effects; all families and members speak at relatively the same rate to the father of the family. However, one specific role effect occurs for the daughter in the well-sibling session. Normal girls speak least often to their fathers, whereas both good and poor well siblings pay more attention to their fathers, with the poor daughters having the highest rate. Therefore in female families there is no general difference in attention paid to the father; only from the point of view of the nonpatient daughter does the father of the schizophrenic have a relatively stronger power position. A coalition between father and his schizophrenic daughter is clearly not apparent in these attention-control data.

Amount of attention paid to the mother in female families is shown in Table 6.5. There is a tendency for family cultures to differ in that more attention is paid to the mother in normal families than in good families. There are no signicant session effects, although again when interacting with each of her daughters the normal mother tends to receive most attention and the good mother least. Although the group and session patterns are only statistical tendencies, there is one significant role effect, for the daughter. Normal daughters speak most often to their mothers, good daughters somewhat less, and poor daughters, least; this effect is not specific to either of the family sessions. Thus normal and good mothers do tend to have distinguishable power positions, with normal mothers receiving most attention and good mothers least. This is especially apparent, from the point of view of daughters, when normal mothers are given more attention by their daughters, good mothers are paid more attention by their daughters than by the whole family, and poor mothers are given less attention by their daughters than by the family as a whole.

Table 6.5 Attention-control Strategies
(families of daughters: group and structural analyses)

Variable	Group Analysis	Roles and Sessions	Roles within Sessions
	$H\,M\,L\ p$	$H\,M\,L\ p$	$H\,M\,L\ p$
Acts directed to father	Fam_c G N P —	Fa_c Mo_c N P G — Ch_c P G N — Fam_{pt} N G P — Fam_{sib} P G N —	Fa_{pt} Fa_{sib} Mo_{pt} P N G — Mo_{sib} $\overline{N\,P\,G}$ — Ch_{pt} N G P — Ch_{sib} $\overline{P\,G\,N}$ .10
Acts directed to mother	Fam_c N P G —	Fa_c N P G — Mo_c Ch_c $\overline{N\,G\,P}$ .20 Fam_{pt} $\overline{N\,P\,G}$ — Fam_{sib} N P G —	Fa_{pt} G N P — Fa_{sib} N P G — Mo_{pt} Mo_{sib} Ch_{pt} N G P — Ch_{sib} $\overline{N\,G\,P}$ —
Acts directed to child	Fam_c G P N —	Fa_c P G N — Mo_c $\overline{N\,G\,P}$ .20 Ch_c Fam_{pt} G N P — Fam_{sib} G/P N —	Fa_{pt} N G P — Fa_{sib} P G N — Mo_{pt} $\overline{\overline{N\,G\,P}}$ .05 Mo_{sib} N G P — Ch_{pt} Ch_{sib}

Further information on control strategies is provided by data on attention paid to daughters, shown in Table 6.5. There are no general group or session effects, indicating that the receipt of attention by daughters is not different in the three types of family. There is, however, a difference between types of mother that is maintained when the mother is with the patient but disappears when the well sibling is present. Normal mothers consistently pay more attention to their daughters than do good mothers, who direct more attention to their daughters than do poor mothers. Thus, from the point of view of the mothers in the schizophrenic families, the schizophrenic daughter has relatively little importance. The patient daughter is isolated from her mother in that neither pays attention to the other at rates equal to those in normal families.

The final target of attention is "no one." This measure, reported in Table 6.6, stands for a strategy in which the speaker avoids eye contact while talking, thus avoiding paying attention to any one family member. Although this strategy is used relatively often, from 11% to 37% of the time depending on the type of family, there are no significant family, session, or role effects.

The final attention-control strategy that families of female patients may use is monopoly of relatively long segments of time by making long speeches; these data are presented in Table 6.6. There are no group or session effects. However, one general role effect shows that the daughters use this strategy at different rates. Good daughters speak in short statements, normal daughters use somewhat longer ones, and poor daughters the longest. However, specification of the daughter's use of this strategy occurs in the session when the patient is present. Relative to normal daughters, good and, to an even greater extent, poor schizophrenic patient daughters speak in significantly shorter statements.

The measures of attention-control strategies suggest the following picture of power-structure in the families of daughters. The three family cultures are not distinguishable in their use of attention-control techniques. However, daughters in schizophrenic families, especially patient daughters, do play a relatively weak power role compared to normal daughters. The low power position of the schizophrenic daughter is apparent in her own participation, when she speaks seldom and in short bursts, as well as in allocation of attention to her by her mother, who pays little attention to her, especially to the poor patient. Fathers in schizophrenic families do not have distinctive power positions except in the eyes of the well daughters, who talk more to them.

Thus in families of normal daughters there is a relatively strong attention-control role for the daughter and a high rate of attention paid between mother and daughter. There is no distinctive power position for the

Table 6.6 Attention-control Strategies
(families of daughters: group and structural analyses)

Variable	Group Analysis				Roles and Sessions					Roles within Sessions				
		H	M	L		H	M	L	p		H	M	L	p
					Fa_c	N	P	G	—	Fa_{pt}	N	G	P	—
					Mo_c	G	N	P	—	Fa_{sib}	P	G	N	—
					Ch_c	P	N	G	—					
Acts directed to no one	Fam_c N P G —									Mo_{pt}	N	G	P	—
					Fam_{pt}	N	G	P	—	Mo_{sib}	P	G	N	—
					Fam_{sib}	P	G	N	—					
										Ch_{pt}	P	N	G	—
										Ch_{sib}	P	N	G	—
					Fa_c	P	N	G	—	Fa_{pt}	P	G	N	—
					Mo_c	N	G	P	—	Fa_{sib}	P	N	G	—
					Ch_c	P	N	G	.20					
Length of statements	Fam_c P N G —									Mo_{pt}	N	G	P	—
					Fam_{pt}	N	G	P	—	Mo_{sib}	N	G	P	—
					Fam_{sib}	P	N	G	—					
										Ch_{pt}	N	G	P	.10
										Ch_{sib}	P	N	G	—

normal father. Families of poor daughters provide the greatest contrast. Again there is no distinct use of attention-control strategies by the father. However, in contrast to other daughters, poor daughters and particularly the patient daughter have weak power positions both in terms of their own participation and the attention paid to them by other family members. Poor patient daughters are especially isolated from their mothers in contrast to the mother-daughter coalition evident in normal families. This isolation, in combination with the lack of attention from the father, points to the degree to which the schizophrenic patient daughter is "out" of the family. Families of good schizophrenic daughters follow the power patterns of the poors, although to a less extreme degree.

Discussion

Attention-control strategies are one of several techniques for exerting power and influence in families. Talking a great deal and maintaining control over long segments of time not only serve to channel and limit the direction of interaction but also allow for exertion of other control strategies as well. We have shown in data derived from participation rate, who-speaks-to-whom, and length of speeches that families having normal and schizophrenic children differ in the use of this strategy, families having male and female children differ, and role players within each type of family also differ. From the point of view of this strategy of control, therefore, there appears to be a differentiated power structure in all of the families investigated.

Theories of normal family structure led us to expect that parents, and especially fathers, would take the high status position and would exercise more control than children, even though the adolescent and young-adult child may have accumulated greater power, and skill in exercising it, than a younger child. Theories derived from clinical work with families of schizophrenic children suggested that power structure in these families is extremely ambiguous; that is, no one clearly takes the powerful or the weak role; or, the normative distribution of control between parents is reversed, with fathers playing the dependent role and mothers dominating the family.

With some exceptions and some ambiguity, these predictions are borne out in the attention-control data, more strongly in the families of sons than in the families of daughters (See Chart 6.1) In the normal male families generational boundaries are clear and in the expected direction; fathers are the high power members, with mothers somewhat lower. The normal son has low status and, in turn, recognizes his father's stronger position by paying him respect. In normal families of daughters there is no evidence for a strong generational difference since these normal fathers do not differ from other fathers of daughters. However, a mother-daughter coalition is clear, with attention being paid back and forth between the two.

In schizophrenic families with sons, both good and poor, we found a reversal of generational roles between father and son. Mothers and their schizophrenic patient sons take the high power positions and the fathers exert little influence. Although some theories might predict a father–patient daughter coalition in the female schizophrenic family, the findings suggest, instead, that the daughter, especially the patient daughter, is isolated from the parents. She receives little attention and respect, par-

Chart 6.1 Summary of Participation Rate and Who-Speaks-to-Whom
Data in Families of Sons and Daughters [a]

Families of Sons	Normal	Poor	Good
Patient Session	Fa⟍ ⟋Mo Son	Fa⟍ ⟋Mo Son	Fa⟍ ⟋Mo Son
Sibling Session	Fa Mo Son	Fa Mo Son	Fa Mo Son

Families of Daughters	Normal	Poor	Good
Patient Session	Fa Mo Dau	Fa Mo Dau	Fa Mo Dau
Sibling Session	Fa⟵Mo Dau	Fa Mo Dau	Fa⟵Mo Dau

[a] Legend:
  Double arrow: significantly high rates of speech to another
  Single arrow: significantly medium rates of speech to another
  Dotted arrow: significantly low rates of speech to another
  Double underscore: significantly high participation
  Single underscore: significantly medium participation
  Dotted underscore: significantly low participation
  No arrow or no underscore: no significant differences across role players

ticularly from her more powerful mother, and attempts little control
herself.

What do these findings mean for the development of schizophrenia in
a family? Specifically, how do they relate to the etiological, responsive, and
situational interpretations we have raised as alternative explanations? Both
Wynne et al. (1958) and Fleck (1963), in their discussions of the relationship between family structure and the development of schizophrenia,
explicitly link parental power roles with the schizophrenic child's development. They assume that a normally developing child requires appropriate parental figures with whom to identify; a son needs a strong, dominant
father while a daughter needs a mother who takes the expressive, more
passive role. In families in which these roles are ambiguous or reversed one
possible outcome is that the child's identity is quite unclear or fragile;

and under family or situational demands he finds the schizophrenic symptoms to be the only feasible response.

The attention-control strategy data supply some support for this etiological argument. Neither the schizophrenic son nor the schizophrenic daughter has the appropriate parental power figure with whom to identify. The father of the male patient does not take the dominant role; instead the schizophrenic son is in this position in coalition with his mother. In the female families the schizophrenic daughter appears to be isolated both from her mother and her father, and her mother is the dominant rather than the more passive parent. In contrast, in the normal families generational boundaries are clear, fathers and mothers are in relatively higher power positions than their children, and mothers pay particular attention to their daughters.

The situational explanation of the findings, that is, that power relationships are a result of the family's response to the experimental context, appears to have less strength here since role differences are limited largely to one family session, when the patient is present. We would expect that families with different orientations to the experimental situation would be affected in the same way in each session and thus show similar patterns both times.

The third alternative explanation of this set of findings is that differences in the use of attention-control strategies result from the family's response to a deviant schizophrenic child. Perhaps mothers pay a great deal of attention to their patient children as a way of protecting or supporting them. However, this pattern occurs only in male families and fails to occur in the families of schizophrenic daughters, where neither mothers nor fathers direct attention to their patient daughters. An alternative parental response to the schizophrenic child might consist of avoiding or ignoring the patient; this appears to occur only in the female families. Since a longer series of inferences must be made in order to support the responsive interpretation—by assuming that parental responses are different toward male and female patients—the etiological argument appears to have somewhat more validity.

To this point we have examined one control strategy, attention control, and have found that the power relationships are largely consistent with theoretical descriptions of normal and schizophrenic families. Since the concept of power is multidimensional and complex it is useful to specify further these family power relationships by examining another control strategy, person control. These data are presented in the following chapter.

Chapter 7

Power:

The Strategy of Person-Control

A second technique used by family members to exert power is the strategy of person control. The defining quality of this power strategy is the direct and explicit confrontation of another person in an attempt to stop the speaker before he has finished his idea, to prevent his being heard, or, more indirectly, to control the direction and content of his interaction. A person-control strategy such as an interruption says to another family member, "Stop talking," or "I am no longer listening to what you say"; a direct question says, "You are being pressed to answer," or, "You must talk about the topic that I am initiating." Each of these strategies, interruptions and questions, is commonly used in interaction and clearly understood as a technique for maintaining control over others. Parents may interrupt to prevent a child from bringing up a topic that is taboo in the family; a group therapist may interject a question to prevent one member from exposing personal content before other members of the group are prepared for it. In all of these strategies an explicit attempt is made to change or stop the behavior of another person.

In his description of interaction in the schizophrenic family Haley (1959) suggests that these family members generally avoid or at best are ambivalent about exercising person control. Attempts to take charge or to make a firm decision are immediately disconfirmed, either by the influencer or by someone else in the family. These family members not only avoid an explicitly labeled role of "leader" but they avoid alliances of two members against a third. "Family members behave as if an alliance between two of them is inevitably a betrayal of the third person" (Haley, 1959, p. 366).

The existence of recognized leadership or labeled alliances in a family imply that power differences exist and that certain strategies of control have been and continue to be exercised in order to maintain these differences. The schizophrenic family member, from Haley's point of view, is unable to exercise control in a clearly defined, unambivalent way that is acceptable and recognized by other members. We might expect, therefore, that these families would avoid the use of person-control strategies. Or when they choose to use them they would select strategies that are less direct or clearly understood or that are easily disqualified.

In contrast, we would expect the normal family to have a clearly defined power structure and the members within the family to support their power positions by the exercise of explicitly labeled control strategies. Thus we assume that person-control strategies are acceptable modes of behavior in normal families, seen as legitimate both by the influencer and the influenced. Legitimacy does not imply that the control strategies are necessarily successful, only that it is acceptable and within the family's rules to confront other members directly in an attempt to change their behavior.

The findings on attention-control strategies, reported in Chapter 6, suggested distinctive patterns of role differentiation within each type of family. Our discussion of generational differences in status and of coalitions drew particularly on findings of the intrafamily and intersession analyses. As shown later, there is less intrafamilial differentiation in the use of specific person-control strategies; rather there appear to be general norms followed by all family members and each type of family follows a different norm. Our emphasis in this chapter, therefore, falls on findings from the across-family analyses.

In this chapter, we look at two person-control techniques, interruptions and questions. Each of these styles of interaction functions to confront another family member in an attempt to control his behavior; each style is also commonly defined and understood to function in this way. Thus both carry with them the qualities that Haley describes as absent from control attempts of schizophrenic family members—direct confrontation and lack of ambiguity. It is important to recognize, however, that these strategies may also have accumulated different meanings in different families, varying from hostility to interest and concern. An interruption in one family may be interpreted and responded to as if it were a personal attack; in another family it may be seen as evidence that the interrupter is excited and responsive. But in either instance the strategy retains its basic function—the control and channeling of another person's behavior.

Our measure of interruptions stands for the more direct technique for controlling other people, one in which clear personal confrontation occurs. The second, indirect technique, is question asking in which the definition of the expected response is more ambiguous. Further investigation of the interruption strategy is possible in our data since we can distinguish between interruptions that are successful (that is, the ones that control the other person's behavior by stopping his speech) and unsuccessful interruptions (the ones that do not prevent the other member from continuing his speech). Finally, we have included a measure of the target of person-control strategies comparable to the target measure in the section on attention-control. Information about the use of these person-control strategies and the persons to whom they are directed add further data on power coalitions as well as preferred control strategies in the families.

Person-Control Strategies: Families of Sons

The families of sons use the direct person-control strategy, interruptions, at different rates that are consistent with the predictions derived from family theories. We will show that the greatest distinction occurs between normal and good premorbid families, when normal families and all of their members use interruptions most often and good families, particularly when the schizophrenic patient is present, avoid using the strategy. Poor premorbid families fall between the two. A set of role differences in the use of interruptions is found within both of the schizophrenic families suggesting that each type of patient son may be following rules for use of direct person-controls that are different from the family rules. In the context of family rules against direct attempts to control others the patient son is either allowed to make these attempts or is avoided as a target of control attempts. In either instance this may be a result of the family's decision to protect the patient from confrontation and thus, indirectly, to protect the family from unacceptable or uncontrollable behavior.

Several measures of the direct person-control strategy of interruption are examined here. We shall look at the source of interruptions, that is, who uses them, and the degree to which they are successfully controlling. Then we will examine the targets of interruptions, that is, who is interrupted, and again, the degree to which targets are successfully controlled.

These data, in combination, will provide a complex picture of the person-control relationships within each type of family.

The first and most general measure of interruptions is attempted interruptions. This measure is based on the proportion of all acts that are intrusions into another person's statement, whether the intrusion successfully stops the other speaker or not. Included here are the statements that break into another person's speech before he has completed his idea. For example,

FATHER: That they were kind enough to ehh to ehh invite me out for any evening/ I would go along. I wouldn' be/
MOTHER: (I) And especially where you like the sport of bowling, too./

Here the mother is counted as intruding into the father's statement; we assume that her act functions to control the father's behavior.

The attempted interruption data in Table 7.1 show that there is no general family culture effect. However, there is a difference between families when the schizophrenic patient son is present. In this setting normal families have a relatively high rate of intrusions, poor premorbid families are medium, and good premorbid families are lowest; median percentages, respectively, are 20%, 21%, and 13%. Since there is also a significant difference between poor and good families in the patient session it is the good families that are consistently lowest.

There are no general role effects. However, in the patient session both fathers' and sons' interrupting rates are congruent with the family pattern, with normal fathers and sons interrupting at a high rate, poor fathers and patient sons medium, and good fathers and patient sons low. Mothers' rates, although not significantly different, follow the same order. These differences in the use of interruption strategies in the patient sessions are not a result of consistent changes of behavior across the two sessions, nor is there internal role differentiation in the use of interruptions in any of the families. Thus the congruence between findings in the patient session and the family roles in that session suggests that all members in each family type are following the same rules about intrusions and these rules differ across family types. The normal family allows or perhaps requires all members to use personal confrontation as a control strategy; the good family, only when the schizophrenic son is present, prohibits all members from using this technique.

The person-control strategy of interrupting may have varying degrees of success. Success of the strategy is inferred by examining whether the target person—the person whose speech is broken into—abruptly stops talking before his idea is completed, in contrast to his continuing to speak simultaneously with the intruding speech. The previous quotation

Table 7.1   Direct Person-control Strategies
(families of sons: group and structural analyses)

Variable	Group Analysis		Roles and Sessions		Roles within Sessions	
	H M L p		*H M L p*		*H M L p*	
			Fa_c	N P G —	Fa_{pt}	N P G .05
			Mo_c	N G P —	Fa_{sib}	N P G —
Attempted			Ch_c	N P G —		
interruptions	Fam_c	N P G —				
					Mo_{pt}	N P G —
			Fam_{pt}	N P G .10	Mo_{sib}	N G P —
			Fam_{sib}	N G P —		
					Ch_{pt}	N P G .20
					Ch_{sib}	N P G —
			Fa_c	G P/N —	Fa_{pt}	G N P —
			Mo_c	P G N —	Fa_{sib}	N P G —
Successful			Ch_c	P N G —		
interruptions	Fam_c	P G N —			Mo_{pt}	G P N —
			Fam_{pt}	G P N —	Mo_{sib}	P G N —
			Fam_{sib}	P N G —		
					Ch_{pt}	P G N —
					Ch_{sib}	N P G —

from a family's discussion exemplified a successful interruption. An unsuccessful interruption is shown in the following segment of interaction.

> SON: I don't know why/ or what it's caused by to (S) *tell you the truth./*
>
> FATHER: (S) *I don't either./* I don't think anybody else knows./

Data for the proportion of all interruption attempts that are successful are shown in Table 7.1. Whereas families of sons differ in the relative use of interruptions as a person-control strategy they do not differ either at the family or role level in the degree of its success. Role players who interrupt often—these are the normal fathers and sons—are no more successful in exercising their power than the role players who use the strategy very seldom.

Some members, however, are more successful in controlling others by interrupting when with one child than when with the other child in the family. The intersession comparisons show that fathers of good patients who generally interrupt less than other fathers are considerably more successful interrupters when with the well son than when with the patient. Furthermore, good family members as a whole are more successful as interrupters in the well sibling than in the patient session. Thus in the good family, when the patient son is present, there are few interruptions in comparison with other families and these are less likely to be effective in stopping the other person from talking. These findings suggest the possibility that interruptions have a less insistent quality when used in the presence of the schizophrenic son.

The role specialization measure provides another indicator of the relative power of the three members. Within the poor premorbid families, when the patient son is present, he is consistently more successful in his use of person-control strategies than are other members of his family, especially his father. This person-control specialization on the part of the poor patient son is further evidence for the relatively powerful position of the poor patient. Not only does he maintain the attention of the family by participating at a high rate, as shown in the preceding chapter, but he is also successful in using person-control strategies.

The other within-family role specialization in rates of successful interruptions is in the normal family in the well-sibling session; here the son is consistently more successful than is his mother. The reason for the limitation of this finding to the second session is not clear; however, it suggests that person-control strategies, in contrast to attention control, may be favored means of control of the normal son.

Thus families of sons differ in their use of the direct person-control strategy of attempted interruptions, and certain family members differ in the degree to which they are successful in using the strategy. Normal families generally interrupt at the highest rate; poor families are medium; and good families low. This finding in itself suggests that the schizophrenic families are ambivalent about or avoid the use of control strategies that directly confront other members in an attempt to control their behavior. The measure of success of the strategy differentiates between the poor and good families and allows for certain inferences about the quality of the few interruptions that do occur. Good families, lowest on attempted interruption rates, have less success with the strategy when the patient is present; this is especially true of the good father. In poor families, medium on attempted interruptions, one family member is highly successful when using this strategy; this specialist is the patient son. These patterns of success, specific to the presence of the patient, indicate that perhaps the quality of the person-control strategy is different when the schizophrenic son is in the family. When the good patient son is present interruptions by the father or the family have an ambiguous or weak impact and therefore are not successful. When the poor patient son is present his attempts at interruption may be successful because of the same ambivalence of family members about responding to a control attempt; rather than resisting the control strategy with strategies of their own, they allow it to succeed.

The fact that control attempts are less clearly defined or more ambivalent in the schizophrenic family when the patient is present may be a result of the parents' decision to treat their patient son with great care. He may be allowed to talk more and he may be allowed to intrude successfully on other people's conversation in accord with the family's implicit rules about protecting him, or for fear of what might happen if he were directly controlled.

The second approach used in the investigation of direct person-control strategies is the examination of the target of these strategies, that is, who is interrupted rather than who does the interrupting.[1] Measures of targets of interruption tell us to whom person-control strategies are directed and, with the addition of measures on degree of success, whether certain role players are successfully confronted.

Data on rates of being interrupted, without regard for the success of the intrusion, are shown in Table 7.2.[2] Both fathers and mothers are differentially interrupted, normal parents most often, poor parents at a medium rate, and good parents least often. Sons in the three kinds of family are not interrupted by their parents to different degrees. It should also be noted that, although not all differences are significant, normal families are highest in rank in all analyses; this was also true on the index of attempted inter-

---

[1] Whereas the group and family session level findings on attempted interruptions and target of interruptions must be identical since one interrupting act always has one target and therefore total percentages for each are the same in each family, the interrupting and being interrupted findings at the role level are independent of each other and can be treated as unrelated measures. Independence results from the fact that the base used for "being interrupted" is the total number of acts of the person interrupted while the base for "interrupting" is the total number of acts of the interrupter.

[2] Whereas the rank ordering at the group and session levels follows the same ordering as found in our measure of attempted interruptions, the variation in significance levels across the two measures is a result of a slightly different set of coding rules for each variable.

Table 7.2 Direct Person-control Strategies
(families of sons: group and structural analyses)

Variable	Group Analysis				Roles and Sessions				Roles within Sessions			
		H	M	L p		H	M	L p		H	M	L p
					Fa_c	N	P	G .20	Fa_pt	N	P	G .05
					Mo_c	N	P	G .20	Fa_sib	N	P	G —
					Ch_c	N	G	P —				
Being interrupted	Fam_c	N	P	G .20					Mo_pt	N	P	G .10
					Fam_pt	N	P	G .05	Mo_sib	N	P	G —
					Fam_sib	N	G	P —				
									Ch_pt	N	P	G —
									Ch_sib	N	G	P —
					Fa_c	P	G	N —	Fa_pt	P	G	N —
					Mo_c	G	P	N —	Fa_sib	P	G	N —
					Ch_c	G	P	N —				
Being successfully interrupted	Fam_c	P	G	N —					Mo_pt	G	P	N —
					Fam_pt	G	P	N —	Mo_sib	N	P	G —
					Fam_sib	P	N	G —				
									Ch_pt	G	P	N —
									Ch_sib	N	P	G —

ruptions (see Table 7.1). This consistently high rate of interrupting and of being interrupted among all members of normal families is one sign of what we have been referring to as a general family norm with regard to person-control strategies.

Parental role differences are further specified in the role-within-session patterns. Only when their patient son is present are there significant differences between types of mothers and types of fathers in rates of being interrupted; again, normal mothers and fathers are interrupted most often, poors at a medium rate, and good premorbid parents least often. Thus the ordering of fathers on being interrupted is the same as their ordering on interruptions. However mothers, all of whom have relatively the same rates of interruption, are interrupted at varying rates, depending on the family type. Normal mothers are often the targets of direct person-control techniques whereas good mothers are least often interrupted.

When role players are compared across the two family sessions, two members of the good premorbid family, mother and son, show consistent differences in the rates at which they are interrupted, depending on which child is present. Good mothers and sons are interrupted significantly more often when the well son is present than when the patient is present. In the context of the good family's tendency to avoid confrontation, indicated by their low interruption rates, this session difference provides even more explicit evidence that it is the mother and patient son in the good families who are not the targets of person-control attempts. Further evidence is provided by the role differentiation measure where, again, in the good families there is a significant distribution of the target of interruption role across the three members. In the well-sibling session the good mother is interrupted more often than the other family members; this difference does not occur in the patient session. Thus lack of confrontation of the good mother is definitely associated only with the presence of her patient son. None of the other types of family, nor the members within them, are significantly differentiated in terms of targets of interruptions.

In Table 7.2 the "rate of being successfully interrupted" is compared across family types. We have pointed out that a successful interruption is one in which the person who is interrupted stops talking before he has completed his idea yielding to the person-control strategy of the interrupter. While family members are interrupted at significantly different rates there are no differences between them in the degree to which these interruptions are successfully controlling.

However, the differentiation within families on this variable provides interesting evidence for the relative effectiveness of the person-control strategy. In the good premorbid schizophrenic family when the patient son is present, this patient himself is less successfully interrupted than other family members, particularly less than the good father. We have previously shown that he is interrupted less often than is his own sibling; now we see that when these few interruptions occur the strategy is not successful. In the good families person control through interrupting is not often used and when it is used, especially with the patient son, it works significantly less successfully than it does for other members.

Within the poor premorbid families there is also a differential allocation of person-control techniques; in each of the family sessions the father is consistently the least successfully interrupted of the three members. Earlier person-control findings showed that poor premorbid fathers are the least successful interrupters; yet when they are interrupted they cannot be successfully stopped as can poor mothers, and sons.

Examination of the targets of direct person-control strategies has shown that in normal families all members are interrupted, especially the parents. In the schizophrenic families, when the patient son is present, the parents are much less likely to be targets of person controls. Within these families, however, there are certain members who are even more consistently avoided; good mothers and their patient sons are not directly confronted and if the good patient is confronted the attempt is not successful.

We have assumed that interrupting another family member functions as a direct person-control strategy; it is an attempt to confront and control the behavior of the other. In the data presented we have shown that the use of this strategy is clearly associated with the type of family yet the differences occur only when the patient son is present. Normal families use interruptions often, and this is true of all members within the family. Furthermore, interruptions are directed to normal parents more than to other parents. The tendency is for every member in the normal family to use this person-control strategy at a high rate and at relatively the same rate. Good families provide the greatest contrast. They seldom use interruptions, particularly when the patient son is present; furthermore, if an interruption is used when the schizophrenic son is present it is not successful, especially when directed toward the patient son or his mother. Poor premorbid families fall between normals and goods on these dimensions. They use direct person-control strategies at a medium rate. Family members do not differ in rate of success except for the poor patient son who uses the interruption strategy at a medium rate and is more successful than other members of his family.

It appears from the findings that norms for behavior having the direct, personally-confronting quality of interruptions vary across types of family but that these varying rules apply only when parents interact with their schizophrenic son. Normal families allow for clearly labeled, explicit confrontations, especially when the source or target of these confrontations is the parents. Good families proscribe the same behavior, especially when the targets are mother or patient son. Poor families fall between the normal and the good. However, the poor patient son, has a special role in terms of personal confrontation, as does the good patient son. Good patients are interrupted less than their siblings and are the least successfully interrupted of all members in their family. Poor patients interrupt at a medium rate, yet are more successful. We have suggested that the schizophrenic sons may be subject to different rules of behavior as a result of parental attempts to protect them or to avoid setting off unpredictable behavior. The good patient is not stopped by an interruption because the interrupter is not as insistent or forceful as he might be with other members; the poor patient is more successful in interruption because family members allow him to "have his way."

An alternative interpretation suggests that the good and poor patient sons are not easily interrupted or are more successful interrupters because they are more powerful in their families. While the person-control data do not consistently support this interpretation it is consistent with the attention-control findings previously presented.

The second person-control strategy, question-asking, is an indirect technique of exerting power. A question directed from one family member to another carries with it the demand that the recipient pay attention to the questioner and respond in a way that the questioner expects. Response to a question may be in the form of a direct answer, or a simple acknowledgment that the question has been heard: in either instance the questioner has succeeded in confronting and setting limits on the behavior of another person. However, in contrast to the interruption strategy, questioning is open and ambiguous and thus explicit evaluation of whether the strategy has been successful is extremely difficult. It is this indirect strategy that might be expected in families having schizophrenic children if we follow Haley's assumption regarding the unclarity and ambiguity of family power structure (Haley, 1959).

Data on question-asking are presented in Table 7.3. This measure includes all questions asked without regard for their content or affective quality; the coding judgment made in the Acknowledgment: Stimulus code takes into account only the grammatical structure of the statement. There is no family culture effect, nor are there differences between families when the well son is present. When the schizophrenic patient is present poor families ask significantly more questions, good families are medium, and normal families are lowest. However good mothers generally ask the most questions, poor mothers fewer questions, and normal mothers the fewest. These findings are congruently specified by the role-within-session patterns where, in the well-sibling session, the same ordering for mothers occurs.

The role of the schizophrenic mother as questioner is further specified in the role allocation within families. Not only do the mothers of good premorbid patient sons ask more questions than other mothers but they also ask more than other members of their own families. The within-family role differentiation measure indicates that when interacting with their schizophrenic patient sons good mothers consistently take the questioning role; the patient is medium in question asking, and the father asks fewest questions. A suggestion that other mothers as well as goods are also questioners is provided by the allocation of roles in the normal families, in which, in

Table 7.3   Indirect Person-control Strategies
(families of sons: group and structural analyses)

Variable	Group Analysis			Roles and Sessions			Roles within Sessions		
	H M L	p		H M L	p		H M L	p	
			Fa_c	P G N	—	Fa_{pt}	P G N	—
			Mo_c	G P N	.20	Fa_{sib}	G N P	—
			Ch_c	G N P	—			
All questions	Fam_c G P N —					Mo_{pt}	G P N	—
			Fam_{pt}	P G N	.20	Mo_{sib}	G P N	.20
			Fam_{sib}	G N P	—			
						Ch_{pt}	P G N	—
						Ch_{sib}	N G P	—
			Fa_c	G P N	—	Fa_{pt}	P G N	—
			Mo_c	G N P	.02	Fa_{sib}	G P N	—
Informational questions	Fam_c G P N —		Ch_c	N P G	—			
						Mo_{pt}	G N P	.10
			Fam_{pt}	G P N	.20	Mo_{sib}	G P N	.10
			Fam_{sib}	G N P	—			
						Ch_{pt}	P G N	—
						Ch_{sib}	G N P	—

the first session, mothers ask more questions than do sons in each of the families.

A second measure of the question-asking strategy adds further clarification to the role of the mother in these families. This measure is the proportion of acts that are questions about information, derived from Interaction Process Analysis, categories 7, 8, and 9. It supplements the previous question measure, which included all questions without regard for whether they had an informational or a predominantly affective quality. These data are shown in Table 7.3. The location of significant differences between families and role players is the same on this question measure as it was on the previous one; differences occur when the patient son is present and are centered on the role of the mother. However, there are two interesting disparities between the two measures in the ordering of differences. Here, on informational or task questions, the poor mothers drop to lowest in their questioning rate especially when their patient son is present. We can infer that the poor mothers ask more questions with affective tone or affective content when their patient son is present than when the well child is present. Furthermore, the families as a whole show different orderings on the two types of question asking. When the patient is present the poor families ask the highest proportion of questions but fewer of these are informational or task questions in quality and thus a larger proportion must be affective questions. In contrast, the good premorbid families are medium questioners but are highest when only the informational questions are examined.

Thus, whereas schizophrenic families, goods in particular, avoid the use of direct person-control strategies, it is apparent from the data on questioning that both poor and good families are more likely to use the indirect technique of control. Again the differential rates tend to cluster in the situation when the patient son is present; when the well son is present all families use indirect person-control strategies to the same degree.

The indirect control strategies appear to be especially useful to the mothers in schizophrenic families. Good mothers generally ask questions at a high rate, poors are medium, and normal mothers are lowest. When they are with their patient sons the good mothers' questions are more likely to be informational ones whereas poor mothers' questions have an affective quality.

We have shown in our examination of the male families that normal families prefer the direct mode of person-control, interruptions; in contrast, the schizophrenic families choose the indirect technique of question-asking. These differences occur only when the patient son is present. Certain role-taking patterns are also striking. The patient son is, to some extent, allowed to deviate from the family norms about direct confrontation. Also the patient's mother seems to be the specialist in the indirect person-control strategies.

Person-control Strategies: Families of Daughters

The use of direct and indirect person-control strategies in families of daughters provides only partial support for the findings presented for families of sons. Female families, in contrast to males, use these strategies to different degrees in both sessions; furthermore, some role players specialize in certain strategies. In Table 7.4 are data on the first direct person-control indicator, attempted interruptions; this measure includes both successful and unsuccessful interruptions. The strategy is used to significantly different degrees across family groups and in each family session, with normal female families using it most often, poor families at a medium rate, and good families at the lowest rate. The ordering of types of family is thus the same in male and female families.

This pattern is further specified in the general roles. Poor mothers when with their patient daughters, and the patient daughters themselves, have an especially high interruption rate in contrast to the poor family as a whole; good mothers and their patient daughters are nonusers of interruptions, as are good families. Fathers in the patient session on the other hand follow the family patterns, with normal fathers breaking into others' statements most often, and good fathers least often. It is apparent that, although the family rates for direct person controls are the same as those in male families, there is a differentiated pattern of role taking within the female families. The poor premorbid patients and their mothers appear to be interruption specialists.

The degree to which a family member is successful when he interrupts others is shown in Table 7.4. In the families of daughters, in the context of differential use of this person-control strategy, there is a tendency for the strategy to be differentially successful as well. Normal families attempt most interruptions but are least successful in controlling the other person; in contrast, although the good families attempt few interruptions they are most often successful in stopping the interrupted person's speech. Differences in the degree of success of intrusions disappear however when the patient daughter is present.

The roles of all three family members reflect the family culture, because good fathers, mothers, and daughters all tend to have high rates of successful person-control attempts whereas normal fathers, mothers, and daughters all have low rates. Again, for all three role players differences in the rate of success disappear in the session with the patient daughter.

Thus, in the families of daughters, normals use the strategy of interruptions most often, good families use it very seldom, and poor families are in-between, just as was found in families of sons. However, these differences encompass both family sessions and although the father generally follows the pattern of the family in interrupting, the mother and patient daughter use interruptions in a way incongruent with the family rates. Mothers of poor daughters, and poor patient daughters themselves, interrupt at a higher rate than would be expected from the family culture, and normal mothers and daughters drop to medium. Although the clinical descriptions of schizophrenic families and the findings in the families of male patients led us to expect that families of female patients would not use these directly

Table 7.4   Direct Person-control Strategies
(families of daughters: group and structural analyses)

Variable	Group Analysis				Roles and Sessions				Roles within Sessions			
	H M L	*p*			*H M L*	*p*			*H M L*	*p*		
				Fa$_c$	N G P	—		Fa$_{pt}$	N P G	.20		
				Mo$_c$	P N G	.20		Fa$_{sib}$	N G P	—		
Attempted				Ch$_c$	N P G	—						
interruptions	Fam$_c$ N P G	.20						Mo$_{pt}$	P N G	.05		
				Fam$_{pt}$	N P G	.10		Mo$_{sib}$	P N G	—		
				Fam$_{sib}$	N P G	.20						
								Ch$_{pt}$	P N G	—		
								Ch$_{sib}$	N P G	—		
				Fa$_c$	G P N	—		Fa$_{pt}$	P G N	—		
				Mo$_c$	G P N	—		Fa$_{sib}$	G P N	.20		
Successful				Ch$_c$	G P N	—						
interruptions	Fam$_c$ G P N	—						Mo$_{pt}$	P G N	—		
				Fam$_{pt}$	P G N	—		Mo$_{sib}$	G P N	—		
				Fam$_{sib}$	G P N	.20						
								Ch$_{pt}$	P G N	—		
								Ch$_{sib}$	G P N	—		

confronting person-control strategies, it is apparent here that two members, the poor mother and patient daughter, do choose to use the strategy.

Families differ in the rate of success of person-control strategies as well. In good families the few interruptions that occur are highly successful, especially when the well daughter is present. In contrast to goods, the normal families of females have high rates of interruptions that tend to be highly unsuccessful. This pattern of success was suggested in the male families, in which we found that good fathers and the family as a whole were more successful interrupters in the well sibling than in the patient session. Thus in families of good female and male patients, success of the direct person-control strategy seems to occur largely in the presence of the well child.

When the good patient is present interruptions are used very seldom, and when they are used they are not successful in controlling the interrupted person's behavior.

A second approach to understanding person-control strategies in families of daughters is through investigation of the targets of interruption, that is, persons to whom person-control strategies are directed.

Data on rates of being interrupted without regard for whether these interruptions are successful or not are shown in Table 7.5.[3] All three members of the family show significant differences in the patient session. Good patient daughters are interrupted at low rates, as are their mothers, normal daughters and their mothers are interrupted at high rates, and poor patient daughters and their mothers are in-between. The father's rates of interruption, however, are incongruent with overall family patterns and with those of mothers and daughters, in that poor fathers tend to be interrupted at the highest rate when their patient daughter is present. The good female families, and all of their members, attempt interruptions at the lowest rate and each member is interrupted at the lowest rate; no one uses person-control strategies and no one is the special target of the strategy if it is used. However, in poor families we have already shown that the mother and her patient daughter choose to use direct person controls, yet they are not the objects of person controls to the same extent. It is the poor father who is most often interrupted by someone else. While we do not have measures of who attempts to interrupt whom we may infer from the set of findings on the poor family that the mother and patient daughter are the sources of interruptions and the father is the most likely target.

Further specification of these role findings is provided by the measure of "being successfully interrupted", or the degree to which the person who is interrupted allows himself to be "talked down." These data are in Table 7.5. (Family culture and session data replicate those presented in Table 7.4.) Only one general role effect occurs, for the father, and this effect is specified only in the session with the well sibling. Good fathers are most successfully interrupted, poor fathers somewhat less, and normal fathers least successfully interrupted. There is a tendency for the poor mother to be most successfully interrupted, the good mother less so, and the normal mother least successfully interrupted, also only when the mother is with her well daughter. Thus, whereas poor mothers generally attempt many person controls and are less often the targets of these controls, when the poor mother is interrupted she does not resist; she stops talking.

The power structures that emerge from our examination of direct per-

---

[3] Group and session findings replicate those for attempted interruptions; the role measures, however, are independent of the attempted interruption measure.

Table 7.5   Direct Person-control Strategies
(families of daughters: group and structural analyses)

Variable	Group Analysis	Roles and Sessions	Roles within Sessions
	H M L p	*H M L p*	*H M L p*
		Fa$_c$ N P G —	Fa$_{pt}$ P N G .20
		Mo$_c$ N P G .20	Fa$_{sib}$ N P G —
		Ch$_c$ N G P —	
Being interrupted	Fam$_c$ N P G .20		Mo$_{pt}$ N P G .05
		Fam$_{pt}$ N P G .05	Mo$_{sib}$ N G P —
		Fam$_{sib}$ N G P —	
			Ch$_{pt}$ N P G .20
			Ch$_{sib}$ N G P —
		Fa$_c$ G P N .20	Fa$_{pt}$ P G N —
		Mo$_c$ P G N —	Fa$_{sib}$ G P N .20
Being successfully	Fam$_c$ G P N —	Ch$_c$ G P N —	
interrupted			Mo$_{pt}$ P G N —
		Fam$_{pt}$ P G N —	Mo$_{sib}$ P G N .20
		Fam$_{sib}$ G P N .20	
			Ch$_{pt}$ G N P —
			Ch$_{sib}$ P G N —

son-control strategies in the female families distinguish most clearly between normal and good families. In normal families direct person-control strategies are used at generally high rates and are least successful. There is role differentiation within the normal families in that the father uses this strategy more often than other fathers; mothers and daughters are medium users. Mothers and daughters are more often the targets of these strategies but these attempts are least successful. Thus normal families of females confront each other directly at a high rate but it is the father who tends to interrupt and the mother and daughter to be the objects of these attempts.

Families of good premorbid schizophrenic daughters use direct person-control strategies very seldom but use them with somewhat greater success than the normal family. All of the good family members follow similar patterns in using very few interruptions when the patient daughter is present, as if avoiding any direct confrontation that might disturb the family equilibrium; when the well daughter is present, again, few people are interrupted, but when this occurs the interruptions are more likely to be successfully controlling, perhaps because of their greater strength or insistence.

The poor premorbid families interrupt at medium rates, generally with medium success but, in contrast to the goods, they divide up the interrupting role. Poor fathers interrupt at medium rates and are most often the target of interruptions; from the point of view of these strategies as indices of relative influence within the family, this suggests a relative lack of power of the father. However, poor mothers and their patient daughters interrupt at high rates and are less likely to be targets of interruptions. The use of explicit control strategies by two members of a schizophrenic family, particularly by the patient herself, contrasts with theoretical predictions regarding alliances and control strategies.

The second, indirect, person-control strategy is question asking. A question sets limits on the possible response of the person being questioned, yet these limits are usually so vague as to allow for a number of quite varied responses. Everything—from answering the question to acknowledging that it has been heard by saying "hmm"—is an appropriate response to the strategy of questioning. Data on question asking in the female families is shown in Table 7.6; this measure includes all statements in the grammatical form of a question without regard for their content or intent. In contrast to findings for male families, in the families of daughters there is a family culture effect in which the good families have significantly high questioning rates, poors are medium, and normal families are low. When the patient daughter is present good families again ask most questions and normals fewest; but when the well sibling of the patient is present the poor families drop to the lowest ranking. An examination of median percents for question-asking suggest that these differences are a result of a substantial drop, from 14 to 4%, in proportions of questions asked by poor families from the patient to the well sibling session.

Only the mother in the female families has significantly different rates of questions. Poor mothers ask more questions than good or normal mothers; however, when mothers are with their patient daughters, the good mothers move to the highest questioning rate and poor mothers drop to medium. Well daughters also have different rates of questions, with daughters in the good families highest, normal daughters medium, and poor daughters lowest. The person-control strategy of question asking thus appears to be a speciality of the good families, particularly of the good mothers.

Table 7.6   Indirect Person-control Strategies
(families of daughters: group and structural analyses)

Variable	Group Analysis		Roles and Sessions		Roles within Sessions	
	H M L	p	H M L	p	H M L	p
			Fa$_c$ G P N	—	Fa$_{pt}$ G P N	—
			Mo$_c$ P G N	.10	Fa$_{sib}$ G N P	—
			Ch$_c$ G N P	—		
All questions	Fam$_c$ G P N	.20			Mo$_{pt}$ G P N	.20
			Fam$_{pt}$ G P N	—	Mo$_{sib}$ P G N	—
			Fam$_{sib}$ G N P	—		
					Ch$_{pt}$ P G N	—
					Ch$_{sib}$ G N P	.20
			Fa$_c$ G P/N	.05	Fa$_{pt}$ P G N	—
			Mo$_c$ P G N	.20	Fa$_{sib}$ G N P	—
Informational			Ch$_c$ G N P	.20		
questions	Fam$_c$ G P N	.20			Mo$_{pt}$ G N P	—
			Fam$_{pt}$ P G N	.10	Mo$_{sib}$ G P N	—
			Fam$_{sib}$ G N P	.10		
					Ch$_{pt}$ G N P	.20
					Ch$_{sib}$ G N P	.05

Data on informational question asking, shown in Table 7.6, provide further evidence for the quality and possible function of this person-control strategy in families of daughters. As on general question asking there are differences in family cultures, with good families high, poor families medium, and normal families low on task-oriented or nonaffective questions. When the patient daughter is present the poor family moves to the highest rank but when the well daughter is present the poor family drops to lowest on rates of task-oriented questions. These patterns suggest that the poor family's use of informational questions as a person-control strategy is specific to its interaction with the schizophrenic daughter.

Role patterns give some evidence about who uses the strategy most often.

While mothers and well daughters use different rates of questions of all kinds the differences in informational question asking are centered on the daughters' role, both patient and her sibling. Good daughters ask most informational questions, normal daughters fewer, and poor daughters the least. Good fathers also generally ask more informational questions, as they do questions of all kinds. It is the good patient daughters who attempt control by specifically focusing questions on the task rather than on affective content.

Thus, in the use of the indirect mode of person-control—question asking —the three types of female family are consistently different. Good families ask most questions and normal families fewest and, as in the families of sons, mothers of the schizophrenic patients are most clearly the "questioners." However, in contrast to the male families, the focus of questions in the female schizophrenic families differs; when the patient daughter is present the poor family asks more informational or nonaffective questions than other families.

While the general patterns in the findings for families of daughters replicate those for male families, there are enough specific differences to suggest that person-control strategies are used somewhat differently by role players in the female families. Both good and poor schizophrenic families avoid the use of direct person-controls, except for the poor mother and her patient daughter, who appear to use this strategy in interacting with the father. Role differentiation occurs in normal families, in which the father tends to take the direct person control, or interrupting, role. Also, just as in the male families, families of female schizophrenic patients choose to use the indirect person control of questioning, with the mother taking this strategy as her specialty. In the female families, however, patterns are not so clearly limited to the patient session as they are in families of sons.

Discussion

The analyses of power structure in schizophrenic families by Haley (1959) and others led to the hypothesis that attempts to control other members' behavior, if present at all in the schizophrenic family, would generally be unclear, ambiguous, or unlabeled. In these families no one would be able to make a family decision or to exert influence in a way that is clear and unqualified. We suggested that the normal family members are, in contrast, able to use control strategies unambivalently and directly in order to maintain the recognized power structure.

The defining quality of the control strategy examined in this chapter— person control—is the fact of one person's confrontation of one other person. Person-control strategies contrast with attention controls in the degree to which a single person's behavior is the target of control. Attention controls, exemplified by rates of participation, focus on the family members as a group. For example, when one person participates at a high rate other people are effectively denied the chance to participate, but this denial is not directed to any single person. Person controls have an identifiable target; therefore any exertion of a person control strategy serves to confront and, furthermore, to involve or entangle the confronter in the interaction to a much greater extent than other strategies.

Because person-control strategies have the qualities of confrontation and direct involvement we assumed that they would be used to a greater extent by the normal than by the schizophrenic families. Also, because the interruption strategy makes more explicit demands on the target than does the questioning strategy, we predicted that the schizophrenic family would choose to use the more indirect technique. In general these are the patterns found in the data.

In families having either sons or daughters, normal families choose to use the direct person-control strategy, interrupting other members; schizophrenic families, the good more than the poor, avoid the use of direct personal confrontations. Instead, the schizophrenic families use the indirect mode of control, questioning. Although there are some differences in degree of role differentiation between families of sons and daughters, these overall patterns are clear.

In both male and female normal families rates of interruptions are high and the relative success of this strategy is low for all members of the family. Parents are the most likely targets of direct confrontations although these confrontations are no more successful than any others. The normal male and female families appear to use the direct mode of person control in preference to the indirect mode, for rates of question asking are consistently lowest in all normal families. Thus almost without exception the normal families and all members within them follow the same set of rules about personal confrontation and involvement. Direct attempts to control other people are allowed, but are not necessarily successful.

Good families provide the greatest contrast with the normals. Whether the child is a son or daughter the good families seem to be following a rule that prohibits direct confrontation of other members but allows for indirect person controls, especially by the mother. Intrusions into another person's speech occur very seldom in a good family, perhaps functioning to avoid the implied personal entanglement or the direct labeling of one person as attempting control.

Poor premorbid families of both sons and daughters fall consistently between normals and goods in the use of person-control strategies. However, some role differentiation occurs to discriminate between the families of poor male patients and the families of female patients. In the families of males the poor patient is a successful user of direct controls while in the female families the poor patient daughter and her mother use the strategy most often. Thus both male and female poor patients use the person-control strategy in a way somewhat different from that of the whole family. Again, as in the good families, mothers of poor schizophrenic patients choose to use the indirect mode of control, question asking.

The fact that the significant differences between families and between role players occur largely in the session when the patient child is present (this is clearer in the male than the female families) leads us to conclude that the use of person-control strategies is not in response to the experimental situation itself. We would have no reason to expect good families, for example to interrupt each other at a very low rate in one session and a somewhat higher rate in another simply as a result of the requirements of the experiment.

Instead we can turn to the etiological and responsive interpretations. Patterns of person-control differences appear, in general, only when the patient child is present; when the well child interacts with his or her parents all families use person controls at similar rates. Furthermore, to some extent the patient child's use of these strategies differs from that of his own well sibling. For example, in the poor family the patient son is a more successful interrupter than other members of his family; in the good family the patient is less successfully interrupted. Thus parents differ from each other only in the presence of their schizophrenic child, and the patient's behavior is different from his sibling. This pattern seems to give equal support to the responsive and the etiological interpretations. The parents may respond differentially to the patient and the well child as a result of the patient child's distinctive behavior and the circumstances around his situation as a patient. However, it is equally reasonable to suggest that the parents' "abnormal" behavior may have caused the patient child's deviance.

There are stronger elements of the "responsiveness" interpretation in our suggestion that the infrequent use of direct person-control strategies in the schizophrenic families, particularly when interacting with the patient, may be the result of the family's need to protect him from direct personal confrontations. They may avoid personal confrontations because these threaten the family with uncontrollable or inappropriate responses that it would rather avoid; or, confrontation may imply greater involvement and entanglement with each other than the schizophrenic family members desire. Whatever the function may be for the family, or whatever the time order of occurrence in the family, it is clear that direct and explicit techniques of person control, characteristic of normal families, are not generally included in the repertoire of the schizophrenic family.

In these chapters we have examined two strategies through which power in families may be exerted, attention control and person control. Attention-control techniques, described participation rates, targets of communication, and speech length, are strategies that serve to maintain the family's attention on one speaker, thus preventing any other person from attempting control and allowing the speaker to use other more direct strategies. The person-control strategy contrasts with attention control in the degree to which one family member is confronted and attempts made to alter his behavior. This latter strategy implies direct and explicit involvement between family members and is indicated by the use of interruptions and questions in interaction.

Findings for attention-control and person-control strategies do not simply replicate each other. Each gives us a basis for inferring something different about the power structures and ways of exercising power in these different families. From the intrafamily analyses of attention-control strategies, such as the rates and targets of participation, patterns of role differentiation were evident. Among normal families with sons, fathers had most power and sons least; the data also suggested a mother-father coalition. Normal families with daughters differed in one important respect, that is, a mother-daughter coalition appeared to be present even though fathers still retained their high position. However, although a hierarchy existed that was clear and recognized, for example, in the deference accorded fathers by sons, power was not exercised in an authoritarian or rigid fashion. Data on person-control strategies, such as interruptions, indicate that family norms permit all members of these families, including the low-status sons and daughters, to make active attempts to influence each other. Thus the clear power structure is accompanied by a norm that allows all members to participate in the decision-making process. The consistency of this picture with other descriptions and theories about normal family functioning is obvious.

In several respects families of good premorbid patients are most different from normals; poor premorbids tend to fall between them. Among the goods, fathers appear to have least power and there is a mother-son coalition; daughters are relatively isolated. Goods are consistently low in their use of person-control strategies, to an extent that suggests that there is a norm against the direct confrontation of others. When attempts are made to influence others, they are indirect in the form of questions rather than interruptions. Further, the use of these strategies tends to be restricted to situations in which the schizophrenic child is present, and the patient himself is allowed to use these influence techniques in ways that differ from other family members. On the whole, the underlying power structure is less clear than in normal families and norms for exerting influence are differential rather than applicable equally to all members of the family.

Taken together, the findings support the use of two different measures—attention-control and person-control strategies—as an approach to understanding the structure and exercise of power in families. The findings further argue for the potential usefulness of this approach in the study of power in other groups.

Chapter 8

Disruptions in Communication

Some theories about families seem to suggest that interaction in normal families (in implied contrast to pathogenic families) is rational and orderly, and that members speak in connected, well-formed sentences, thus allowing for purposeful activity and organized task behavior. In contrast, disrupted, fragmented communication in speech is sometimes assumed to be characteristic of families having schizophrenic children (Wynne and Singer, 1963) and is associated with conflict and disorganization. This chapter presents data that are not compatible with this point of view.

Instead, the position argued in this chapter is the following: disruptions in the flow of communication and variation from ordered, complete sentences are more likely to occur in normal families and, further, these modes of communication function to allow for greater adaptibility to changing situations. Variable patterns of speech, indicated by the use of incomplete sentences, pauses, fragments, repetitions, and laughter, provide an interaction environment with high stimulus variability and many opportunities for changing the course of the discussion, for interjecting rewarding and punishing sanctions, and for introducing new information. This style contrasts with the rigid, ordered, almost ritualistic form of communication that requires fully completed sentences and correct constructions and that provides little opportunity for spontaneous changes; it is this latter mode that is more often characteristic of the families having schizophrenic patients.

The interaction codes for communication variability were selected and developed for the study with the first hypothesis in mind—that disconnected, fragmented speech stands for "conflict" or "anxiety" and thus would be found more often in schizophrenic families. However, observations of the families in our study and the patterning of findings led us to reconsider and to reject this hypothesis. Instead, basing our new conception on studies of the adaptive value of response variability, we began to emphasize the potentially positive functions of apparently "disruptive" aspects of communicative behavior.

Originally, following Mahl (1956), we selected measures of speech disruption such as repetitions, incomplete sentences, and fragments, the first two of which Mahl had shown to be related to physiological indicators of anxiety. Our data showed that normal families, particularly families with sons, tend to have highest rates on these measures, yet observations of these normal families suggested that the fragmented and disrupted styles of speech are probably not related to "anxiety" but instead are indicators of spontaneity and flexibility. These normal family members interrupted each other, failed to complete their ideas, talked all at once, and yet appeared to maintain continuity in content and enough organization to solve problems. We would not have expected this ablity of "anxious" family members. Thus the combination of data from interaction codes and observations of family interaction suggested that the "anxiety" or "conflict" formulation probably has little validity.

Two other lines of theoretical and empirical work have been more helpful in providing a framework for interpreting our findings. Both provide grounds for the assumption that some level of "disorder" or "discontinuity" in communication is more functional for a family than is "order" and "continuity." Fiske and Maddi (1961), working from physiological-arousal and psychological-activation data, have hypothesized that a certain level of variability in the stimuli in a person's environment is necessary for his development, is sought out by him if not readily available, and contributes to his affective state. Further, the level of stimulus variability in the environment is directly related to the individual's arousal level, both of which are predictive of the individual's ability to produce on a task. Fiske explains, "at low levels of activation, the organism may be inattentive, easily distracted, and not concentrating fully on the task. At somewhat higher levels, the organism is alert and attentive; it mobilizes its resources and is oriented toward coping with the situation. It performs to the best of its abilities. Still higher levels of activation are associated with excessive tension or hyperactivity. Anxiety and other strong emotional states appear, and behavior is less efficient" (Fiske and Maddi, 1961, p. 32). Furthermore, an individual is able to alter his own arousal level by seeking out or avoiding variability in his environment. The Fiske and Maddi model thus points to the positive function of a certain level of change, disturbance, or unpredictability in an individual's environment; variability serves to maintain the individual's attention and leads to production.

Other work, more closely related to the content of this study and having as its basis a similar assumption regarding the function of variable, disrupted communication, has been done by Goldman-Eisler (1958). She found that one indicator of discontinuity in speech—the use of pauses—is associated with the introduction of new and unpredictable words. In other words hesitations in speech, while breaking the even flow of communication, also allow the speaker the choice of changing the course of his speech, and of introducing new information following the pause. Variability in speech is thus associated with the introduction of change.

These bodies of work provide a set of concepts, hypotheses, and data giving support to our assumption that communications varying from ordered, continuous speech serve a positive function in family interaction. The presence of such phenomena as incomplete sentences, pauses, fragments, repetitions, and laughter provide stimulus variability, and, following Fiske and Maddi, a certain level of variability may be useful, particularly in maintaining the family's production on a task. This kind of stimulus variability, furthermore, may be monitored and altered by the family to serve its own purposes. Not only should a certain level of disrupted speech be related, in general, to productivity, but, more specifically, we may predict that it is related to the introduction of new information. Deviations from well-informed sentences provide more choice points at which the family can change, and thus adapt, to new situations.

For example, in a family system in which the norms require complete, unbroken sentences, each precisely stated in an orderly way, the variability in speech patterns is very low. This system puts rather severe limits on all kinds of change in the flow of interaction and thus places severe limits on the family's ability to adapt to new situations, because sanctions pushing toward change cannot be interjected at the point at which they will have an effective impact; spontaneous responses to an individual's communications cannot be easily made; and time-saving alterations in the direction of interaction cannot be introduced. New roles, new ideas, new procedures have to wait for the end of the speaker's paragraph. The "ritual" of interaction is altered only with great difficulty.

In contrast, a family having an extremely high level of speech variability may also lack the ability to adapt to changing situations. An excessive number of fragments, repetitions, incomplete sentences, and laughter in a family's interaction may lead to a situation in which expectations about "who will do what next" become unclear since little organized information is available for family members to make accurate predictions. Under this condition of chaotic interaction then, any sanctions for change that a member may choose to apply or any new information he may interject may not be clearly understood or responded to by others in the family, and thus may be largely ineffective. Therefore chaotic speech patterns as well as rigid speech patterns prevent change and adaptation.

In the family system having moderate amounts of variability in speech patterns there are many more possibilities for changes in roles, norms, and content of interaction—in other words, for adaptation to new situations. Basically this pattern of interaction allows sanctions to be interjected at their most effective point in time in a system in which patterns of interaction are moderately predictable. For example, the inclusion of some incomplete sentences in the family repertoire allows for unformed ideas to be presented, which can then be responded to immediately and further molded by the whole family. The use of some silences provides time for consideration, choice, or rest. A moderate amount of laughter serves as an immediate sanction, punishing or rewarding and thus modifying the family's solution to a problem. The use of these "disrupting" styles of speech, at moderate rates, thus provides the family with an optimum level of flexibility in which many alternative directions are possible.

The speech disturbance phenomena stand here as indicators of the stimulus variability in the family's environment; they are also seen as sanctions that family members may use to introduce change in the system. Thus not only do variable speech patterns allow for change; some may also, in themselves, provide this change. We have chosen to cluster our measures of speech disturbance into two groups, one in which the sanctioning qualities of the speech pattern are clearly understood in the common culture, and the other in which sanctioning qualities are not so clearly understood. These are the "direct" and "indirect" types of speech disturbance.

The direct modes of speech disturbance include the following variables.

1. Tension release: Percentage of all acts in categories 2+11 of Interaction Process Analysis; these include acts containing laughter, sarcasm, jokes, stuttering, for example
2. Laughter: Percentage of all acts containing laughter; Fragment Code
3. Pauses: Percentage of all acts containing silences; Pause Code

Each of these types of speech is commonly understood to serve as a reward or punishment, or as a technique for eliciting change in a situation. When laughter or a pause or an attacking joke occurs we assume that members of the family understand that a sanction is being applied. Furthermore we assume that these kinds of sanctions, because they are clearly understood, may also be consciously maniupulated by family members.

The indirect modes of speech disturbance include the following variables.

1. Total speech disturbance: Percentage of all acts with one or more of the following: incomplete sentence, incomplete phrases, repetition, laughter; Fragment Code
2. Repetitions: Percentage of all acts that include repeated words or phrases; Fragment Code
3. Incomplete phrases: Percentage of all acts that contain speech fragments, or noncontent sounds and groups of disconnected words; Fragment Code
4. Incomplete sentences: Percentage of all acts that are incomplete sentences; Fragment Code

The indirect modes of speech disturbance represent styles of speech that are disruptive or fragmenting but that are not defined in the common culture as sanctions, or as reward or punishment techniques. Family members who use many incomplete sentences, for example, may be relatively unaware that they are communicating in a way that effectively influences other members and the sequence of events in the group.

This organization of speech disturbance variables into direct and indirect modes is for convenience in later interpretation of findings. It should be made clear, however, that the division of variables into two types is secondary to the major assumption, that the pattern of speech disturbance in a family may be one kind of stimulus variability in the family's environment.

Summary of Findings on Disruptions in Communication

Before proceeding to a detailed analysis of the speech variability data we summarize briefly the major patterns in the data for the comparison across three types of families of sons. These patterns are highly consistent across all of the speech disruption indicators, and, as we will notice later, are strikingly different from those found in families of daughters.

Eight speech disturbance measures were analyzed, using the standard group and segmental format. Then the number of times that a family (or role player) held a statistically significant "high," "medium," or "low" position relative to other families (or role players) was counted. The summary of these significant patterns is shown in Table 8.1.

This overall comparison across families of sons provides graphic evidence

Table 8.1 Distribution of Rank-orders of Statistically Significant Across-family Comparisons on All Speech Disruption Measures

(families of sons)

	Normal	Poor	Good
High rank	17	4	0
Medium rank	1	15	5
Low rank	3	2	16

for the differences in rates of speech disruption. Although the table does not indicate whether significant differences derive from family culture comparisons or role differences, it does point to the fact that normal families have consistently more than good families. This pattern immediately raises questions related to the hypotheses about variability: Are normal families more adaptable than good families? Is the disrupted speech a contribution of one role player within a family? Do family types vary in their use of direct and indirect sanctions? Each of these questions we may examine in more detail when we look at the eight measures of speech disturbance. It should be noted that the consistency of rank-ordering shown in Table 8.1 is based on only a subset of the statistical comparisons, those that were statistically significant. As will be seen below, these statistically significant patterns themselves are scattered rather than clustered in particular types of analysis.

Direct Modes of Speech Disruption: Families of Sons

Three indicators of speech disturbance have been classified as "direct." These are the speech patterns that are understood in the common culture to function as sanctions; they are used and experienced as techniques for rewarding or punishing, or for eliciting change in a situation. At the same time they are generally disruptive of the even flow of communication and thus provide variability in the family environment.

The first of these is the measure of tension release. Included here are spontaneous expressions of relief, joking, laughter, stuttering, and anxious giggles; for example, "Y-y-your mother or father ehh ehh you figured ehh blamed you for fighting in the first place," or, "(Laughter) This is quite a room, isn't it?" An important aspect of this variable is that coding is done from the typescript and the tape recording; therefore intonation and interaction context are taken into account in making a judgment about the presence of tension and disruption. We need make only a small inference to the assumption that these actions are likely to serve as sanctions in the family since their implicit reward or punishment connotation is one criterion for inclusion in the code categories.

Findings for tension release in families of sons are shown in Table 8.2. Across the three types of family there are consistent differences, congruent with the general findings for all speech disturbance variables. At the group level normal families have highest rates of tension release (approximately 5% of all of their acts), poors are medium, and good families are low (with a median of 3%). Findings in the patient session are statistically significant and congruent with the group level findings; differences in the sibling session are not significant.

Role differences on tension release also occur. Normal fathers are significantly higher than poor fathers, who are higher than good fathers, in the role analysis and when with the patient son. A similar tendency occurs for mothers, especially when with their patient son. A similar tendency occurs for mothers, especially when with their sons; normal mothers have highest rates of tension release, poor mothers are medium and good mothers are lowest. Sons also have significantly different patterns of tension release: normal sons have the highest rates, as do both of their parents. However, there is a reversal of the ordering of sons in the schizophrenic families; good sons move to the medium position and poor sons drop to lowest.

Thus when the rates of tension release, seen as an indicator of disrupted speech and as a sanctioning technique, are compared across a set of families we note that the normal-poor-good ordering is consistent, that the differences occur largely when the patient son is present, and that these are replicated in the roles of the father and mother. The children have different patterns of tension release, with the poor child dropping to lowest rates.

The clustering of differences between families in the patient session and the fact that family differences seem to derive largely from the behavior of the parents suggest that the parents of schizophrenic sons may play different "tension-release" roles with their two children; in other words, they may alter their styles of speech depending on which of their sons is present. Examination of the across-session findings shows that two parents do significantly alter their rates of tension release. Mothers of good premorbid patients have significantly fewer tension-release acts when their patient sons are present than when the well child is present. The controlled, rather rigid style of communication characteristic of good parents interacting with the schizophrenic son is partially a result of the controlled communication style that the mother chooses to effect. Normal fathers also have higher tension-release rates in the patient session than in the sibling session and are, in general, more variable in their rates than other fathers.

Further examination of the patterns of tension release within each

Table 8.2 Direct Modes of Speech Disturbance
(families of sons: group and structural analyses)

Variable	Group Analysis		Roles and Sessions		Roles within Sessions	
		H M L p		*H M L p*		*H M L p*
			Fa_c N P G .10		Fa_{pt} N P G .05	
			Mo_c N P G —		Fa_{sib} N P G —	
			Ch_c N G P .20			
Tension release	Fam_c N P G .02				Mo_{pt} N P G .02	
			Fam_{pt} N P G .01		Mo_{sib} P N G —	
			Fam_{sib} N P G —			
					Ch_{pt} N G P —	
					Ch_{sib} G N P —	
			Fa_c N P G —		Fa_{pt} N P G .20	
			Mo_c N P G .10		Fa_{sib} P N G —	
			Ch_c N G P —			
Laughter	Fam_c N P G .20				Mo_{pt} N P G .10	
			Fam_{pt} N P G .10		Mo_{sib} P N G —	
			Fam_{sib} N P G —			
					Ch_{pt} N G P .20	
					Ch_{sib} N G P —	
			Fa_c P G N .20		Fa_{pt} P G N —	
			Mo_c P G N —		Fa_{sib} P G N .10	
			Ch_c P G N .20			
Pauses	Fam_c P G N —				Mo_{pt} G P N —	
			Fam_{pt} P G N —		Mo_{sib} P G N —	
			Fam_{sib} P G N —			
					Ch_{pt} P G N —	
					Ch_{sib} P N G —	

type of family provides evidence for family role specialization in good premorbid schizophrenic families. When the well son in the good family is present he is consistently the tension-release specialist, while his parents, and particularly his father, have lower rates. In all other families in both sessions no one role player varies consistently from the others.

Thus it is apparent that the high rates for normal families and the medium rates for poor families apply to all members approximately equally and that these patterns are most clearly distinguishable in the family's interaction with the patient. Only the normal father varies consistently in his tension-release rate, yet he is not the tension-release specialist when compared with the other members of his family. It is the good families that show a differentiated structure in relation to this mode of sanctioning. In the context of significantly low rates of tension release good mothers consistently lower their rates even more when with the patient, thus taking the lead in maintaining a controlled atmosphere. On the other hand the well child in the good family takes tension release as his role specialty. We may hypothesize that this role is "delegated" to him by the family and thus he may act for all.

More evidence for these conjectures can be found in the other speech disruption measures classified as direct sanctions. The second is our measure of laughter. Laughter, whenever it occurs, serves to break up the continuous, ordered sequence of events in interaction and thus provides for variability in communication patterns. But it may also have explicit meaning as a positive or negative sanction. Here we refer to the commonly understood strategies of "laughing with" or "laughing at"; for example, "That's, that's not a qualifying excuse for being late. (Laughter)," or "But I don't think you did that (Laughter), much."

Table 8.2 shows significant and consistently patterned differences between family types in amount of laughter similar to those found for tension release. At the family culture level normal families have the most laughter, poor families are medium, and good families are low. These consistent rankings occur even though median percentages are not highly variable; 3% of normal families' acts include laughter whereas 1.5% of the good families' acts do. The pattern is specified congruently in the two sessions, where only in the session with the patient son is there a significant difference in proportion of laughter; again, normals are high, poors in the middle, and goods are low.

When we examine family members' rates of laughter we see that patterns for mothers and fathers are congruent with overall family differences, especially when they interact with their patient sons. With the patient present, normal parents are highest, poors are medium, and good parents are lowest in rate; when with their well sons all parents have relatively equal rates. Sons in these families, however, have different patterns of laughter. When the schizophrenic son is present, poor premorbid sons drop to the lowest rate, with normal sons high and good sons medium; there are no differences between the well siblings.

The across-session comparisons indicate that no person consistently changes his rates of laughter from one family session to the next, nor is any one member more variable in laughter rates than another. Thus the clustering of family and role differences in the interaction with the patient son is not the result of role players altering their laughter rates but instead is a result of the family norms that serve to differentiate one family type more clearly from another.

Within the poor premorbid family, however, when the patient son is present, there is a "laughter" role specialist—the mother. Poor families have medium laughter rates compared with other families; poor mothers have medium rates when compared with other mothers. Yet, when compared with their husbands and patient sons, the poor mothers consistently lead the family in laughter. This specialty may be related to the poor mother's affect behavior where, we have shown, her role combines negative affective qualities and interpersonal references. Laughter, for her, may function as a negative sanction.

The third direct mode of speech disturbance is our measure of silences or pauses, shown in Table 8.2. The occurrence of a pause clearly breaks the continuity of interaction. Further, as Goldman-Eisler (1958) has shown, words following pauses are less predictable than words not following pauses; silence thus introduces "new" information. Therefore the presence of pauses in a family's speech provides greater variability in its environment. Pauses may also serve as sanctions, designed to move a person or the family group in a desired direction. For example, a person who persistently pauses in the middle of his ideas maintains active control over time in interaction and thus prevents others from acting; he sanctions by forcing others to continue to listen to him, to wait for him to finish. Also, a pause interjected into a sentence at the right "psychological moment" may have the same impact as a direct verbal order; it serves to emphasize; for example, "I'm going back to the instance of Johnny and those darn foolish Italian shoes with those Cuban heels and everything he brought home that we made him bring back, (Pause) He wanted, I, all right, we were willing to negotiate with him," or, "Cause the books are always about 'make sure he does get enough love.' Let's face it. (Pause) That's the way I look at it anyway."

One characteristic that differentiates pauses from the other speech disruptions is its passive quality. Pauses serve to sanction—to reward or to punish—even though the speaker does nothing, in contrast to laughter, which demands active, and in a sense more committed, behavior. As we shall see, this distinction may be an important one because families tend to use pauses at rates different from their rates for other modes of speech disruption.

When comparisons are made across types of family in their use of pauses there are no family culture or session differences. All families use pauses at approximately the same rate, 2% of all their acts. Fathers and sons, however, have varying pause rates. At the role level, poor fathers have higher rates than goods, who have higher rates than normal fathers. The same ordering is found for the sons, although it is not replicated in the role-within-session data. Although the differences are not overall family ones there is a suggestion that, in contrast to the active speech disturbances, the passive mode of sanctioning is used most often by the schizophrenic families, at least by the men in these families.

Data from the across-session comparisons provide evidence for only one role difference that is dependent on the presence of a particular child. Even though there are no significant differences between types of mothers, the mothers of good premorbid schizophrenic sons significantly alter their rates of pauses with the two children. When with their patient sons they have higher pause rates than when with their well sons. We have suggested that the good mother may play the "controlling" or "controlled" role when her sick son is present; her high pause rate adds another dimension to this interpretation, pointing to the passive qualities of this role. While good mothers show different rates across the two sessions they are not the pause specialists in their own families; all good family members share this role equally. Only in the normal families is there a hint of role specialization, where, in the first session, normal mothers have higher rates than fathers.

We began with the assumption that these direct modes of speech disturbance provide variability in external stimuli and thus may be related to the family's ability to change the course of its discussion; they also serve as sanctions that elicit change. The data show that there are systematic differences across families in the amount of variability generated or accepted as well as some differentiation within families among sanctioning roles. The strongest and most consistent finding, to be further replicated in other data, is the difference between families in rates of speech disturbance, where the ordering from high to low is normal-poor-good, and where greatest differences are concentrated in the patient session and in the parents', rather than the patients' behavior. If we assume that the level of stimulus variability is monitored by family members and may be altered by them then we may conclude that parents interacting with their schizophrenic sons find it useful to maintain a relatively lower level of variability than normal parents, yet the usefulness is only strong enough to create differences when the schizophrenic patient is present.

The opposite is true for the passive mode of disturbance, pauses, where normal fathers and sons drop to low rates in comparison with schizophrenic fathers and sons. Perhaps the only acceptable sanction in the schizophrenic families is the diffuse and poorly defined type, the kind of behavior that is open to ambiguous interpretation.

It is the mothers in the schizophrenic families who appear to play different roles in relation to the two children and thus may be the "leaders" in maintaining the family's level of variability when the patient son is present. Good mothers consistently lower their rates of tension release and raise their rates of pauses when with the patient sons, thus taking the lead in maintaining the polite and organized interaction style characteristic of the good family as a whole. Poor mothers, when with their patient sons, are the specialists in laughter in their families, also aiding in maintaining the family stimulus variabilty level. No other family member consistently takes such a differentiated role.

The patient son, especially the poor patient son, appears to avoid the use of active sanctioning modes and specializes in passive ones—in pauses. This occurs in the context of the poor family having medium rather than low levels of speech disturbances. The poor patient, therefore, chooses to sanction in ways that are not clearly defined and not commonly understood.

Finally, there is a suggestion in the data that the well sibling in good premorbid families plays a role differentiated from other members of his family and perhaps fulfilling a function that is necessary for the family but impossible for other family members to carry out. His specialization in tension release is a hint that he may be the family's change agent or the family's specialist in negative affect. Whatever its function, his behavior seems to be different from the others in his family.

Indirect Modes of Speech Disruption: Families of Sons

The indirect modes of speech disturbance are styles of speech that provide variability in communication and thus allow for change and adaptation in the situation but are not commonly understood as sanctions. These are the measures of incomplete phrases, incomplete sentences, repetitions, and the index combining these three, along with laughter.[1]

---

[1] Although laughter is used as a separate indicator of direct modes of disturbance it is also included in the index of total speech disturbance.

Although the measures taken singly do not show strong patterns of family differences, when considered as a group they add further evidence for the interpretations already suggested.

The first is the "total speech disturbance" measure, shown in Table 8.3 and derived by combining the codes that use the written typescript as a source; the coder makes no inference about sanctioning qualities of the actions. On this measure there are no family culture, session, nor general role differences. Only fathers when interacting with their patient sons have significantly different rates, with normal fathers having most speech disturbances, poors medium, and good fathers least. This ordering replicates those found on other speech disruption measures.

The fact that fathers are different from each other when with their patient sons is not a result of consistent change in their rate from the sibling to the patient session, nor is it related to role differences within families, because no role player is the family's speech-disturbance specialist in the patient session. There is a tendency, however, for the good father to take this specialty role within his family in the well-sibling session and for the good mother to be consistently low.

Incomplete phrases, one of the single measures of speech disruption, are not used differentially by any families or role players, do not occur in one session more than another, and are not used by one family member more than other members of the same family (data are in Table 8.3). The speech style exemplified by the following quotations is apparently common in all families, occurring in approximately 25% of all acts: "Uh you must have some good uh valid reasons for it," or, "That ah they could ah in some fashion give to the kids."

Repetitions are another indicator of speech disturbance counted directly from the written typescript. Included are acts containing repeated syllables, words and phrases that are not obviously added for emphasis; for example, "You got you got to get out," and "Uh that that it wasn't necessary for it to be brought up." Only the fathers show consistent differences in use of repetitions; see Table 8.3. The significant role effect is replicated in the session findings where, in both situations, normal fathers are high, poors are in the middle, and good fathers are low. Median percentages range from 16% for normal fathers down to 7% for good fathers. Again, the ordering of rates replicates the ordering found on the other speech disturbance measures.

Although the three types of mother are not different from each other in their use of repetitions, one set of mothers, in the poor families, consistently changes its repetition role across the two family sessions. When with their patient son poor mothers' use of repeated words is higher than when with their well child. However, at the same time they are not the

Table 8.3 Indirect Modes of Speech Disturbance
(families of sons: group and structural analyses)

Variable	Group Analysis		Roles and Sessions		Roles within Sessions	
		H M L p		H M L p		H M L p
			Fa_c	N P G —	Fa_{pt}	N P G .20
			Mo_c	N P G —	Fa_{sib}	N G P —
			Ch_c	G P N —		
Total speech disturbance	Fam_c	N P G —			Mo_{pt}	N P G —
			Fam_{pt}	N P G —	Mo_{sib}	N P G —
			Fam_{sib}	N P G —		
					Ch_{pt}	G P N —
					Ch_{sib}	P N G —
			Fa_c	N P G —	Fa_{pt}	N P G —
			Mo_c	N P G —	Fa_{sib}	G P N —
			Ch_c	P G N —		
Incomplete phrases	Fam_c	N/G P —			Mo_{pt}	N P G —
			Fam_{pt}	N P G —	Mo_{sib}	N P G —
			Fam_{sib}	N P G —		
					Ch_{pt}	N G P —
					Ch_{sib}	P N G —
			Fa_c	N P G .10	Fa_{pt}	N P G .05
			Mo_c	N P G —	Fa_{sib}	N P G .20
			Ch_c	G P N —		
Repetitions	Fam_c	N P G —			Mo_{pt}	N P G —
			Fam_{pt}	N P G —	Mo_{sib}	N P G —
			Fam_{sib}	N P G —		
					Ch_{pt}	P G N —
					Ch_{sib}	G N P —

repetition specialists within the family when with the patient; other family members are equally likely to take this lead. Only when the well sibling is present do the poor mothers drop to lowest rates and the well sibling takes the top position. Normal families also show role differentiation in this mode of speech disorder. Fathers in interaction with each of their normal children take the high repetition role and the child drops to lowest in each of the families. This occurs in the context of normal fathers' high rates, where the median is 16% in comparison with other fathers, where the median is 9% for poor fathers and 7% for good fathers. Thus normal fathers consistently use repetitions as a form of speech disruption more often than any member of any family type. The important finding regarding the use of repetitions is the replication of the same normal-poor-good ordering found for the other active speech disorders, along with the fact that differences here are not family-wide but are centered in the father's role.

The final measure of indirect speech disturbances is incomplete sentences, in Table 8.4. This style of speech is analogous in its passive quality to the direct speech disturbance measure, pauses, since when either of these techniques is used the speaker does nothing rather than carry out some action as in the other techniques. An incomplete sentence is one in which the speaker fails to complete his idea even though he had not been interrupted; essentially the sentence is allowed to "run down," for example, "Yeah, but that was . . . ," or "you don't wear your play clothes going to school. It's not ah . . .". An incomplete sentence may serve a

Table 8.4 Indirect Modes of Speech Disturbance
(families of sons: group and structural analyses)

Variable	Group Analysis		Roles and Sessions		Roles within Sessions	
	$H\ M\ L\ \ p$		$H\ M\ L\ \ p$		$H\ M\ L\ \ p$	
			Fa_c	P N G —	Fa_{pt}	P N G —
			Mo_c	P N G —	Fa_{sib}	N P G —
			Ch_c	N P G —		
Incomplete sentences	Fam_c	N P G —			Mo_{pt}	N P G .20
	Fam_{pt}	P N G —			Mo_{sib}	P N G —
	Fam_{sib}	N P G —				
					Ch_{pt}	P N G —
					Ch_{sib}	N P G —

sanctioning function just as does a pause in forcing others to continue to listen or to ask questions in order to clarify meanings.

All families in all situations tend to use incomplete senetences at approximately the same rate: 3% of all statements are unfinished. On the other hand, goods are found consistently in the lowest rank position. Only mothers, when interacting with their patient sons, have significantly different rates. In this instance normal mothers are highest, poor mothers medium, and good mothers are low. Again the ordering of differences replicates the ordering for other speech disturbance measures.

The differential use of incomplete sentences by mothers in the patient session is partly a result of the good mothers' alteration of roles when interacting with two different children. When she is with her well child she uses more incomplete sentences than she does when with the patient son. The fact that she speaks in a more orderly and grammatical style with the patient adds further support to our suggestion that the good mother may feel it necessary to maintain a controlled, fully predictable environment when the patient is present.

While mothers vary from each other in their use of incomplete sentences they are not specialists in the speech style within their own families. For example good mothers have no more incomplete sentences when with the patient than do other members of the good families.

Across all of the indirect speech disturbance measures there are fewer significant differences between types of family or role players. Yet when differences do occur they consistently follow the ordering found for the direct modes of disturbance. Members of normal families have most disruptions, poors are medium, and good families have lowest rates. We noted in examining the direct modes, also, that differences seemed to be clustered in the roles of the parents rather than in the child's role, and the same pattern occurs in the indirect measures. Although not so consistent, when differences between role players do occur it is the mothers or the fathers who use different rates of speech disturbances. Furthermore, these differences tend to cluster in the patient rather than the well sibling session. Thus the indirect modes of speech disturbance are not strongly differentiating but their patterns follow those of the direct modes. Again the lower level of stimulus variability in the schizophrenic, and particularly the good premorbid families, suggests their need to maintain a nonchanging environment when the patient is present.

As we noted for direct modes of speech disruption, mothers in these families appear to play differentiated roles in their families. Mothers of poor premorbid patients are either highly variable or consistently change their speech disturbance rates across sessions, whereas other members of the poor family do not change. Good mothers also show a tendency to switch roles with the presence of a different child; other members do not change in this way.

Disruptions in Communication Style: Families of Daughters

We have shown for the families of sons that there are consistent and significant differences among the three types of family in speech disruption patterns. In general normal families show most disruption, poors are medium, and good families show least. Families of daughters, while providing fewer statistically significant differences, show patterns that are different from families of sons.

If we make the same kind of gross comparison of statistically significant findings for female families that was made for the families of males, we see that the good families have the highest rates of speech variability, the normal families are medium, and the poor premorbid families are consistently low. These data are shown in Table 8.5. A further breakdown of findings shows however, that the orderings vary, depending on whether we look at the direct or the indirect modes of speech disturbance. On direct measures good families are high, normals medium, and poor families are lowest; this effect comes most strongly from our measure of pauses. On indirect measures, poor families are high, normals in the middle, and good families are low. Thus it is apparent that families of good premorbid schizophrenic daughters use the direct, clearly understood sanctioning methods, whereas poor premorbid families use indirect, subtle modes of speech disruption and normal families of daughters are medium in the use of both of these methods. All families of daughters use one or another of the speech disturbance modes and there is no family type that consistently uses none of them, as is the case in the good premorbid male families.

Examination of each of the direct and indirect variables will show the source of the differences, whether they occur largely in interaction with the schizophrenic patient, and whether they are a result of the behavior of the parents, as they are in families of sons.

As on all of the variables previously presented, statistical comparisons

Table 8.5   Distribution of Rank-orders of Statistically Significant Across-
family Comparisons on All Speech Disruption Measures
(families of daughters)

	Normal	Poor	Good
High rank	3	6	12
Medium rank	16	3	2
Low rank	2	12	7

for families of daughters are limited to those made across families and to the measures of across-session variability. The small sample may introduce enough unreliability into the summary measures that findings are less patterned and consistent than in families of sons. Therefore all data on families of daughters must be interpreted conservatively.

Direct Modes of Speech Disruption: Families of Daughters

On the first direct mode of speech disturbance, tension release, only the fathers in families of daughters differ, with normal and good fathers having similar rates but poor fathers being significantly low (see Table 8.6). When we take into account the trends in the data along with significant differences, it is apparent that poor premorbid families consistently use fewer tension release mechanisms than do other families.

The second direct mode of speech disturbance is the measure of laughter. Here again, in Table 8.6, there is only one significant role difference, for the patient daughter, which follows the same ordering as the other direct modes. Good premorbid patients have higher laughter rates than normal daughters, who, in turn, have higher rates than poor premorbid patients. Median percentages range from 5% for goods down to 0% for poors, indicating, in general, that poor premorbid schizophrenic daughters do not laugh at all. While other comparisons are not statistically significant there is a tendency for families in both sessions to follow the same good-normal-poor ordering.

The use of pauses in speech is the third direct mode of speech variability, one that is more passive than the other direct measures (see Table 8.6). Families of daughters do not differ in their general family culture but in each of the interaction situations there are significant differences; good families consistently use more pauses, normal families are medium, and poor families are lowest. Furthermore there are role and role-within-session differences that provide some evidence for an inference about the usefulness of pauses in families of daughters.

Fathers in families of daughters have significantly consistent patterns in both sessions, with good fathers pausing most, poor fathers least, and normals being in the middle. Daughters, in general, show the same differences. However, when we look at patients and well siblings separately there is evidence that the poor premorbid patient uses pauses more than would be expected by the family pattern as a whole; she moves up to the middle rank. The same pattern occurs for mothers of patients. They follow the good-normal-poor ordering when interacting with the well child but when interacting with their patient daughter poor mothers move up to the middle rank. Supporting evidence for the change in the poor mother's role is found in the across-session variability measure, where poor mothers are consist-

Table 8.6 Direct Modes of Speech Disturbance
(families of daughters: group and structural analyses)

Variable	Group Analysis				Roles and Sessions				Roles within Sessions			
	H	M	L	p	H	M	L	p	H	M	L	p
					Fa$_c$ N/G P .20				Fa$_{pt}$ G N P —			
					Mo$_c$ G N P —				Fa$_{sib}$ G N P .10			
					Ch$_c$ G N P —							
Tension release	Fam$_c$ N G P —								Mo$_{pt}$ N G P —			
					Fam$_{pt}$ N P G —				Mo$_{sib}$ G N P —			
					Fam$_{sib}$ G N P —							
									Ch$_{pt}$ P N G —			
									Ch$_{sib}$ G N P —			
					Fa$_c$ N P G —				Fa$_{pt}$ N G P —			
					Mo$_c$ N/G P —				Fa$_{sib}$ N G P —			
					Ch$_c$ G N P —							
Laughter	Fam$_c$ G N P —								Mo$_{pt}$ N G P —			
					Fam$_{pt}$ G N P —				Mo$_{sib}$ N/G P —			
					Fam$_{sib}$ G N P —							
									Ch$_{pt}$ G N P .20			
									Ch$_{sib}$ G N P —			
					Fa$_c$ G N P .20				Fa$_{pt}$ G N P .05			
					Mo$_c$ G P N —				Fa$_{sib}$ G N P .20			
					Ch$_c$ G N P .20							
Pauses	Fam$_c$ G N P —								Mo$_{pt}$ G P N .05			
					Fam$_{pt}$ G N P .05				Mo$_{sib}$ G N P .10			
					Fam$_{sib}$ G N P .20							
									Ch$_{pt}$ G P N .10			
									Ch$_{sib}$ G N P .20			

ently more variable than goods, who are more variable than normal mothers. Relative to other mothers and daughters, poor mothers and their patient daughters tend to use this passive mode of direct sanctioning more than they use more active modes (tension release and laughter). This use of pauses by patient children and by mothers when with their patient children is the same in both male and female families. Good and poor mothers and their schizophrenic children consistently have more silences than do normal mothers and children.

Across all of the direct measures of speech disturbance the most striking finding is that poor premorbid schizophrenic families use direct modes of speech disturbance least often, in contrast to the pattern for male families, where good premorbid families are low. The general tendency is also for families of good premorbid daughters to use direct modes of disruption most often in contrast to the pattern for sons, where normal families are highest.

In contrast to families of poor premorbid sons who used pauses most often, poor premorbid families of daughters use pauses least often. The overall picture of the three types of family is one in which there is most disruption and direct sanctioning in good premorbid female families; we would see more laughter, tension release, and generally understood disturbance in these families. In contrast, poor families have little clearly understood tension release, except for a somewhat greater use of the passive technique of pausing by the mother and patient daughter.

We found in families of sons that differences between families centered in the session with the patient son and were largely a result of the behavior of the parents rather than the children. Families of daughters, perhaps because of the reduced sample size, do not show these clusterings. Instead all three family members seem to have some effect on the differences, and there are only a few instances in which the presence of different children seems to influence the direct modes of speech disturbance differentially.

Indirect Modes of Speech Disruption: Families of Daughters

The indirect and direct modes of speech disturbance in families of sons showed similar patterns. However, in families of daughters there are patterns that are internally consistent and yet different from those found for the direct modes in these families. Generally poor premorbid families use the indirect modes most often, normals are in the middle, and good families are lowest.

On the summary measure, total speech disturbance, which combines all indirect modes of speech disturbance, only when the patient daughter is present are the families different (see Table 8.7). Here poor families are high, normals are in the middle and good families are lowest, as they are on

Table 8.7   Indirect Modes of Speech Disturbance
(families of daughters: group and structural analyses)

Variable	Group Analysis				Roles and Sessions				Roles within Sessions			
	H	M	L	p	H	M	L	p	H	M	L	p
					Fa$_c$ P N G —				aF$_{pt}$ P N G —			
					Mo$_c$ G P N —				Fa$_{sib}$ P N G —			
Total speech					Ch$_c$ G P N —							
disturbance	Fam$_c$ P G N —								Mo$_{pt}$ P N/G —			
					Fam$_{pt}$ P N G .10				Mo$_{sib}$ G N P —			
					Fam$_{sib}$ G N P —							
									Ch$_{pt}$ P N G —			
									Ch$_{sib}$ G N P —			
					Fa$_c$ P N G —				Fa$_{pt}$ P N G .10			
					Mo$_c$ G P N —				Fa$_{sib}$ P N G —			
					Ch$_c$ P N G —							
Incomplete phrases	Fam$_c$ P G N .10								Mo$_{pt}$ P N G —			
					Fam$_{pt}$ P N G .10				Mo$_{sib}$ G P N —			
					Fam$_{sib}$ G/P N —							
									Ch$_{pt}$ P N G —			
									Ch$_{sib}$ N P/G —			
					Fa$_c$ P N G —				Fa$_{pt}$ P N G —			
					Mo$_c$ N G P —				Fa$_{sib}$ N G P —			
					Ch$_c$ N P G —							
Repetitions	Fam$_c$ N P G —								Mo$_{pt}$ P N G —			
					Fam$_{pt}$ P N G .20				Mo$_{sib}$ N G P .10			
					Fam$_{sib}$ N G P —							
									Ch$_{pt}$ P N G .10			
									Ch$_{sib}$ G N P —			

most of the indirect measures in the patient session. No other role or session differences occur; therefore the effects on the family differences do not appear to come from any one role player, yet are associated with the presence of the schizophrenic daughter.

The second indirect measure of speech disturbance is our measure of incomplete phrases that includes the use of "filler words" such as "uh," "ah," and "uhm", (see Table 8.7). Overall group differences indicate that poor premorbid families use these most often, good premorbid families next most, and normal female families least often. However, there is a pattern of findings incongruent with these in the patient session where poor families are high, normal families in the middle, and good families are low, supporting the general trend for the indirect measures. Only fathers in this session follow the same pattern significantly.

Similar patterns are found for the use of repetitions in families of daughters but this patterning is limited to the session when the patient daughter is present (see Table 8.7). Poor families use repetitions most often, normals are in the middle, and good families are lowest. This pattern is partly a result of the speech of the patient child since poor patient daughters use repetitions more than normals, who use them more than good patients. The relationship of this ordering to the presence of a specific child is apparent when we examine the use of repetitions in the well-sibling session. Here, for the poor family as a whole and for each of the poor family members, the use of repetitions drops to lowest rank and the normal family moves to the high position. Differences in the use of repetitions in the two sessions may occur partly as a result of changes in speech pattern of the mother and daughter in the schizophrenic families, who are consistently more variable across sessions than the normal mother and daughter.

The final indirect speech disturbance is incomplete sentences where, again, when the patient daughter is present, there is a tendency for poor premorbid families to be highest (see Table 8.8). This pattern is not clearly related to any one role player. However, in the sibling session normal families use repetitions most often, poors are medium, and good families are low, with this effect coming from the well child, who follows the same ordering. Again, therefore, the presence of a particular daughter appears to have an effect on the patterns of speech disturbance in these families.

Thus across all of the indirect modes of speech disruption in the families of daughters there is a generally consistent difference between families in their use of these sanctioning techniques that appears when the patient daughter is actually present. Poor premorbid families use these techniques most often, normals are medium, and good premorbid families are lowest.

Table 8.8   Indirect Modes of Speech Disturbance
(families of daughters: group and structural analyses)

Variable	Group Analysis				Roles and Sessions				Roles within Sessions			
	H	M	L	p	H	M	L	p	H	M	L	p
					Fa$_c$	N P G		—	Fa$_{pt}$	P G N		—
					Mo$_c$	G P N		—	Fa$_{sib}$	N G P		—
Incomplete sentences					Ch$_c$	N G/P		.20				
	Fam$_c$	N G P		—					Mo$_{pt}$	P G N		—
					Fam$_{pt}$	P G N		—	Mo$_{sib}$	P N G		—
					Fam$_{sib}$	N P G′		.20				
									Ch$_{pt}$	P N G		—
									Ch$_{sib}$	N P G		.05

When the well child is present, however, in instances when there are significant differences, normal families are the most frequent users of indirect modes, as they were in families of sons.

In contrast to families of sons, the effects on the whole family seem to come about not as a result of the parents' use of indirect speech disturbances, but from all family members. When the differences in the patient session are taken into account then we can infer that the presence of the specific child calls forth a certain norm for behavior from all members of the family. Since we lack within-family comparisons like those made in the families of sons only this general statement can be made about family role-taking.

Across all of the speech variability measures it is apparent that neither type of female schizophrenic family fully avoids variability in communication style as did the good premorbid male families. Thus neither of the female schizophrenic families interacts in such a rigid, controlled way that some adaptation and change is not possible. Instead, female families seem to specialize in the type of variability they allow in their interaction. Good premorbid families use direct modes of disruption most often, those that are more clearly understood as sanctions; in allowing direct sanctions good families of daughters are strikingly different from good male families, who follow an unbroken, precise mode of speech. Poor premorbid female families, on the other hand, use the indirect modes of disturbance, whereas the good families tend to avoid these, particularly when the patient daughter is present. On these variables, when the well child is present, the families of daughters tend to look more like families of sons. Thus we can conclude that all three types of female family provide for some variability in their communication, although the styles of variability may differ according to the family type. We do not see the same kind of perhaps defensive avoidance of variation and change that we have assumed good premorbid families of sons use to control the patient or the parents-with-the-patient.

Discussion

We have organized our data around the idea that disruptions in the smooth flow of speech stand for one kind of stimulus variability in the family's environment. Further, following Fiske and Maddi (1961), we suggested that a certain level of variability in the family's environment is required in order to adapt quickly to changing situations. Thus deviations from ordered, coherent conversation may serve a positive function in a family's discussion. The mechanism through which disordered communications may lead to adaptation is outlined by Goldman-Eisler (1958) in her discussion of hesitations; each break in the flow of speech provides a choice point at which sanctions for change can be introduced and new directions taken. Not only does broken speech open up many more possibilities for change than rigidly organized conversation, but also some kinds of broken speech serve, in themselves, as rewards or punishments leading to alterations in the interaction that follows.

The findings for families of sons and daughters are generally not congruent with each other. We have shown, in a large proportion of instances in which there are significant differences between families of sons, that the normal families have the highest rates of disruption, poor premorbid families are medium, and good premorbid schizophrenic families are consistently lowest. In contrast, the families of daughters are ordered with good families highest, normals medium and poors lowest in communication disruptions. Because the sample size of families of sons is larger and the findings probably more stable than in the families of daughters, our interpretive discussion will focus on the former.

The consistent patterning of findings in our data for families of sons and the support from related studies appear to provide a certain level of validity to the guiding hypothesis. As was implied in the introduction of this chapter there may be extreme levels of disordered speech in families that are dysfunctional for the family in the sense that they prevent adaptation. We have no independent measure of adaptation but may use evidence from our observations of these families to estimate the degree to which the families are able to organize themselves and maintain flexibility. Whereas normal families have the highest rates of disorder in their communication patterns these disruptions do not appear to be so great as to create chaos and thus unpredictability and inability to adapt. In fact, even though normal family members interact in a fragmented, disorganized way they also clearly understand and respond to each other and seem to have the capacity to make family decisions and to change opinions in the face of changing information.

The good premorbid families of sons, on the other hand, clearly have patterns of speech that provide very little opportunity for alterations in the flow of interaction. From our observation it appears that the precision and orderliness of interaction in the good families sets severe limits on the degree to which any spontaneous action is taken by family members. Sometimes a rigid "taking turns speaking" occurs with each family member waiting patiently while one person "makes a speech." Observers noted that in good premorbid families strict control over all actions is maintained by the family norms, and that this control is extended from the content of behavior—"what" can be talked about—to the style of behavior—"how" it can be discussed.

The next question is: Do these different styles of communication, associated with the presence or absence of pathology in the children, serve certain functions for the families and for the patients within the families? In speculating about functions we need to keep in mind the particular empirical patterns we have found. Not only do the three types of families of sons differ in general in their use of disrupted speech but there are patterns within the findings that point to the importance of the behavior of certain role players. In general differences between families occur only when the schizophrenic son is present with his parents; when parents are with their well children families and role players do not differ in style of speech. Also in the family's interaction with the schizophrenic child it is the parents' rather than the patient son's style of speech that appears to contribute most strongly to the family pattern. Moreover there is evidence that mothers in the schizophrenic families more consistently alter their communication styles when with two different children. These patterns of differences, finally, occur most often in the speech styles we have classified as "direct," that is, those disruptions that are commonly understood to function as sanctions.

This patterning in the findings immediately recalls the earlier discussions of the etiological, responsive, or situational interpretations that may be inferred from the data. We suggested that when significant differences between family types cluster in the patient rather than the sibling session, and when these differences are largely a result of the two parents' rather than the child's behavior this supports more parsimoniously either an etiological or responsive argument rather than a situational one. Good premorbid parents may have chosen rigid patterns of speech to use especially with one child who later became schizophrenic; this etiological interpretation is in accord with theories about the pathogenic influence of rigidity and control in these families. Or, parents may respond with these patterns to one child, already deviant, and therefore be no different from normal parents when the well sibling is present.

If these patterns of speech are selected by the parents for use with one child, they may serve a special function for the family. In normal families the higher rates of active disruptions may function to allow extensive expression of a wide variety of actions, feelings, or ideas. The result is that content of interaction is constantly fluctuating, is unpredictable, is ambiguous, and therefore must be constantly reorganized and reinterpreted. The system demands new adaptations and each new adaptation then requires further adaptation. The way into the normal family's ambiguous situation is led by the parents who consistently provide uncertainty by their styles of speech. Thus the role that the parents take may serve the family in maintaining unpredictability and in establishing a continually open interaction situation, one that provides a challenge to all members to respond, to adapt, to reorganize their perceptions and actions.

In contrast to normal families, the good premorbid families of sons have consistently low rates of speech disruption, with the exception of their tendency to use pauses in interaction more than normal families. The unbroken quality of the good family's speech reflects a high degree of predictability in the sequence of events; there is little uncertainty or ambiguity and also little opportunity for a family member to break out of the rigid sequence and to change the order of events. This pattern in good families is, again, largely reflected in the parents' behavior, particularly the mothers'. The extent to which good families follow a rigid interaction pattern—speaking in complete sentences with little laughter, few fragments and false starts—suggests that a strong and consistent effort is being made, especially by the parents, to avoid uncertainty. We may speculate that the parents of the good premorbid schizophrenic patient feel the necessity of avoiding any situation in which uncontrollable events might occur, or unacceptable feelings might be expressed, or forbidden topics might be broached, particularly in relation to the patient. Thus we are suggesting that this ritualistic style of speech serves a defensive function for the good premorbid families, and, as is the case with all defenses, it puts severe limits on the family's adaptability. Order and predictability are maintained at the expense of challenging uncertainty and change.

Our finding that families with good premorbid schizophrenic sons allow less disruption of their communication than do families with poor schizophrenic sons (who have less disruption than normal families) recalls another body of theory and research that appears to be related to these findings and interpretations. These works can be grouped under the heading of "disorders of perception and sensation in schizophrenia." Venables has labled them "studies of input dysfunction" (1964). One important characteristic of most of these studies and the theories developed out of them is resultant classification of patients would be sufficiently similar to our classification of patients as good and poor premorbid schizophrenic types that investigators have generally distinguished between process and reactive schizophrenia or between acute and chronic illnesses. Although the indicators for type of schizophrenia vary across studies, we are assuming that the resultant classification of patients would be sufficiently similar to our classification of patients as good and poor premorbid schizophrenic types to allow for meaningful comparison of our findings with those of other studies.

The perception theories vary in their statements about the process of development of schizophrenia, although as Venables writes, "These theories . . . describe rather similar clinical pictures, the acute stage with its excess of sensory input, and overgeneralization followed by a transition to a chronic stage with diminished awareness of outside stimuli and withdrawal" (Venables, 1964, p. 8). Acute schizophrenic patients, comparable to our good premorbids, appear to be flooded with stimulus inputs that they are unable to organize or to select. Not only do these inputs come from the environment, but they also come from the patient's own body movements and sensations. On the other hand, the chronic schizophrenic patient, similar to our poor premorbid, has a diminished awareness of external stimuli and his attention is narrowed. Experimental studies by Payne (1962) and Payne and Friedlander (1962) show that it is the acute schizophrenics who stand out from other groups, including normals, in their degree of overinclusive thinking; poor premorbid schizophrenic patients do not differ from normal individuals in breadth of attention.

These theories and their supporting data propose that the good premorbid schizophrenic patient is bombarded with stimuli that he cannot organize and therefore cannot selectively respond to; the poor premorbid patient, on the other hand, has successfully narrowed his range of attention and put limits on incoming stimuli. Considering our findings on the degree of stimulus variability allowed by families of these patients, particularly by the parents, we may hypothesize that the parents of good premorbid sons have taken over the filtering and selection process that their schizophrenic patient sons cannot carry out. Good premorbid parents have developed control techniques that successfully limit the range and strength of incoming stimuli to the patient and the family; their rigidity in patterns of speech is an example of this stimulus control. How this pattern of interaction has come about remains unclear. A question that cannot be answered with our data is whether good premorbid parents have taken over a function that their patient child has lost, perhaps to protect the child from a disturbing or overwhelming situation, as would be argued in a responsive interpretation or whether they have so successfully filtered and controlled incoming events that the child has never learned this skill, as an etiological view would hold.

In comparison with good premorbid families, who consistently have rigidly organized and coherent patterns of speech that seem to serve a defensive function for patient and family, poor premorbid families are closer in interaction patterns to the disrupted, fragmented speech style characteristic of normals. The theories of schizophrenia focusing on attention would suggest that the poor premorbid patient son has successfully diminished his awareness of incoming stimuli; thus he may not need the family's aid in carrying out this filtering function.

Findings from families of daughters have been ignored in our discussion of the possible functions of variable speech styles, partly as a result of the small sample and thus greater unreliability in the findings. The overall patterns in the data, however, suggest that the good premorbid female families have the highest rates of disrupted speech rather than the lowest, as was true in the male families. Whether this pattern indicates unpredictable and chaotic interaction in good families is not clear from our data. Furthermore, the literature on attention and filtering mechanisms in good and poor premorbid schizophrenic patients is not especially helpful in understanding the differences between families of daughters since these studies of individuals have not investigated male and female patients separately. Therefore we cannot make inferential links between the female schizophrenic's perceptual deficiencies and the possible function of her family's style of communication. We can conclude, however, that it is essential to maintain both the good-poor distinction and the male-female distinction in the investigation of input dysfunctions in schizophrenia, at least until it is shown that these variables are not important.

Chapter 9

Responsiveness

A recurrent theme in reports of the quality of life in families of schizo-phrenics is that their members are not responsive to each other's needs or wishes; in the extreme they are not responsive to each other's existence as persons. Imperviousness, for example, is one of the prime characteristics of the "schizophrenogenic" mother; she does not listen to what her child is "really" saying nor does she attend genuinely to his needs but behaves to-wards him on the basis of her own needs (Fromm-Reichmann, 1948). A closely related but more complex conception views the schizophrenic mother as responding to an image of her child composed largely of her own projected wishes and fantasies, rather than to a realistic figure with his own needs and requirements (Brodey, 1959). Laing has coined the term "mys-tification," thus focusing attention on the function of such communica-tions and their impact on the recipient, to refer to situations where one's response to another is in terms of one's own needs but at the same time one acts as if it is really a response to the other's needs (Laing, 1960).

The common element of these various descriptions is that there is a lack of recognition of the other person's particular qualities, a nonacknowledg-ment of his presence, an indifference to his motives and intentions. We shall use the term responsiveness to refer to this dimension of behavior; its meaning is identical to Bateson and Reusch's term "acknowledgment" (1951). Responsiveness is not restricted to agreement with another or to behavior oriented, specifically to need gratification. To be responsive to, or to acknowledge another's behavior does not require that one behave as the other wishes but only that one show an understanding of his intention. To agree and to disagree are equally responsive in that they both firmly acknowledge what the other person has been saying.

As is the case with our other variables we are using both direct and indirect measures of responsiveness. The direct measures come from our Acknowledgment code; here a statement was coded in terms of its degree of acknowledgment of the previous statement, taking into account the nature of the stimulus statement. The indirect measures come from our Focus code; here an attempt was made to distinguish among various aspects of the situation to which the speaker referred for example, to the experimental procedures, or to other persons, or to expressed opinions. As before, findings on families of sons will be reviewed before going on to those for families of daughters. In both instances analyses of direct measures will be reported first.

As noted above, the Acknowledgment code takes into account the properties of the stimulus statement as well as degrees of acknowledgment in the response. In contrast to some of our other codes, the Acknowledgment code uses a speaker's full statement as the basis for coding both stimulus and response aspects of the statement; there are two Acknowledgment codes, one a stimulus code and the other a response code. Full or complete acknowledgment in a response includes an explicit recognition of both the content and intent of the previous speaker's statement; moderate acknowledgment involves a reference to either the specific content of the previous statement or to the speaker's intent or expectations. An example of a statement coded as showing complete acknowledgment is the response in the following interchange.

STIMULUS: And in the long run free advice isn't any good.
RESPONSE: No. You're not asking for advice. All you're doing is telling your problems.

An example of less complete or more moderate acknowledgment is as follows.

STIMULUS: I always had to do everything—the man's work, the woman's work, and everything around the house.
RESPONSE: Oh dear, this is a lecture.

The lowest degree of acknowledgment is recognition of the previous speaker having said "something" but neither the intent nor the content receives explicit response. Thus simple and unelaborated agreements or recognition of the fact that another has spoken are coded here. For example,

STIMULUS: Well it had something to do with it and I think it's a combination question.
RESPONSE: Ya.

The degree of coded acknowledgment of a response depends on the demand quality or specificity of expectation of the previous statement. Each statement is coded for the type of expectation that it carries which the next speaker may acknowledge or not. In the stimulus code statements are classified as: (a) inductions—direct demands on others to change their opinions or do something; (b) questions; (c) affirmative statements—where full content is explicit; (d) elliptical affirmative statements—these lack explicit content but are complete meaningful acts in terms of the common cultural understanding of them, for example, "Yes", "All right;" (e) fragments. Each statement is coded both according to its own stimulus properties and for its degree of responsiveness to the immediately preceding stimulus statement. Two statements with identical content may be coded as showing different degrees of responsiveness, depending on the stimulus properties of the preceding statements. Thus a simple agreement or disagreement response such as "Yes" or "No" will be coded as a complete acknowledgment if it is in response to an induction, such as, "Do you agree with me now?"; or coded as showing only moderate acknowledgment if in response to a question like "Can't add anything to that can we?" or finally, as showing minimum acknowledgment if in response to an affirmative statement, "It's his own business." Although the code is limited to the relationship between statements that follow each other and does not deal either with longer chains of reciprocal acknowledgment or with more distant connections, by attempting to take into account the different degrees of expectation set up in stimulus statements we hoped to capture some of the complexity of the underlying notion of acknowledgment. It is evident from this description and our discussion of other index scores why the measures of responsiveness derived from the Acknowledgment code are considered as "direct" measures. They refer to what we would assume would be participants' views of and understandings of the statements.

An index of fragmentation, or noncodability, will also figure prominently in the findings in addition to indices for acknowledgment and nonacknowledgment. Responses that are not codable do not contain enough information for coding the degree of acknowledgment to the previous statement; either they are fragments or the previous statement itself is not complete enough to permit a determination of whether and to what degree the response acknowledges it. This may occur if the stimulus statement is either, in terms of our codes, a fragment or an elliptical affirmation. Noncodable responses differ from nonacknowledgments in that the latter contain sufficient information for us to state that the previous statement was explicitly not acknowledged. For most of our codes rates of noncodable responses are trivial and may be ignored; as will be seen below, they are far from trivial in this instance.

The Acknowledgment response code is similar to the Bales IPA code in the degree of inference it requires and the extent to which coding is based on minimal and often ambiguous cues. It might be expected that coding reliability would be a problem here as it was in the case of the IPA code. Average act-by-act coding reliability for response acknowledgment, based on a one-ninth sample of tasks discussed by each family, is 67%; this is considerably lower than the reliabilities of 85% and above achieved for other codes but similar to the reliability levels achieved for the IPA code. Reliabilities for index scores that group together several of the code categories are higher than basic coding levels of agreement. It is particularly germane to our purposes that most difficulty was encountered in coding the several degrees of positive acknowledgment, that is, whether low, moderate, or high; reliabilities are considerably higher for the grosser distinctions, that is, whether a statement is or is not codable and whether it acknowledges or does not acknowledge the previous statement. Thus despite the poor overall reliability of the code, the index scores for codability and for acknowledgment that are emphasized in this chapter have mean act-by-act reliabilities that are adequate for our purposes—91% and 97% respectively.

Responsiveness: Families of Sons

Table 9.1 contains analyses for male families on indices of fragmentation, that is, the proportion of acts on which a judgment can be made about acknowledgment, and positive acknowledgment, that is, the proportion of codable acts that include some degree of acknowledgment.

One feature of the table stands out immediately: all but two of the 24 comparisons are within the .20 level of statistical significance. Further, there is a high degree of consistency in the rank-order patterns across the different levels of analysis, most strongly in the index of positive acknowledgment. The findings are as follows. First, normal families—as groups, in each of the two experimental situations, and for each of the separate roles—are highest in level of fragmentation; good and poor premorbid families vary between being lowest or middle in rank but in no instance are they significantly different from each other in this variable. Second, normal families—in all but one comparison—are highest in their levels of positive acknowledgment, good premorbid families are in the middle, and poor premorbids are lowest in rank.

The percentages of acts in these categories and differences between family types are of interest. Approximately one-third of the acts produced in normal families are coded as fragmentation; one-fourth of the acts in both good and poor premorbid families fall into the fragmentation cate-

Table 9.1   Responsiveness: Direct Measures of Acknowledgment
(families of sons: group and structural analyses)

Variable	Group Analysis	Roles and Sessions	Roles within Sessions
	H M L p	*H M L p*	*H M L p*
		Fa_c N G P .20	Fa_{pt} N G P —
		Mo_c N G P .01	Fa_{sib} N G P .20
		Ch_c N P G .10	
Fragmentation	Fam_c N P G .05		Mo_{pt} N P G .05
		Fam_{pt} N P G —	Mo_{sib} N P G .05
		Fam_{sib} N G P .02	
			Ch_{pt} N P G .05
			Ch_{sib} N P G .10
		Fa_c N G P .05	Fa_{pt} N G P .20
		Mo_c N G P .02	Fa_{sib} N G P .20
		Ch_c N G P .05	
Positive acknowledgment	Fam_c N G P .01		Mo_{pt} G N P .10
		Fam_{pt} N G P .01	Mo_{sib} N G P .02
		Fam_{sib} N G P .05	
			Ch_{pt} N G P .02
			Ch_{sib} N G P .20

gories. Levels of positive acknowledgment are uniformly high with median values for families, members, and sessions all falling above 90% for all types of families; this would be expected, since there could hardly be continued interaction without such high levels of responsiveness. However, the range of percentages for positive acknowledgment among families varies for different family types with all Normal families between 90 and 99%, good premorbids between 88 and 98% and poor premorbids between 80 and 97%. It is apparent that families can achieve high levels of responsiveness whether or not they have a schizophrenic child, but that there is a marked decrement for some schizophrenic families, particularly for some with poor premorbid patients. It is this phenomenon of skewing toward the lower end of the range for the poor premorbids that results in the statistically significant differences in the comparisons.

Compared to both types of schizophrenic families, interaction in normal families would be marked by higher rates of brief interjections some of which are clearly understood, such as "yes," "no," "all right," and "OK," which would be coded as elliptical affirmations, and other less clearly understood fragments and incomplete comments. Because of our rules for coding response acknowledgment, these elliptical and fragmented speech patterns result in high rates of fragmentation. However, when enough information is present in a statement for us to code its stimulus demand quality, the responses of normal family members to these codable statements show a higher degree of acknowledgment than the responses of members of schizophrenic families. Thus, paradoxically, normal male families' highly fragmented speech occurs along with clearly responsive speech, whereas the speech of schizophrenic families, although it contains more adequate information for coding, is less responsive.

We noted above that the codability of a response for its degree of acknowledgment is a function of the amount of information available in both the stimulus and response statements. By our coding rules, fragments are defined as "combinations of words with unclear content either from the context or the common culture." [1] Response statements are not codable if they are fragments or if they follow stimulus statements that are fragments. The second source of noncodable responses are elliptical affirmations; responses to these statements might or might not be codable for acknowledgment, depending on the particular context. The frequency of fragments may be associated with differential rates of interruption; these features of interaction may be helpful in understanding the differentials in fragmentation and acknowledgment found in Table 9.1.

Normal families are highest in rank, although not always significantly so, on all comparisons for attempted interruptions, are significantly highest on all comparisons except those for children for rates of elliptical affirmation, and are highest in rank (though rarely significantly different) on all but one comparison for fragments (Table 9.2).

As we have indicated, it is possible for responses to elliptical affirmations to be coded for degrees of acknowledgment. Normal families, however, are

---

[1] The definition of fragments in the Acknowledgment code differs from that used in our discussion of fragments as measures of speech disruption in Chapter 8. This reflects the use of the full statement as the coding unit for acknowledgment; a statement is a fragment only if the full statement itself is incomplete or fragmentary. In the Fragment code used in Chapter 8, incomplete phrases are counted even if they are included in acts or statements that are otherwise complete.

Table 9.2 Attempted Interruptions, Elliptical Affirmations, and Fragments
(families of sons: group and structural analyses)

Variable	Group Analysis				Roles and Sessions					Roles within Sessions				
		H	*M*	*L*	*p*		*H*	*M*	*L*	*p*		*H*	*M*	*L*	*p*
						Fa$_c$	N	P	G	—	Fa$_{pt}$	N	P	G	.05
						Mo$_c$	N	G	P	—	Fa$_{sib}$	N	P	G	—
						Ch$_c$	N	P	G	—					
Attempted											Mo$_{pt}$	N	P	G	—
interruptions	Fam$_c$	N	P	G	—	Fam$_{pt}$	N	P	G	.10	Mo$_{sib}$	N	G	P	—
						Fam$_{sib}$	N	G	P	—					
											Ch$_{pt}$	N	P	G	.20
											Ch$_{sib}$	N	P	G	—
						Fa$_c$	N	P	G	.10	Fa$_{pt}$	N	P	G	.01
						Mo$_c$	N	G	P	.05	Fa$_{sib}$	N	G	P	—
						Ch$_c$	N	G	P	—					
Elliptical											Mo$_{pt}$	N	P	G	.20
affirmations	Fam$_c$	N	P	G	.10	Fam$_{pt}$	N	P	G	.05	Mo$_{sib}$	N	G	P	.02
						Fam$_{sib}$	N	G	P	.20					
											Ch$_{pt}$	P	N	G	—
											Ch$_{sib}$	P	N	G	—
						Fa$_c$	N	G	P	—	Fa$_{pt}$	N	P	G	—
						Mo$_c$	N	G	P	—	Fa$_{sib}$	N/G	P		—
						Ch$_c$	N	G	P	—					
Fragment											Mo$_{pt}$	N	G	P	—
stimuli	Fam$_c$	N	G	P	.20	Fam$_{pt}$	N	P	G	—	Mo$_{sib}$	N	G	P	—
						Fam$_{sib}$	N	G	P	.20					
											Ch$_{pt}$	G	N	P	—
											Ch$_{sib}$	N	G	P	—

apparently less likely to give codable responses to such statements than either type of schizophrenic family; a cross tabulation for a small randomly selected sample of sessions shows that only 3% of normals' statements following elliptical affirmations are codable compared to 12 and 9% respectively for poor and good premorbids' responses to statements in this category. Thus the higher rate of noncodable responses for normals is not only a concomitant of the greater frequency of fragments, but reflects a lower rate of codability of responses to elliptical affirmations; further, it is accompanied by a higher interruption rate.

Although interruptions have been viewed by some observers as a type of nonacknowledgment, for example, as a "devious" acknowledgment (Reusch, 1957), this is a far from adequate formulation of their meaning and function. It is clear that in normal families high rates of acknowledgment, hence of responsiveness to others, can accompany high rates of interruption and the fragmentation of statements.

On the index of Fragmentation, good premorbid families tend to be lowest; this is associated with a low rate of attempted interruptions, elliptical statements, and fragments. This pattern is strongest for mothers and children in these families as may be seen from the role-within-session analyses in Table 9.1. In these comparisons there are significant differences in each instance between the members of normal and good premorbid families. The pattern is weakest for fathers; poor premorbid fathers tend to be highest and tend also to be weaker in the patient session.

The findings on levels of positive acknowledgment among male families reported in Table 9.1 are among the strongest and most consistent results of the study. All comparisons are significant and in all but one instance (mothers in the patient session) the rank-order patterns are identical, that is, normals are high, poors low, and goods in between. The pattern at the family group level is replicated for each member of the family, for each of the experimental sessions, and for each member within each of the sessions with one exception noted for mothers in the patient session, where good mothers are highest in rank when with their schizophrenic sons. The internal consistency of these findings and their consistency with other observations of schizophrenic families provides firm support for the view that members of these families, particularly those of poor premorbid patients, do not "listen" to each other and are impervious to the needs and intents expressed by others. This is clearly not the sole domain of the mother since patterns of nonresponsiveness appear for other family members, for siblings as well as patients.

The combination of low to moderate levels of fragmentation with a low level of acknowledgment for members of poor premorbid families suggests a pattern of confused communication similar to that described by Wynne (1963); that is, the surface of the discussion seems coherent and clear—each statement is completed—but there is little connection between one person's statements and the next. This is a more autistic form of interaction than in either of the other families. Good premorbid families are more likely than poors to take into account what others have said, while at the same time, as indexed by a low rate of interruptions, they try to minimize a response that might be too direct and potentially disruptive. Normal families, as noted above, appear to be able to maintain a continuous and coherent conversation responding to each other's intents and meanings despite a relatively high level of disruptive and fragmentary statements.

There are no significant findings in any of the intersession or intrafamily comparisons on these direct measures of responsiveness. Thus no signs of role differentiation are evident nor do the members of these families alter their behaviors in marked ways in the presence of a schizophrenic child. These styles of responsiveness reflect general norms within each of the families, norms that are differential across family types.

We turn now to analyses of the indirect measures of responsiveness derived from the Focus code. The focus of an act is that part or aspect of the situation to which the act refers. Among the main foci distinguished are the opinions of other individuals in the group. As defined in our scoring manual, (Appendix B) acts are included in this category that are: "Explicit comments on, references to, and questions about others' opinions or the opinion of the group as a whole." These include acts like the following: "I see your point," "Why did you pick that," "All right." This category is related to our general definition of responsiveness in that comments on another person's opinion are one clear way of being responsive to that person. Findings on the distribution of acts into two other Focus categories will also be presented. One includes acts that make explicit reference to the experimental situation including comments on the state of agreement in the group and on the rules and procedures to be followed, and the other category contains explicit references to personal experiences in one's own or others' lives; both of these are considered to be less responsive than comments on opinions. It should be emphasized again that the reason for describing these as indirect measures, in contrast to the direct acknowledgment measure of responsiveness, is that the ongoing real context of interaction is not taken into account in their coding; rather each act is coded in terms of its manifest and explicit meaning with only the speaker's statement in which it is embedded used as a context. Thus although a statement about how they are to proceed in reaching agreement might be directly responsive to another's question in the group and might be coded as reflecting a high degree of acknowledgment, it would be coded here in the focus category that includes references to the experimental situation: as will be seen in our discussion below, this would not be considered as showing as high a degree of responsiveness as a comment that referred explicitly to another's opinion. On the basis of past work and the findings on acknowledgment reported above we would expect normal families to be relatively high on references to others' opinions.

Table 9.3 includes analyses on these three Focus indices—others' opinions, the situation, and personal content as foci of acts.

The three measures vary in their power to discriminate significantly across family types but some patterns are apparent for each of them. In overview what we find is as follows: normal families are highest in their references to others' opinions in the present group and are particularly low in the extent to which they introduce personal experiences into the discussion; they also tend to be low on the amount of attention they give to the experimental situation or the task. Good premorbid families are highest on the introduction of personal content into the discussion; they tend to be low on their references to others' opinions, and this is particularly true for fathers and mothers in the patient session. Poor premorbid families tend to be highest in the degree to which they focus on the rules, procedures, and the task situation; they tend to be relatively low in commenting on the opinions of others.

The consistently high rank for members of normal families in their references to others' opinions suggest that the norm for responsiveness that we noted in our discussion of acknowledgment indices pervades relationships among members of these families. They not only respond to one anothers' intents but they explicitly take into account one anothers' meaning. Whereas poor premorbid family members had been lowest in responsiveness on the direct measure, they and the good premorbid families alternate in the low rank on this indirect index of references to others' opinions. The poor premorbid parents are lowest in the well sibling session; the good premorbid parents are lowest in the patient session. Both poor patients and their siblings are consistently lowest in this behavior, although the differences are significant only for the patients. Good fathers are particularly low when with their patient sons. This is one of the few instances in which there is a significant difference in the behavior of fathers from session to session with good fathers being significantly higher in their rate of comments on others' opinions in the well sibling session. This intersession difference is similar to one found for interruptions reported in Chapter 7; it appears that there is less defensiveness in good families about directly confronting each other when the well sibling is present than when his patient brother is present.

Poor premorbid families give relatively more attention than either of the

Table 9.3 Responsiveness: Indirect Measures of Focus of Attention
(families of sons: group and structural analyses)

Variable	Group Analysis				Roles and Sessions				Roles within Sessions			
		H	M L	p		H	M L	p		H	M L	p
					Fa_c	N P G		—	Fa_{pt}	N P G		.10
					Mo_c	N G P		.01	Fa_{sib}	G N P		—
					Ch_c	N G P		—				
Focus on others' opinions	Fam_c	N P G		.02					Mo_{pt}	N P G		.05
					Fam_{pt}	N P G		.02	Mo_{sib}	N G P		.01
					Fam_{sib}	N G P		.20				
									Ch_{pt}	N G P		.20
									Ch_{sib}	G N P		—
					Fa_c	G/P N		—	Fa_{pt}	P N G		—
					Mo_c	P G N		.05	Fa_{sib}	G P N		—
					Ch_c	G P N		—				
Focus on situation	Fam_c	P G N		—					Mo_{pt}	P G N		—
					Fam_{pt}	P N G		—	Mo_{sib}	P G N		—
					Fam_{sib}	G P N		—				
									Ch_{pt}	N P G		—
									Ch_{sib}	P N G		—
					Fa_c	G P N		—	Fa_{pt}	G P N		—
					Mo_c	G P N		.05	Fa_{sib}	P G N		—
					Ch_c	G P N		.10				
Focus on personal content	Fam_c	G P N		.20					Mo_{pt}	G P N		.20
					Fam_{pt}	G P N		—	Mo_{sib}	G P N		.01
					Fam_{sib}	G P N		.20				
									Ch_{pt}	G N P		—
									Ch_{sib}	G P N		.05

other families to the characteristics of the experimental situation and of the task confronting them. On the whole, normals tend to be least attentive to these aspects of the situation. This pattern is similar to one remarked on in our discussion of expressiveness. There it was noted that members of poor premorbid families tended to be concrete and particularistic in expressing their affect toward persons present in the situation. Here this relative concreteness of orientation is expressed again in their stronger tendency to focus on the features of their current environment, namely, the experimental situation.

Finally, members of good premorbid families are consistently high on the extent to which they introduce personal content into the discussion of the item. The low rank of normal families on this index deserves equal attention since there are no significant pair differences between good and poor families but on several of the comparisons both of them are significantly higher than normals. The strongest replications of the group level findings are for mothers and children and for the well sibling session. No significant differences appear in comparisons across fathers although normal fathers remain consistently low in rank.

This is one of the few measures on which there are significant role differences within families. In both normal and poor families (in the second session for the former and in both sessions for the latter) the mothers are significantly higher than either fathers or sons in the degree to which they introduce personal content into the discussion. The children in these families tend to be the least active in this way. There are, however, no role differences within the good premorbid families; their high rank tends to reflect behavior that is normative for all members of the family.

We have suggested in discussing other findings, notably those for expressiveness and the direct measures of responsiveness, that good premorbid families tend to avoid direct expressions of feelings or the confrontation of other persons in the situation in preference to indirect expressions of feeling. Do these findings on the use of personal content as a prominent focus of their discussion fit with this interpretation? A more detailed description of the category and the acts that typically fall into it helps to answer this question. This category is defined to include "References to experiences or incidents in one's own life, in the lives of others in the group, or in the lives of other real people whom group members know. This category includes real, conditional, and hypothetical experiences" (Appendix B, Focus Code). Typical examples of acts coded into this category are "If I had a party/ and I asked you to leave"; "I've come across this problem in my family"; "My mother said/ when you're old enough to buy your own loafers/ you buy them." Contrast this with acts coded into the category of references to other's opinions in the group; for example: "I see your point"; "Why did you pick that?" or "So why bring it up?"

It is apparent from these examples that the personal content introduced by good premorbid families tends to be at least one remove from the immediate situation. Normals, who are high on references to opinions, are more oriented toward each other in the here and now. The poor premorbids, although also concerned with the immediate situation, are more impersonal in that they give relatively more emphasis to the experimental situation and the task rather than to other persons.

The few instances in which the intrafamily and intersession analyses resulted in significant differences have already been referred to in our discussion of across-family analyses.

The findings for the families of sons on direct and indirect measures of responsiveness are consistent with each other. Norms for levels and styles of responsiveness tend to be generalized within families since on the whole the differences across family types tend to be repeated for mothers, fathers, and sons. Within normal families the members are directly responsive to each other and actively refer to what others have been saying. Continuity in the discussion is ensured by the immediate acknowledgment of the previous speaker and by overt and explicit reference to content that has been introduced by others. Good premorbid families are well mannered and orderly but less directly responsive to each other. They are less likely to talk directly about what others have said and any personal content they introduce is likely to be abstract and hypothetical rather than reflecting the immediate interpersonal situation. Poor premorbid families are least directly responsive to others in the group; they tend to be relatively more concerned with the impersonal and concrete task requirements.

Some speculation is in order following the emphasis on data and description in the preceding pages. From the summary description it might be said that the different types of family define the experimental situation in markedly different ways. We are not referring to conscious and explicit views but to implicit and tacit assumptions about the nature of the task, the rules that are to be followed in solving the problem, and the aim of the discussion. The aim that appears to underly the performance of normal family members is that of trying to reach substantive agreement on the issue, or at least to achieve an understanding of one another's point of view. Their approach requires that they pay attention to expressions of opinion and try to persuade each other of the rightness of a particular position. They engage in a give-and-take discussion that resembles the ideal model of a democratic decision-making group. The good premorbid families provide a striking and interesting contrast to the normals in that they seem to be most concerned with keeping the interaction going according to form; they are, in a sense, ritualistic and appear to be going through the motions of a discussion without really addressing themselves to each other or to the substance of the issues. They assume that if they keep going for a "proper" amount of time that a solution will present itself or that it will be legitimate to stop; in either case they will be free to leave and to escape from a situation that is somewhat stressful. In addition to not responding to each others' intentions and meanings, poor premorbids show some confusion and lack of clarity regarding the requirements and the goals of the task, and perhaps do not have shared internalized rules to depend on for appropriate behavior in this situation. They seem to be intent on discovering the rules of the game; once they understand the rules, the problem will be solved.

Responsiveness: Families of Daughters

We turn now to the analysis of findings on direct and indirect measures of responsiveness for families of daughters. Table 9.4 contains findings on the indices of fragmentation and positive acknowledgment.

In contrast to the strong and consistent findings for families of sons, we find little consistency in rank order patterns for families of daughters on fragmentation and only two significant differences. In the latter instances, for mothers in each of the two experimental sessions, the significantly high rank for normal mothers is similar to what was found for male families. However, this parallel is striking because of its singularity. It may be noted that absolute levels of fragmentation do not differ between male and female families; median values for combined family scores are approximately 30% in both types of family. We return below, after discussing other measures of responsiveness, to a more detailed examination of the sources of these differences in findings between male and female families.

On the positive Acknowledgment index the findings are internally consistent and congruent with those found before but are less strong than the patterns among male families. Normal families of daughters are consistently highest in rank through each level of analysis. Further, when differences are statistically significant the poor premorbids tend to be lowest (with the exception of the rank pattern shown for families in the patient session where, however, an inspection of ranges and median values for goods and poors shows they are almost identical). As was true in the case of families of sons, overall rates of positive acknowledgment are very high with median values over 90% for each of the different types of family.

Thus a generally high rank for normals and a low rank for poors on this direct measure of responsiveness is found in both families of sons and

Table 9.4   Responsiveness: Direct Measures of Acknowledgment
(families of daughters: group and structural analyses)

Variable	Group Analysis	Roles and Sessions	Roles within Sessions
	H M L p	*H M L p*	*H M L p*
		Fa_c P G N —	Fa_{pt} P N G —
		Mo_c N P G —	Fa_{sib} N P G —
		Ch_c P N G —	
Fragmentation	Fam_c G P N —		Mo_{pt} N P G .20
		Fam_{pt} P N G —	Mo_{sib} N G P .10
		Fam_{sib} N G P —	
			Ch_{pt} N P G —
			Ch_{sib} G N P —
		Fa_c N P G —	Fa_{pt} N P G —
		Mo_c N G P .20	Fa_{sib} N G P —
Positive		Ch_c N G P .05	
acknowledgment	Fam_c N G P .05		Mo_{pt} N G P .05
		Fam_{pt} N P G .10	Mo_{sib} N P G —
		Fam_{sib} N G P —	
			Ch_{pt} N G P .10
			Ch_{sib} N G P —

daughters, although with less strength in the latter. Differences between findings for male and female families appear in comparisons across fathers in the well-sibling session. Among families of sons differences between fathers and between families in the well-sibling session are congruent with and as strong as findings at the group level analysis and the segmental analyses of other roles and the patient session; in families of daughters no significant differences appear in comparisons across fathers and in any analysis involving the well-sibling session. Thus differences that are pervasive among families of sons, and which we interpreted as reflecting a general family norm, tend among female families to be specific to mothers and their patient-daughters in interaction with each other.

We may approach the question of why differences found to be generalized in male families appear here only for mothers and schizophrenic daughters in interaction with each other by focusing either on the pattern of no differences between fathers or on the differences for mothers and daughters. If we focus on fathers, it would seem that fathers of schizophrenic daughters are deviating from the over-all family pattern in the direction of normalcy; this is indicated by the lack of differences between fathers in normal, good, and poor families of daughters. There is additional evidence here (found earlier in the findings on strategies of control) that the father in female patient families is isolated from the more pathological patterns of behavior manifested by his wife and schizophrenic daughter. When mothers and their patient daughters are together they differ from their normal counterparts in ways that are similar to normal-schizophrenic differences among all the members of male families. The pattern that we have to this point been referring to as a pervasive norm within families of sons might be thought of in terms of pathogenic functioning; in male patient families the pathology pervades all members, while in female patient families it seems to be restricted to the mother and her schizophrenic daughter. This is consistent with the mother-daughter coalition reported in our discussion of who-talks-to-whom patterns in Chapter 5.

Findings for families of daughters on the indirect measures of responsiveness derived from the Focus Code are presented in Table 9.5.

The results are familiar; the patterns of findings among female families are similar to but weaker than those found among male families. Parallels to the families of sons are clearest if we look at the lowest rank positions in the three measures. Thus on the Focus index of reference to others' opinions, members of normal female families appear in the lowest rank in only one comparison; among male families this could be stated more assertively, that is, normals appeared almost always in the highest rank position. Similarly, whereas good and poor premorbids are both found in the lowest rank position on this index, the goods never appear in the highest rank. This is a loose reading of the findings but the overall pattern for families of daughters is weak on this index and in this instance they are of most interest when they are compared with that found for families of sons.

On the second Focus index of references to the task and experimental situation the pattern is clearer, although again it is the low-rank positions that are most consistent. Normal families here, as with male families, pay relatively little attention to the structural features of the experimental situation; the differences are strongest across mothers and between normal and patient daughters.

Table 9.5 Responsiveness: Indirect Measures of Focus of Attention
(families of daughters: group and structural analyses)

Variable	Group Analysis		Roles and Sessions		Roles within Sessions	
	H M L	p	H M L	p	H M L	p
Focus on others' opinions			Fa$_c$ P N G	—	Fa$_{pt}$ N P G	—
			Mo$_c$ P N G	.20	Fa$_{sib}$ N P G	—
			Ch$_c$ N G P	—		
	Fam$_c$ P N G	—			Mo$_{pt}$ G/P N	—
			Fam$_{pt}$ N P G	.20	Mo$_{sib}$ P N G	.20
			Fam$_{sib}$ P N G	—		
					Ch$_{pt}$ N G P	.10
					Ch$_{sib}$ G N/P	—
Focus on situation			Fa$_c$ G P N	—	Fa$_{pt}$ P N G	—
			Mo$_c$ P G N	—	Fa$_{sib}$ G N P	—
			Ch$_c$ G P N	—		
	Fam$_c$ P G N	.02			Mo$_{pt}$ P G N	—
			Fam$_{pt}$ P G N	.05	Mo$_{sib}$ P G N	.05
			Fam$_{sib}$ G P N	—		
					Ch$_{pt}$ P G N	.02
					Ch$_{sib}$ G P N	—
Focus on personal content			Fa$_c$ G N P	.10	Fa$_{pt}$ G N P	.10
			Mo$_c$ N G P	.05	Fa$_{sib}$ G N P	.20
			Ch$_c$ G N P	.20		
	Fam$_c$ G N P	.20			Mo$_{pt}$ G N P	.10
			Fam$_{pt}$ G N P	.05	Mo$_{sib}$ N G P	—
			Fam$_{sib}$ N G P	—		
					Ch$_{pt}$ G N P	—
					Ch$_{sib}$ N G/P	—

On the third index that includes references to personal experiences, the good premorbids tend to be high, with the exception of the comparison across mothers, when normals are significantly high; poor premorbid families are lowest in rank in each comparison. A general pattern found in analyses of other variables reappears here: the two types of female schizophrenic family tend to differ markedly from each other, with the normals often falling between them in the analyses; among families of sons it is the normals that tend to be different from both types of schizophrenic families. For this reason, although the pattern of findings on these Focus indices for female families appears to fit with those found for male families—normals being directly responsive to each other, goods introducing personal content not related to the immediate interpersonal situation, and poors more concerned with concrete and impersonal aspects of the situation—this general trend is blurred and complicated by the tendencies for the two types of schizophrenic family to be different from each other in the comparisons for families of daughters. The differences between male and female families in this regard may be seen if we count significant differences between pairs of families for the three Focus indices. Among families of sons, of the 24 significant differences (at the .20 level or better) between any pair of families, only one is found between the good and poor premorbids; among families of daughters, 12 of the 32 significant differences are found between good and poor premorbid families.

We return now to the analysis of fragmentation patterns among families of daughters (Table 9.4) and attempt to locate a possible source of the difference between these findings and those for male families that showed strong and consistent differences across different types of family. It will be recalled that among male families, differences in fragmentation were associated with parallel differences in fragment stimuli, elliptical affirmations, and attempted interruptions.

Differential between types of female family in rates of attempted interruptions are similar to those found for males. However, these rates among female families are not accompanied by a similar pattern of rates for fragment stimuli, where the patterns vary relatively randomly. We may ask whether there are conditions under which an increase in attempted interruptions might be associated with an increase in fragments. One possibility lies in the extent to which attempted interruptions are successful. Being "unsuccessfully interrupted" means that the speaker has continued talking. There may be a greater likelihood that his statement will contain sufficient information to be coded for degree of acknowledgment. Although our analyses do not include direct correlation of interruptions and acknowledgment, some relevant evidence on this may be found by

Table 9.6 Attempted Interruptions, Fragments, and Elliptical Affirmations
(families of daughters: group and structural analyses)

Variable	Group Analysis		Roles and Sessions		Roles within Sessions	
		H M L p		*H M L p*		*H M L p*
			Fa_c N G P —		Fa_{pt} N P G .20	
			Mo_c P N G .20		Fa_{sib} N G P —	
			Ch_c N P G —			
Attempted interruptions	Fam_c N P G .20				Mo_{pt} P N G .05	
			Fam_{pt} N P G .10		Mo_{sib} P N G —	
			Fam_{sib} N P G .20			
					Ch_{pt} P N G —	
					Ch_{sib} N P G —	
			Fa_c G N P —		Fa_{pt} G N P —	
			Mo_c P G N —		Fa_{sib} G N P —	
			Ch_c G N P —			
Fragment stimuli	Fam_c G N P —				Mo_{pt} P N G —	
			Fam_{pt} P G N .20		Mo_{sib} P G N —	
			Fam_{sib} G N P —			
					Ch_{pt} G P N —	
					Ch_{sib} G N P —	
			Fa_c N P G —		Fa_{pt} N G P .20	
			Mo_c P N/G .20		Fa_{sib} N G P —	
			Ch_c N P/G —			
Elliptical affirmations	Fam_c P N G —				Mo_{pt} N P G —	
			Fam_{pt} N P G .05		Mo_{sib} P G N .20	
			Fam_{sib} N P G —			
					Ch_{pt} N P G —	
					Ch_{sib} G N P —	

examining rates of being successfully interrupted for male and female families.

Although both male and female normal families tend to be low on rates of being successfully interrupted, it is only among the females that we find the normals significantly so on several of the comparisons. Thus we may hypothesize that the differentials found in fragmentation for families of sons and the differences in findings between families of sons and daughters are associated with, and perhaps mediated by, rates of success in interrupting behavior. The exact nature of this relationship would have to be determined by more detailed correlation and sequential analyses.

Table 9.7 Successful Interruptions
(families of sons and daughters: group and structural analyses)

Variable	Group Analysis	Roles and Sessions	Roles within Sessions
	H M L p	H M L p	H M L p
		Fa_c P G N —	Fa_{pt} P G N —
		Mo_c G P N —	Fa_{sib} P G N —
Successful interruptions: Families of sons		Ch_c G P N —	
	Fam_c P G N —		Mo_{pt} G P N —
		Fam_{pt} G P N —	Mo_{sib} N P G —
		Fam_{sib} P N G —	
			Ch_{pt} G P N —
			Ch_{sib} N P G —
		Fa_c G P N .20	Fa_{pt} P G N —
		Mo_c P G N —	Fa_{sib} G P N .20
Successful interruptions: Families of daughters		Ch_c G P N —	
	Fam_c G P N —		Mo_{pt} P G N —
		Fam_{pt} P G N —	Mo_{sib} P G N .20
		Fam_{sib} G P N .20	
			Ch_{pt} G N P —
			Ch_{sib} P G N —

Differentials in rates of elliptical affirmation among male families also entered into our interpretation of differentials in fragmentation; normal males were high on these types of statements and high on fragmentation. The lack of differences in fragmentation for female families is associated with few and less consistent differences among them on elliptical affirmations (Table 9.6). This finding fits with our discussion of the basis for fragmentation differentials among male families, that is, fragmentation varies directly with the frequency of elliptical affirmations; where there are minimal differences in the latter there are no differences in fragmentation.

We may now bring together the several threads of the argument regarding the basis and meaning of different levels of fragmentation. It is evident from an examination of actual percentage scores that the statistically significant differences among families of sons on the fragmentation index reflect consistently high rates for Normal male families and their members (in each comparison, rates for normal families of sons are also higher than any of the rates for families of daughters). These high rates in turn appear to be associated with relatively high rates among normal families of sons for being successfully interrupted and having fragment stimuli and elliptical affirmations. These differential rates—for fragmentation, interruptions, fragments, elliptical statements—with the distinctive position of the normals vis-a-vis the two types of male schizophrenic family, tend to be present for all members of these families in both experimental situations. Thus norms regulating these behaviors seem to be diffuse and general. They result in relatively homogeneous and undifferentiated behavior on these dimensions within the normal male family in the sense that the same patterns appear for all members in both experimental sessions. This feature of less differentiation within families of sons as compared to families of daughters has been remarked upon before in our discussion of differences in expressiveness.

It might be argued that a high rate of elliptical statements reflects a general norm about behavior that functions in normal families in the presence of sons. Elliptical statements represent a matter-of-fact, nonembellished pattern of interaction; they are more direct, more to the point, more masculine, as Hemingway's prose is in comparison to the richer, more complex texture of Virginia Woolf's. Another characteristic of elliptical statements must be taken into account; many of the statements coded in this category express agreement—"sure," "yes," "all right." These are unqualified agreements where the substance is implicit; there is the reciprocal assumption among interactants that the intended meaning of the agreement is understood without further elaboration. Again the contrast between male and female families is instructive; while overall median levels of elliptical affirmatives are about 6% for both types of normal family, the distribution of scores for families of sons is skewed sharply toward the high end with some families having as high as 19 and 20% of their acts coded in this category. Two additional alternative possibilities suggest themselves to account for this pattern. Either levels of mutual understanding are sufficiently high for meaningful communication and a continuous conversation, so that the "obvious" need not be stated explicitly since all understand it, or the surface of agreement is a defensive facade below which family members do not wish to penetrate.

Among the three alternative and speculative lines of interpretation, that is, that normal families of sons differ from normal families of daughters and all types of schizophrenic family, in style, or in depth or shared values, or in strength of shared anxieties, we lean toward the interpretation of differences in style. This seems to us both more parsimonious and more consistent with other findings that do not suggest either greater understanding or greater anxiety among normal families of sons.

Discussion

Two sets of strong findings have been reported and reviewed in this chapter. First, there are differentials in levels and types of responsiveness between normal and schizophrenic families of both sons and daughters; briefly, normal families are more responsive and more likely to focus their comments on the opinions of others, whereas the least responsive poor patient families orient toward the features of the immediate experimental situation and the goods, who are moderately responsive, tend to introduce somewhat abstracted personal experiences. Second, levels of fragmentation vary markedly among families of sons, with normals being particularly high, but these differences are not present in comparisons among families of daughters; these differentials are related to an interaction style among normal male families, that is they are high on interruptions, fragment stimuli, and elliptical statements—a combination that may be associated with the high levels of fragmentation found.

This combination of findings could be consistent with either of two alternative types of interaction. It is possible that the fragments and disruptive speech events of normal families are themselves not codable and that a high proportion of their codable statements are acknowledging. We would then observe, particularly among the normal families of sons, sequences of complete, clear, and responsive statements interrupted by bursts of unclear, meaningless, and unresponsive disruptions. Our observations of normal families, however, point to a different pattern. That is, both disruptions and complete, clear statements occur together, with each kind of statement being equally responsive. Normal family members appear to be responsive even while they are interrupting and seem to understand the intent and meaning of others' speeches even when these are highly fragmented. Thus we would assume that the fragmented speeches that we could not code and about which we could make no judgment of responsiveness would actually show the same rates of positive response as do the coded statements. The same interpretations may be made for the schizophrenic families of sons. Their lower rates of fragmented speech, associated with lower rates of responsiveness could indicate long sequences of clear and complete speech, only some of which is responsive, interrupted by only a few disruptions. On the other hand, our observations suggest that the disruptions, if they could be coded, are as nonresponsive as the complete statements. These alternative conceptions of the flow of interaction will be examined more directly in correlational and sequential analyses.

Each of the alternative frameworks that we have been using to interpret findings—etiological, responsive, and situational—receives a measure of support from one or another aspect of the findings. The pathogenic importance attributed to nonresponsiveness by many investigators was noted early in the chapter. Among specialists concerned with personality functioning and development we would expect to find a broad concensus regarding the destructive impact of a nonresponsive family environment with its associated lack of sensitivity to the child's own needs. Our findings on levels and types of responsiveness fit easily within this etiological view. Not only is the level of resonsiveness higher in normal families of both sons and daughters but for both sexes degree of pathology is related to degree of nonresponsiveness, that is, families of patients with poor premorbid histories are less responsive than those with good histories. Thus some level of attentiveness to each other would seem both to reduce the pathogenic effect and at the same time to be an indicator of a better prognosis. Further, the findings suggest that the level of responsiveness is an all-family norm and is not restricted to the mother's role. Finally, the degree of pathology appears also to be related to whether other persons can be objects of attention: normal family members address themselves to the comments and opinions of those with whom they are interacting; goods, at one remove, tend to refer to more abstract situationally-distant personal experiences; poors concentrate relatively more on the impersonal rules and concrete features of their situation.

Differentials in fragmentation may also be thought of in etiological terms. The polarization among male families of normals and goods, for example, is similar to the findings on disruptions in communication reported in Chapter 8; there the goods showed a rigid and nonvariable style of interaction that parallels their low levels of fragmentation and normals showed a highly variable style that is consistent with their high fragmentation levels. In interpreting the findings on disruption within an etiological framework, it was suggested that the parents of good premorbid patients may tend to filter out and modulate environmental stimulation with the result that the child's capacity to do this for himself does not develop adequately. Such an interpretation could be used as well here, but a responsive model appears to provide a better fit for the full range of findings. Two sets of findings must be taken into account: first, that among families of sons normals are highest on fragmentation and goods lowest; second, that there are no significant differences among the families of daughters. The highly variable staccato style of interaction in normal families has been discussed in other chapters and contrasted with the formal and overorganized style among the goods. Our interpretation in responsive terms of other findings is relevant here—the goods are defensive and particularly anxious about directly confronting others and this results in a discussion with a surface texture that is well-ordered and clear but that at the same time lacks both meaningful continuity and clear reference to each other's ideas. In marked contrast, normal families are more labile and relatively nondefensive about discussing their ideas with each other even when they are in disagreement. When normals and goods have been found to be most different from each other, with the poors falling in between, we have argued that this supports a responsive interpretation; that is, the defensiveness of the goods is viewed as a response to a current stress, to the more recent appearance of the illness, and the pattern of rigidity and overcontrol reflects their attempts to manage their problems with a minimum of overt disruption.

This argument applies only to the male families since it is only among them that we find differences in fragmentation. The differentials in findings between the families of sons and daughters, when no differences are found for the latter between normal and patient families, must be taken into account by any interpretive model; these differences would seem to fit as well with either a responsive or situational model. In either case an assumption must be made about culturally based differential norms for interacting with daughters and sons. The assumption is that when daughters are present the style of interaction is more polite and orderly, with less intrusions into each other's speech. We find also that the families of male patients are distinctively low on fragmentation. We may speculate that anxiety about the potentially disruptive effects of the behavior of schizophrenic sons might lead to an increase in the level of control over and orderliness of interaction. Whether this increased control over interaction is specific to the experimental situation or is a more general family response to a sick son is difficult to assess. The fact that the findings are identical in the well sibling and patient sessions and that there are no significant intersession differences would support either a responsive or a situational model, and the data do not permit us to distinguish between them.

The findings on responsiveness reviewed in this chapter and discussed in the last section are among the strongest in the study. Even here, however, it is apparent that each of the alternative models of interpretation has a degree of plausibility. We have exaggerated to some extent the peculiar "fittingness" of certain findings with each model in turn in order to make the point that an adequate interpretation must take all of the findings into account and still remain reasonably parsimonious and internally consistent. Clearly, none of the models meets these ideal criteria. We believe, and the work reported in this monograph testifies to the belief, that an understanding of their particular limitations is a useful step in the direction of a more valid, more comprehensive, and more useful theory of relationships between family interaction and schizophrenia than is presently available.

Chapter 10

Family Discussions:
Illustrations of Findings

The indices of interaction, on which findings have been reported in the several preceding chapters, are abstract measures of the concrete phenomenon of family members interacting with each other. In focusing our attention exclusively on statistical analyses of differences between and within families, we have, to this point, omitted detailed descriptions of how families would appear to an observer. Such descriptions would seem useful for several reasons. First, they serve to return us to the concrete reality of the family in action, toward the understanding of which such studies as the present one are ultimately directed. Second, they help to clarify the relationship between our indices and the flow of interaction. Third, they indicate the patterning of interaction from which our separate indices have been selected and abstracted and thus suggest next steps in analysis and investigation. With these aims in mind, this chapter will present a series of illustrative examples of family interaction drawn from our protocol typescripts.

These segments of interaction are selected specifically to illustrate findings from the study, that is, the ways in which affect is expressed, and the patterning of power relationships, speech disruptions, and responsiveness. In our discussion we suggest some of the functions of certain interactions, show how patterns may be maintained, and point out some of the ways in which independently measured variables may be associated with each other.

Certain qualifications must be kept in mind in reading the chapter. The typescripts themselves and our comments and suggestions about the functions and meanings of certain behavior are not "findings." They are only included to illustrate findings presented in the previous chapters. Segments of family interaction were selected, not because the particular family had the "highest" or "lowest" percentage on a certain interaction variable, but because the observers watching the family through a one-way mirror or the coders working from the tape and/or typescript noted striking interaction patterns in that family that later seemed to exemplify the patterns in the data. Moreover, the focus in this chapter is largely on families of sons and on the session when the patient is present, since it is in this situation that most of the significant differences between families were found. When particular points are to be made about families of daughters or parents' interaction with their well child we will include interaction segments from them. Finally, since our statistical analyses were made on single variables, that is, since each variable was taken one at a time, it is quite possible that no family of any one type exemplifies all of the interaction characteristics of that type of family. For example, a single good premorbid family may have very low rates of interruptions, characteristic of our findings for all good families, but that same good family may have high proportions of positive affect, not characteristic of good families as a group. The amount of overlap in the styles of interaction is such that no "ideal" good or normal family can be used to exemplify all findings.

Moving from the statistical differences between families at the interaction code level back to the experiential level serves to develop new and more complex hypotheses about the family's interaction. Some of these are hypotheses that we feel can be investigated by the use of multivariate analyses. For example, correlations between whether the interrupting act has negative affect qualities may measure the function of certain control strategies. Examination of the family typescripts also points to the importance of sequential patterns of interaction in understanding how modes of communication are used and responded to in the family. These types of analysis are now under way and will be reported in future publications.

We will look at normal, poor premorbid, and good premorbid families in turn in order to provide a picture of each type of family. In the presentation of each we will examine patterns of expressiveness, control strategies, disruptions in communication, and responsiveness.

Families of Normal Children

One major quality of normal families that differentiates them from both types of schizophrenic family is the extent to which affect is directly expressed by all family members. Normal families are both more expressive and more positive in their interaction than are the schizophrenic families, especially when these parents are with their patient children. We have interpreted these findings in terms of the degree to which the schizophrenic families must defend against warmth and closeness in contrast to the normal families, who can express feelings directly. The expressiveness of the normal family is apparent in the degree to which members support each other, protect each other, laugh together, and seem to enjoy each other's company. In certain instances one member of the family is "weak" in some sense—he lacks knowledge or information necessary for the task, he does not understand the experimental instructions, he has difficulty expressing his ideas clearly, or finds himself in the position of supporting an opinion that is obviously unsupportable. Normal family members openly protect and help each other.

One observer noted [1] about a Normal father-mother-daughter triad, ". . . both mother and daughter seemed to have more education and more information than the father did. [They] gave the father quite a lot of nonthreatening support around the fact that he is less informed. The daughter explained what 'IQ' meant, and why it (IQ) couldn't be changed, in a way that allowed her father to retain his opinion on the item but give more reasonable arguments."

Another normal family, this time with a son, when discussing a problem having to do with parents who do not speak English well, recognized the fact that they did not speak English well themselves; this led to the father's explicit support of his wife.[2]

---

[1] Observers who watched the family interaction through a one-way mirror were asked to write a one-page description of the family at the end of the session. These informal notes are used in this chapter as supplementary information to the interaction protocols.

[2] The form of the quoted typescripts has been altered from that used for coding and processing of data to a form more easily read. Here statements are ordered in the sequence in which they occurred. Three dots and italics indicate that the statement was spoken simultaneously with the one adjacent to it. Pauses, interruptions, and laughter are inserted where they occur. Double asterisks are included at the point at which something was said but it was not ascertainable to the typist. All proper names have been changed to insure anonymity, and a minimum of punctuation added for clarity. No other content or form has been changed.

Their discussion is about the following item:

> Theresa, who is 23 years old, lives with her mother and father who are honest, hard-working people but who have never learned to speak English very well. Theresa feels uncomfortable about inviting young men into the house and is afraid this will spoil her chances of finding a good husband. She wonders if she shouldn't move into her own apartment with a friend. What should she do? Here, Mother said, "Move into her own apartment." Father and Son said, "Stay with parents."

MOTHER: *Mmm*

FATHER: No, she was thinking of herself. And that's the way the question is given down, to. . . .

MOTHER: *Mmm*

FATHER: . . . Which would have been b- which would have been better for her. To go out and then l- live in her own apartment living herself to abide the uhh *p-ehh the poor English* that her father and mother *is talking when she's entertaining her friend?*

MOTHER: . . . *Well she was ahh, she was living ahh* with her friend. She was living with a friend. She wasn't going to live by herself. She was living with a friend.

FATHER: Suppose you and I couldn't talk good English and we don't talk, you don't talk too (Laughs) *too good English* . . .

SON: *Hmm*

MOTHER: *Well we don't.*

SON: *Yes* (Laughs)

FATHER: . . . *We don't talk very good English. We don't. We* . . .

MOTHER: *Well we don't* (Laughs) *We don't talk*

SON: *Yeah ehh. But would you want, would you want Sally* to move out to a new apartment just because you didn't *speak good English?*

MOTHER: *Well if if she wanted to* I wouldn't No I because I I

SON: (Interrupts) But y- would that would you like that for a reason?

MOTHER: No I wouldn't. I know *she wouldn't*

FATHER: *You're on Yes.* (Pauses) You're on, you're on Candon Camera. (Laughs)

MOTHER: That's all right.

FATHER: That's right. Don't talk (Pauses)

MOTHER: But I I mean she I I know she wouldn't move out on that account, but I'd

SON: (Interrupts) I know. But you wouldn't want her too, either.

MOTHER: Well not on that account. No.

SON: So?

MOTHER: No, I wouldn't want her to move out because I I didn't speak good English, which I don't (Laughs)

FATHER: Well you talk good English enough and and they're not referring to neither you or I *in this case.* . . .

MOTHER: *No, no.*

FATHER: . . . But at the same time I'm I'm just saying that every if umm m- my English was even worse that it 'tis that you didn't hardly understand me and no-one-body else understood me . . .

MOTHER: Mmm

FATHER: . . . Still she, if if she was going to bring in a boyfriend like that, that's her home *and I'm her* father and you're her mother . . .

MOTHER: *Yes*

FATHER: . . . so there was nothing she could do only (Pauses) That's what I, that's what I'd say *and I think you,* I think you'll agree with me *on it.*

Noticeable in the previous excerpt is a sense of warmth generally more characteristic of the normal families. There is pleasure in joking, laughter, asides, and references to family members. The father's reassurance to the mother is typical of normal families. This freedom to laugh and tease as well as be supportive, by all three family members, is evident in the following normal family, also discussing the problem of the daughter whose parents speak poor English. Here, originally, the daughter felt the girl should move to her own apartment and the parents disagreed.

DAUGHTER: (Laughs) *Oh Father, I I I change.*

MOTHER: (Laughs) ** *Oh but I mean, no, no, no. Let's face it. Now there I think is a perfect example.* (Laughs)

FATHER: (Laughs)

DAUGHTER: (Laughs) *You want to know anything,* I'll teach you . . .

MOTHER: Yeah, she'll teach you how to speak bop. But *uh basically I mean to say,* to me . . .

DAUGHTER: . . . (Laughs) Anything else you want to learn . . .

FATHER: (Laughs)

DAUGHTER: . . . *I'll teach you.*

MOTHER: . . . *there's no question there at all.*

FATHER: No, I don't think I don't think they shouldn't ah . . .

MOTHER: As long as they're not being narrow-minded, intolerant, *not letting her bring her friends home* . . .

FATHER: Y-yeah.

MOTHER: . . . *not being, you know, polite to them* . . .

FATHER: *Yeah. Yeah.*
MOTHER: *. . . but the fact* that they don't just speak a a another language
             to me is *utterly ridiculous . . .*
FATHER: *Yeah, yeah.*
MOTHER: *. . .* Actually can uh other people coming in probably can't
             speak their language either.
FATHER: *Anybody, anybody anybody can ** what do you mean?*
DAUGHTER: *As far as I was concerned I wouldn't be happy with a daughter*
             like that at home. *As a matter* of fact I'd be happier with her
             gone fft.
MOTHER: *No*
DAUGHTER: *. . . Didn't say the kids would be . . .*
MOTHER: *What's what's, yeah*
DAUGHTER: *. . .* it didn't say the parents would be unhappy with her gone
             if they want her to go.
MOTHER: *Yeah, no. But what I mean*
DAUGHTER: *. . .* if she wants *to go, go.*
MOTHER: *What has your* whether your parents speak English or not
             got to do with meeting uh *meeting someone?*
DAUGHTER: *It's got nothing to do with it.* But if she it makes her happier,
             it may *make her more tolerant, too . . .*
MOTHER: *I mean actually, no.* (Laughs)
DAUGHTER: *. . . I think she may realize how unimportant it is.* (Laughs)
FATHER: *Well er my* brother *is it isn't a question of my brother don't*
             speak English, he speaks English with a continental accent.
             (Laughs)
MOTHER: (Laughs) Yeah, but but *you know, listen, . . .*
DAUGHTER: (Laughs) *Father, you ** (Laughs)
MOTHER: Face it. What does (Laughs) what does whether (Laughs)
             your parents ** (Laughs) have to do *with meeting anybody?*
FATHER: (Laughs)

In addition to the positive support for each other evident in the previous excerpt, and although normal families have lower rates of negative
affect of all kinds and particularly of antagonism, disagreement, anger,
and personal attacks nevertheless do occur. The quality of disagreement
tends to be direct yet benign. Normally family members discuss opinion
differences in a way that differentiates these opinion differences from the
members who hold them. This is in contrast to one common quality of
schizophrenic family interaction that we note later; in the latter instance
the family member's opinion, particularly the patient child's, tends to

be treated as identical to his behavior and thus opinions are not dealt with as if they were objective ideas to be manipulated.

In the family discussion below, members began by disagreeing about whether an adolescent girl has the right to choose her own friends, even though the parents disapprove of the friends the girl selects. The son in the family took the position that the girl has the right to select her own friends; the parents disagreed. Quickly the discussion moved from the questionnaire item to this son's choice of friends, with the parents subsequently pressuring him to bring his friends home to meet them or to find friends in the neighborhood of whom they approved. Although this became a heated and involving sequence it was explicitly disconnected by all three members from the differences of opinion on the questionnaire item.

FATHER: (Interrupts) And the story is George O'Connell u- used to see you down the other side, and then Mildred my old teacher at Dorchester High use to see you when you were b- , you and Jimmy when you were going in there beside the railroad tracks up beside the new group of houses. So I used *to keep pretty good track.* (Laughs) . . .

SON: (Laughs) *How did you know we were up there?* (Laughs)

FATHER: . . . *That's what I'm trying to say* . . .

SON: (Laughs) *We only went up there a couple of times.*

FATHER: . . . *Re- regardless what you have to say* I know that but I happen to have enough friends around the neighborhood that I can keep pretty good track of you. *Of what you're doing* . . .

SON: (Laughs)

FATHER: . . . *which is- s nothing to do with the question involved* . . .

MOTHER: *Well that has nothing to do with the question.*

FATHER: . . . The story is if you're going with kids that seem to be all right I have no arguments. I don't have to individually meet each one of your friends. I'm not saying that. If you're going with a neighborhood group that seems to have a good neighborhood name I got no arguments. But the story is *this one particular boy isn't the one.*

SON: *But getting back to* . . .

MOTHER: *All right. If you i- if your parents,* if your parents think that you're running around with somebody that is definitely a bad influence on you . . .

SON: If the ahh daughter a- *agrees partly, yes.*

MOTHER: . . . *Do you think you should go along with their* way of thinking?

SON: . . . Getting back to the question, *I do agree 'cause ahh* if if if they have proof that she really is an idiot and and the girl herself knows that she is, they I think the girl should not. But if like the the instance with Marvin. I think he's changed.

MOTHER: Well the thing to do is to, ahh if your parents are right in what they say

SON: I think they should talk it over then. Have 'em meet the person himself. I

MOTHER: (Interrupts) And then if they decide that they're not a good influence on you.

SON: Ohh if then stop hanging around with him. (Pauses) Don't push him off all together though. (Pauses) Like if you meet him in the street. If he says don't if y- you don't you're ** of course, you're going to say I don't yeah.

FATHER: No, you can't *ignore him. No one's expecting you to.*

SON: *Oh yeah.*

MOTHER: *Well I don't mean that . . .*

SON: *Then I agree on the question.*

MOTHER: . . . I I don't mean that. I mean getting so buddy-buddy with him that you're spending time all the time with him. You're young. You should be flipping around.

In normal families, differences between members can be discussed without direct antagonism yet with personal involvement. One normal family, present with their daughter, exemplifies the quality of benign disagreement generally found in the normal families; here a family is concluding its discussion of the following item.

> Some people believe that there is nothing a person can't do or be if he wants to, and if he really works hard. Do you agree or disagree?

Here father and daughter agreed and mother disagreed.

MOTHER: I I don't think that everybody can attain anything they want. I I say *no to that.*

DAUGHTER: *Oh you c-* well that's just it. *You never get everything you want but I mean i-*

MOTHER: (Interrupts) *That was the question.* No. Any- a- everybody or anyone can attain anything they want in life. Isn't that it? Wasn't that the question?

FATHER: Yeah.

MOTHER: If they really want it bad enough. And I say everybody can not attain what they *want in life.*

DAUGHTER: *Hmm, No,* the question was, *it has been* said . . .
MOTHER: *What?*
DAUGHTER: . . . that if you try hard enough to get something then you will attain it. If you want something bad enough *you will try hard enough* to get it. . . .
FATHER: *And you work hard enough* for it.
DAUGHTER: . . . *That's what is s- it didn't say* everybody or anybody or anything like that. . . .
MOTHER: *It said an- anybody.*
DAUGHTER: . . . it just said that if you want something bad enough you'll try to get it and you'll get it ann-
MOTHER: You'll *try perhaps* but I won't say you'll always get it. All right? . . .
FATHER: *And you're thinkin thinkin' it*
MOTHER: *Let's* leave it at that. . . .
DAUGHTER: *Okay.*
MOTHER: . . . You two think that you can but I *for ev- for everybody.* . . .
FATHER: *Well we have to agree. We have to agree.*
MOTHER: . . . *No I don- I don't see how we could.*
DAUGHTER: *No I don't*
MOTHER: We'd stay here all night maybe and I I would still say that everybody can't have can't get what they want in life.

Our findings have shown that the power structure in normal families of both sons and daughters is clearly differentiated. In families of sons fathers generally take the high power position, whereas sons are in the low position, participating less and paying attention most often, when they do participate, to their father. In families of daughters a mother-daughter coalition is apparent. However, within these quite clearly structured power relationships we have noted that every family member is able and is allowed to confront others with his own arguments. These personal confrontations are shown in the family example on pages 221–222 in the form of a very high rate of interruptions, by the normal daughter as well as the two parents. Other forms of personal confrontation are also apparent in the discussions of normal families. One common one is the open clash of ideas and opinions often supported by strong arguments that are clearly taken into account by all family members. These strong task-focused arguments are just as likely to be initiated by the children as by the parents in the family, especially by the daughter, who tends to be in coalition with her mother.

In the following excerpt the family is discussing whether obedience and respect for authority are the prime virtues to teach one's children, and the daughter has disagreed with this judgment. In contrast to the usual pattern in the schizophrenic families the daughter here is allowed to confront her parents with a differing opinion that they listen to seriously.

DAUGHTER: *No. It says* it doesn't say do you respect and authority. It says do you think these are the most important virtues, values which well anyway

MOTHER: Well, supposing you say well oh, I do love my parents or I do love my family or this or that ehh but I don't have to do what they say. I can still

DAUGHTER: (Interrupts) I didn't say they weren't important at all. I just said I don't think *they should be the most important value.*

MOTHER: *Well, would you think that the fact that love* was more important in that respect because uhh

DAUGHTER: I think that that should just be with it. I'm not saying that they shouldn't be important, they are important but just the same I don't think they should be the only ones. *I can't see that.*

FATHER: *Well, what was it.* It was respect and what?

DAUGHTER: *Obedience..............*

FATHER: No, no, it it wasn't obedience. No.

MOTHER: Authority.

FATHER: Ss, yeah, yeah respect for authority, yeah. Well, the way I look at it you should have the respect for the authority and and if you have ahh (Pause) good argument against the authority well that's that, and uhh but you still have to respect the authority.

DAUGHTER: Yeah, but the point is they said that those are the most important virtues to instill in your child and I don't see that. (Pause) It's not an army or a dictatorship or anything else where command just *passes down.*

Although it is the interrupting, or, as in the above example, the directly confronting person-control strategies that most clearly distinguish normal from schizophrenic families in our data, observation of the families provides examples of other, less direct and explicit, control strategies. However, the differences between normal and schizophrenic families lie in the fact that all of the control strategies occurred in the context of clearly defined roles governed by rules calling for direct confrontations by all members, low- and high-power, in an atmosphere having greater positive affect.

The normal families' characteristic style of interaction is evident in their high rates of disruptive communications along with their high degree of responsiveness to each other. This combination of qualities suggests that normal family members clearly understand what to expect from each other and can pick up the meaning of fairly subtle and fleeting cues given in fragments of speech. The ability to predict and understand each other in the face of highly disrupted speech patterns allows family members to respond to or acknowledge each other to a greater extent than do the schizophrenic families. An example of responsiveness in the face of disrupted speech is the discussion by a normal family on the problem of whether parents should give some of their life savings to their son to start a business or whether they should use the money to go to Florida. Here the content of the discussion is carried on even though rates of interruptions and simultaneous speech are extremely high.

MOTHER: (Interrupts) But if he had had other failures and wasn't capable of it, *wasn't trustworthy that's what well th- the it isn't see, I think, see, it didn't say that* . . .

FATHER: *Oh yeah. Oh if he wasn't capable or if he was, oh yeah. Yeah. Yeah.*

MOTHER: . . . and that's what I had in mind I didn't know ah I had no experience and

FATHER: Well that *well that's why I answered the way I did w- w- I* . . .

MOTHER: *See, there were two answers.*

FATHER: . . . Ah (Pauses) assuming that he was a good *a responsible fellow,* (Pauses) that . . .

MOTHER: *Was responsible* ** *certainly you don't* . . .

SON: **give him the money.*

MOTHER: . . . You know very well I would give it (Laughs) in that case, but I had in mind

FATHER: (Interrupts) Set him up, yeah. Because h- h- he would, if he was that type of fellow then he'd (Pauses) he'd aim

MOTHER: (Interrupts) Oh to help him out. I would certainly help him out. But I had in mind that at that age if he hadn't

FATHER: (Interrupts) And if they had a considerable amount they, *it seems* to me that they could

MOTHER: *Yes.* (Pauses) Well certainly if he was responsible and

FATHER: (Interrupts) Although ther- th there's other ways I mean

MOTHER: (Interrupts) That's what I was thinking, that if they had earned

FATHER: (Interrupts) If he was going to be a business man why he could probably ah go to a bank and and get his, *you know, and be on on his own. I mean its an awful hard question, see.*

High rates of responsiveness in the normal families also are indicative of the ways in which normal family discussions are organized or structured. Within the rules for direct confrontation and the pattern of variable communication normal families also tend to have a continuously moving and changing argument in which each person's contribution is taken into account and has a modifying effect on the opinions of each of the other members. Consequently the discussion follows a constantly changing course as new ideas are interjected. The final decision therefore is most likely to be a new opinion representing a melding of opinions and ideas of all members. As might be expected, because the schizophrenic families tend to have lower rates of positive acknowledgment and more rigid or orderly patterns of interaction, the structure of their arguments appears to be different with the extreme pattern being one in which all members express their originally stated opinions in sequence and no new idea serves to modify or add to previously stated arguments. The result is a circular discussion ending with the same opinions with which it began.

The effect of acknowledgment and taking into account the opinions of all members is shown in the following discussion of a normal father-mother-daughter triad in which the original disagreement was between the mother and the other two members. They are talking about whether a doctor should tell a patient he has an incurable illness or whether this should be postponed as long as possible. At the outset of the discussion the father's and daughter's argument was represented by this statement of the daughter: "I don't think you have the right to make the judgment yourself. I think that you should tell the person and let them take it." The mother said, "But I think that, I think it's the individual. Some people you can tell and some you can't." After 10 minutes or more of talk about the topic, the solution is represented by the following excerpt.

FATHER: No? Well, what are you going to do? Would you put it off as long as possible, or not?

MOTHER: I can't say. I uhh it would be eh the individual. I still say that d- depends on the person that you're to tell. Would they collapse an- and not live for the next two *years at all?*

FATHER: *So what difference does it make?* So what difference does it make?

MOTHER: They'd just pine away or would you wait

DAUGHTER: (Interrupts) All right. Yeah, but that isn't the question. (Pauses)

FATHER: Look at the good part of it. As Kathleen says, why you'd be be able t- to you could d-d-do something in a in a month.

MOTHER: (Laughs)

DAUGHTER: Uh no, no. I think that the thing is like n-n-now somebody that's going to school, say, like me. I found out I had two years to live. Do you think I want to stay in school and study, work all summers, Saturdays? I you know I just have completely all my time taken up with things that I have to do because I'm only doing this to prepare myself for something that I'm going to do later.

FATHER: That you're not even going to do because *you're going to go out of the picture.*

DAUGHTER: *But I'm, yeah*

MOTHER: Well, in that case then I think that you should be told.

DAUGHTER: Yes.

MOTHER: Some cases you should be *told.*

FATHER: So *you* shouldn't hold off as long as possible *in other words. In that instance. Okay.*

DAUGHTER: *I don't think you should. Unless, un-less* you know that the person would go into some deep state of depression.

FATHER: *Hmm*

MOTHER: *Yeah.* Well, that's what I'm saying, the *circumstances.*

DAUGHTER: *Yes.* But th- the way the que the question was worded I think *was if you* the doctor tells you . . .

MOTHER: *You should tell them.*

DAUGHTER: . . . and he says, now would you tell this oth so and so.

MOTHER: Hmm

FATHER: *What should you*

DAUGHTER: *All right. The doctor* knows that they're in a physical position to take this. They're *you know* . . .

FATHER: *Hmm.*

MOTHER: *Yeah*

DAUGHTER: . . . they're in the position to take it. And then if you're putting it off, you're putting it off because of your own selfish reasons I think

MOTHER: I think that it could be told in such a way that the person could (Pauses) ther cou it would would not be too definite. They may collapse completely but if they said that ahh the-eh-there's a possibility that you may go in two years.

DAUGHTER: Yeah

MOTHER: Then I think it there's still a little hope. I don't know *maybe I'm escaping from reality or something but*

DAUGHTER: *Well, there's always a little hope. Yes, yes, yes, I I think you're right.* All right I think the both actually, there is there's always some hope. No mat no matter how hopeless a disease it is *ther's* always . . .

FATHER: *Hmm*

DAUGHTER: . . . you know there always is some hope.

FATHER: There's a way of telling it too, don't forget. (Pauses)

DAUGHTER: Hmm. (Pauses) But I

FATHER: But I think they should be told.

MOTHER: Okay.

FATHER: Do you agree?

DAUGHTER: (Laughs)

MOTHER: Eh dehh in a modified way.

DAUGHTER: (Laughs)

MOTHER: (Laughs)

DAUGHTER: Oooooooh

MOTHER: It it depends on the person an- and ahh I think that they should have some idea and then

FATHER: (Interrupts) So then you agree that it shouldn't be held off as long as possible. That's the question. Yes or no. Do you think it should be held off as long as possible?

MOTHER: Well where they said as pos long as possible that would give me the idea that ahh it would be held off for a while. (Pauses)

FATHER: It isn't that wasn't the question.

DAUGHTER: Oooohuh

MOTHER: It would be held off for a while and then you would tell them because *or give* them some idea another time

FATHER: *Well*

DAUGHTER: (Interrupts) Yeah, but why are you holding off for as long as possible?

MOTHER: Depending on the person.

FATHER: Why? *Why are you holding out?*

DAUGHTER: *Why though?*

MOTHER: Because they might collapse an-an

FATHER: (Interrupts) So what of it?

MOTHER: I think that eh eh they could be told that perhaps ahh you may only live two years. Perhaps.

FATHER: *All right. . . .*

DAUGHTER: *All right.*

FATHER: . . . Supposing the guy I'm in bed after six months, right? I'm laying down in bed *then you come in and say* . . .

DAUGHTER: *All right then you have to tell them.*

FATHER: . . . you then you'd come in. You'd say to me, well you'd better prepare yourself, you're going out and you should have told me eight months ago. (Laughs) When I could have enjoyed myself.

MOTHER: (Laughs) Well all right I'll tell you an-and and anybody that wants to

FATHER: (Interrupts) Yeah, do you want to be told?

MOTHER: I don't want to make that decision right now. I I don't know.

FATHER: Or do you want to be

DAUGHTER: You just want to

MOTHER: (Interrupts) I'd want to know within a eh want to know a little ahead. I think well, I don't know. I can't

FATHER: (Interrupts) You have to face it.

DAUGHTER: W-well that's it. Some people don't want to *face it.*

FATHER: *Face it.* That's right.

DAUGHTER: The thing is, this is the way I look at it. I think if you told the person they were going to die and they were the type of person that couldn't face it. They wouldn't face it. *The- they'd* just say think . . .

FATHER: *Yeah*

DAUGHTER: . . . the person was *lying* . . .

FATHER: *Yeah*

DAUGHTER: . . . or they would ahh decide well I feel good there's nothing wrong with *me.* . . .

FATHER: *Yeah*

DAUGHTER: . . . you know. But uh all right that that the person has come to this conclusion *themselves see.* . . .

FATHER: *Yeah*

DAUGHTER: It isn't somebody else saying.

MOTHER: Then it could be the same way. I think that the person should be made to realize themselves and let them think it themselves.

DAUGHTER: Yeah, but uhn they should be told

MOTHER: Yes. eh eh

DAUGHTER: And then they can think whatever they please *but at least they've been told.*

MOTHER: *All right, yes, yes, all right.*

This discussion provides a clear picture of the quality of the ongoing argument in normal families. Each person's opinion is seriously taken into account, modifications of earlier opinions occur, and the family concludes with a new judgment of the issue.

In summary, our illustrations of interaction in normal families have attempted to show the observable qualities of the families from which the interaction code findings were drawn. It is clear that there is a variety of relationships and a range of interaction styles within the sample of normal families, yet certain common factors differentiate them from families with schizophrenic patients. While working on a task that requires the exchange of opinions and information, normal family members give each other more positive support and agreement and generally appear to enjoy each other's company. There is laughter, teasing, and joking among themselves. We have pointed especially to the help that family members give to each other when one person is in some way weak. Thus normal families do not appear simply as highly organized, task-focused, serious workers on a problem; they enjoy the problem and each other as well.

The giving and receiving of attention in these families is as the cultural norms would predict: fathers hold the high power position and sons the low, with attention and respect being exchanged between them. Mothers and daughters form an attention coalition in families of daughters. However, within this clearly defined power structure there is a second interesting pattern of control evident in the segments of interaction as well as in the data. All normal family members, including the children, are allowed to directly confront the other members with questions, pressures to change opinions, interruptions, strong arguments, and comments or interpretations about motives and personal interests. Indirection and avoidance of each other are not characteristic qualities of the normal families.

In reading the segments of interaction from the normal families the most striking quality is the degree to which their communication is broken into fragments, incomplete sentences and what appears to the reader to be incomprehensible statements. Yet a second quality is also present; each member seems to be able to respond to the other without a completed idea as a cue. The rate of responsiveness and acknowledgment is high. We have pointed to this high rate of disruptive communication and the high degree of responsiveness as an indicator of the normal family's ability to adapt to constantly changing situations. Sanctions for change are easily interjected into interaction and the continual response to these sanctions results in an ever-changing flow of interaction. This sequence clearly differs from the circular, non-changing argument that the schizophrenic families favor.

Families of Poor Premorbid Schizophrenic Children

In general, poor premorbid schizophrenic families fall between normal families and good premorbids on a large proportion of the interaction variables examined. In the area of expressiveness poors have a medium level of all types of affect and are also medium in the ratio of positive to negative affect. However, they differ more clearly from both normal and good premorbid families in the extent to which they use both positive and negative affect directed toward other family members. When with their patient sons, in particular, the poor families have significantly high rates of support, help, and agreement with other family members as well as high rates of direct hostile attacks on others. Our observations of the poor families reflect the findings from the interaction codes; this concrete form of support of family members as well as overt hostility were often noted. The notes made by observers and by coders add information about the tone, meaning, context, and general function of some of these expressions of interpersonal affect.

The medium level of expressiveness in the poor families, we assumed, functions to avoid more direct involvement of family members with each other; the focus on the narrowly defined "tasks" of giving and asking for opinions about the questionnaire item allowed the poor families, when the patient was present, to skirt the problems that might arise from a more personally engaging discussion. In some of the poor families it seems clear that intellectualized or cliché-ridden conversations are avoiding rather poorly controlled hostility.

For example, in the following family having a poor premorbid schizophrenic son, the son shocked his parents by saying on one questionnaire item that "parents should use strict discipline." This was clearly felt by the parents to be an attack on their own mode of child training which they think is permissive. In the first few minutes of the discussion the mother asked her son, "Do you feel that our discipline has been adequate, Bobby? . . . Well for instance, ahm, would, everytime you're late would you prefer that you got sent to bed without your supper? Or had your (Laughs) b-b-behind warmed or something of that sort?" Very quickly the discussion moved to an intellectualized level that served to avoid further talk about the family's disagreement. Avoidance of each other is even more clearly apparent when it is noted that the father's long speeches were all spoken while his eyes were closed. A segment of this non-expressive discussion follows.

MOTHER: (Interrupts) in the house by eight o'clock every night regardless of what's going on in town and

FATHER: (Interrupts) Because then they'd l-l-learn their responsibility on their own. I think we -we understand that pretty much. A a person has to ahm develop his own wings as a fledgling. He has to learn how to ah (Pauses) make his own decisions. He has to learn the consequences of his own action or or lack of action and uh basically a parent is is around to guide children, supposedly in a sensible direction assuming the parent has more than average amount of sense or at least an average amount of sense. I think that strict discipline though, is ah gone out of style pretty much. Whether it's going to swing back and come r-r-return, I don't know.

MOTHER: Well we agree that there should be discipline ah but it should be ahm ah restrained ah to the extent that it fits the occasion, I suppose you might say.

FATHER: Well incidentally, this is all part of a a a broader social picture too. Because children and and any any adolescents who will shortly become adults are going to be disciplined one way or another by all kinds of external forces whether they like it or not. And if it and if parents don't as indicate that they have to fol follow certain rules and regulations well, society will. And sometimes it will be a very harsh process to have the corners rubbed off you because all of us actually are now (Pauses) being guided by too much discipline. I think our laws are becoming more strict and certainly are ah limitations

MOTHER: (Interrupts) Freedoms **

FATHER: Freedoms

SON: Well I guess I I can go to your side. I I mean I qualified this in my footnotes and ah I wasn't really against uh. I wasn't very very uh for strict discipline in the first place. And ah and like you say, uh take away some of our ee freedom and everything. So I, I ah I like the kind of discipline I get and I guess uh well *we all* agree on the same kind just a

FATHER: (Interrupts) *Well* what the degree is, then.

SON: Ya, the degree of discipline

MOTHER: Okay

FATHER: But one of the best disciplining most most uh universal and widespread universal eh rather ahm disciplinary actions that we all get exposed to is that of uhm a traffic regulation. Every place we have to stop, we have to thirty-five, we have to do this and not do that and so on. It it it's beaten into us from the day we, the minute we walk out of the door in the morning or till we come back in the afternoon or evening. Isn't that true? And we're all we're all conditioned to a certain degree and if a person doesn't at least have a little freedom within his own (Pauses) confines of his own home why I guess he's going to have a pretty miserable life. Well then we agree for the most part that discipline has its place.

Within the context of medium rates of all kinds of expressive acts exemplified in the previous intellectualized task-oriented discussion, the poor premorbid families, especially when the patient child is present, have the greatest numbers of both positive and negative affect acts directed toward other family members. Solidarity and support of other members seem to have a variety of functions and to occur in a variety of forms in the poor families. In some instances it appears in the form of protection of one member, very often the patient child; in others, the positive expressiveness has undertones of hostility; sometimes it is clearly warm and supportive, especially of someone who is in some way "weak." In the selection below both parents use directly supportive statements toward their poor patient son in a way that functions to prevent his continuing to defend his own, from their point of view, "unsupportable" argument, that anyone ("he") could do anything he wants to if he works hard enough.

SON: But, I do say I'm I'm up the top class, I think, as far as intelligence is concerned and I can become probably a intelligent worker some day and get myself a good job. And I believe that ah I can possibly ah do well enough to re to retain a status of of being an educated white collared ah man. And I do believe this cause I think I have the ability to do some of the things but not all of the things. Nobody can do everything.

MOTHER: No, that's right. You know, Jim, *you know the expression that sometimes you use, the early bird, the early bird is the one that catches the worm . . .*

FATHER: *Well now we all agree then. Then we all agree that nobody*

MOTHER: . . . and I - you know, in a way its right. If you work hard enough, Jimmy, and you are gifted and you've got the ability and you work hard at something you want to be and then you do achieve it, Jim. (Pauses)

SON: I think you're right. Ge- I think if I'm not lazy I I will I can accomplish something.

FATHER: Okay

MOTHER: Well

FATHER: Okay, that's it. Ahh

SON: That's it

FATHER: Ahh

SON: What do you think of that one?

MOTHER: Very good, Jimmy.

SON: And I'm not lazy and I'm doing good in school today cause I'm not lazy. *I'm putting the effort in* in school today and I'm not lazy.

FATHER: *You don't have to*
SON: *And I'm doing well*
FATHER: (Interrupts) *Well all right so* (Pauses) Good, Very good.
SON: Isn't that right? You saw my ppapers.
FATHER: Very good. You're doing good school work.

Often, as well as having controlling qualities, these interpersonally positive acts carry with them great ambivalence. For example, one poor
family with a patient son disagreed on the questionnaire item about
whether to send a 4½-year-old child to nursery school even though she
cries each day. After some discussion the patient son found a rather
artificial way of agreeing with his mother; her sarcastic-supportive response
to his agreement is included in the following excerpt.

MOTHER: But the child comes first. If the mother can't give the child
          her time at four and a half, if the child desperately needs it,
          then the mother is not a mother. (Pauses) At that time. We're
          not talking about fifteen, sixteen or eighteen, we're *talking of
          four and a half.*
SON: *Well I'm not qualified to talk on this problem because at least
          sixteen at* sixteen I I at fifteen I remember . . .
MOTHER: *Well then, that, thank you, John. That's very sensible.* . . .
SON: because that was only nine years ago. But I but when at four
          and a half it was much too far back for me to remember.

Poor premorbid families, when the patient is present, have the highest
rates of interpersonally expressed negative as well as positive affect; that is,
more hostility and antagonism are directed toward family members who
are present than in the other families. Noted most often by observers
was antagonism directed toward the patient child. In the same poor family
talking about whether a 15-year-old boy has the right to decide on his own
bedtime, the father overwhelmed both his wife and his son with a barrage
of legalistic, disorganized arguments for his own point of view and then
attacked his son for his lack of courage in standing up for his own opinion.

FATHER: *You see, you're floating around. You see, you have a bad* habit
          of ahh ehh I'm trying to ss- . . .
MOTHER: and *ah Dad ahh*
SON: *You say*
FATHER: You you haven't changed me at all but I apparently *you're
          ahm* . . .
MOTHER: *You can't change Dad and yy and*
FATHER: . . . No, it isn't it isn't a question of changing. He hasn't sub-
          mitted any arguments from my point of view.

MOTHER: (Interrupts) Oh his arguments were good.

FATHER: Www- well I don't know. *That's a matter of opinion.* . . .

MOTHER: *He's had good arguments.*

FATHER: . . . I have I found no good arguments but I asked but he has told me as to why a fifteen year old child should not make the decision as to when he goes to bed **

SON: (Interrupts) Who owns the house? Who pays the bills? Who does all the work? (Pauses) Who brought the child up? Who nursed him? who had to change his diaper? Who had to bear him? *Who had to pay the doctor bills?*

MOTHER: *Well when. Just a minute*

FATHER: *Ahh hav-having* all that in mind, it does not give me a right, or your mother a right at a child when he reaches with all those arduous duties that we have performed ahh for the child ahh the child ahh ahh. I think in my opinion at the age of fifteen should be able to know by then if we if we gave him the proper upbringing as to when to go to bed.

MOTHER: And another thing, when do you think a child should have his own right or his own decision on going to bed?

SON: That is not the question. The question is *when should a fifteen year old*

MOTHER: Ohh.

FATHER: *It's mmm Naw he's avoiding it.*

MOTHER: Ohh all right

FATHER: He's avoiding it and I and *I feel very unhappy* . . .

MOTHER: *Well shall*

FATHER: . . . that you are. I hoped that you'd have the strength and the courage to stand up and say fifteen or fourteen or sixteen or eighteen. You think an eighteen year old boy should be told when he goes to bed?

SON: That's not the question.

FATHER: No, I'm asking you whether it is or it isn't. As long as *you wait*

SON: I'll discuss that with you outside. But while we're va-wasting valuable time and using up somebody's tape recorder and . . .

Another frequent mode of expressing negative affect in poor premorbid families, in addition to direct attacks, as exemplified in the previous excerpt, is in the form of reasonably phrased, calmly stated, but devastating attacks on other's opinions. In the following discussion this mode of "reasonable" argument is clearly apparent. It occurs along with a sequence of acts that were coded as interpersonally directed hostility, which in the coded data are shown to be most often used by poor families. In this sequence the patient son, who originally disagreed with his parents, was subsequently shown by them to be quite wrong in his opinion, began to cry quietly; at this point both his father and mother demanded that he speak up since "they (the experimenters) don't hear the nod of the head." This family is discussing the following questionnaire item.

> The parents of a 14-year-old girl want to buy their daughter a new coat. The girl would like to pick out the coat herself to be sure it is in the same style as her friends wear. Her parents want to get a more practical coat for her, one that will last for several seasons. Should the girl pick out the coat herself, or should the parents have the final word? On this one, Mother and Father said, "Parents should have final word." Son said, "Girl should pick coat herself."

FATHER: That girl's 14 years of age.

MOTHER: Well girls 14 years of age today are pretty well grown up. And they know pretty much what they want. But, on the other hand, they don't have the money in their pockets to pay for these things.

FATHER: Yeah, well but they also want sometimes to go to extremes when they see them.

MOTHER: (Interrupts) They want very extreme ahh

FATHER: (Interrupts) They see things in the paper and *they want them.*

MOTHER: *Something that ahh* they want very extreme styles. Something that ahh perhaps they could only get one season out of, which would be very impractical especially if there's ahh ahh several children in the family. It ahh runs into a good deal of do-re-mi. Now what is your opinion? (Pauses)

SON: Well I felt that the girl was old enough to pick out a coat for herself. (Pauses)

MOTHER: I surely do. If she has earned the money baby-sitting to pay for it, ahh I would think she could go in

SON: (Interrupts) That's what I had in mind.

MOTHER: I would think she could go and ahh get anything she wanted any any foolish-looking thing regardless of whether it looked well or not. I would feel that she could go ahead and get it. But if her parents are sss still buying her clothing at 14, lots of parents are not buying their daughter's clothes at 14, because they are baby-sitting and earning their clothing. Ahh if they have earned the money ahh then I feel they have a right to ahh have the final to have the final say. There again you there has to be some guidance. (Pauses) Ahh you have to try to tell this child ahh how much good she will get out of this sort of thing, and how much good she will get out of another sort of thing, and then let the child to make up their own mind. They must learn to make up their own mind at some time or other. But if a child goes in the store with the parents and decides, Oh I want the $50 coat, ahh ahh and the child is not working, the child is not earning any money to help pay for that coat, and there are other children in the family, I don't feel that that child should have that coat.

FATHER: Especially if it's not a *practical thing*.

SON: *I agree.*

MOTHER: At the expense of ahh perhaps stinting on the food bill or stinting on one of the other children.

FATHER: Well if if the coat was something of real value, could last, you could get a lot of things out of it, very practical, it might pay you because it could be used.

MOTHER: But on the other hand, ahh young young children don't want to wear ah the styles are changing rapidly and they they they don't want to wear things ahh more than one or perhaps two seasons. Therefore you don't put a lot of money into ahh clothing like that because they want a new one. They want a difference. They want a change in style. They never wear things out. They want a change. (Pauses) Ahh this was ahh my reason for answering the question the way I did. Now you go ahead, Jack. (Pauses)

SON: Well I still say the child should be old enough to pick out the coat herself within reason. (Pauses)

MOTHER: Mmmhmm

FATHER: It's old enough to pick it out, there's no question about that

MOTHER: Sure, sure.

FATHER: But it's what what are they picking out. (Pauses) As Mummy said, if they earned everything for themselves, they could do any old thing. Something that'll look foolish as could be and they and they only wear it about twice and don't like it anymore. And they they're stuck with it for the rr for that season. That's all they have. They're stuck with it. Next time they go out and buy something, you can rest assured that they'll ask a little advice before they buy it.

MOTHER: That's right. Because they will learn a lot by that experience.

FATHER: I'm not saying they can't pick out their own. If they they're paying, as Mummy said, if they're payin for it themselves, they can have pp have the final say. But if they're not paying for it themselves then they haven't got the final say. You'd give them a choice and say, there you are, this is free, take your choice. (Pauses) Then they have their own pick. They have their pick, but you've put them in the category that they can have it in. (Pauses) That's why we ss that's why we say they shouldn't the fff say, ahh *to pick out* their own.

MOTHER: You'll have to say something, Jackie. shh nod of the head doesn't go on the

FATHER: (Interrupts) They don't hear the nod of the if ahh

MOTHER: (Interrupts) They don't hear that nod.

SON: I know (Pauses)

FATHER: Well if that's that's the way (Pauses) I look at it and I guess Mummy looks at it the same way. (Pauses)

SON: I guess I'll have to agree.

MOTHER: You don't have to. Umm Umm (Pauses)

FATHER: We didn't say anything about not being able to pick out their own. It all depends upon who how it'd be paid for. If it's their own money they they can pick anything they want if they can pay for it. Because if they make a mistake uhh

SON: (Interrupts) But if the ss but if the parents are payin for it

FATHER: (Interrupts) Then it's up to the pare-

SON: (Interrupts) Then the parents should have the final say.

FATHER: Then it's up to them, not to have the final say. But the parents will put it into a group of perhaps three, and say there are three coats. You can have any one of them. (Pauses) That they've known perhaps they've looked at the coats that the child should wear. L L L L L little L L sort of like this. Maybe this one. Maybe that one. So you say, all right, there's the three, now take your pick. And the and the child still takes his own uhh ddd- decides which one he wants.

SON: Umm hmm

FATHER: All the parents have done was put it into a category and say there it is, that's as far as we'll go with it. (Pauses) And it's what the parents have done is picked out something that's of value, something that looks good instead of some ahh flashy thing that is of no value at all, that

MOTHER: (Interrupts) And something serviceable.

FATHER: That they would pick out. But if they had the money, they can do that. Because they'll never do it again. (Pauses) Maybe help realize how foolish they were, and how messed up they made it everything and how they spent their money for, hard-earned money for nothing. They won't do it the next time.

Next time they'll ask questions. And ahh listen a little bit. (Pauses) So we don't say you can't pick it out. We both, Mummy and I both say you can pick out your clothes. But if you're paying for it, you have all the say, as far as that. But if you're not payin for it we'll put it into a group, then you take your pick from there.

SON: Yeah. (Pauses) I agree with that. (Pauses)

MOTHER: Awright.

Apparent in the preceding segment of interaction is a characteristic mode of argument in the schizophrenic families, a type of "double-binding," about which we will say more later. Briefly, after their patient son has finally agreed with them, the parents discount his agreement by saying "You don't have to agree." This leaves him momentarily confused about what his parents want him to do, until they repeat their argument and make clear by their behavior that there is only one answer that is acceptable.

Moving on to power strategies, we showed that poor premorbid families consistently fall between normal and good in the extent to which direct and indirect person control strategies, such as interruptions and questions, are used. The tendency to use indirect modes of confrontation was evident in relatively low rates of interruptions, as shown by our data, and in other ways as well. In some poor families members spoke in what could be described as a set of successive monologues that were polite, orderly, and rigid, preventing any true confrontation of each other. Avoidance of direct confrontation or attempts to influence others' behavior took the form, in one family, of inability to decide to *stop* talking about a questionnaire item; this family exemplifies Haley's hypothesis that in some schizophrenic families no one is able to take charge in an explicitly defined way. Only after 45 minutes could the family bring itself to stop talking about the first item, and in a way that negated the whole discussion; the patient son, who originally disagreed with his parents ended by saying, "I really agreed with you all along."

Further evidence for the lack of confrontation of family members is shown in several families where one member obviously understood that the other two had misperceived or distorted the questionnaire item, yet he did not interrupt to make a correction. The use of confrontation strategy in order to correct errors was, in contrast, often evident in normal families. Other strategies for avoiding direct confrontations occur in the form of "giving in" before any discussion is possible so that only agreement and restating of the questionnaire item remains.

The fact that personal confrontations, especially in the form of interruptions, are not often used or acceptable in the poor premorbid families is apparent from an examination of the phenomena that occur when these confrontations *are* used. For example, in the following family, when his patient son interrupts to say that he agrees with his father, the interruption is labeled as illegitimate. The family is discussing whether to talk to a stranger on a train; mother and son agreed that this was acceptable and the father disagreed.

MOTHER: I don't think *that they mean*
FATHER: (Interrupts) *I wouldn't*—I don't mind if I was going to talk to them about the weather, or about ah something that we ah might have ah something in common or no or no some ah be able to talk to each other about something in common but ah, just to speak about myself, I don't think I go along with it. I'd just as soon read my newspaper than to start telling her about my ah my own personal business. If I start telling her about my wife, my children, she'll start asking more questions and ah I don't think I want to ah *I don't want to*
SON: (Interrupts) *Well I agree* with my *father.*
FATHER: *Jimmie* ah Jimmy ah - w- we allow each other a *little time to finish here.*
SON: *Oh Oh.*
FATHER: Don't bust in, would you please.
SON: Okay.
FATHER: So I I would rather ah talk (Pauses) talk about things other than myself.

Family members find it difficult or not acceptable to confront other members directly by interrupting them, pressing them for explanations, or seriously taking into account differences of opinion or understanding of the problem being discussed. In fact, in some instances when these attempts occur, as in the previous example, they are negatively sanctioned.

We have shown in the interaction analyses that the patterns of attention giving in the poor families suggest that power structures differ depending on the sex of the patient child. When the schizophrenic son is present there is evidence of a mother–son coalition; when the patient daughter is present she is isolated and is the low-power person.

The mother–son coalition occurs in several forms. One form is as an alliance that acts to force the father to change his opinion rather than simply to isolate him by paying no attention. In another form the poor mother and her son take a large proportion of the interaction time talking to each other, with the mother providing opinions and ideas and the son agreement with her, effectively eliminating the father from the discussion.

In the segment below, in which the latter coalition type is apparent, the family is discussing whether a 20-year-old boy should go with his parents to visit their friends.

MOTHER: Well I I ah definitely agree with Jim, and of course, Jim, ah I'm sure that you realize a lot of times, I mean just so that you could be occupied that you do come with Mother and Dad on the weekend because you don't like to be home alone. During the week naturally you're busy at the hospital and you're surrounded with a lot of people. But if you had friends I'm sure Jimmy that you wouldn't want to drag along with Mother and Dad. Would you?

SON: No I wouldn't. I think that you're a hundred per cent right, Mother.

This sequence of events in which the poor premorbid mother supplies opinions and her patient son agreement with them is a coalition pattern noted often. It appears to function as a control strategy for the patient's mother, who maintains her son's attention and, at the same time, isolates her husband.

Families of poor premorbid schizophrenic daughters contrast with families of sons in that the patient daughter is isolated and a low power member. Isolation was evident in patterns of attention giving and in body movements as well. For example, one observer noted: "The mother seemed reluctant to give much of anything. Even when it came to giving her daughter matches for which the daughter had asked, the mother pushed them only a quarter of the way across the table. When the mother reached to take the cigarettes and matches from her daughter, she reached the entire distance of the table. Toward the end of the experiment, however, when the daughter asked for cigarettes, the mother handed them about three-quarters of the way back." The patient daughter was also effectively ignored by one or both parents' turning away from her as she spoke or their not looking at her as they talked.

The low participation rate of the patient daughter is apparent in one sequence when, even though the daughter disagreed originally with her parents, and might be expected to participate in order to defend or explain her own opinions; she spoke very little until she finally said rather helplessly, "Can I change my mind?"

We pointed out in the discussion of normal families one characteristic power strategy used in resolving disagreements in these families that is strikingly different from the schizophrenic families: in normal families a member's opinions are clearly differentiated from his behavior. The following segment from a poor premorbid family shows how the objective discussion item (about the 20-year-old boy who leaves home without telling his parents where he is going) is restated in terms of this schizophrenic patient's behavior and, without it being made explicit, the son is forced to justify his own behavior rather than his own opinion. The second striking quality of interaction in these families, briefly mentioned earlier, is also exemplified in the same segment. In many families we noted the following pattern: the person who stood alone, in the sense that he disagreed with the other two members, was pressured persistently and strongly to change his opinion on an issue that seemed to be of special importance to him and his family. After being subjected to several strategies of control the isolate finally gave in and agreed with the majority; their response to his agreement was "You don't have to agree." This double-binding strategy when used by parents on their schizophrenic children was then often followed by a disintegration in the child's interaction—sometimes in the form of stuttering, squirming, giggling, or bewilderment. It is important to note that when this strategy is used by the schizophrenic families it is used to control any of the members, not just the patient.

In the poor premorbid family included here both personalization of the original opinion difference and this peculiar double-binding strategy are evident, the latter followed by a further negation by the patient's father who indicates that he really didn't mean what he had been saying all along. (On this item, originally, the mother and son agreed that the 20-year-old son had a right *not* to tell his parents where he was going, and the father disagreed.)

FATHER: Well, that's that's the gist of the question, *come and go as he pleases, for days.*

SON: *Well, I don't think*

MOTHER: *Would you do* that? (Laughs)

SON: *I don't know.* (Laughs) Depends on where I was going.

MOTHER: *I mean,* would you just leave the house without saying anything?

FATHER: *Well look*

SON: No

MOTHER: And not show up?

SON: No

MOTHER: No, well see I don't, Lew, would do

FATHER: (Interrupts) Well, put yourself on on on my side and on your mother's side. You live in one in one household and if you had children that just disappeared, say you had five kids that they were always on the go, and you never knew what they were doing or where they were going.

SON: I'd throw them out of the house.

MOTHER: (Laughs)

FATHER: That's right, you'd get eaten out of the house, you'd you'd do that, right? You'd eat me out of the house, because I say this, the responsibility of a parent ceases when the person goes on his own. Once the person is on his own then then they have a right pretty much to do what they please, but up til up until the time they all live in the same roof, I believe out of courtesy anybody should at least vaguely say, well look, Pop, I'm going here and if it's a good place to go no parent says no, you can't go, and uh that's all there is to it, it's as little as all that.

MOTHER: So well uh so listen.

SON: (Interrupts) I don't believe that for one day that say if the kid just wants to go for a night that he has to tell his parents where he's going. *I didn't tell you where I was going then*

FATHER: *Well say you're* No, I didn't care.

MOTHER: You mean for an evening, not for a night, a full night, *for an evening.*

SON: *Yeah, for an evening.*

FATHER: *Yeah,* No.

MOTHER: All right, Lew, so look it stands to reason when I leave the house I say to Daddy, I'm going here, or I'm going there, right? . . .

SON: Yeah

MOTHER: . . . He does the same thing, so you know where the person is. *I mean to me that's just perfectly natural.*

FATHER: *Isn't it better* Isn't it better than to, than to be shocked into something I mean to get a call in the middle of the night, or two days later and say look, we picked up your son or you been in an accident or *something like that.*

MOTHER: *Oh you're a pessimistic* character

FATHER: I'm not pessimistic, Jean, because you are going to worry until he come home.

MOTHER: All right, so you're going to, naturally you're *going to worry.*

FATHER: *Sure you're going* to worry but why should we worry about it. If he don't worry about it the rightful thing for us to do is to say look we don't want to worry any more, you uh you want to lead your own life and you don't feel as though uh you owe us any respect of any kind, we feel you should pick up your clothes take your clothes and go live on your own. It's as simple as all that . . .

SON: Well

FATHER: . . . then you could do as you please and and a lot of kids do it.
MOTHER: Yeah, but don't tell me you wouldn't worry about it.
FATHER: Sure you'd worry about him.
MOTHER: Well then you wouldn't tell him a thing like that.
FATHER: Well uh, Jean, if it gets to the point that that uh it's going to be on your mind all the time and he's going to be running your life for you uh where where where do you where do you stop at this thing. If he's going to be running your life you can't always let uh people that live under the same roof, just because they are 20 years old, run your own life.
SON: Well I agree partially with that, I agree.
FATHER: *Well I say*
MOTHER: *You don't have to agree, Lew.* (Laughs)
SON: Yuh?
MOTHER: You don't have to agree, Lew.
SON: I'm not agreeing, I know it.
MOTHER: (Laughs)
FATHER: Look, Don't listen to me, Lew, be- because I talk too much sometime, but these are my own personal opinions. I mean as I know that uh good kids do it, so lets face it, it's a natural thing in my estimate.

In the preceding family's discussion there is evidence of blatant distortion of one family member's speech by another person. Although this characteristic was not measured by our interaction codes it was noted by observers and coders. Distortion of both the content of interaction and the original questionnaire items occurred, and usually remained uncorrected. Here the patient son agreed with the implication of his father's opinion by saying "I'd throw them out of the house." His father turned this into, "That's right, you'd get eaten out of the house . . . You'd eat me out of the house . . ." In another poor family, discussing whether to pick up a crying infant described in the questionnaire item as being three months old, the father's original statement was, "I said pick the baby up," while his wife began with "I say definitely not." After talking about what to do, what they had done with their son, and why, and it was clear that neither would change his opinion, the mother suddenly said,

MOTHER: By the way the child is two years old.
FATHER: Ohh (Pauses)
SON: That's not a **
FATHER: *Oh that's different. Yeah.*
MOTHER: Isn't it?
SON: I ahh lost *track of that too.*

FATHER: *Well that's that's different.*
MOTHER: *I think* it's two years old.
FATHER: *Yeah.*
SON: I lost *track of the age, too.*
FATHER: *Oh if it's two years old* I shouldn't think that that *I thought it was an infant . . .*
SON: *That's even more reason for*
FATHER: *. . . I thought* it was an infant.
MOTHER: I think the child is supposed to be *two years old by the way.*
SON: *It's even that's even that's even a stronger ahh*
FATHER: *Two years ohh well* two years old that would be different. *I thought I thought it* was an infant.
MOTHER: No I think it's I think it was two years old. I'm not sure. I think it was two years old.
FATHER: Huh well if it's two years old I'd say let him cry it out. But I thought it was an infant.

In addition to differences in expression of affect and the use of control strategies, our data suggest that the poor premorbid families' interaction style is somewhat less variable than the normal families but not as extremely rigid as the good premorbid families. In the excerpts of poor families we have included it is evident that fragmented speech, interruptions, laughter, and other broken speech patterns are not completely avoided by the poor families. Thus we might predict a medium level of adaptation and a variety of styles of adaptation to new and changing situations.

One common stylistic pattern in the poor families, differentiating them clearly from normals, is the extent to which discussions tend to be circular. An extreme form is one in which each person's opinion is stated in a long, unbroken speech, and these opinions are then restated several times, with the final outcome being no change in opinion but instead another restatement of positions. This circular pattern we would assume would be less likely to occur if the family rules allowed for direct confrontations of members and positive and negative sanctioning at the moment when it would have an effect. The extreme form in which lack of variable communication occurs is shown in the following poor family, in which there is a rigid "taking of turns" and long unbroken statements that have the flavor of formal public speeches.

Some people believe that there is nothing a person can't do or be if he wants, and if he really works hard. Do you agree or disagree?
On this one Mother and Father agreed and Son disagreed.

FATHER: Go ahead, Kent.

SON: Well, uh, the main thing here I think is ability. I think, I think if someone has a lot more ability and intelligence than another person that uh this other person is going to be limited No matter how bad or how hard he tries. If he just doesn't have the intelligence or the ability he's not going to make it as uh high as the other, the next guy that has more ability and more intelligence.

FATHER: Yeah, but do you think

SON: (Interrupts) This is evident in grades in school, A, B, C, and D. (Pauses) The order of awards and merit is based on your grades. Why do some people get higher grades than others? They have more ability. Both the one that gets, that doesn't get the higher grades may work even harder than the fellow that gets gets the highest grade. I know in college there was instances instances like this (Pauses) where a fellow would work ten times harder than the next guy but not get anywheres near as high a grade because the other fellow was just smarter, had more ability.

MOTHER: Well you know I had two uh trains of thought on that also and uh, no matter how how hard some people try they never can make it. They haven't got what it takes. So I think probably I'll go along with Kent's idea there.

FATHER: Well the reason I answered it the way I did was this. Uh, he talks about uh one kid having more ability than another which is true. But I don't think a kid, uh regardless of his ability, reaches for something that he doesn't wish to accomplish. Uhh, I was unfortunate enough not to be able to go to college. It was something I wanted and uh there was only a hairline spread of me not getting a college education through (Pauses) some misfortunate happening. But that didn't hold me back from wanting to go ahead and uh without an education I fell into something which I was happy with and I strived to hit the top and uh I think I come pretty well uh hitting it. I know uh percentagewise I did very well, without patting myself on the back. I don't think an individual growing up will reach out for anything that he is not capable of handling A-1. And surely you can't be successful in doing anything unless it is something you like. If a child is forced into education along the lines of some science we'll say that he (Pauses) is not accepting or would not enjoy, I don't think he'll every be successful at it. Because you've got to enjoy your work or it's impossible.

(Pauses) As far as ability goes, like Kent said, I'll agree with him a hundred percent uh some have it and some don't but I still don't think they'd strive for something they really wanted without getting it if they wanted it bad enough. They surely wouldn't go after a scientist's degree if uh they knew nothing about science and didn't care anything about it because if they like science I know they'd be successful at it and not find it a hardship. This has often come up with the family uh. We've talked over Kent's situation. We don't know to this day whether he accepted the right uh (Pauses) science. He started out with one, we'll say uh was it chemical engineering, Kent?

SON: Electrical

FATHER: No . . .

SON: Oh

FATHER: . . . you you had in mind something else. Chemical wasn't it?

SON: No

MOTHER: *Civil?* Was it

FATHER: *And you changed your mind*

SON: Civil.

MOTHER: Civil.

FATHER: Civil? Yeah, civil engineering. And his brother happened to go into electrical ahead of him and uh I don't know whether that has any bearing on it or not but he at the last minute changed his mind and went into electrical. Whether he should have or not (Pauses) that's beyond me. (Pauses) So we all thought that he was uh very favorable to the idea and that he would be very successful at it cause he could have been successful at anything he handled. Any more?

MOTHER: And, well, no.

Closely related to the poor family's style of communication—its medium rates of disrupted and variable speech—is the poor family members' patterns of responsiveness to each other. It is the poor family and all of its members who have the lowest rates of acknowledgment; that is, members do not take into account the intent or content of other speakers' contributions. Sequences of interaction seem not to follow in any predictable order; there are obvious misunderstandings of levels of meanings or of referents, or, in some instances, there is "acknowledging behavior" in response to communications that are clearly meaningless. Not only is nonresponsiveness a descriptive quality of some of these family patterns, but in some families it is clear how nonacknowledgment is maintained. Certain members sustain the fragmented, unpredictable flow of communication by stopping, through interruptions or other sanctions, any act that attempts to acknowledge. The previous interaction segment in which the son attempted to interrupt in order to agree only to have the fact of his agreement ignored and his action labeled as illegitimate is an example of one mechanism used to maintain nonacknowledgment. In the poor family below nonacknowledgment occurs when the son's statement is distorted by his father so that its intent—to gain a compromise agreement by "meeting halfway"—is completely lost. (Here the family is talking about whether it is better for a committee chairman to get the work done or make sure that people get along well together, with mother and son originally selecting the first alternative and the father the second.)

FATHER: You may have the short end of it an entire scale where people totally disagree with each other. And still something has to be accomplished. It either has to ah a given bill or a given ah (Pauses) motion has to be either carried or lost. Otherwise you'll spend you'll be there for ever. (Laughs)

SON: Well you will you agree that ah there has to be some understanding? 'Cause then ah ah, I think, we could meet half *way here*.

FATHER: *I think it* would be idea, I could ya, I would say so. You could go halfway. I think it would be ideal. I think that all of the work would would go along much more swimmingly. But, where I think that you'd also agree that if you were to ehh have a specific problem and were a member of a committee of eight or twelve that gathered for the first time, and then you discovered that every member on the committee got along very nicely with every other member and was in substantial agreement with the basic principles, I think somebody would make a motion that the there'd be no more meetings and that one person could draw up a draft and then come together the next time and vote on it. What'd you think of that?

A number of qualities of the poor premorbid family found in our interaction code data have been illustrated in the segments of interaction. The way that the poor family deals with the task and with each other seems to be relatively concrete. These families focus on the topic provided in the questionnaire item, in a relatively intellectualized or narrow way, sometimes in a way that seems to defend against hostility or closeness. Their modes of expressiveness are also relatively concrete, with both support and hostility directed toward family members. It is the lack of variety in their affect that differentiates them from normal families, and the relative closeness of members to each other that differentiates them from the goods.

The poor premorbid families generally avoid confronting each other directly by using rigid procedures of interaction and strategies for "giving in" before a conflict comes into existence. Other strategies also functioning to control, which were noted in the family's discussion but not directly measured in interaction codes, were personalization of opinions to the point at which one family member is required to defend his own behavior rather than his own opinion, and is thus more easily forced to agree, and undercutting of the member's agreement once it occurs. These strategies are used within a context of power relationships in which the mother–patient son coalition successfully isolates the father or the father–mother coalition isolates the daughter.

The style of communication in the poor family consists of a medium level of disruption associated with relatively unchanging but constantly restated arguments by the family members. The fact that poor families are lowest in levels of responsiveness to each other may be reflected in the misunderstandings and distortions of communication that we have pointed out. Although the poor family members speak in relatively well formed sentences their understanding of and responses to each other are often tangential and unclear; and, very often, these "errors" in responses remain uncorrected.

The Families of Good Premorbid Schizophrenic Children

As our data have shown, the families having schizophrenic children with good premorbid histories are, on many interaction variables, distinctly different from the normal and poor families. These differences are in large part confined to the good parents' interaction with their schizophrenic child and do not extend to interaction with a well sibling of the patient. One of the major differences is in the area of expression of affect. The discussions of the good families are task-centered and avoid direct expressiveness, a pattern we have suggested to be defensive in function. However, when affect is expressed it is more likely to be negative in quality than positive; thus there is a high proportion of disagreements, critical comments, or negatively toned laughter and joking. Compared to other family types the goods have medium levels of positive affect directed toward other people in the family.

The combination of an instrumental or task focus with a high proportion of all kinds of negative affect suggests that the good family has a controlled and limited discussion, largely concerned with the questionnaire item, interspersed with disagreements and indirect and overt hostility. In some instances narrow focus on the task may defend against hostility and in other instances it appears to be a strategy for controlling expressions of closeness. In the example that follows, the defensive quality of the family discussion is notable, especially in the father's statements, even without the additional information that might come from intonation and pacing of speech. The sarcastic criticism that is expressed is deflected from family members to the questionnaire item and to the situation in which the family finds itself.

The problem that this family has been asked to discuss is the following.

> Mrs. Burns' husband died two weeks ago and since that time she has spent most of her time sitting at home and feeling sad. Her daughter insists that it would be much better right now for her to find things to do and keep busy so that she won't think about her husband's death. Which do you think?
>
> On this one Father said, "Take time to get over his death," Mother and Son said, "Keep busy and not think about him."

MOTHER: Take an example of Ma. Would you want her to be sitting around now? *Or is it better* for her to go off **

FATHER: *Yeah but.* The question is ah ah a question that ah is, it's incomplete. All of the questions are incomplete. They they leave to figure things. So I read into it something else than *perhaps* . . .

MOTHER: *Mmm*

FATHER: . . . naturally I expect her to sit around and do something, not just bite her fingernails or something like that. But ah do something seems to ah, I can't remember the question but it ah was the idea that ah go right off and try to completely forget. That's ridiculous and *that's why* . . .

MOTHER: *She had been sitting around for some time anyway*

FATHER: . . . *that's what* I mean. As far as I'm concerned the question is such that ah ah I could have answered it the other way and it wouldn't have *made any* difference to me . . .

MOTHER: *Mmm*

FATHER: . . . as far as I'm concerned. Because the wording of the question is such that you cannot forget. It says *to forget* . . .

MOTHER: *Mmm*

FATHER: . . . and and that's ridiculous so you just let a person take time to *forget* . . .

MOTHER: *Mmm*

FATHER: . . . and at the same time you expect that they're doing something. Ah you're never possibly as far as I'm concerned could

go right out and do something to completely forget. Now sure
it should possibly help to ah be doing something. But ah the
question was such that I read it to be ah ah rather than try to
make a complete effort to completely forget, take time to *forget that's all.* . . . .

MOTHER: *Mmm*

FATHER: . . . Just take it easy and I think that's exactly what happened
with Marilyn ah and ah

MOTHER: Well Marilyn now even though she's out of work she's perhaps
has to ride by the cemetery every day so she's not forgetting
even though she went out to work.

FATHER: Oh no, you can't forget. That's the point. I mean the word to
me ah such that *no matter* what you do you could have
answered it the . . .

MOTHER: *So we really*

FATHER: . . . and it would have been the same as regards agreement.

MOTHER: How about you? Do you think we agree on that set up?

SON: Well, having something to do would take her mind off the death
naturally. I mean it wouldn't take it off completely but it
would help I think.

MOTHER: Yes, I think we're about in agreement on that. That was more
or less a

FATHER: Well the fact I answered it differently is simply that ahh to
me the act of forgetting is going to take a long time and it
also is going to take or it is not going to take place automatically by trying to do something else. *That's the* reason . . .

MOTHER: *Hmmm*

FATHER: . . . I answered it that way.

MOTHER: Then we agree on that, so raise your hand **

FATHER: *Heh heh you agree that I'm right then . . .*

MOTHER: *No.*

FATHER: . . . *but* I don't say that *I am.*

MOTHER: *No. No.*

FATHER: . . . *These are opinions.* That's another thing ah in answering
here. It was opinion and ah attitude and things of that nature.

MOTHER: It's more or less the understanding.

Note, for future comparison with his own well sibling, that the patient
son in this discussion speaks only once and that speech is to affirm his
original opinion.

When negative feelings are expressed directly in good families they appear in the form of disagreements about the questionnaire item with

fewer critical comments about other family members than found in the poor families. Disagreement with the opinions of others is rather polite, restrained, and task-focused. Ideas, not people, are attacked. In the following family the good patient son's argument about whether to bring a bed-ridden grandparent into the home is in clear disagreement with his parents' opinion, yet it is treated with a lack of personal involvement that differs from the direct and pressing arguments that the poor families use. In fact, when there is a chance for the argument to become personalized and direct, the patient son as well as his father makes a clear differentiation between ideas and past occurrences.

FATHER: Another thing too. When I looked at that question was that eh there were young children in the house. And *if you have an older person* . . .

MOTHER: *And that's*

FATHER: . . . that's sick in there it's a lot that'll upset your children too.

MOTHER: Upset everybody eh where there's children, if there's not children

FATHER: I mean you're tryin' to keep the children quiet and so forth.

SON: I don't, this is another thing, but I don't unhh I don't think children should be hidden from this type of thing.

MOTHER: What do you mean?

SON: I don't think they should be protected.

MOTHER: From what?

SON: From things like this. Havin' a elderly lady or man that is ill.

MOTHER: Well you never were.

SON: Pardon?

MOTHER: You never were.

SON: No, but

MOTHER: What'da you mean? I don't

SON: (Interrupts) I'm not makin', well let me finish

MOTHER: Unhh. (Pauses)

SON: I think children are hidden from too many things in this world. I'm not, I'm not voicin' my opinion of what *I would happen to me.*

MOTHER: Ya. Ya.

SON: These are my thoughts. (Pauses) I think it would do more good for a child to see that the mother is helpin' the grandmother than it would be for—for a child—Children aren't the same age. Maybe it would be all right for one but with some a little

<table>
<tr><td></td><td>older. To see the sick person all alone. This is just the impression that I get.</td></tr>
</table>

MOTHER: To see the sick person what?

SON: Livin' alone. I know every time y you went away, I always wanted to stay with Grampy. And he always said, "No." But he was always happy that I came. Cause it kept him gave him somethin' to do all day instead of just sittin' around.

MOTHER: But but he wouldn't have come down to the house. Emh Gordon. I asked him to the first time.

SON: Well he didn't want me to go up there either.

MOTHER: Well I couldn't.

SON: But I still went.

MOTHER: Ya, how could I force

SON: (Interrupts) Well I'm not sayin' ya

MOTHER: (Interrupts) No. But I'm just sayin'

SON: (Interrupts) force somebody

MOTHER: But how could you. *If they didn't* that's what this says

SON: *You can't.*

MOTHER: *I*

SON: *Didn't* say anything about forcing.

MOTHER: No. That's right.

SON: You can't force a person but you can sternly appeal.

FATHER: See that's your viewpoint Gordon. Not and the other is ours eh and

SON: (Interrupts) I'm not arguin'

FATHER: No I I and I we're not arguin but we're basin' on how far away does our parents live from you and the necessity of keepin that parent healthy, right? You can keep a parent healthy. What I mean -healthy is is keep goin' all the time and the proper attention tha you know they're sick. It's accordin' how close you live to them.

We have pointed out the good family's characteristic lack of positive affect, particularly their low rates of interpersonal support. One way the good family maintains its task focus is to avoid coming to grips with the fact that family members truly disagree or have different opinions that must be resolved. When the original disagreement is denied or not recognized, there is no need for one member to approve or disapprove of another member's opinion in the course of attempting to get him to change his opinion. Another strategy for maintaining low rates of positive affect is apparent in the brief segment from a family discussion included below. Here, when the father clearly approves of his son's statement and says so, this support is effectively stopped and, in a sense, the whole sequence is denied importance, by the mother's lack of acknowledgment and her switch to another topic. Over a period of time it thus might be expected that being nonresponsive acts as a negative sanction against many forms of closeness.

MOTHER: *Ya.*
SON: along with the other thoughts . . .
MOTHER: Yeah
SON: . . . (Pauses) My goal is hap- happiness, with my family. (Pauses) That's my biggest goal.
FATHER: That's a good goal. (Pauses)
MOTHER: I know that last one question. I've forgotten what it was ** the next to the last and the last one, I had a terrible time answerin' them.

Although the good families generally limit themselves to the task or instrumental area with little expression of affect and particularly avoidance of interpersonally supporting or directly antagonistic statements, this pattern occurs only when the patient child is actually present. When the well sibling is present goods are, in general, not different from the normal families. The change, particularly the change in rates of personally directed hostility, is traceable in part to the behavior of the good patient's well sibling, who seems to be able to express the negative feelings that the other family members cannot express. Compare the well sibling's active, disagreeing, and sometimes attacking role in the following discussion with his own patient brother's passive agreement in the segment in pages 252–253. The family is talking about the following problem.

> Mrs. Collins is taking Peter to kindergarten for the first time. Peter says that he wants to wear his old cowboy hat. Mrs. Collins would like to let him wear it since he wants to, but she knows that the other children will be dressed in their best clothes and she'll be embarrassed in front of the other mothers if he wears the old hat. Should she let him wear it, or not?
> On this one, Mother and Father said, "She should let him wear it." Son said: "She should not let him wear it."

FATHER: (Laughs) I don't
SON: (Laughs)
MOTHER: Now get yourself out of that.
FATHER: (Laughs) I don't even remember it.
MOTHER: Why should he wear it?
SON: What difference does it make if he wears a cowboy hat or not?

She's worried about what the others will think.

MOTHER: Well that's why we said

SON: (Interrupts) Who cares if what the others think (Laughs) for crying out loud? *It would make no difference at all.* It ahh I

FATHER: *Well a funny thing Freddy* (Interrupts) It would make the kiddo stand out like a sore thumb *right from the start and this would*

SON: *So what? So what?*

MOTHER: (Interrupts) Well I thought we were the ones that agreed that he could wear it. You and I agreed that he could wear it and Freddy *ahh said . . .*

FATHER: *Yeah*

MOTHER: . . . that he coul- he shouldn't wear it.

FATHER: And ahh

SON: (Interrupts) Oh no. No. I said he could, and you said he shouldn't. (Pauses) I said it would all it was all right if he wore it.

FATHER: Yeah. *And we say . . .*

SON: *And you said*

FATHER: . . . No.

SON: Yeah.

FATHER: And that's why I say he would stand out like a sore thumb and *he would he would be tagged now.*

MOTHER: *It's like if you wanted to wear something* to that prom the other night and we know that you shouldn't wear it.

SON: It's not something like that. The kid is a lot younger.

MOTHER: I know but it's *a comparison . . .*

FATHER: *But it's his first day at school, Freddy.*

MOTHER: *. . . it's a comparison . . .*

SON: *No. It's no sort of a comparison.*

MOTHER: *. . . It's* the first prom. You went to it ahh

FATHER: (Interrupts) No. Wait a minute *now. You get* ahh forget the prom there. . . .

SON: *No. It wasn't*

FATHER: . . . Don't get it off onto a tangent. Get it back into the kindergarten. He's going to school for the first time. Now ahh he's he's had his own way and now he's coming into a situation where he is not *going to have his own way.*

SON: *Who said, it didn't say anything,* who said anything about having his own way?

MOTHER: He has to *conform. When he goes to school.*

Not only are good families different in their expression of affect, they also use power strategies in ways different from normal and poor families, but only when the patient child is present. Patterns of attention control suggest a mother–patient son coalition in which the father is isolated but attending to his wife in the families having female children the patient daughter is isolated both from her father and her mother. These family members also avoid direct confrontation of each other as if to retain a rather precarious family system that might fall apart or explode if members engaged each other in a personally involving discussion.

When we examine the coalition patterns in the good families it is apparent that these may result from several different types of relationship. The mother–patient son coalition in families of sons, for example, in some instances reflects a differentiation of mother–son roles, with the mother providing opinions, ideas, and suggestions, and the son providing agreement with his mother's contributions, while the father is passive and ignored. Further, in some families the isolation of the father from his patient son appears to be a result of the father's lack of acknowledgment of his son's attempts to pay attention to him. Each time the patient son tries to speak to his father, his father interrupts, changes the subject or does not hear. Thus, he is the isolate in the triad; the father takes an active role in maintaining his isolation. In other instances there is a protective attention of the mother for her son that also succeeds in isolating the father. The following excerpt exemplifies this latter pattern; here the father and son agreed that a 20-year-old boy should be pressured to spend time with friends his own age while the mother said, "Let him come with his parents as long as he wants to." A large segment of the discussion is carried on between mother and son, with the father simply observing.

MOTHER: Well on that one I figure sometimes I was the one who disagreed, right?

SON: Yeah.

FATHER: Usually.

MOTHER: I (Laughs) you just cut it out. I ah figure that you co- supposing somebody ah let them come but don't pressure them —but try to ah get them to ah go with other people and ah (Pauses) ah make friends. But not pressure them because if he really wants to come well then you'll probably do him more harm than good by pressuring him. Right? (Pauses)

SON: Ah I believe the kid's—you know—how old is he?

MOTHER: You have to talk up, honey.

SON: How old is the guy?

MOTHER: Twenty.

SON: He should be getting out with groups his own age.

MOTHER: He should be. Yes. We understand that part.

SON: I should—I would—if I was the parent I would try to pressure him because in later life he'll need these friends.

MOTHER: But I don't figure you can pressure anybody, Davie. You can't force. Pressure is force. And you can't really force get much out of forcing somebody. You could force somebody to go to a dance but they're not going to have a good time. Right?

SON: Yeah. But I would still p-pressure him that you know to get in with a group his own age. *Because* it's not good to have him to mix with older people.

MOTHER: *Nope. Right.*

SON: *He should*—should mix with his own age.

MOTHER: But don't you think the word pressure is a little bit ah—the word was pressure, Davie.

SON: Yeah. (Pauses) I wouldn't say pressure though.

Families of daughters with good premorbid histories fall into a very different pattern of power relationships. Here the patient daughter is effectively isolated from both of her parents. Examination of the good families in order to understand how this isolation occurs suggests that in some instances parents simply monopolize the amount of talking time available; in other instances the isolation of the daughter is an active process constantly attended to by one or both parents. The daughter is interrupted, talked over, not heard, questioned when someone else is talking, or overwhelmed with questions that allow no time for an answer. The following segment of a good family's discussion with their patient daughter is an extreme example of this active mode of isolation.

Mrs. Johnson's mother is a widow who is now bedridden and needs someone to take care of her. Mrs. Johnson is thinking of having her mother come to live with her. However, she has three children at home who are still in school and she wonders if it might be better for her mother to go into a nursing home. Which do you think she should do? On this one: Father said, "Have her mother come to live with her." Mother said, "Have her mother go into a nursing home." [3]

FATHER: Did you get that question, Ann?

DAUGHTER: What? No.

MOTHER: You know actually ahh this ahh relates to that one about whether to go to Florida or not, I think, (Pauses)

[3] This good patient daughter answered only a small proportion of the questionnaire items; for this reason some items were used on which only disagreement between parents was available.

DAUGHTER: What was the question *it again?*
FATHER: *Why?* In what way?
DAUGHTER: *What was it again?*
MOTHER: *Well* What?
DAUGHTER: Wha-what was it again?
MOTHER: The question was this ahh Mrs. Johnson's *mother* isn't well . . .
DAUGHTER: *(Sighs)*
MOTHER: . . . And she needs somebody to take care of her. Should Mrs. Johnson take her to her home where she has three little children to take care of or should she send the mother to a nursing home?
FATHER: What do you think, Ann?
DAUGHTER: (Pauses) (Sighs) ** (Pauses) Well ** it seems to me what to really feel you need the grandmother
FATHER: *Well but ahh*
MOTHER: *To know you'd see the three children?*
DAUGHTER: *Because if*
FATHER: (Interrupts)No. The children are at school so they're not at home, Ann. *They're school* children. . . .
DAUGHTER: (Sighs)
FATHER: . . . So they're away all day. What do you think about that? If they're *away all day?*
DAUGHTER: ** (Sighs) (Sighs) Well I was
FATHER: (Interrupts) It won't be noisy so *much of the day,* will it?
MOTHER: *Hmmm?*
DAUGHTER: (Pauses) Uh uh uh, when it is your mother? When it's her mother **
MOTHER: What?
DAUGHTER: (Pauses) When it is her mother.
MOTHER: Where is her mother?
DAUGHTER: We- well, well, it is her mother. Well, well, it is her mother.
FATHER: It is her mother. *That's right.*
MOTHER: *Yes.* And she should take care of her. Is that it? What what do you mean, Ann?
DAUGHTER: (Pauses) Well (Pauses) well well she ahh (Sighs) she ** if she if she um maybe she should have her *if she can't,* she can't, she can't
MOTHER: (Interrupts) *Well I agree, we agree.* But ahh ahh but if possible if it isn't going to be working a hardship on her and her family that it is far better to bring the mother into the home and have her in the family and ah take care of her.

Although this segment of interaction provides evidence for the parental modes of isolation of their patient daughter it is also quite evident in some of the good female families that the patient daughter has developed other, much more subtle strategies for control. For example, in the previous family the patient daughter effectively controlled her parents by consistently asking her mother to repeat the questionnaire item just read; in the one instance when her father attempted to repeat the item, rather than the mother, she followed his repetition with, "What was that again?" in a way that forced her mother to repeat the item once more. The part that the patient daughter may play in the sequence of interaction must therefore not be minimized simply because she is not a member of the high-participation, reciprocal-attention coalition.

The second control strategy we have investigated—person control—clearly distinguishes between the good premorbid families and others. Goods avoid the use of interruptions and tend, instead, to use indirect strategies such as questions. The lack of interruptions and simultaneous speech in the good families implies also a more ordered, rigid mode of interaction. Instead of directly confronting others when there is a problem to be solved, as there is in the experimental situation, good families tend to use other strategies for resolving conflicts.

The lack of direct confrontation and the substitution of questions are evident in the following section of a good family's discussion. Here the rather polite, controlled interaction results in somewhat longer, more complete speeches, more pauses, and a clearer sequence in the task-focused discussion. It should be compared with the normal family's high rates of interruptions and direct confrontations of each other, shown in the segment on pages 221–222.

The family is discussing the following questionnaire item.

> Mrs. Rogers wants to send her 4½-year-old girl to nursery school. The little girl is afraid to be with the other children unless her mother is with her, and she has cried each time Mrs. Rogers has left her at the school. Do you think it is better to send her to school even though she cries about it, or would it be better to wait until she's older?
> And on this one, Mother and Father said, "Better to wait until she's older." Son said, "Better to send her to school."

MOTHER: They're outnumbered. (Pauses) No, I vote I I wrote the first one and 'rased it I'm pretty sure. And then changed it and the only reason I changed it was because if it was going to school they would have to anyhow. But where it was nursery school what's the harm, they're little, in keepin' em home one more year?

FATHER: Well if I had thought that out a little more I might've changed my mind too. Because one thing on on nursery school is gettin' along with other other children, which I didn't think about when I answered th when I answered the question. Gettin' out and gettin' with other kids and eh gettin' away from their parents for a for a short time. Durin' the day and gettin' with other people. I didn't even think of that. I might've checked it the other way. (Pauses) What were your feelings on that, Gordon, when you answered?

SON: Unh well my main feeling was (Pauses) it doesn't matter that much if a child does go to nursery school.

FATHER: No, it isn't *the idea of* going to school.

MOTHER: No.

SON: But ah I mean even the idea of mixing with it doesn't matter at that age that much. She has enough love at home and she she's not grown up enough to go out yet if if the decision was made. But the family did make a decision, too, to send the child to nursery school. So they went to nursery school. And she started cryin' and the the thought that came into my mind was ah

FATHER: Upset?

SON: No. Anything anything ups this is this is an important age. (Pauses) and she kind of cried her way out of it. You see what I mean?

MOTHER: Oh, you thought she cried to get her own way.

SON: Well she she cried cause she didn't like it but she got her own way (Pauses)

FATHER: Well, well, the question was whether the mother should take her out or leave her in, so *she really* didn't get her own way . . .

SON: *Right.*

FATHER: . . . until you answer the question, right?

SON: Right.

FATHER: So ah (Pauses) anhhnh well of course, you're right then at a at a kid like that at that age, if they don't like somethin' they'll cry to get out of it.

MOTHER: Hmmm. But like take Judy's sister now. ** Ah Marion started kindergarten Lexington. They, do they have to go? They don't have to go, do they?

SON: Yes. Lexington.

MOTHER: Well anyhow she started kindergarten. At least for three weeks that child has cried cause she has gone every place with Judy. To church—you know Judy's in everything down. Just like that one it was only a twenty year old, this was the four year old. Every place with Judy. Meetings, this place, that place. At least three weeks she's cried. I said why don't you let her stay home a day and see what she says. She's been home with supposedly a cold. Now if that wasn't public kindergarten going into the first grade—if that was just a nursery school, would you put up with it? I mean put the child up through it? Wouldn't it make the child feel that you disliked him, you were trying to get rid of him? Where it won't a necessity, you were only doin it for your convenience?

SON: Eh what the question wasn't that this woman was doin' it for her own convenience. I read into it like I said. This was the decision made that they thought was best for the child.

MOTHER: Ya, but how is it

In the good families direct power strategies such as interruptions are seldom used. This raises the question of how these families resolve the conflicts between members that must arise from time to time. If direct confrontations are not allowed, have the good families developed other mechanisms for satisfactorily resolving or avoiding the differences between members? Several strategies that avoid personal confrontation were evident in family discussions. In some families the "conflict" was quickly redefined as a "mistake" as in the following discussion.

Some parents feel that obedience and respect for authority are the most important virtues children should learn. Do you agree?
On this one mother and son disagreed. Father agreed.

MOTHER: I remember that.
FATHER: Well
SON: What was the question again?
FATHER: The question is obedience.
SON: Yeah
FATHER: To parents
MOTHER: Authority
FATHER: And authority is one of thef- is the fundamental virtue that anybody could have. In other words, everything is based on obedience to parents *and law.*
SON: (Laughs)
MOTHER: Do you remember—that was the one that I che I checked *by mistake wrong.*

FATHER: *You checked that* one wrong.

MOTHER: and ah then we had to ahh ah I *I made a mistake.*

FATHER: *Well if you agree* that ah obedience is the prime virtue that *anybody could have*

MOTHER: *Well does he? Does he or not?*

FATHER: *I'm asking him* eh *I'm as*

MOTHER: *Hmm*

FATHER: Do you agree that that's true? I

SON: (Interrupts) Yes.

FATHER: Well then why did you say "no"?

SON: Did I say "no"?

MOTHER: *Hmmm. You said "no". Your mother checked it wrong too.*

FATHER: *You must have you must have ah* you may have checked it wrong. You may have read the question wrong. *But I mean if you don't have a* you have to have obedience.

MOTHER: *I mean you have to have authority*

FATHER: Obedience is *fundamental.*

SON: *I thought you,* I thought you *checked it.*

MOTHER: *No, was y- you and me.*

FATHER: *I agreed* that that's the quest, that *that was right.*

MOTHER: *I had checked it wrong* last *time, Jimmy.*

SON: (Laughs)

FATHER: *Mummy* checked it wrong. You chec—you either checked it wrong or you didn't agree, *one or the other.*

MOTHER: *I mean you have to-* you have to be

SON: (Interrupts) I must have checked it wrong then.

FATHER: (Interrupts) But the idea is that obedience has to start, you have to have obedience for parents, *law* and church.

SON: *Law*

FATHER: And I mean becomes church is *first* . . .

SON: *First.*

FATHER: . . . because it governs the home. The home is there because it governs the respect for outsiders. And I mean

MOTHER: (Interrupts) Well church and law is the same because if you break an- either law against the church it's also a law -practically always a law against

FATHER: (Interrupts) Well law is well I mean if you didn't have any laws what would you have? *You'd have nothing.*

SON: *You—you'd have ah*

FATHER: You'd have a—you'd have places like the—well

SON: You'd have places like Puerto Rico. An not like Puerto Rico ah

FATHER: Well you'd have, you have Japan when when the students up uprise when they're when all the those, *see . . .*

MOTHER: *Yeah. I mean there has to be authority . . .*

FATHER: *. . . that's that's the ah that's the biggest thing today is lack of obedience towards laws. . . .*

MOTHER: *. . . And there has to be obedience.*

FATHER: *. . .* I mean you settle your differences through sitting down and and arguing. Or have somebody else go through with you find you can find a way to overcome an ah an unjust law. You can always find a way to overcome it. But if you in itself disagree and won't obey authority you you'll break this law first, then you'll break another one, then then you'll lose *respect for . . .*

SON: * *

FATHER: *. . .* somebody else. So therefore its law, *obedience,* that's all.

SON: *So ah*

MOTHER: But I checked that wrong last time.

SON: I think I did too.

FATHER: Okay. Raise your hand.

Another strategy used to resolve conflicts in a way that avoids the recognition of the conflict itself is a specialty of some of the good families. In the following family, several times, disagreements were resolved by explicitly allowing one or two members to make the decision because of their assumed experience in that area; the disagreeing member abdicated any influence he might have by saying "I've never been in that situation," or "You know more than I do about that." For example, in the following excerpt, when discussing whether obedience and respect for authority are the prime virtues to teach a child, one good patient daughter tries to avoid confronting her parents with her disagreement by abdicating her position; however, her parents prevent her from giving in too soon.

FATHER: *You're not in ahh pa-par* you're not ahh you're not *running a home* like a prison. . . .

MOTHER: *Undisciplined*

FATHER: *. . .* You're, there are certain requirements that a child has to meet. (Pauses) You try to teach them what's right and what's wrong. (Pauses) And they refuse to learn the difference and you know they're going to be undisciplined at all times. (Pauses)

MOTHER: They have to know right from wrong and ahh and being-disciplined ahh is a little along that line too.

FATHER: In other words if a parent is wrong, the child shouldn't turn around and say you're wrong, I'm right, regardless. (Pauses)

MOTHER: When you're very young you see we *don't know about the age.*
DAUGHTER: *I can't say. I I'm not* married so I don't know *what I hi how how can I say what I'd be like if I w- I'm well I was never a mother* . . .
MOTHER: *It's really hard to ahh. Another thing is we don't know what age.*
DAUGHTER: . . . so I don't know (Laughs) *wh- how I'd be* . . .
MOTHER: *I know it.*
DAUGHTER: . . . *It's hard to say where I'm not a married* person . . .
MOTHER: *You see it's hard to say.*
DAUGHTER: . . . *See if* I was a married person with children of my own . . .
MOTHER: *Mmm.*
DAUGHTER: . . . I could get a give a better opinion *because I'd know* . . .
MOTHER: *I know it.*
DAUGHTER: . . . How I am and *not how ahh to say* . . .
MOTHER: *That's right.*
DAUGHTER: . . . how I would be is silly because you don't know how you're going to act in a situation. You can only surmise. And I don't think I'd be that strict. So I. *Well raise your hand* . . .
FATHER: Well
DAUGHTER: It's all *over* (Laughs) . . .
FATHER: Well all over, I guess.
DAUGHTER: Dead issue. (Laughs)

To this point we have examined the good premorbid families' power relationships and their modes of expressing affect. Our data have also shown that good families have clearly distinguishable styles of speech and levels of responsiveness. The families of good male patients follow the most rigid and precise patterns of speech, with few broken sentences, a low rate of interruptions, and least use of laughter and other tension release mechanisms. However, although good families speak in ordered and predictable ways, they are, at the same time, less responsive to other members' communications than are normal families. Lack of acknowledgment of others in the context of a "ritualistic" style suggests that each good family member tends to make clear and organized speeches that are not related to the speeches of the others. If this is the case then we would expect that there are only limited possibilities for affective sanctions and thus for adaptation or change; the course of the good family's discussion might consist simply of a series of restatements of original opinions, with no member altering his opinion on the basis of what has gone before. We have pointed several times to the possible defensive functions of these communication styles.

The same patterns of findings are shown for families of good premorbid daughters with the exception of the precise and rigid speech styles. The families of good female patients tend to have high rates of disrupted, disorganized speech. Thus they use laughter, pauses, and other tension-release mechanisms to the extent that the flow of interaction is more difficult to predict. Their patterns of responsiveness are the same as in the male families.

We have already included segments of good families interacting that exemplify the long, unbroken speeches that are associated with the avoidance of direct confrontations. This pattern is particularly true of families of sons, such as the one in pages 261–263. One common correlate of this ritualistic pattern in good families is a rigid and circular argument in which no member changes but opinions are simply restated until, for example, an "appropriate" amount of time has been filled. In the following segment taken from a good family interacting with their well daughter this kind of non-changing argument is evident; very few new interpretations or ideas are added and the three family members finish their discussion with opinions similar to those with which they began. One characteristic of these circular arguments is the observer's inability to predict when the discussion will end; the rules for ending in some of the schizophrenic families appear to be unrelated to the member's change of opinion or the family's state of agreement.

The family is discussing the following problem.

You are traveling on the train by yourself when a middle-aged woman sits down next to you and begins to talk about her trip and ask questions about you. Would you talk to her about yourself or would you begin to read your newspaper so she would stop talking to you?

Here, mother and daughter said, "Talk to her about yourself." Father said, "Read your newspaper."

DAUGHTER: (Laughs)
MOTHER: That's right, that's typical.
DAUGHTER: (Laughs)
MOTHER: Shall we talk?
FATHER: You can talk.
DAUGHTER: (Laughs)
FATHER: But why would you say ah talk about yourself.
DAUGHTER: She's probably lonely and she is, I don't know.
FATHER: Well you can pick up *any subject* and asking about yourself
DAUGHTER: (Laughs)
MOTHER: Well she's went on a trip and she's gonna ask us ask me if I enjoyed my trip, I'd be so happy to tell all about the trip and
DAUGHTER: *I don't think she*

FATHER: *Well then you assume* she was gonna ask you one personal question

DAUGHTER: *Well maybe she actually*

MOTHER: *Ah I thought the questionnaire* said that she's gonna ask me about my trip.

FATHER: She's gonna ask you about yourself.

DAUGHTER: She's gonna ask you about yourself.

MOTHER: Oh. I'd be glad to tell her.

DAUGHTER: Cause you're never going to meet her again. I mean she's going away and

FATHER: Oh you'd be surprised how small the world is. I mean she's liable to turn right up in your parlor the next night.

DAUGHTER: *So it*

MOTHER: *Oh well,* no if she'd ask me questions about myself I'd say I was the mother of five children and ah the house we lived in. I don't see *harm to. Then I'd tell about the baby and everything. . . .*

DAUGHTER: *There's plenty of times I've been on the bus and they've come up to me and start talking to them.*

MOTHER: . . . Oh no I'd be too happy to talk about it.

FATHER: Well, I I didn't mean that I, I'd deliberately start reading the paper. But I'd pass a nice piece of hello, how are you, and about the trip and ah before I'd get involved about ah *about . . .*

MOTHER: (Laughs)

DAUGHTER: (Laughs)

FATHER: . . . how many lumps of sugar I take in my coffee or something. I'd just read my paper.

MOTHER: Well you're a man. I think (Laughs) *you're women* (Laughs)

DAUGHTER: *Yes. Me and Mom like to talk anyways.* (Laughs)

FATHER: Nah.

DAUGHTER: We like to talk anyways **

MOTHER: (Laughs)

FATHER: Well I, I can see that you ah you'd talk about yourself awhile. Whether you're married or not married, whether you're enjoying the trip, why you're taking the trip but ehh if it cut ah into a personal ah (Pauses) question game, I, I, I just as soon read my paper.

MOTHER: (Laughs)

DAUGHTER: I wouldn't read my paper. I'd bring up another subject.

MOTHER: I would too. *I'd* change the subject on to . . .

DAUGHTER: *Yes*

MOTHER: I'd do that anyway when someone

DAUGHTER: (Interrupts) Cause you don't want to answer the question, just talk about something else. Yeah (Laughs)

FATHER: Well it's really gonna depend how you feel on that day.

MOTHER: (Laughs)

FATHER: Some days you just pick up your papers and reading ehh. You don't feel too much about talking about yourself or anything else. I agree then that you talk about yourself to a certain extent.

MOTHER: Mmm hmm.

DAUGHTER: Yeah. (Pauses) (Laughs)

FATHER: And then would you, would you answer personal questions?

MOTHER: Well what's what's *person what personal* what would be a personal question? . . .

DAUGHTER: *Yeah, what's personal question?*

MOTHER: . . . What would you say?

DAUGHTER: I mean what she doesn't know you, what could she

FATHER: (Interrupts) Beyond the questions of hello and how are you, are you married and you

MOTHER: (Interrupts) well what else? I mean she's a stranger.

DAUGHTER: (Interrupts) She doesn't know anything about you. What could she ask you? (Pauses)

FATHER: Well I don't know what she could ask me. I don't know what

DAUGHTER: (Laughs)

MOTHER: I'd just as soon talk to her

DAUGHTER: Sure, yeah I'd talk to her (Pauses)

FATHER: (Pauses) O.K. *We agree on that you talk* to the girl.

DAUGHTER: (Laughs)

MOTHER: Shall we raise our hand now?

DAUGHTER: (Laughs)

FATHER: Yeah, you can raise your hand.

DAUGHTER: (Laughs)

MOTHER: (Laughs)

This pattern of the continued restatement of original opinions without alteration or revision is common in good families. Also, although the good families, when interacting with their patient children, generally have patterns of ordered, coherent, relatively rigid speech, in some instances it is apparent that the clear style still allows very fragmented, unclear meanings. The incoherence of the content may, in turn, account for the lack of responsiveness or acknowledgment of one member to another; it is impossible to respond clearly to a statement that is unclear in itself, although grammatically well structured.

In some instances the relatively infrequent responsive statements appear to be used as a reward, especially to the other members of one's own coalition. The use of nonacknowledging statements as control strategies was apparent, also, in the family segment in pages 259–260, where the patient daughter was effectively discouraged from stating her opinion because what she had to say was not recognized or paid attention. Lack of responsiveness in some good families takes the form of "not hearing"; as an observer of one good premorbid family, present with their patient daughter, noted, ". . . this family showed the degree of disorganization that must be present just below the surface of their politeness. The father and mother talked almost constantly and at the same time. The father would speak in a rather low voice, looking at the corner of the room, while the mother, at the same time, talked louder to her daughter. They seem not to hear each other at all."

In summary, the families of good premorbid schizophrenic patients are distinctly different from normal families on many of the coded variables. The affective tone of the good family is relatively cold and emotionless with considerable attention paid to the narrowly defined "task" and much less attention paid to the members of the family themselves. Even when family members do air their own feelings these are attached to the ideas and opinions being discussed rather than to the people. One hears polite disagreements, devaluation of opinions, sarcasm, and critical jokes, not attacks on others' motives or personalities. The presence of hostility thus appears as an undercurrent in the flow of discussion. The good family's focus on the task may serve the purpose of avoiding a more direct expression of hostility that threatens fragmentation of the family, or it may avoid the closeness that may similarly be a threat to the family structure. The well child in the good family in some instances may play the role that other members cannot or will not take—the expresser of feelings, particularly negative feelings.

Power coalitions in good families are much like those in poor families in that, in the case of the male child, there is a mother–son coalition with the father isolated; in the family of daughters the patient is the isolate. We have pointed to several ways in which these patterns occur and are maintained, varying from simple monopoly of time and attention to active sanctioning techniques that prevent one member from participating. However, family members are not completely powerless even when they are effectively isolated from the giving and receiving of attention; they may use subtle strategies not requiring more than a sentence or a gesture to obtain what they want. The good family members avoid confrontation of each other as well; no one interrupts, no one presses anyone else, no one demands clarification, and no one pushes for a true change in another's opinion.

One correlate of the good family's task focus and its avoidance of clear confrontation between members is the family's style of speech. Long speeches, many pauses, few disruptions such as fragments and repeated words, provide a form of interaction, orderly and precise, that appears to aid in avoiding the reality of the opinion differences between members. These families follow the required form for discussion and, in doing so, skirt the real differences that might become apparent if a freer, less ritualistic style were used. Instead of a pattern in which each person's statement is built on and takes into account all that has gone on before, the good family's arguments tend to move in a circle; members continually restate their own original opinions, little new information is introduced and no one changes, except in a clearly artificial way.

Conclusion

In this chapter we have reviewed some of the major findings derived from interaction coding of small, concretely defined units. These findings have been illustrated with segments from the family typescripts, selected to bring the richness, variety, and reality of the family relationships into view. Although these segments of interaction should in no way be considered "findings," they help to show how the different relationships and styles of communication might be experienced or observed. In indicating possible functions of different behaviors and the dynamics of family relationships, we have also implied that approaches to the analysis of data other than those reported in this book, namely multivariate and sequential analyses, would also be appropriate to the study of these complex phenomena. These are currently in process.

Chapter 11

Review and Implications of the Study

The preceding chapters constitute a report of the empirical findings of the study. Methods and data have been described in detail. The extent to which the study contributes to a fuller understanding of relationships between family processes and schizophrenia depends on the validity of these findings. The usefulness to other investigators of our approach and methodology will reflect judgments based on their examination of the technical accounts of methods, analyses, and results that are to be found in the text. This chapter is intended neither as a substitute for the data nor as a rhetorical epilogue. Rather, the aim is to review a number of general issues and questions that have been neglected or bypassed in the detailed presentation. Persistent problems of research in this problem area are discussed, as are some advantages and limitations of our particular approach; overall trends in the data are noted, along with general implications of the study for both theory and research. The relevance of our findings to clinical observations are also discussed, but no implications are drawn for clinical practice.

Review of the Study

Aims and Primary Features

It may be useful to recall at this point that the explicit aims of the study, as stated in the introductory chapter, were to develop general methods and concepts for the experimental investigation of natural social groups and to apply them to the study of relationships between family interaction and schizophrenia. We conceived the study as linking the tradition of experimental social psychology with that of clinical research on family pathology. The relevance of our general approach, of particular methods of experimentation and analysis, and of specific results for the study of other types of groups and social processes has been discussed at a number of points. However, the relationship of our findings to clinical observations of schizophrenic patients and their families, to clinically based theories, and to the possibilities of clinical intervention has on the whole not been treated explicitly in this report. Although Chapter 10 includes material on the family as an interacting group and is an effort at placing abstract variables and findings into their human context, it is not oriented toward clinical issues. Relationships between this study and the observations, needs, and interests of clinicians require further discussion.

The obvious question is whether our findings are consistent with clinical observations. It is frustrating but instructive to discover that this is not an easily answered question. The typical complaints of researchers and clinicians about each others' work no doubt apply here. Clinicians often argue, particularly when research findings are not in accord with their observations, that researchers—by emphasizing precision, reliability, objectivity, and quantification—define the basic clinical problems out of existence; that is, researchers are accused of excluding the really important phenomena with which clinicians are concerned by focusing only on those variables that can be measured. In the present instance, for example, clinicians might view the index of expressiveness, based on the proportion of unit acts falling into a subset of the Bales IPA code-category system, as so different from what they usually mean by interpersonal affect and feeling that the results could not be relevant to their concerns with the emotional quality of family relationships.

This is a serious and a difficult problem. The relationship between operational and conceptual definitions is complex as is the relationship between the score produced by a standard measurement procedure and the intuitively grasped sense of phenomenon. However, the work of resolving the problem must be shared by the clinician and is not solely the task of the researcher. For the countercriticism of the researcher to the charge that his measures and his results are only distantly related to clinical observations is that clinicians' statements of concepts, hypotheses, and theories are so imprecise and vague that it is necessary to translate them into other terms so that they can be studied. If clinicians and clinical investigators are interested in increasing the relevance to their work of findings from studies such as that reported in this volume, they have a responsibility to clarify their concepts and to report their observations with due attention to their methodological context.

The notions of pseudomutuality and of the double bind are two interesting formulations that exemplify the difficulty of translation into researchable questions. How we are to judge whether expressions of support, agreement, and positive regard are "pseudo" or "truly" mutual is not described in the original discussion of pseudomutuality as a prime feature of the schizophrenic family. (Wynne, Ryckoff, Day, and Hirsch, 1958). Thus in measuring what appeared to us to be the basic components of mutuality— support, agreement, positive affect—it was not possible to make a clear prediction regarding differences to be expected between normal and patient families. When we find, as we did, that members of normal families show higher rates of positive affect than members of patient families this could be interpreted in one of two ways; either normal families are more pseudomutual and our findings are inconsistent with the original clinical observations or our measures reflect true mutuality and do not bear on the question of pseudomutuality. These difficulties of prediction and interpretation suggest that the clinical observations that led originally to the distinction between these two types of mutuality be specified more precisely. This specification of concepts that require further clarification is one of the ways in which research findings feed back to the clinical situation.

The problem is equally difficult with regard to double binds (Bateson, Jackson, Haley, and Weakland, 1956). There are many different types of contradictory message and of ways of metacommunicating so as to avoid or escape from the psychological situation of the double bind. Further, since contradictions may appear between "levels" of a message as well as within its explicit content, all messages may be seen as self-contradictory from one or another perspective. We were not able to develop a direct measure of double binds because there seemed no way of establishing clear criteria consistent with the original definition. At best we were able to indicate that certain comparisons, such as between results for direct and indirect measures of affect, seemed not to be inconsistent with the idea. However, this did not permit using our results as a direct test of the hypothesis that the patient families would show a higher rate of double binds, but only of pointing out whether the two levels of affect were consistent or not.

Translating a concept derived from and applied to clinical observations into a researchable question is a subtle and delicate process; we must expect some change in meaning between the original concept and the measures actually used in a study. This would not be serious provided the problem was recognized, but researchers, for their part, often seem to forget that their scores and measurement procedures are related to the original concepts through a series of intervening and complicated steps and inferences;

they tend to treat their findings as if they represented direct measures of the original concepts. We have already noted the problems of interpreting our findings on indices of expressiveness as if they represented measures of pseudomutuality, or of the consistency between levels of affect as if this was a valid measure of the double bind. We have tried throughout the report to be explicit about the relationship between conceptual and operational definitions of the dimensions of interaction with which we have been concerned such as expressiveness, power, and responsiveness. Nevertheless there is a critical sense in which the measures cannot be evaluated simply in terms of their validity as empirical signs or representatives of clinically-derived concepts. In part this reflects the design and objectives of the study. The study was not designed as an instrument-validation study; if nothing else, the lack of clear criterion measures would have prevented this. In addition, as the measures produce findings they take on a conceptual meaning of their own, sometimes as a specification of the initial global concept but sometimes, as was true with the measures of what we came to call disruptions in communication, by generating an entirely new conceptual dimension.

In addition to this gap between a clinical concept and its operational measure, there is the further problem that variables are included in this study because they are of general sociological or social psychological interest rather than only because of an assumed clinical significance. Thus our use of the Bales IPA code, and of indices of expressiveness and instrumentality computed from it, derives in part from our interest in comparing findings for families with the body of data and related hypotheses that has accumulated in research on small experimental groups where this coding system has had extensive use. The same grounds apply for other variables and codes such as the use of participation as a measure of one type of control strategy, or of various speech-disruption measures as indicators of variability and adaptiveness. It would seem to us that it might be useful and productive if variables, dimensions of interaction, and hypotheses developed in studies of various types of groups were to be used by clinicians and family researchers in their investigations of pathogenic families. However, until more work is done using these more general dimensions of group interaction there will be the problem of relating such findings to the functioning of pathogenic families as clinicians typically observe and conceive of them.

This orientation of the study to general aspects of group functioning rather than to specific clinical problems of families is reflected not only in the concepts and variables studied but also in the fact that the research was not connected in any way with the clinical work that was part of the patient's and the family's association with the hospital. Families were not in treatment with the research investigators, the discussions that form the basic material for analysis were not derived from therapeutic sessions but from experimental situations set up solely for the purposes of the study, and, finally, it was made clear to the families that the information collected would not enter into the patient's clinical record and would not be available for use by those engaged in the clinical work that went on. We do not know in what particular ways families may behave differently when in a clinical situation than in an experimental situation, but there is no doubt that there would be differences. We have argued that our measures of interaction may be used to describe general characteristics of family structure and functioning. These abstract descriptions of families may then be used as a source of hypotheses about how families are likely to behave in other situations such as a family therapy session. In generalizing or extrapolating our findings, however, it is necessary to proceed by moving from descriptions of actual behavior to this more abstract level. We would not expect families to behave in the same way in other situations. Rather, what we learn about a family or type of family from their behavior in this one clearly defined situation leads us to a conceptual level that in turn allows us to predict how they are likely to behave in other situations. In comparing the results of different studies with each other, or in relating findings from research and clinical settings, much of the misunderstanding that arises could be avoided if this distinction were observed between behavioral and conceptual levels. In the first instance the question is whether the behaviors are the same in the two situations. We would hardly expect similarity if the situations were radically different, and yet the question seems often to be asked in this form. In the second instance we are asking whether the behaviors in the different situations are both predictable and understandable on the basis of an abstract description or model of the family. The latter is surely a more useful question.

To this point we have focused on the relationship between clinical concerns and the concepts, methods, and findings of the study. In stating that an aim of the study was to link traditions of sociology and social psychology with clinical psychiatry we intended that the implications of the work would flow in both directions. In emphasizing the investigation of *ad hoc* groups, experimental social psychologists have tended to ignore aspects of interpersonal relationships that are more evident in and critical to the functioning of natural groups with enduring relationships among their members. The problem we discussed above (cf. Mishler and Waxler, 1967a) of relating the behavior of a family in one situation to its behavior in another situation does not arise in the study of *ad hoc* groups since their life cycle is bounded by the temporal requirements of the study and they have no other existence except that which is called forth in the experimental situation. The fact that families exist as social units independently of the laboratory, that family members enter the laboratory with a history of relationships to each other and leave it to continue their lives together, directs our attention to features of their interaction that have been neglected in experimental social psychology. For example, characteristics of pathogenic families such as nonacknowledgment or nonresponsiveness, which have had a prominent place in the clinical literature, have received little attention in studies of *ad hoc* groups. Our success in measuring this dimension of behavior and its potency in discriminating between types of families suggests that it merits more intensive study in the functioning of other types of groups. A similar point may be made about several other variables included in the study.

Methods and Procedures

There are no longer any grounds for seriously doubting that experimental methods can be applied to the study of significant aspects of family functioning. It is evident from our own work reported here and the work of others (in Mishler and Waxler, 1968) that this can be done. Standard procedures can be used to generate interaction among family members and techniques for observing, recording, coding, and analyzing verbal interaction can be developed that are as reliable and objective as other procedures such as questionnaires and interviews that have been used to study family relationships. Further, the adequacy of these methods does not suffer in comparison to their use in studies of small *ad hoc* groups.

The experimental study of families is only one research strategy and our particular study is but one of the methodological variants of the general approach. In evaluating its promise and usefulness, there are problems and limitations that must be taken into account along with its advantages. In this section some of the more general problems of the approach are discussed.

Typically, in the concluding section of a research report, the methods used are ignored. We are including a discussion of methodology for two reasons. First, one aim of the study was to develop methods that were appropriate and useful for the study of family interaction; a report on the results of this attempt and on its problems would seem to belong here. In addition, as the reader has no doubt learned from the text, we believe that the findings can only be understood by explicit reference to the methods that generated them. Thus, on this ground as well, methods belong in a concluding discussion of substantive findings.

The research design of a study is intimately connected to the types of analysis that may be undertaken and to the scope of appropriate generalization from the findings. This study was unique among studies of families

and schizophrenia (see Mishler and Waxler, 1968) in the number of variables simultaneously controlled Included in the study are the families of
male and female schizophrenic patients with good and poor histories of
premorbid social adjustment. None of the patients had histories of chronic
or continuous hospitalization. There are two normal control groups—an
intrafamilial control of a well sibling matched for sex and age with the
patient and a separate control group of families in which the children, also
matched for sex, had no history of psychiatric treatment.

The use of multiple controls leads to several important problems. There
is, for example, the initial problem of locating and recruiting eligible families for the experiment; the more restrictive the controls, and using several
controls imposes further restrictions, the more difficult it is to find eligible
families. The number of young schizophrenic patients with a sibling near
the same age and of the same sex was expected to be considerably smaller
than the total number of schizophrenic patients. As it turned out, only 13%
of all schizophrenic patients admitted to the hospital were eligible by all of
our criteria for inclusion in the study (cf. Chapter 2).

The problems do not stop with the selection and recruitment of eligible
families, but continue into the analysis, where the small number of cases
and the multiple comparisons require the use of less efficient statistical
procedures; because of the complexity and the number of comparisons
made, the findings are not always clearly consistent with each other. These
inconsistencies are among the problems posed for the interpretation of data
in complicated experimental designs. Our approach to the analysis of families as social systems, detailed in Chapter 4, was an attempt to maximize
the benefits of this complicated design. It allowed us to locate the source of
differences between families, that is, whether the differences depended on
group, situational, or member role effects, and to determine the nature and
significance of consistencies and inconsistencies across levels of analysis.

There is the additional problem of generalizing or extrapolating from the
findings. The use of experimental and statistical controls is designed primarily to clarify theoretical relationships between variables, to permit the
separate effects of different variables to be determined more easily and
more clearly, and to locate patterns of interaction. Paradoxically, however,
controls that are theoretically relevant may at the same time make it more
difficult to generalize findings to real populations of interest. To use an
example, we know from this study that differences between the behavior
of parents of schizophrenic and normal children are stronger when the
former are interacting with their patient son than with their well son. Given
this finding, is it possible to generalize to the behavior of parents toward
schizophrenic sons in families where there is no other male child? More
generally, is it possible to move directly from this finding of differentials in

parental behavior in these two highly specific situations to a statement about the general pathogenic consequences of certain types of parental behavior? Such generalizations require the assumption that the variables excluded from direct study would at most have trivial effects. The aim, for example, of including a well-sibling control was to determine in what ways the behavior of parents toward schizophrenic children was distinctive. If we had observed parents only when with their schizophrenic children this would not have permitted us to conclude that the observed behavior appeared only when with the patient but not at other times. Such statements are the aim of scientific research and depend on possibilities of comparing behavior across situations. Thus the use of well-sibling and normal controls serves to extend rather than to restrict the range of theoretical generalization. The applicability of the generalization as an empirical description of real families must take into account, however, other variables that have been excluded by the research design but remain effective in the real world. In other words the assumption often made that "all other things are equal," or that the effects of other variables are random or trivial, is clearly not true in the present case and great care must be exercised before generalizing theoretical relationships to real situations. This is a general problem of research in the social sciences (See Blalock, 1961, for an analysis of the problem of making causal inferences from empirical data.)

The main features of our approach to eliciting and recording information on family interaction may be summarized as follows. Strodtbeck's revealed-difference procedure was used to generate family discussions. Three members of a family, parents with their sick child on one occasion and his/her well sibling on another, discussed together a number of situations about which they disagreed in privately stated opinions and tried to reach agreement. The experiment was carried out in a room equipped for sound recording and observation in the research wing of the hospital; families came to the hospital for this purpose. A multichannel tape recorder was used for recording the discussion and an observer monitored the who-to-whom behavior from behind a one-way screen. The family was left alone during their discussion. Finally, to avoid systematic experimenter effects, the two experimenters (the authors) each ran sessions of all types of family included in the research design; to avoid order effects, we varied whether families came to the first experimental session with their patient or well child.

The influence of the experimenter on the types of information generated in experimental situations has been well documented (Rosenthal, 1966). Our procedures were designed not so much to eliminate the effect of the experimenter, something which we do not believe to be possible, but to neutralize or standardize his effect. This was done primarily in ways that served to guard or protect him from entering into particular personal relationships with families, because we believed that such relationships would by definition have to be different from family to family with resultant differential and unmeasurable effects on the data. As much as possible, we wanted the situation to be one in which family members had to deal with problems they set for each other rather than with problems set for them by the experimenter or with or by their relationship to him. Thus the task itself required them to talk together about their own privately expressed opinions; this is a problem produced by themselves rather than by the experimenter. In leaving the room the experimenter avoided being a direct participant, even a quiet one, in the discussion. Finally, the laboratory setting provided an impersonal though nonthreatening atmosphere. It is our impression from postexperimental discussions with family members that they treated the situation as a scientific study, accepted the experimental requirements in these terms of reference, and on the whole were pleased at having been given an opportunity to participate in the research. Our attempt to create a neutral, standard, and relatively impersonal situation seems both to have been successful and to have been an acceptable and understandable situation for family members.

Our stress on and our procedures for producing a neutral and impersonal situation have been spelled out in some detail to permit an easier and more direct contrast with an alternative set of assumptions that underlies the work of a number of other family investigators, particularly those who approach the families within a clinical perspective. In brief, their argument is that significant and critical family processes will appear only when issues of particular importance to the family are raised and when the family has been observed over an extended period of time. There is no doubt that families will behave differently in other situations, as we have recognized in an earlier discussion, and that issues that emerge in intensive long-term family therapy will be of more profound subjective significance than those discussed in our time-bounded and neutral situation. However, the aim of research is not simply to involve the family in its problems but to learn something about its basic structure, and, more specifically, to determine the distinctive structures of different types of family. We are interested in creating a reliable and valid diagnostic procedure and not a mode of therapeutic intervention. The usefulness of the approach depends neither on its power to generate behavior in agreement with a priori assumptions about significant processes, nor on the family's experience of it as personally relevant and meaningful. Its usefulness depends instead on whether it permits us to discover and establish reliable differences between families that can be used to predict other aspects of families in which we are interested, such as whether they have a schizophrenic child. It may also be noted that in more clinically oriented investigations too little attention has been given to the effects on family functioning of the therapist and of other aspects of the therapeutic situation.

One last point about procedure merits emphasis. As far as we can determine, ours is the only family study in which a multichannel tape recorder was used that permitted each member of the family to be tuned in independently of the others by the typist who transcribed the tapes. Our decision to use this more elaborate equipment was based on comparisons between the typescript that resulted when only a single microphone was used and the typescript obtained from multichannel equipment; about 25% of codable acts were lost in the single-microphone arrangement. This problem is most serious if coding procedures focus on small unit acts of the type we studied and if there is an interest in the sequence of interaction. When either of these objectives is present a single microphone for a group of three or more persons seems to us to be totally inadequate. Most important, there is not only an overall reduction in the number of total acts, but the loss is differential; persons who speak quietly or are interrupted by others or speak unclearly or in a fragmented way tend to be those on whom most information is lost. If dyads are studied, or if the interest is in an overall trend of the discussion, or if the aim is only to determine the final decision then the use of multichannel equipment may be less necessary. However, even in these instances there is no doubt that a single microphone hookup provides a less accurate recording of the family's discussion.

Considerable attention has been given in the text and in the accompanying coding manual (Appendix B) to the details of our coding procedures. A few general comments about the approach are in order.

We have stressed the importance of reliability and there is surely no need to argue for focusing on this problem of measurement in a field where reliability of measures has been difficult to come by. However, when we have reported our procedures to other investigators they have often expressed concern about the costs involved in such a coding operation. Adequate reliabilities depend not only on clear and well-defined code category systems but on intensive code training, supervision of coders, and a continuing monitoring of the coding process. There is no evading the costs for this in funds and in professional staff time. Nevertheless it should also be recognized that it has been possible to use untrained personnel as coders because their work and competence depended on in-service training. Costs, therefore, should be compared with the costs of using trained clinicians, with expensive training and high current fees. In addition, it is our experience, and that of other investigators, that the costs saved through a less closely controlled coding operation with resultant unreliable findings are then lost several times over in the costs of analysis where professional time is wasted in an effort to salvage poor data.

Our coding procedures are an exercise in the microanalysis of verbal behavior. The units to which the codes are applied are assumed to be the smallest meaningful acts that are put together and arranged by persons in sustaining meaningful discussion with each other; in this respect they are like the kernel phrases of the linguists, although their approach was not used systematically in developing our codes. We depart further from the linguists in not concerning ourselves with the syntax of the discussion but in treating these primary unit acts as if they occurred in isolation from the ongoing interaction process. At most, the preceding statement or act has been used as context, but often acts were coded without reference to what came before or after. Carried to its limit, the assumption is that the codes could be applied to these unit acts even if they were arranged randomly rather than in the actual context within which they occurred. The implicit model of human behavior is that certain important characteristics will be expressed regardless of the overall context; or, more narrowly, that an adequate interpretation may be made on the basis of markedly restricted contexts. For example, it is assumed that differentials in levels of expressiveness will appear throughout a sequence of verbal behavior and will not be specific to particular contexts. We would not argue for this as a comprehensive model for human social behavior; it has clear and obvious limitations that do not need to be detailed here. It seems to us important, however, to test the limits of this simplified model, to determine whether we can find interesting and important differences between pathological and normal families, before dismissing it in preference to more complicated approaches. Further, as we discover the limitations of this model we will also learn about the particular ways in which the model must be elaborated and made more complex.

One useful consequence of this approach to coding is the flexibility of the data field as it is finally arranged on computer tape. With each unit act multiple-coded and with acts numbered in sequence through the course of a discussion, the numbers of ways in which the material can be aggregated, indexed, and compared is almost limitless. This flexibility was critical in permitting the range of detailed analyses reported in the data chapters.

The multilevel approach to the analysis of families as social systems has been described in the text in detail. It allowed comparison of normal and patient families as collective social units and a comparison of the individual members of these families in each of the two experimental sessions. The presence of statistically significant differences across families could be determined separately for family members and for the families as wholes in either session and for combined sessions. These multiple comparisons could be interpreted within a unified and comprehensive framework that permitted us to distinguish between group effects, when differences were located only in the families as collective units; role effects, when differences were located in specific member roles; and a number of group-role interaction effects. We believe that the general usefulness of the approach has been demonstrated by the clarification that has resulted. Further, it seems to us that more precise theories about family processes and personality development can develop only when it is possible to link concepts more directly with empirical units of analysis. That is, propositions about overall family processes must be linked directly to a set of empirical operations for describing such processes; similarly, propositions about mothers and fathers as members of these families must be tied to a different set of operations that are appropriate to the description of individual behavior. A specification of the links between conceptual and empirical units as is provided by the multilevel approach cannot help but be beneficial in a field that tends to be dominated by loose and vague theorizing.

Analyses and Findings

The large number of interaction indices calculated from the many codes were reduced to five conceptual domains, or variable clusters, and the extended analyses of these clusters form the central data chapters of the report. These are: expressiveness, strategies of attention and person control, speech disruption and responsiveness. For purposes of this discussion it is convenient to group these further into two large classes—variables that are substantive in the sense that they refer to qualities of relationships and interaction, and structural variables that denote the more formal or stylistic aspects of interaction. Under the former heading we would place expressiveness and the strategies of attention and person control; these are analogous to the typical and frequently observed general dimensions of social relationships that traditionally are referred to as affection and power. In the second class of structural variables are the domains of communication style and responsiveness.

In the chapter summary on expressiveness we noted that in comparison to both types of schizophrenic family the normal families were both more expressive and more positive in the quality of their expressed affect. More precisely, this is a pattern for the normal male families, for although there are no radical reversals in the findings for female families, the range and strength of the differences between the normals and the schizophrenic families decrease considerably in the latter comparisons. In particular, there are no instances on measures of expressiveness in which normal and poor premorbid families of daughters differ significantly from each other. This finding supports the points made above about the importance of introducing controls for the sex and premorbid history of patients in studies of schizophrenia. Even in the comparison of families of sons there are fewer differences between the normals and the poor premorbids than there are between the former and the good premorbid families. This is among the most important of the findings from the analysis of expressiveness measures, namely, that good premorbid families are instrumental in their behavior and relatively negative in the quality of their expressed affect. Again, this is a statement that applies primarily to families of male patients since differentials on expressiveness are rarely significant in the analyses of female families, although the goods tend to maintain a consistent position on the negative side of the affect measure among these families as well as among the males.

In examining the direction of expressed affect, that is, interpersonal affective orientations, we found consistency between direct and indirect measures for both male and female patient families on general levels of interpersonal expressiveness and on the expression of positive interpersonal affect. On these measures normal families were consistently low and poor premorbid families consistently high. We interpreted this to mean that members of normal families could direct their affect toward a variety of targets other than persons immediately present in the situation and that they were consistent in their direct and indirect expressions; and further, that the degree to which poor premorbids focused their affect on persons was an indication of a more concrete and particularistic mode of expression.

There was one important difference between the findings for families of sons and daughters, however, and this was on the index of negative interpersonal expressiveness. In families of sons good premorbids tended to be low and we interpreted this as an indication that they were unwilling to risk direct confrontation of others in the situation; however, in comparisons across families of daughters, good premorbids were consistently high. These differences appear to be consistent with reports of other investigators (Fleck, Lidz and Cornelison, 1963) who found that male patients came from what were referred to as skewed families in which patterns of conflict and hostility are less manifest, and female schizophrenics from schismatic families in which conflict among members is more open.

In distinguishing between two types of control strategy, attention and person control behaviors, we moved beyond traditional discussions of power in small social groups where the focus has tended to be limited to relative amounts of power, that is, to the hierarchy of power and authority within a group. At best the idea of power applied to a family is an ambiguous and uncertain concept. It is clear that parents possess much more power than their children and that their power to compel or to coerce behavior is supported and legitimized by cultural norms and institutional practices. It seemed to us particularly important, therefore, to examine the ways in which members of a family attempt to influence each other, that is, their strategies of control, rather than to concentrate primarily on a quantity notion of power.

As was true on expressiveness, the normal and good premorbid families provide the sharpest contrasts on measures of control strategies. The power structure of normal families is revealed most clearly in the analysis of attention control strategies. Here patterns of role differentiation are consistent with what would be expected from theory and the observations of other investigators. There is a parental coalition with mothers and fathers attending to each other; the father has the highest status and receives respect and attention from his son who has the lowest status in the family. The father's role is somewhat weaker and more peripheral in normal families with daughters, where there is some evidence for a mother–daughter coalition.[1] The existence of a clear hierarchy of power and authority in the normal families does not, however, bring with it patterns of authoritarian or coercive control. Rather, it is within these families that we find most evidence of direct attempts at interpersonal influence in that all members of these families, including the low status children, are more likely to use person-control strategies such as interruptions, than are the members of either of the schizophrenic patient families.

There are important differences in power structure between the male and female patient families. In families with schizophrenic sons we find a reversal of generational roles between fathers and sons; the patient and his mother take the relatively high power positions and tend to defer to each other with the father exerting little influence and being somewhat outside of the system. In the families of patient daughters, on the other hand, the daughter appears to be most isolated in that little attention and respect is accorded her and she, on her part, does not try to influence the proceedings. Further, the mother in these latter families appears to be generally more powerful than the father. Within schizophrenic families, particularly the good premorbids, where the distribution of power deviates from normative role prescriptions, the exercise of power as reflected in control strategies is itself impersonal and indirect. In our detailed discussion of these findings we pointed out that these patterns of role differentiation in patient families did not provide suitable parental models for identification for either sons or daughters. The schizophrenic son is allied with his mother vis-a-vis

---

[1] In interpreting differences between families of sons and daughters here and elsewhere, we must not forget that these terms are a shorthand way of referring to the index case and to the sex of the patient-sibling pair of children who participated in the study. There were other children in many of the families and they were often not of the same sex as the patient. Thus in discussing parental role differences in male and female families there is always an implicit qualification to the effect that we are referring only to situations in which they are interacting with a son or daughter.

a weak and peripheral father; an isolated and relatively powerless schizophrenic daughter has to contend with a powerful mother.

We noted earlier the tendency for significant differences between family types to be restricted to the experimental session where the patient was present. This pattern is strikingly evident in the analysis of attention- and person-control measures. It appears as if the dimension of power, of who has it and of how it is used, is particularly sensitive to the presence of the patient.

The measures that we have grouped together under the concept of speech disruption—fragments, repetitions, incomplete sentences, and pauses—provide some of the most interesting and exciting findings of the study, in part because they were unexpected and seemed at first to diverge from other findings about these types of family. As we re-examined our initial expectations, it appeared that we had made the assumption that psychological normality would be expressed in behavior by orderly and continuous speech; and, as a corollary to this, that disruptions of speech marked by such behaviors as fragments and repetitions could be viewed as departures from normality and as signs of tension and stress. Following this line of reasoning, our initial hypothesis was that families of schizophrenic patients would show more of these disruptions than would the normal families. As the reader knows, these expectations were not borne out. For families of sons, the findings were consistent: normal families were significantly more likely to show evidence of disruption and deviation from orderly, continuous speech and good premorbid families were found to be the most orderly and well controlled in their speech.

These findings led us to reconsider the social and psychological functions of change and variability in speech patterns. We suggested that there may be an optimum level of such variability that serves an adaptive function for the family and its members. Variability provides opportunities for change, for the introduction of new information, and for movement and development within the group. It may be contrasted with an extreme form of nondisrupted speech, namely, ritualistic language, which neither provides new information to the listener nor permits the possibility of change. In this sense good premorbid families are more ritualistic in language and behavior and may therefore be expected to be more rigid and less adaptable than normal families. The other pole of this hypothetical continuum of variability in communication, a nonadaptive overvariability reflecting a chaotic and possibly random flow of behavior, does not appear in our data. Clearly the level of variability exhibited by normal families is not disruptive of organized, purposive activity; they are able to deal adequately with the amount of disruption they generate for each other.

We believe that these findings can be linked to studies of cognitive processes in schizophrenia. In particular, we suggested that the experimental and clinical evidence on input dysfunction in acute schizophrenics, that is, their difficulty in dealing with multiple sources of stimulation and their sensitivity to disorganization when bombarded with stimuli, fit with our findings (Venables, 1964). That is, it appears as if in good premorbid families the function of controlled, orderly behavior might be to reduce the possibility of disorganization by reducing the multiplicity and intensity of stimulation. This is treating the finding within a responsive model of interpretation; it might also be argued that the effect of growing up within a nonvariable environment would be the type of thought disorder found to be typical in schizophrenia. The findings would also seem to be related to experimental studies that suggest the need for stimulus variability in order to maintain normal adaptive behavior (Fiske and Maddi, 1961).

Like speech disruption, responsiveness is a structural aspect of interaction. Here we are concerned not with what is said in response to others but simply with whether the fact that something has been said is acknowledged in another's response. Findings for measures of this variable are among the strongest and most consistent in the study. They are also intimately related to those just discussed. To summarize the main findings: normals are most responsive and poor premorbids least. One of the more interesting secondary findings was that among the families of sons the normals had a higher rate of fragmentation, which was associated with their higher levels of interruptions, fragment stimuli and elliptical affirmations. In conjunction with the findings on speech disruption, what we see is a pattern of interaction that is noisy, in that it includes high rates of interruptions, speech disruptions, and changeable behaviors but that at the same time, is highly responsive to what is going on, particularly to the opinions of others as they are expressed in the situation; it is thus effective and adaptive. Poor premorbid families are most different from the normals on responsiveness and exhibit a pattern of relatively nonresponsive behavior where they focus their attention on the rules of the experimental situation; they behave as if somewhat confused and are concerned with discovering a rule that will tell them what to do. The good premorbids show again a pattern of controlled and rigid, though only moderately responsive, behavior with a tendency to conduct their relations with each other in a somewhat impersonal and abstract way.

Examination of the findings within each conceptual area tends to mask certain patterns that cut across areas. These patterns provide interesting insights into the nature of family and role differences. Some of these general patterns have been referred to in the discussions of particular variables. Here we bring them together and discuss their implications.

First, many of the statistically significant differences found between the normal and patient families are restricted to comparisons of parents and to their behavior in the experimental session with the schizophrenic child; by our rules of inference, these findings are instances either of patterns congruent with the group analysis or are role effects. It is a matter of great importance that differences between parents of schizophrenic children and parents of normal children are more striking than are differences between schizophrenic patients and normal children serving as research controls. There are evidently many ways in which schizophrenic patients can behave in interaction with their parents that are indistinguishable from the behavior either of children from families with no known psychiatric pathology or of their own well siblings. In our discussions of these similarities in behavior we suggested that they were evidence for pervasive and strong cultural norms regulating the behavior of children within families, or at least their behavior when interacting with their parents. The strength of such norms is shown further by the fact that we almost never found significant differences between the behavior of the two siblings in the two experimental sessions, either in normal or patient families.

That these similarities found in our data across the behavior of children are not simply a function of the insensitivity or the irrelevance of the measures used is shown by the patterning and frequency of significant differences found between parents in these different types of family. Mothers and fathers of good and poor premorbid schizophrenic patients differ from each other and each differs from normal parents on a large number of variables. As previously noted these differences across families emerge more strongly in sessions with their patient child. However, these intersession differences do not reflect major alterations in parental behavior; significant differences between sessions in the behavior of parents are rare. On the whole, what appears to happen is that there is a slight exaggeration of a general style or a reduction in variability of behavior when with their schizophrenic child; thus nonsignificant trends in the well-sibling session comparisons become significant in the patient session comparisons. Perhaps this is a way of saying that the parents behave like themselves, only more so, when with their schizophrenic children.

Findings for specific variables have been discussed in earlier chapters and some of the main threads of our interpretation will be reviewed below. First, however, we may note come general implications for theories of family behavior and schizophrenia of this overall pattern of differences between parents and similarities between children. First, we have shown that schizophrenic children can behave with their parents in ways that are not deviant with reference to prescribed norms for children of their sex and age. Put another way, appropriate age-sex role performance vis-a-vis their parents is within their behavioral repertoire. Moreover, they behave appropriately in circumstances where their parents' behavior deviates from that of normal parents and from the parents' own behavior when with the patient's well sibling. Two possibilities suggest themselves. Either the parents are responding in anticipation of deviant performance on the part of the patient (or to some actual behavior not measured by our instruments) and act so as to bring their schizophrenic child's behavior within the normal range, or their children are attempting to perform adequately but must do so under the additional strain and burden of deviant parental behavior. These alternative possibilities are related to the three frameworks of interpretation we have proposed to account for specific findings—the etiological, responsive, and situational models.

On the basis of others' theories and studies, we had expected to find many instances of role differentiation between mothers and fathers and between them and their children. There were few findings of intrafamilial role patterning, and on the whole, these expectations were not confirmed; their lack of confirmation constitutes one of the major negative findings of the study. Generalized family styles of interaction and family norms expressed in behavior appear to be stronger than intrafamily role differentials for the dimensions of behavior under study. These findings fit with much other data on family resemblances in such areas as psychological and biological traits, cognitive styles, social values, and even political behavior. They lend support to the emphasis placed by many investigators on the family unit as a focus for research and theory. There is clearly a "strain toward consistency" within a family and when different behaviors are socially required and supported, such as for mothers and fathers in their different roles within and outside the family, there is an apparent similarity in styles of interaction.

Two of the control variables built into the design were shown to be of considerable importance in that the results confirm the hypotheses of expected differences between families of male and female patients and families of good and poor premorbid patients. Some of the differences between findings for male and female cases have remained difficult to interpret in part because of the small size of the female patient sample. The differences uncovered in the study between good premorbid, poor premorbid, and normal families are more consistent and reinforced the argument that led to the research design, namely that it is important to include two subtypes of schizophrenia in such research.

We were surprised to find, particularly among male families, that the good premorbids were most different from the normals. Our surprise reflected our naive and simple assumption at the beginning of the study that degrees of premorbidity represented degrees of pathology and that these in turn would be directly correlated with the extent of family pathology. Thus the poor premorbids were expected to differ most from the normals, with the goods falling between them. Our results depart from these expectations but are consistent with the findings of other similar experimental studies, for example, Caputo (1963), and Farina (1960). In addition, they are remarkably similar to Goldfarb's findings in his research on families of schizophrenic children. He found that the families who were not different from the families of normal children in any significant way had schizophrenic children who showed evidence of organic damage and displayed the most severe clinical pathology, whereas schizophrenic children without such neurological signs had families who were markedly disturbed in comparison to normal families. (Goldfarb, 1961) We have already discussed in the data chapters some of the problems these findings pose for etiological and responsive interpretations.

It is clear that had we included in the study only what on clinical grounds would be considered the sickest patients, fewer differences would have been found between normal and schizophrenic families. There is no doubt that the similarity between families of poor premorbid patients and of normals is at the root of contradictory findings from different studies and of frequent reports of negative findings, that is, of no significant differences between schizophrenic and normal samples.

As a final general point, we must again stress the fact that all of the analyses and the findings reported and interpreted depend on aggregate scores, that is, on sums across a discussion of certain kinds of participation. We have focused entirely on total outputs in certain categories of interaction and in this report have not in any way examined sequential patterns nor intercorrelations among various dimensions. Both of these types of analysis will be reported in future publications.

Implications for Research and Theory

Frameworks for Interpretation:

The initial impetus for this study came from theories that were etiological in tone and emphasis. Clinical investigators with primary interest in the course of pathology and in possibilities of therapeutic intervention hypothesized that faulty family relationships were etiologically relevant and critical to the development of schizophrenia. (For a review of these theories, see Mishler and Waxler, 1965.) Although concepts and hypotheses drawn from these several theories markedly influenced our own work, we have been less committed to an etiological point of view. It has seemed evident to us that questions of etiology cannot be settled by fiat simply because differences are found empirically between normal families and families of patients. Alternative explanations of such findings can be proposed that are equally plausible and reasonable on a priori grounds; we have proposed responsive and situational models as viable alternatives to an etiological approach to the interpretation of findings. In the body of this report we have argued that the appropriateness of each of these models to each set of findings must be examined, their relative plausibility and parsimony compared, and the different assumptions of each model clarified.

Discussing these issues in an earlier paper (Mishler and Waxler, 1967b), we pointed out that the problem of sorting out and comparing these types of explanation with each other is common to all ex post facto studies. These models differ critically in the assumptions that are made about the time ordering of variables. Do the family interaction patterns displayed in the experimental situation precede in time the onset of schizophrenia, as would be required by an etiological interpretation? Or do the family patterns reflect a response to the development of schizophrenia in a child, as would be assumed in a responsive model? Or, finally, are the ways in which family members interact with each other affected primarily by the hospitalization of the patient, as is implied by a situational interpretation? (See Bell, 1959–60, 1967 for a parallel discussion of problems of interpretation in child development studies.)

In comparing these alternative models with each other we recognized that the ex post facto design of our study and the types of variables measured would not permit a definitive choice between them. This is not, of course, a limitation of our study alone since all other studies of family processes that begin with a defined and diagnosed patient as an index case share the same design and the consequent problems of interpretation. However, in specifying control variables and in making explicit the inferences and assumptions that seemed to be required to fit a model to the data, we hoped to clarify the basic requirements of a theory that could adequately account for relationships found between schizophrenia and family interaction patterns.

As it turned out, comparing the fit of each model to the data and to each other took several different forms: the use of other variables as statistical controls in the analysis of data, an assessment of the congruence of the data with theoretical expectations, and the introduction into the line of argument of additional inferences and assumptions about the populations studied and the variables measured. Our research design permitted us to control, for example, for the presence of the patient or his/her well sibling as a factor influencing parental interaction. Differences in the behavior of parents across the two experimental sessions, we argued, would not be consistent with a situational interpretation since there was no change in the status of the family vis-a-vis the hospital nor in experimental conditions and research setting from session to session. Such a finding would, however, be consistent with either an etiological or responsive model since both interpretations emphasize the importance of one child's status as a schizophrenic patient.

Choosing between etiological and responsive interpretations was more difficult. Particular patterns of findings were not sufficient in and of themselves to support one rather than the other approach to interpretation, and other information external to the findings had to be introduced in assessing their relative merits. For example, findings for families of sons on the index of positive acknowledgment (Chapter 9), on which normal families were consistently high and poor premorbid families consistently low, with goods in-between, are congruent with many other observations about the imperviousness of interpersonal relationships in families of schizophrenic patients and with relatively well-developed theories about the effects of such patterns on personality development. For these reasons the findings were treated as supporting an etiological interpretation even though a responsive model could also fit the data. That is, it could as well be argued that parents who have had to live with a chronic schizophrenic child have learned to ignore, that is, fail to acknowledge, his behavior so as to minimize disruption and disturbance in the family; they would then appear at least acknowledging. The good premorbids, faced with a more recent problem, would fall between the poors and the normal families. This would be a responsive model of interpretation applied to these findings.

In other instances, particularly when good premorbids were most different from normals, a responsive model gained in plausibility. Here, too, the argument rested on other data and theories.

For example, in our discussion of speech-disruption patterns, we suggested that the tendency toward rigidity among good premorbids might reflect the stress of the recent appearance of illness and the consequent efforts to control the situation or the patient's behavior.

The conclusion that we have reached is that within the limitations of our own and other similar ex post facto studies, a definite choice cannot be made between these alternative models of interpretation. Even with a relatively large number of control comparisons built into the research design—patient and well-sibling experimental sessions, patients with different histories of premorbid social adjustment, normal families, male and female patients—a judgment about the time order of variables requires additional inferences based on other data and theories. Although we found a situational interpretation least plausible, the limitations of an ex post facto design did not permit us clearly to sort out an etiological from a responsive interpretation.

The state of our knowledge about schizophrenia and about the role of

family processes makes it a foregone conclusion that a study of their relationships must end with suggestions for further research rather than with
a catalogue of definitive findings. From our analysis of problems of interpretation we think certain types of study take on more importance and
therefore that some priorities can be established. In the following section
emphasis is given to various types of research design rather than to particular variables. This is because the solution to general interpretative questions, that is, to the relative credibility of etiological or responsive models,
lies in the area of research design. The usefulness of particular substantive theories for our understanding of families and schizophrenia can be
assessed only when these variables are studied empirically within strong
research designs focused specifically on these general questions of interpretation.

Considerations for Further Research

Given the problems of interpretation that inhere in ex post facto designs, it is natural to turn to longitudinal studies. On the face of it, longitudinal studies would seem to solve many of our problems since the time
order of variables could be determined directly and etiological and responsive explanations could then be clearly separated from each other. The
benefits of such designs are undoubtedly great and we do not mean to
diminish their importance by noting that they are hypothetical and ideal
values; the practical and empirical difficulties of longitudinal studies
make it likely that ex post facto research will continue to have a dominant
place in future work. Among the numerous and well-known problems of
longitudinal research are: sample attrition over time, the low incidence of
schizophrenia with the consequent requirement of large study populations,
the critical importance of the variables chosen for initial study, the effects
on the data of repeated observation requiring complex multipanel designs,
the turnover of members of the research team, and the long delay before
the analysis of data can be undertaken and findings generated. In addition,
in studying schizophrenia there is the problem of determining its onset:
can we state when it begins so that "before" and "after" measures can be
separated from each other? We shall return below to some modified longitudinal designs, but these comments provide the grounds for beginning
with a discussion of ex post facto designs that will continue to have a contribution to make to this area of study.

As we noted above, the objective of this section is to suggest designs that
would help us to evaluate the relative usefulness and validity of situational,
responsive, and etiological interpretations of differences in interaction between patient and normal families. A situational interpretation assumes

that the facts of patienthood and hospitalization have been primary determinants of family behavior. Designs to test this model would be relatively easy to develop, since their primary feature would be the inclusion of control groups with illness and treatment histories similar to schizophrenic patient samples. The use of nonschizophrenic psychiatric patients such as those with character disorders (Reiss, 1967; Stabenau, Tupin, Werner, and Pollin, 1965) is focused on this problem of separating out the specific features of schizophrenia from more general effects of patienthood, as is the use of patients with unspecified but nonpsychiatric illnesses (Lerner, 1965) or with a specific nonpsychiatric illness such as tuberculosis (Farina, 1960).

Such designs could be further strengthened if they included two subtypes of schizophrenia, because such subclassification—whether good and poor premorbid as in the present study, or chronic and acute or paranoid and nonparanoid as in other studies—has been shown to be of critical importance. In such a design the nonschizophrenic patient sample should also be divided along a similar dimension so that in the end one would be able to compare, for example, families of chronic and acute schizophrenics with families of chronic and acute nonschizophrenic patients.

One modification of the usual experimental procedures could provide data in support of or counter to a responsive interpretation. If, when with a schizophrenic patient, normal parents modified their behavior in the direction of the behavior of his real parents, this would be evidence that the patient could evoke such behavior and a responsive interpretation would gain in credibility. One experiment with normal families has been reported (Leik, 1963) in which families were rearranged into a number of different three-person groups; the extension of this type of design into the study of schizophrenics and their families would undoubtedly provide important data relevant to the problem of alternative interpretations of the relation of family processes to schizophrenia. Also of particular usefulness to the understanding of the responsive interpretation are studies of interaction processes in families where there is a child with an illness known to have a genetic or physiological cause that results in a behavior. Examples of these are phenylketonuria and cerebral palsy, the occurrence of which may force the family to alter role structure and develop new techniques for handling deviance. (See Blumenthal, 1967 and Schaffer, 1964 for data on families of these children.) If these families are no different from families with schizophrenic children then evidence for the responsive interpretation would become stronger.

Modifications of usual approaches to measurement and data analysis would also be useful in this connection. In particular, more attention to sequential patterns in interaction would allow us to determine whether, for example, parents actually do respond differently to certain types of behavior depending on whether it is produced by their patient child or his well sibling. One investigator has reported differences in rates of intrusion by third parties into an ongoing two-party discussion (Lennard, 1965); this is one approach to sequences. We are currently engaged in extended analyses of sequential patterns, moving beyond the findings on aggregate scores reported in this book.

The design modifications suggested above still rely essentially on data collected at one point in time. Even ex post facto studies can be extended in time to cover distinct phases in the course of illness such as onset or recognition and diagnosis of the illness, hospitalization, symptom remission, return to the family, relapse, or continued recovery. Studies of families through these phases would provide evidence with regard to the functional and adaptive significance for the family of the development of schizophrenia and of hospitalization. At this time, alternative hypotheses remain largely speculative—is the patient selected for patienthood and extruded so the family can maintain itself as an ongoing system, or can the patient no longer be contained because the system of internal controls and patterns of management have broken down, or does the patient himself initiate and force the process either to escape from the family or as a way of expressing his hostility to his parents. Repeated investigations of families at different points in time would be a recognition of the fact that illness is not a static state but that there are changes over time and these changes are likely to be linked to changes in family behavior.

Such repeated studies of families after the onset of illness offer some of the advantages of longitudinal designs without some of the major practical difficulties, and if they incorporate some of the control groups suggested earlier would help to determine the relative power of a responsive model as an interpretive approach. The use of high-risk groups is another strategy for longitudinal research (cf. Mednick, 1967) that deserves more attention. These and more traditional longitudinal studies would gain from the inclusion of variables that located families within a wider social context. One of the peculiar omissions in the work on family interaction is its isolation from work on the social epidemiology of schizophrenia. Social class, social mobility, migration, and ethnicity, are among the factors found to be associated with differential incidence rates of schizophrenia (cf. Mishler and Scotch, 1963). Given the high cost and the difficulties of longitudinal studies, it is particularly important that their designs be constructed in ways that permit us to determine the role of these macrosocial variables and their relationship to patterns of family interaction in the development of schizophrenia.

Concluding Note

This volume summarizes five years of work. Although, in the perspective of the long history of interest in the problem of schizophrenia, this does not represent a particularly significant segment of time, it does represent in absolute terms a relatively heavy investment in time, energy, and resources. The findings reported here, the methods of study and analysis developed, and the conceptualizations and interpretations proposed are the initial returns on this investment. The results of the study provide further evidence that hard knowledge does not come easy in this area, no more so than in any area of scientific work.

For us, the investigators, this is a progress report describing what we have been able to learn and understand to this point in time. Further analyses of the data are underway that focus more directly on intercorrelations among variables and on sequential patterns of interaction. Other studies, stimulated by the findings and the questions they raise, are underway or in preparation including studies of relationships between cognitive processes in parents and children, of special features of speech in families and schizophrenia patients, and of the general functions of deviance in social groups. We believe that the study enters into and, depending on other investigators' judgments of its relevance and usefulness, may help to shape the relatively new tradition of family studies, namely, the direct observation of family interaction under standard controlled conditions and the systematic measurement and analysis of behavior.

Implicit in our work is the assumption that progress in our understanding of general psychological and interpersonal processes and an increase in the depth and breadth of our knowledge about relationships between family interaction and schizophrenia depend upon the development of rigorous methods of measurement and analysis, on the clarification of concepts and interpretive models, and on more powerful research designs directed toward well-defined questions. This is not an argument for the use of particular methods, such as the revealed-difference technique, nor for quantification and statistical analyses of the type used here. A variety of studies using other, though no less systematic, methodologies are urgently needed. For example, we lack detailed studies of the natural history of the schizophrenias in the absence of drugs or other modes of clinical intervention; ethnographic accounts of patients and their families in their natural settings have not been collected; detailed records of the language of schizophrenic patients and of the temporal patterning of their symptoms are rare. Experimental studies have different strengths and weaknesses than these other approaches; they are not urged as substitutes for but as complements to them.

Hopefully, the findings of this study and the problems that are posed will guide other investigators toward the formulation of critical questions and the development of appropriate methods. It is less important that particular features of the study be replicated or adapted than that others take the work seriously enough to read it closely, and, discerning its faults and limitations, go on to their own work.

Study Procedures, Sample Characteristics, and Index Score Data

A. 1 Scoring Method for Phillips Scale of Premorbid Adjustment (See Phillips, 1953)

As described in Chapter 2, this scale was applied to schizophrenic patients' case records to discriminate between patients with good premorbid social adjustments and those with poor premorbid social adjustments. The scale is composed of five subscales, each of which can have a value of 0 through 6; the total score for a patient is obtained by summing subscale scores. In instances where information for one or more subscales was lacking in the case records the patient was given a score equal to the mean of his other subscale scores.

Because of uneven information in the patient records, lack of clarity of category definitions, and inappropriateness of some scales to adolescent and female patients, a satisfactory scoring reliability was difficult to obtain. Instead each case record was scored by two independent raters and discrepancies discussed and resolved. Whereas possible Phillips scale scores range from 0 to 30, with 0 standing for a good premorbid adjustment, our patient sample scores range from 6 through 28 with a median of 22.

The cutting point selected to distinguish goods from poors is somewhat higher than that used by Phillips, falling between 18 and 19, thus giving us 11 patients classified as having good premorbid social adjustment and 21 patients classified as poor. This cutting point was selected after approximately half of the schizophrenic families had participated in the study. Scoring of case records was postponed until that time so that the experimenters, who were also the case record scorers, could run a number of family sessions "blind" to the good-poor dimension. At the time that the cutting point of 18/19 was selected this was the median score of the sample of schizophrenic patients. A disproportionate number of poor premorbid patients was added after this time because fewer good premorbid patients meeting all sampling criteria were available. The skewed distribution, with more poor than good patients, is largely a result of our selecting only unmarried patients, when marriage is an important criterion for obtaining a low scale score.

The distribution of Phillips' scale scores is listed below.

Scale Score	Numbers of patients
6	1
8	1
13	1
14	2
15	3
16	2
18	1
19	1
20	1
21	1
23	5
24	6
25	3
28	4

A. 2 The Relationship between the Patient Population and the Sample of Schizophrenic Patients

From the total listing of admission to the Massachusetts Mental Health Center, the following selective steps were taken to obtain the final sample of schizophrenic patients who, along with their families, participated in the study.

1. Population of all hospital admissions listed, from which all schizo-phrenic patients were selected, on basis of diagnosis.
2. Population of all schizophrenic patients listed, from which all patients meeting sampling criteria were selected, on basis of social characteristics.
3. Sample of all schizophrenic patients meeting sampling criteria listed; some families refused to participate.

The following tables provide information about the characteristics of the sample at each of these steps.

Population of Admissions

Table A.1 All MMHC Admissions (Inpatients and Day Hospital), January 1, 1963, Through December 31, 1963, by Diagnosis

Diagnosis	N	Percentage
Schizophrenia	276	28.4
1. Schizophrenic reaction	93	9.6
2. Paranoid	71	7.3
3. Catatonic	12	1.2
4. Hebephrenic	3	0.3
5. Simple schizophrenia	4	0.4
6. Schizo-affective	45	4.6
7. Mixed and undifferentiated	21	2.2
8. Chronic	6	0.6
9. No subtype	21	2.2
Borderline schizophrenia	6	0.6
Other psychoses	114	11.7
Neurosis		
psychoneurotic	30	3.1
depressive reaction	112	11.5
Character disorder	244	25.1
Organic disorder	50	5.1
No diagnosis or no mental illness	139	14.3

Sample of all Schizophrenic Patient Admissions

The 276 schizophrenic patients admitted during the year January 1, 1963 through December 31, 1963 were supplemented by 97 patients diagnosed as schizophrenic who were admitted following this period. We have no reason to believe that there are significant differences between these two samples. The sample of schizophrenic patient admissions, presented in Table A. 2, consists of 373 patients.

In Table A. 2 the distributions of cases according to the sampling criteria indicate that the largest number of patients is lost because the well

Table A.2   Number and Percentage of Patients Diagnosed as Schizophrenic Lost through Disqualification on Sampling Criteria

Sampling Criteria	N	Percentage
1. Race		
a. Caucasian [a]	343	92.0
b. Negro, Oriental, other	30	8.0
2. Marital status of patient		
a. Single [a]	238	63.8
b. Married	88	23.6
c. Separated, divorced, widowed	47	12.6
3. Residence of patient		
a. Living with parents [a]	163	43.7
b. Other: With spouse, school, institution	210	56.3
4. Area of residence		
a. Boston area [a]	154	41.3
b. Outside Boston area	219	58.7
5. Status of parents		
a. Living together [a]	192	51.5
b. Other: dead, divorced, etc.	181	48.5
6. Number of siblings		
a. 1 + [a]	298	79.9
b. 0 or NA	75	20.1
7. Sex of siblings		
a. Like patient, like and unlike [a]	225	60.3
b. Unlike, NA	148	39.7
8. Marital status of siblings		
a. Single, single and married [a]	219	58.7
b. Married, no sibs, NA	154	41.3
9. Residence of siblings		
a. With parents, spouses, and parents [a]	148	39.7
b. With spouses, no sibs, NA	225	60.3

[a] These characteristics meet the sampling criteria.

sibling does not live with the parents, the family lives outside the Boston
area, the patient lives away from home, and the parents are dead or
divorced.

Of the 373 schizophrenic patients in the sample, 50 (13.4%) met all of
the sampling criteria. The failure to meet sampling criteria was usually a
result of disqualification for more than one reason.

Sample of Schizophrenic Patients in the Study

The qualified sample of 50 schizophrenic patients, along with their families, were asked to participate in the study. Of these 18 (or 36%) refused;
36 participated at least once. Background data for both refusing and participating families were obtained from the patient's hospital record. Table

Table A.3   Number and Percentage of Schizophrenic Patients Disqualified from the Sample by Sampling Criteria

	N	Percentage
Patients qualified for sample	50	13.4
Patients not qualified for sample	323	86.6
Three or more disqualifying criteria	126	33.8
Two disqualifying criteria	86	23.1
One disqualifying criterion	86	23.1
Other [a]	25	6.6

[a] These patients were eligible for the study according to case records but a further check revealed reasons for their disqualification, e.g., recent death of a parent, the well sibling's return to school outside the state, etc.

Table A.4   Comparison of Schizophrenic Patient Families Who Refused with Those Who Participated, on Four Background Characteristics

	Refused		Participated	
	N	Percentage	N	Percentage
Sex of patient				
Male	8	44.4	21	65.6
Female	10	55.6	11	34.4
			$\chi^2 = 1.34$	
			df = 1; NS	
Age of patient				
15–19	4	22.2	10	31.2
20–24	9	50.0	17	53.1
25 +	5	27.8	5	15.6
			$\chi^2 = 1.207$	
			df = 2; NS	
Religion of patient				
Catholic	11	61.1	17	53.1
Protestant	4 ⎫	22.2	6 ⎫	18.8
Jewish	2 ⎬ 7	11.1	5 ⎬ 15	15.6
Other	1 ⎭	5.5	4 ⎭	12.5
			$\chi^2 = .006$	
			df = 1; NS	
Education of father				
NA	0 ⎫	0.0	1 ⎫	3.1
1–12 years	10 ⎬ 10	55.5	14 ⎬ 15	43.8
12 + years	8	44.4	17	53.1
			$\chi^2 = .16$	
			df = 1; NS	

A. 4 compares the two sets of families on four variables, sex, age, religion of patient, and educational level of the father.

Chi-square tests indicate that there are no significant differences between the schizophrenic families participating in the study and those that refused to participate. Those families that chose to participate tended to be more likely to have patient sons rather than daughters, younger patients, and a somewhat higher educational level. These differences, however, are assumed to be too small to have had an important effect on the degree to which findings from the sample can be generalized to the 50 qualified patient families.

A. 3 The Relationship between Background Characteristics of Schizophrenic and Normal Families

Information on background characteristics was obtained by a questionnaire given to parents at the second session. In instances when the family participated only once, partial background data were obtained from the patient's hospital record.

The following tables compare the sample of schizophrenic families (all types combined) with the sample of normal families on family income, father's occupation, father's education, mother's education, family religion, parents' birthplace, and grandparents' birthplace. Chi-square tests show that on none of the variables are there significant differences between the samples. (Families for whom data were not available, the Not-Ascertainable category, are not included in the chi-square tests.)

Table A.5   Yearly Family Income of Schizophrenic and Normal Families

	Schizophrenic		Normal		
	f	Percentage	f	Percentage	
0 - $6000	6	18.7	3	17.6	
6 - 10,000	14	43.7	8	47.1	
$10,000 +	3	9.4	6	35.3	
NA	9	28.1	0	0.0	$x^2 = 2.83$
					df = 2; NS

Table A.6   Father's Occupation in Schizophrenic and Normal Families

	Schizophrenic		Normal		
	f	Percentage	f	Percentage	
Professional and clerical	12	37.5	9	52.9	
Skilled, unskilled labor	15	46.9	8	47.1	$x^2 = .06$
NA, retired	5	15.6	0	0.0	df = 1; NS

Table A.7   Father's Education in Schizophrenic and Normal Families

	Schizophrenic		Normal		
	f	Percentage	f	Percentage	
High school or less	14	43.7	7	41.2	
Some college or college graduate	12	37.5	10	58.9	$\chi^2 = .25$
NA	6	18.8	0	0.0	df = 1; NS

Table A.8   Mother's Education in Schizophrenic and Normal Families

	Schizophrenic		Normal		
	f	Percentage	f	Percentage	
High school or less	13	40.6	9	52.9	
Some college or college graduate	11	34.4	8	47.0	$\chi^2 = .06$
NA	8	25.0	0	0.0	df = 1; NS

Table A.9   Family Religion in Schizophrenic and Normal Families

	Schizophrenic			Normal			
	f		Percentage	f		Percentage	
Catholic	17		53.1	11		64.7	
Protestant	6 ⎱		18.7	5 ⎱		29.4	
Jewish	5 ⎰ 15		15.6	0 ⎰ 6		0.0	$\chi^2 = .186$
Other	4 ⎰		12.5	1 ⎰		5.9	df = 1; NS

Table A.10   Parents' Birthplace in Schizophrenic and Normal Families [a]

	Schizophrenic			Normal			
	f		Percentage	f		Percentage	
United States	23		71.9	13		76.5	
Canada	2 ⎱		6.3	1 ⎱		5.9	
Northern Europe	2 ⎰ 7		6.2	2 ⎰ 4		11.8	
Southern Europe	3 ⎰		9.4	1 ⎰		5.9	$\chi^2 = .112$
NA	2		6.3	0		0.0	df = 1; NS

[a] Birthplace classification: if combination of United States and foreign birthplaces occurred, the foreign one was used; if two or more foreign birthplaces for parents were mentioned, the father's was used; if two or more foreign birthplaces were mentioned for grandparents the one most "foreign" to the United States was used.

Table A.11   Grandparents' Birthplace in Schizophrenic and Normal
Families [a]

| | Schizophrenic | | Normal | |
	f	Percentage	f	Percentage
United States	4	12.5	5	29.4
Canada	3⎤	9.4	2⎤	11.8
Northern Europe	9⎬ 22	28.1	8⎬ 12	47.0
Southern Europe	10⎦	31.2	2⎦	11.8	$\chi^2 = .508$
NA	6	18.7	0	0.0	df = 1; NS

[a] Birthplace classification: if combination of United States and foreign birthplaces occurred, the foreign one was used; if two or more foreign birthplaces for parents were
mentioned, the father's was used; if two or more foreign birthplaces were mentioned
for grandparents the one most "foreign" to the United States was used.

A. 4 Letter to Families of Patients

The Commonwealth of Massachusetts
Department of Mental Health

JACK R. EWALT, M. D.
SUPERINTENDENT

MASSACHUSETTS MENTAL HEALTH CENTER
BOSTON PSYCHOPATHIC HOSPITAL

SOUTHARD CLINIC   COMMUNITY CLINIC   CHILDREN'S UNIT

72 - 76 FENWOOD ROAD

BOSTON, MASS. 02115

Dear Mr. and Mrs.————:

As you know, the professional staff at the Massachusetts Mental Health
Center is interested in the families of patients as well as the patients themselves. In order to gain more understanding about families so as to improve
hospital programs, we are asking many families to participate in a special
project. An important aim of this project is to learn more about the ideas
and opinions of different members of the same family. In order to do this,
we need to have families come to the hospital together so they have a
chance to tell their ideas and to talk them over.

Your family is among those selected for the research and we are writing
to ask for your cooperation. It is necessary that we see both of you on two
separate occasions, once with your daughter————, and a second time with
your daughter————. Each meeting will be held at the hospital and will

take about an hour and a half. Meetings will be scheduled any time at your convenience. In order to obtain a true picture of the many different points of view in different families, it is important to the success of the study that each selected family participates in the study.

This research has the approval of the Massachusetts Mental Health Center. As is the case with all scientific studies, the findings will be put into a statistical report so that no individual person's views can be identified.

Within the next few days a member of my research staff will call you to arrange an appointment to come to the hospital. If you have any questions about the project feel free to call me. I think you will find that participating will be an interesting experience and will also be a useful contribution to the future work of the hospital.

Sincerely,

Elliot G. Mishler, Ph.D.
Director of Psychological Research

A. 5 Letter to Families of Normal Children

Harvard Medical School
Department of Psychiatry
74 Fenwood Road, Boston 02115

Massachusetts Mental Health Center
(Boston Psychopathic Hospital)
Department of Mental Health

JACK R. EWALT, M.D.
BULLARD PROFESSOR OF PSYCHIATRY
SUPERINTENDENT

Dear Mr. and Mrs.————:

As you know, the American family has become the object of widespread study. There is growing interest among family sociologists and other students of family life in the different ideas and opinions of families about the issues that come up in their daily lives. In order to gain a more scientific understanding of family opinions we are asking many families to participate in a special research study. In this study, families are asked to come to our office together so they have a chance to tell us their ideas and to talk them over.

We are writing to ask you for your cooperation. Your family's name was randomly selected from lists of names obtained from schools, churches, and clinics in the Boston area. The study requires that we see both of you on two separate occasions, once with your daughter————, and a second time with your daughter————. Each meeting is held in our research offices at 74 Fenwood Road, Boston, and takes about an hour and a half. These meetings can be scheduled at a time that is convenient for you, including in the evening and on weekends. In order for the findings of the study to show a true picture of the many different points of view in different families, it is very important that each selected family participates in the study.

This research is supported by a grant from the U.S. Public Health Service to the Harvard Medical School. As is the case with all scientific studies, the findings will be put in a statistical report so that no individual family's or person's views can be identified.

Within the next few days a member of my research staff will call you to arrange an appointment to come to our offices. If you have any questions about the study, feel free to call me. I think you will find that participating will be an interesting experience and will also be a useful contribution to the future understanding of American families.

Sincerely,

Elliot G. Mishler, Ph.D.
Director of Psychological Research

A. 6 Revealed Difference Questionnaire

Opinion Questionnaire

Here are a number of situations that people face in their lives. People have different ideas about what to do in these situations and we are interested in your own personal opinion about them.

Please put a check mark ($\checkmark$) next to the alternative that comes closest to your own opinion.

Also, please answer the following questions:

Your age: _____
Sex: M   F

1. The parents of a 14-year-old girl want to buy their daughter a new coat. The girl would like to pick out the coat herself to be sure it is in the same style as her friends wear. Her parents want to get a more practical coat for her, one that will last for several seasons. Should the girl pick out the coat herself, or should the parents have the final word?

Girl should pick coat herself _____
Parents should have final word _____

2. Mrs. Jones has a problem with her 3-month-old baby, who often cries when nothing is wrong with him, even after he's been fed and changed. The doctor says the baby is in good health, and says that all babies cry sometimes. The baby's crying upsets Mrs. Jones and she wonders what to do. What would you advise her?

Pick up the baby, or play with him, when he cries _____
Let him cry, and try to get used to it   _____

3. Some people believe that there is nothing a person can't do or be if he wants to, and if he really works hard. Do you agree or disagree?

Agree   _____
Disagree _____

4. Margaret has been seeing a man whom she likes very much and they are starting to get serious. She has never told him that she was engaged once before, several years ago, and that it ended unhappily. She hesitates to tell him now because it might seem strange that she never mentioned it before. Do you think she should tell him about it or just remain silent?

Tell him about previous engagement _____
Remain silent   _____

5. A 20-year-old boy who lives at home prefers to go with his parents when they visit their friends and relatives rather than to spend time in social activities with friends his own age. The parents feel that this is not good for him but do not know what to do. Do you think they should let him come with them as long as he wants to, or should they put more pressure on him to spend time with friends his own age?

Let him come with them as long as he wants to   _____
Pressure him to spend time with friends his own age _____

6. A foreman sees one of his crew taking some company materials home from work. Should he report him or should he just ignore it?

Report him _____
Just ignore it _____

7. Theresa, who is 23 years old, lives with her mother and father who are honest, hard-working people but who have never learned to speak English very well. Theresa feels uncomfortable about inviting young men into the house and is afraid this will spoil her chances of finding a good husband. She wonders if she shouldn't move to her own apartment with a friend. What should she do?

Move into her own apartment _____
Stay with parents   _____

8. You are traveling on the train by yourself when a middle-aged woman sits down next to you and begins to talk about her trip and asks questions about you. Would you talk to her about yourself or would you begin to read your newspaper so she would stop talking to you?

Talk to her about yourself _____
Read your newspaper   _____

9. George has just begun a new job and doesn't know anyone in his crew. A few of the men get together to go bowling after work and have asked him to join them. Should he join in with them right away or would it be better to wait a while before getting involved with one particular group?

Join in right away _____

Wait a while   _____

10. Since her husband died, Mrs. Green has been living alone. She has not been feeling well lately and her daughter is worried about there not being anyone there to take care of her. She wants Mrs. Green to give up her house and come to live with her. Mrs. Green wants to stay in her own house. Do you think it would be best for her to stay in her own home or go to live with her daughter.

Stay in her own home   _____

Live with her daughter _____

11. A 6-year-old boy comes home from school crying. He tells his mother that another little boy in his class hit him. His mother tells him to stop being a crybaby and to hit the other boy back next time. Do you think that was the right thing to tell him or not?

Right thing to tell him _____

Not the right thing   _____

12. Mrs. Allen, a widow, has asked her son to wallpaper some rooms in her house and to do some repair work for her. His wife wants him to do work around their own house that needs to be done. Do you think his mother has a right to expect him to do work at her house?

Yes _____

No _____

13. When a 19-year-old girl has a party at her house, should her parents go out for the evening to give her and her friends privacy, or should they stay home?

Should go out   _____

Should stay home _____

14. A Boy Scout group plans to enter a magazine subscription contest. Under the rules of the contest a boy can either try for the individual prize of a bicycle or put his subscriptions in with the other boys in his group to try for the TV set. Some boys think that they should all put their subscriptions together to try for the TV set, other boys think they should each have a chance to try for the bicycle. What do you think they should do?

Put subscriptions together for TV set _____

Let each boy try for the bicycle   _____

15. Mrs. Jones is worried about her 11-year-old son, who very often talks back to her when she asks him to do something. She feels that if she lets him talk back he will lose respect for her. But she also wonders if it isn't sometimes good to let a child express how he feels even when it is toward his parents. Do you think it would be a good idea to let him talk back sometimes?

Yes _____

No _____

16. Some parents think children should not be disciplined very strictly; others feel children should be strictly disciplined so they learn early about what things are right and wrong. What do you think parents should do?

Not use strict discipline _____

Use strict discipline   _____

17. Now that Johnny is two years old, his mother has decided to take a part-time job because the family needs extra money. While she is at work, an older woman comes over to take care of him. Johnny likes this woman but misses his mother a lot, and doesn't feel like playing when she isn't there. What do you think his mother should do?

Stop work and stay home with him   _____

Continue working and let him get used to her being away _____

18. Mrs. Thomas is concerned about her 19-year-old son who she feels is always making plans that he does not carry out. For instance, he may decide in the evening to look for a job the next day, but when morning comes she cannot get him out of bed. Do you think Mrs. Thomas should try to pressure him or should she let him carry out his plans in his own way?

Pressure him   _____

Let him carry out plans in his own way _____

19. Jim is very worried about his job and his girlfriend. One day when he meets a friend, he tells him about the whole problem. Afterward, he reconsiders and thinks that he should have kept his personal problems to himself. Which do you think he should have done?

Told his friend about his problems   _____

Kept his personal problems to himself _____

20. Mrs. Burn's husband died two weeks ago and since then she has spent most of her time sitting at home and feeling sad. Her daughter insists that it would be much better right now for her to find things to do and keep busy so that she won't think about her husband's death. Which do you think is better?

Keep busy and not think about him _____

Take time to get over his death   _____

21. The question of bedtime is an issue in many families. Do you think a 15-year-old boy should be allowed to have the final word about what time he goes to bed, or should his parents have the last word?

15-year-old should have final say ⎯⎯

Parents should have last word   ⎯⎯

22. The doctor has come to the conclusion, after many tests and examinations, that his patient, Mr. Weber, has an incurable illness. Should he tell Mr. Weber the truth or should he put off telling him as long as possible?

Tell him the truth ⎯⎯

Put off telling him ⎯⎯

23. Mr. and Mrs. Adams have saved a considerable amount of money during their 35 years of marriage. Mrs. Adams suggests that they give some of this money to their son, who needs it to go into business for himself. Mr. Adams thinks they should use the money themselves to enjoy some of the things they have worked hard for, like going to Florida in the winter. What would you advise them to do?

Give some of the money to their son   ⎯⎯

Use it to enjoy things they worked hard for ⎯⎯

24. Jean is 19 years old and has been going with one boy, whom she likes, steadily for the past year and feels that she has gotten to know him well. Sometimes she feels, though, that it would be better to go out with many boys and not get too involved with one person yet. Which do you think is better?

Go out with one boy ⎯⎯

Go out with many   ⎯⎯

25. Children often are disturbed when they find out that their own parents sometimes tell "white lies," that is, small lies to avoid an embarrassing situation or hurting someone's feelings. Should parents try to explain why they have to tell these lies so the children will not be disturbed when they hear them, or should they always avoid telling any kind of lies when the children are around?

Explain "white lies" to children ⎯⎯

Avoid telling any lies   ⎯⎯

26. Mrs. Collins is taking Peter to kindergarten for the first time. Peter says that he wants to wear his old cowboy hat. Mrs. Collins would like to let him wear it since he wants to, but she knows that the other children will be dressed in their best clothes and she'll be embarrassed in front of the other mothers if he wears the old hat. Should she let him wear it, or not?

She should let him wear it   ⎯⎯

She should not let him wear it ⎯⎯

27. Mr. and Mrs. Carter's 20-year-old son sometimes leaves the house for long periods of time without telling his parents where he is going and refuses to tell them where he's been when he returns. His father and mother feel they have a right to know how he spends his time. Do you think he has a right to keep this to himself, or should he tell his parents?

Has a right to keep this to himself _____
Should tell his parents   _____

28. Human nature being what it is, there will always be wars and conflicts. Do you agree with this?

Agree   _____
Disagree _____

29. Mrs. Johnson's mother is a widow who is now bedridden and needs someone to take care of her. Mrs. Johnson is thinking of having her mother come to live with her. However, she has three children at home who are still in school and she wonders if it might be better for her mother to go into a nursing home. Which do you think she should do?

Have her mother come to live with her   _____
Have her mother go into a nursing home _____

30. Janice has been spending a lot of time with a girl in her high school class that her parents disapprove of. They feel this other girl is a bad influence and want Janice to stop seeing her. Janice feels she has a right to pick her own friends. Do you think Janice is right in this?

Yes _____
No _____

31. Mrs. Rogers wants to send her 4½-year-old girl to nursery school. The little girl is afraid to be with the other children unless her mother is with her, and she has cried each time Mrs. Rogers has left her at the school. Do you think it is better to send her to school even though she cries about it, or would it be better to wait until she's older.

Better to send her to school   _____
Better to wait until she's older _____

32. Margaret loves to play the piano but she knows that she does not have enough talent to become really good no matter how hard she practices. She has decided to stop taking lessons and to spend her spare time doing volunteer hospital work. Do you think she is wise to stop taking lessons?

Yes _____
No _____

33. Mrs. Williams discovers that a 10-dollar bill that was on her dining room table has disappeared. Suddenly she notices that her daughter's 5-

year-old playmate has the bill sticking out of her back pocket. The child refuses to admit that she took the money. Mrs. Williams knows her mother will punish the girl very harshly. Should she tell her mother about this or not?

Should tell child's mother   _____
Should not tell child's mother _____

34. A 15-year old boy has ideas about religion that differ from those of his parents. His father becomes annoyed when he expresses these ideas and many arguments have arisen. Do you think he should keep his ideas to himself to avoid arguments, or does he have a right to express his own ideas if he wants to?

Should keep ideas to himself   _____
Has right to express his own ideas _____

35. At what age do you believe it is proper for a girl to begin dating? That is, going with a boy to a movie or going out with him when they're not with a group their own age? Sixteen or older, or under sixteen?

Sixteen or older _____
Under sixteen   _____

36. When a committee is working together, is it more important for the chairman to help people get along well together or is it more important for him to make sure that the job gets done regardless of how people feel?

Help people get along well together _____
Make sure the job gets done   _____

37. Mrs. Watt has 10 years to go before retirement. She is due for a promotion and has her choice between two jobs. In the first job she will supervise all the clerical workers in her department and will teach new employees how to do their jobs. If she takes the second job, she will have her own office and her own work to do without getting involved with new employees. If you were Mrs. Watt, which job would you choose?

Supervise and teach new employees _____
Do her own work   _____

38. Some parents feel that obedience and respect for authority are the most important virtues children should learn. Do you agree?

Agree   _____
Disagree _____

BACKGROUND QUESTIONNAIRE

We would like to get a few background facts about you and your family so that we can have a true picture of your family situation.

1. Who lives in your household? Please list all of the people, including yourself, who ordinarily live there. Include their ages and their relationship to you.

Relationship	Age
a.	
b.	
c.	
d.	
e.	
f.	
g.	

2. Besides people in your own household, which of your own relatives live in the Boston area? (Like your mother, your uncles, married children, etc.)

_____	_____
_____	_____
_____	_____
_____	_____

3. How often do you visit with your relatives at their homes?
   _____ Once a year or less
   _____ Several times a year
   _____ Once a month or more
   _____ Once a week
   _____ Twice a week or more
   _____ Every day

4. Do any of the family's relatives live in the same building as you do?
   _____ Yes
   _____ No

5. In what country were you born? _____

6. In what country was your mother born? _____

7. In what country was your father born? _____

8. Do you belong to any clubs, church groups, lodges, unions or other organizations?
   _____ Yes
   _____ No

9. How often do you attend meetings of these groups?

_____ Regularly

_____ Sometimes

_____ Rarely

OCCUPATIONAL INFORMATION

> For husbands: Please answer the following questions.
> For wives: If you do any work other than your own housework, please answer the following questions.

10. What is your occupation?
11. Specifically, what kind of work do you do on your job?
12. What business or industry to you work in?
13. How many grades of school did you finish?

_____ Grades 1-3

_____ Grades 4-6

_____ Grades 7-8

_____ Part of high school

_____ Graduated from high school

_____ Part of college or other adanced training

_____ Graduated from college

14. What is your religious preference?

_____ Protestant

_____ Catholic

_____ Jewish

_____ Orthodox

_____ Other

_____ None

15. About how often on the average do you attend religious services?

_____ Once a year or less

_____ Several times a year

_____ Once a month or more

_____ Once a week

_____ Twice a week or more

16. Into which of these groups did your total family income fall in 1962?

_____ 0-$2,000

_____ $2,000-$4,000

_____ $4,000-$6,000

_____ $6,000-$10,000

_____ $10,000 plus

17. Is there another language besides English that is sometimes used in your home?

    _____ No

    _____ Yes.   What is it? _____

18. Who usually speaks this other language?

19. Each family works out its own way of doing things. We would like to know how some things are done in your family. For example, how do the husband and wife divide up some of the family jobs?

    a. Who does the grocery shopping?

        _____ Husband always

        _____ Husband more than wife

        _____ About the same

        _____ Wife more than husband

        _____ Wife always

    b. Who gets the husband's breakfast on weekdays?

        _____ Husband always

        _____ Husband more than wife

        _____ About the same

        _____ Wife more than husband

        _____ Wife always

    c. Who disciplined the children when they disobeyed?

        _____ Husband always

        _____ Husband more than wife

        _____ About the same

        _____ Wife more than husband

        _____ Wife always

    d. Who takes out the trash?

        _____ Husband always

        _____ Husband more than wife

        _____ About the same

        _____ Wife more than husband

        _____ Wife always

    e. Who keeps track of the money and bills?

        _____ Husband always

        _____ Husband more than wife

        _____ About the same

        _____ Wife more than husband

        _____ Wife always

    f. Who repairs things around the house?

        _____ Husband always

        _____ Husband more than wife

        _____ About the same

    _____ Wife more than husband

    _____ Wife always

g. Who washes the evening dishes?

    _____ Husband always

    _____ Husband more than wife

    _____ About the same

    _____ Wife more than husband

    _____ Wife always

h. Who makes complaints when complaints have to be made, such as to the landlord?

    _____ Husband always

    _____ Husband more than wife

    _____ About the same

    _____ Wife more than husband

    _____ Wife always

20. In every family somebody has to decide such things as where the family will live and so on. Many couples talk such things over first—but the final decision often has to be made by either the husband or the wife.

a. For instance, who usually makes the final decision about what house or apartment to take?

    _____ Husband always

    _____ Husband more than wife

    _____ About the same

    _____ Wife more than husband

    _____ Wife always

b. Who usually makes the final decision about whether or not to buy life insurance?

    _____ Husband always

    _____ Husband more than wife

    _____ About the same

    _____ Wife more than husband

    _____ Wife always

c. Who usually makes the final decision about what car to buy?

    _____ Husband always

    _____ Husband more than wife

    _____ About the same

    _____ Wife more than husband

    _____ Wife always

d. Who usually make the final decision about what time the children should go to sleep at night.

    _____ Husband always

———— Husband more than wife
———— About the same
———— Wife more than husband
———— Wife always

e. Who usually makes the final decision about whether the wife should go to work or should quit work?
———— Husband always
———— Husband more than wife
———— About the same
———— Wife more than husband
———— Wife always

f. Who usually makes the final decision about what doctor to have when someone is sick?
———— Husband always
———— Husband more than wife
———— About the same
———— Wife more than husband
———— Wife always

g. Who usually decides what to do on a Saturday night or Sunday?
———— Husband always
———— Husband more than wife
———— About the same
———— Wife more than husband
———— Wife always

h. Who usually decides how much money your family can afford to spend per week on food?
———— Husband always
———— Husband more than wife
———— About the same
———— Wife more than husband
———— Wife always

These are some questions about family life and children. Read each of the statements below and then rate them as follows:

A	a	d	D
strongly	mildly	mildly	strongly
agree	agree	disagree	disagree

Indicate your opinion by drawing a circle around "A" if you strongly agree, around the "a" if you mildly agree, around the "d" if you mildly disagree, and around the "D" if you strongly disagree.

There are no right or wrong answers, so answer according to your own opinion. Please work as quickly as possible.

Agree Disagree

1. Children should be allowed to disagree with their   A a   d D
   parents if they feel their own ideas are better.
2. Playing too much with a child will spoil him.   A a   d D
3. A good mother should shelter her child from life's   A a   d D
   little difficulties.
4. A child should not plan to enter any occupation   A a   d D
   that his parents don't approve of.
5. The home is the only thing that matters to a good   A a   d D
   mother.
6. Too much affection will make a child a "softie."   A a   d D
7. A watchful mother can keep her child out of all   A a   d D
   accidents.
8. It is frequently necessary to drive the mischief out   A a   d D
   of a child before he will behave.
9. Children should realize how much parents have to   A a   d D
   give up for them.
10. All young mothers are afraid of their awkward-   A a   d D
    ness in handling and holding the baby.
11. If children are quiet for a little while a mother   A a   d D
    should immediately find out what they are think-
    ing about.
12. People who think they can get along in marriage   A a   d D
    without arguments just don't know the facts.
13. A mother has to suffer much and say little.   A a   d D
14. A child will be grateful later on for strict training   A a   d D
15. Children will get on any woman's nerves if she   A a   d D
    has to be with them all day.
16. When the father punishes a child for no good   A a   d D
    reason the mother should take the child's side.
17. It's best for the child if he never gets started   A a   d D
    wondering whether his mother's views are right.
18. More parents should teach their children to have   A a   d D
    unquestioning loyalty to them.
19. A child should be taught to avoid fighting no   A a   d D
    matter what happens.
20. Parents should sacrifice everything for their chil-   A a   d D
    dren.
21. One of the worst things about taking care of a   A a   d D
    home is a woman feels that she can't get out.

22. A mother should make it her business to know everything her children are thinking.   A a   d D

23. Parents should adjust to the children some, rather than always expecting the children to adjust to the parents.   A a   d D

24. There are so many things a child has to learn in life there is no excuse for him sitting around with time on his hands.   A a   d D

25. A parent must never make mistakes in front of the child.   A a   d D

26. If you let children talk about their troubles they end up complaining even more.   A a   d D

27. Mothers would do their job better with the children if fathers were more kind.   A a   d D

28. Most children are toilet trained by 15 months of age.   A a   d D

29. A young child should be protected from hearing about sex.   A a   d D

30. Children should not annoy parents with their unimportant problems.   A a   d D

31. Children and husbands do better when the mother is strong enough to settle most of the problems.   A a   d D

32. A child should never keep a secret from his parents.   A a   d D

33. Children who take part in sex play become sex criminals when they grow up.   A a   d D

34. Children would be happier and better behaved if parents would show an interest in their affairs.   A a   d D

35. A devoted mother has no time for social life.   A a   d D

36. The sooner a child learns to walk the better he's trained.   A a   d D

37. Children should be taken to and from school until the age of eight just to make sure there are no accidents.   A a   d D

38. Taking care of a small baby is something that no woman should be expected to do all by herself.   A a   d D

A. 8 Distribution of Experimenters within the Experimental Design

Table A.12   Distribution of Two Experimenters Across 88 Experimental Sessions

	Male Families		Female Families	
	EGM	NEW	EGM	NEW
Schizophrenic families:				
Good premorbid	2	8	5	5
Poor premorbid	6	23	2	4
Normal	12	8	9	4
Total: EGM 41%				
NEW 59%				

A. 9 Numbers of Questionnaire Items Discussed

Table A.13   Distribution of Number of Revealed-Difference Items Discussed in 88 Family Sessions

No. of items	No. of sessions
2	1
3	1
6	11
7	6
8	7
9	59
10	1
12	2
	N = 88

A. 10 Technique for Computing Reliability of Index Scores

The mean percentage agreements between two coders for a number of interaction index scores are presented in Table 3.2. Index scores are in the form of a percentage with acts falling into certain categories forming the numerator of the proportion and acts falling into other categories forming the denominator. For example, one Affect index score consists of all acts in categories $1+2+3$ in the numerator and the total number of acts in all categories in the denominator. We are concerned with the reliability of the coding judgment when categories 1, 2, and 3 are combined, rather than considered separately.

This agreement level is computed in the following way: The total number of agreements that an act is or is not in the numerator of the index is divided by the total number of acts in the denominator of the index score. Using the above index score as an example, all of the acts coded as either 1, 2, or 3 by *both* coders plus all acts coded as non-1, 2, or 3 by *both* coders are divided by the total number of acts under consideration. If the data were as follows:

		Coder A	
		Categories 1, 2, 3	Categories 4, 5, 6, 7
Coder B	1, 2, 3	17 A	2 B
	4, 5, 6, 7	D 4	C 27

N = 50

then the percentage agreement for the index score 1+2+3/Total would be obtained by summing cells A and C (44) and dividing by the total (50). Reliability for this data is thus 88%.

A. 11 Interaction Index Scores

Listed below are the formulas and names for each of the 79 index scores derived from the interaction codes. Scores are computed by summing the frequencies of acts coded in the categories listed in the numerator and dividing this value by the summed frequencies of acts coded into the categories listed in the denominator.

Interaction Indices	Name of Index
Acknowledgment: Stimulus	
1/Total	Inductions
2/Total	Questions
3/Total	Affirmative statements
4/Total	Elliptical affirmations
5/Total	Fragment stimuli
Acknowledgment: Response	
5+6+7+8+0/Total	Fragmentation
1+2+3/1+2+3+4	Positive acknowledgment
1/1+2+3	Acknowledgments that are complete
2/1+2+3	Acknowledgments that are partial
3/1+2+3	Recognitions
Affect	
1+2+3/Total	Positive affectivity
5+6+7/Total	Negative affectivity

Interaction Indices	Name of Index
1+2+3+5+6+7/Total	Affectivity
1/1+2+3	Positive interpersonal affect
7/5+6+7	Negative interpersonal affect
1+7/1+2+3+5+6+7	Interpersonal affect
1+2+3/1+2+3+5+6+7	Positive/negative affectivity
Focus	
1+2/Total	Focus on situation
4/Total	Others' opinions
5/Total	Own opinions
7/Total	Personal experiences
8/Total	General opinion and evaluation
Fragments	
Incomplete sentences	
1/Total	Incomplete sentences
Repetitions	
1/Total	Repetitions
Incomplete phrases	
1/Total	Fragments
Laughter	
1/Total	Laughter
Number of fragments	
1+2+3+4/Total	Total fragmentation
2+3+4/1+2+3+4	Multiple fragments
Interaction Process Analysis	
1+2+3+10+11+12/Total	Expressive
4+5+6/4+5+6+7+8+9	Giving information
1+2+3/1+2+3+10+11+12	Positive/negative ratio
1/1+2+3	Positive interpersonal expressive
7+8+9/Total	Informational questions
12/10+11+12	Negative interpersonal expressive
1+12/1+2+3+10+11+12	Interpersonal expressive
2+11/Total	Tension release
Interruptions: interrupting others	
1+2/Total	Attempted Interruptions
1/1+2	Successful interruptions
Interruptions: being interrupted	
1+2+3+4+5+6/Total	Being interrupted
4+5+6/1+2+3+4+5+6	Being successfully interrupted
1/1+2+3	Father speaks simultaneously
2/1+2+3	Mother speaks simultaneously
3/1+2+3	Child speaks simultaneously

Interaction Indices	Name of Index
1+4/1+2+3+4+5+6	Father intrudes
2+5/1+2+3+4+5+6	Mother Intrudes
3+6/1+2+3+4+5+6	Child intrudes
4/4+5+6	Father interrupts
5/4+5+6	Mother interrupts
6/4+5+6	Child interrupts

Metacommunications

1+2+3+4+5+6+7/Total	Total metacommunications
2+3+4+5/1+2+3+4+5 +6+7	Qualifying and disqualifying metacommunications
6+7/1+2+3+4+5+6+7	Metacommunications on rules and roles
2+3/2+3+4+5	Qualifying metacommunications
2+4/2+3+4+5	Metacommunications on others' statements

Negations and retractions

1+3/Total	Negator
2+3/Total	Retractor

Pauses

1/Total	Pauses

Statement length

1/Total	Proportion of acts that are new statements

Objects

0/Total	Acts with no objects
1+2+3+4+5/1+2+3 +4+5+6+7+8+9 +11	Objects internal to the family
1/1+2+3+4+5	"Me" as internal object
2+3/1+2+3+4+5	"You" as internal object
4/1+2+3+4+5	"We" as internal object
5/1+2+3+4+5	Impersonal internal objects
11/6+7+8+9+11	Impersonal external objects

Subjects

0/Total	Acts with no subjects
1+2+3+4+5/1+2+3+ 4+5+6+7+8+9+11	Subjects internal to the family
1/1+2+3+4+5	"I" as internal subject
2+3/1+2+3+4+5	"You" as internal subject
4/1+2+3+4+5	"We" as internal subject
5/1+2+3+4+5	Impersonal internal subjects

Interaction Indices	Name of Index
11/6+7+8+9+11	Impersonal external subjects
Speaker	
1/Total	Father's speeches
2/Total	Mother's speeches
3/Total	Child's speeches
To whom	
1/Total	To father
2/Total	To mother
3/Total	To child
4/Total	To no one

A. 12 Median Percentage Scores

In the table below are listed the median percentages for each interaction index score. These median scores are presented for each of the three family types in each of the two sessions. The family types (indicated by N, G, and P, standing for normal, good premorbid schizophrenic and poor premorbid schizophrenic) are ordered as high, medium, or low according to their relative mean ranks on the Kruskal-Wallis "H" test.

The Kruskal-Wallis "H" test takes into account only the relative rankings of the percentage scores, not the absolute percentages themselves. Therefore it is possible, as shown in the first row of scores for families of daughters, for one type of family to have a low mean rank and yet have a median percentage higher than another family type. This pattern occurs when there is a skewed distribution of percentage scores on the interaction index.

	Families of Sons				Families of Daughters			
Index	Session	High Rank	Medium Rank	Low Rank	Session	High Rank	Medium Rank	Low Rank
Chapter 5								
IPA expressiveness	pt	N 33.2	P 29.7	G 21.1	pt	N 37.3	G 29.3	P 32.8
	sib	N 27.6	P 27.3	G 27.7	sib	G 35.2	N 29.7	P 33.0
Affectivity	pt	P 51.2	N 49.3	G 45.6	pt	P 50.3	N 48.3	G 47.7
	sib	N 52.0	P 49.4	G 48.8	sib	N 48.3	P 46.8	G 42.0
IPA pos/neg	pt	N 70.3	G 62.3	P 53.8	pt	P 57.5	N 53.8	G 43.0
	sib	N 63.9	P 63.5	G 53.9	sib	P 66.2	G 51.2	N 56.6
Affectivity pos/neg	pt	N 65.2	P 64.2	G 59.4	pt	N 66.8	P 68.0	G 62.8
	sib	N 65.5	P 63.5	G 63.2	sib	P 67.6	N 59.5	G 63.2
IPA interpers. expressiveness	pt	P 5.6	N 1.9	G 2.3	pt	P 8.7	G 3.9	N 2.3
	sib	P 5.2	G 2.7	N 1.8	sib	G 5.3	P 4.9	N 2.6
IPA pos. interpers. expressiveness	pt	P 6.2	G 3.6	N 1.8	pt	P 12.9	G 1.5	N 1.5
	sib	P 6.5	G 2.2	N 1.9	sib	P 6.7	N 1.7	G 2.6
IPA neg. interpers. expressiveness	pt	P 2.4	N 1.2	G 0.0	pt	G/N	5.8/4.6	P 0.0
	sib	P 2.8	G 2.4	N 1.1	sib	G 7.3	N 0.9	P 1.7
Interpers. affect	pt	G 30.2	P 31.3	N 28.3	pt	G 40.7	P 40.1	N 32.9
	sib	G 34.9	P 33.0	N 27.5	sib	N 36.0	G 37.9	P 34.6
Pos. interpers. affect	pt	G 31.8	P 32.9	N 29.9	pt	G 40.0	P 39.8	N 36.1
	sib	G 35.8	P 35.1	N 30.4	sib	G 42.9	N 36.9	P 42.0
Neg. interpers. affect	pt	N 26.1	P 26.4	G 28.3	pt	G 29.5	P 32.7	N 27.8
	sib	G 33.2	P 29.3	N 25.6	sib	N 35.8	P 22.8	G 29.4

Index	Session	Families of Sons			Session	Families of Daughters		
		High Rank	Medium Rank	Low Rank		High Rank	Medium Rank	Low Rank
Chapter 6								
To father	pt	N 22.5	P 14.3	G 11.8	pt	N 14.0	G 15.8	P 10.7
	sib	N 16.4	P 21.8	G 20.2	sib	P 21.3	G 13.7	N 12.9
To mother	pt	G 25.3	P 22.7	N 18.7	pt	N 26.7	P 25.9	G 24.1
	sib	N 22.2	P 19.8	G 18.7	sib	N 28.3	P 18.1	G 18.9
To child	pt	P 25.5	G 21.6	N 12.3	pt	G 22.3	N 16.3	P 10.9
	sib	P 20.7	G 22.9	N 16.3	sib	G/P 19.0/17.8		N 16.3
To no one	pt	N 28.4	P/N 27.0/22.4		pt	N 18.4	G 16.4	P 10.9
	sib	G 23.0	N 25.3	P 24.3	sib	P 37.3	G 18.2	N 22.1
Statement length	pt	G 69.7	P 69.1	N 61.3	pt	N 64.6	G 62.0	P 60.0
	sib	P 64.8	N 62.6	G 60.6	sib	P 66.7	N 65.4	G 63.0
Chapter 7								
Attempted interruptions	pt	N 20.3	P 21.3	G 12.9	pt	N 26.4	P 16.9	G 13.3
	sib	N 22.2	G 22.6	P 19.9	sib	N 24.2	P 21.7	G 18.5
Successful interruptions	pt	G 21.8	P 18.8	N 17.0	pt	P 18.2	G 15.5	N 12.2
	sib	P 21.3	N 21.1	G 14.2	sib	G 28.0	P 15.5	N 14.9
Being interrupted	pt	N 19.6	P 17.2	G 12.3	pt	N 22.3	P 15.9	G 14.2
	sib	N 19.5	G 20.1	P 18.3	sib	N 21.8	G 18.6	P 17.5
Being successfully interrupted	pt	G 22.9	P 19.3	N 17.0	pt	P 17.7	G 17.2	N 12.6
	sib	P 21.4	N 22.5	G 17.0	sib	G 26.5	P 20.5	N 17.2
Questions	pt	P 11.1	G 8.8	N 7.4	pt	G 11.1	P 14.4	N 7.7
	sib	G 10.6	N 9.6	P 9.2	sib	G 11.1	N 5.9	P 3.6

Index	Session	Families of Sons			Session	Families of Daughters		
		High Rank	Medium Rank	Low Rank		High Rank	Medium Rank	Low Rank
Informational questions	pt	G 6.5	P 5.8	N 4.2	pt	P 12.8	G 7.5	N 4.0
	sib	G 6.3	N 4.9	P 5.3	sib	G 7.9	N 3.9	P 1.9
Chapter 8								
Tension release	pt	N 5.4	P 3.0	G 2.9	pt	N 6.3	P 5.6	G 4.4
	sib	N 4.6	P 3.3	G 3.0	sib	G 4.9	N 5.9	P 1.6
Laughter	pt	N 2.8	P 1.8	G 1.2	pt	G 3.2	N 2.8	P 1.8
	sib	N 3.2	P 2.8	G 1.8	sib	G 3.0	N 3.1	P 1.2
Pauses	pt	P 1.9	G 2.2	N 2.0	pt	G 5.2	N 1.7	P 1.3
	sib	P 2.8	G 1.8	N 1.7	sib	G 2.6	N 2.1	P 0.5
Total speech disturbance	pt	N 34.6	P 31.9	G 31.8	pt	P 39.8	N 31.0	G 34.1
	sib	N 34.0	P 32.1	G 32.7	sib	G 34.3	N 31.1	P 30.0
Incomplete phrases	pt	N 24.5	P 23.3	G 25.1	pt	P 33.0	N 22.6	G 22.7
	sib	N 24.4	P 23.8	G 24.6	sib	G/P 24.1/24.5		N 22.4
Repetitions	pt	N 12.1	P 9.8	G 8.2	pt	P 11.5	N 8.6	G 7.4
	sib	N 11.2	P 9.1	G 6.4	sib	N 8.3	G 7.7	P 5.9
Incomplete sentences	pt	P 2.8	N 3.2	G 1.8	pt	P 4.1	G 3.3	N 2.8
	sib	N 4.1	P 3.8	G 2.4	sib	N 3.4	P 2.5	G 2.6
Chapter 9								
Fragmentation	pt	N 35.5	P 29.0	G 24.4	pt	P 31.6	N 32.4	G 31.5
	sib	N 35.2	G 29.6	P 27.0	sib	N 31.0	G 32.9	P 24.7
Positive acknowledgment	pt	N 96.4	G 94.1	P 91.0	pt	N 96.4	P 94.2	G 94.1
	sib	N 96.9	G 95.4	P 92.2	sib	N 96.6	G 95.5	P 93.1

Index	Session	Families of Sons			Session	Families of Daughters		
		High Rank	Medium Rank	Low Rank		High Rank	Medium Rank	Low Rank
Attempted interruptions	pt	N 20.3	P 21.3	G 12.9	pt	N 26.4	P 16.9	G 13.3
	sib	N 22.2	G 22.6	P 19.9	sib	N 24.2	P 21.7	G 18.5
Elliptical affirmation	pt	N 8.5	P 5.9	G 3.3	pt	N 7.3	P 5.0	G 4.0
	sib	N 6.8	G 5.1	P 4.2	sib	N 5.9	P 4.1	G 5.2
Fragment stimuli	pt	N 5.0	P 3.7	G 3.6	pt	P 6.8	G 5.5	N 4.6
	sib	N 6.2	G 5.3	P 4.6	sib	G 5.4	N 5.0	P 3.8
Others' opinions	pt	N 20.2	P 15.1	G 13.9	pt	N 19.7	P 17.0	G 15.5
	sib	N 17.9	G 16.6	P 14.7	sib	P 18.0	N 17.5	G 14.7
Focus on situation	pt	P 10.7	N 8.0	G 7.2	pt	P 15.8	G 9.4	N 7.1
	sib	G 9.0	P 8.0	N 7.7	sib	G 10.2	P 10.2	N 7.1
Focus on personal experience	pt	G 13.9	P 12.7	N 9.8	pt	G 13.2	N 12.2	P 5.9
	sib	G 16.4	P 13.1	N 8.7	sib	N 14.7	G 12.0	P 6.7
Being successfully interrupted	pt	G 22.9	P 19.3	N 17.0	pt	P 17.7	G 17.2	N 12.6
	sib	P 21.4	N 22.5	G 17.0	sib	G 26.5	P 20.5	N 17.2

Appendix B

Interaction Code Book

Contents

Introduction to the Code Book

This Appendix is the coding manual used in the study. It includes all of the procedures and rules used to convert the tape recordings of family discussions into the quantitative interaction scores analyzed and reported in this volume. With only minor revisions in the arrangement of sections the rules are presented in essentially the way in which they were actually used. The reader will find that in some instances the name of the inter-action code category has been changed in discussions in the text; for example, the Tension code is referred to as a code for Speech Disruptions in the text. Changes in labels involve only that; there are no changes in content of the code as presented here. All of the examples used to illustrate code categories were taken from pretest groups.

We include here a summary of the coding method and some technical information about the organization of coding work that will provide a context for the specific codes.

Recording Equipment

Family discussions are recorded using a four-track Viking tape recorder. Four unidirectional microphones are used, three by the three family members, and the fourth by the observer sitting behind a one-way mirror. The tapes are transcribed from a four-track Viking transcriber that allows each track (and thus each family member) to be heard separately or all members and the observer to be heard together. Comparison of this recording technique with a standard one-track recording method indicated that approximately one-fourth of the interaction was not audible with the latter method.

General Data Processing Procedures

Tape recordings are transcribed onto ditto masters by the typist, using a set of standard typing rules. Typescripts are then checked by another person who listens to the tape, makes corrections on the typescripts, and inserts appropriate symbols as well as the information from the observer's record of "who speaks to whom." Following the checking operation, the interaction is broken into standard "units" or "acts" and these units are numbered sequentially. Several copies of each session typescript are dittoed.

Coding

With the exception of the Interaction Process Analysis and the Pause codes all coding is done directly from the typescript; IPA coding is done from the typescript while the coder is listening to the tape recording. Although there are many codes, each of which is independent and each of which is applied to all units, the coding operation consists of the coder working on groups of codes in a single reading of the typescript. Codes are grouped according to the degree of complexity and the level of inference required to make a coding judgment. Coding operations are as follows.

1. Tension
   Incomplete Sentences
   Repetitions
   Fragments
   Laughter
   Negation
   Retraction
2. Subjects
   Objects
3. Focus

4. Affect
5. Who Speaks to Whom
6. Interaction Process Analysis
   Pauses
7. Breaking-into-Speeches
   Interruptions
8. Acknowledgment: Stimulus
   Acknowledgment: Response
9. Metacommunications

Coders' Training. The coders were young women with bachelors' degrees whose prime characteristics were intelligence and interest in research; they were not necessarily psychology or sociology majors. Groups of coders (two or more) were trained by a process that consisted of practice on pretest materials, meetings to discuss code problems, and more practice, until a consistent level of 85% act-by-act agreement was reached for a code. Amount of training time ranged from two days for simple noninferential codes up to three to four weeks for the complex codes. Further, because a running reliability check was kept on all complex codes, if the per cent agreement level fell below 85% coding was stopped for further practice and discussions.

Coders were not explicitly told the hypotheses of the study nor the exact purpose of our expectations about the codes. They were also not told the type of family being coded; only family numbers identified the typescripts.

Reliability of Coding. A report of coding reliability and the method used for computing reliability is included in Chapter 3 and Appendix A. Throughout the total coding operation reliability measures were obtained by an independent recoding of one-ninth of each session typescript. One questionnaire item out of the nine given to each family was randomly selected for recoding and was randomly assigned to a coder. For codes in which only clerical errors contributed to unreliability (Pauses, for example) no standard ongoing reliability check was made.

Materials.

1. *Typescripts.* Sessions were typed on ditto masters so that several copies of the same session were available. This allowed flexibility in coding in that two coders could work on the same session at one time. Pages of type-

scripts were stapled together by discussion task; that is, the typescript for each family session consisted of nine packages, one for each of the items that the family discussed. This also allowed for flexibility and for control over the "halo" effect in coding; no one person coded a full session but instead coded only the even- or only the odd-numbered task items.

2. *Code sheets.* Code numbers were recorded on mimeographed code sheets having IBM column numbers recorded vertically down the left margin; the sequential act numbers were punched into the first four columns of the IBM cards. A "duplicate" set of code sheets for each family session was also used to record the data for reliability checks. For the sake of coding flexibility, each set of code sheets applied to one-half of the columns used on the IBM cards, that is, data coded into Columns 1–21 were recorded on Set 1 code sheets and data for the same session coded into Columns 22–40 were recorded on Set 2 code sheets. After coding of the session was completed, the two sets of code sheets were taped together to be punched on one deck of IBM cards.

Preparation for Data Processing

Code sheets were in the form appropriate for keypunching onto IBM cards. Each "act" was put on a separate IBM card, sequentially numbered. On the card were punched all code numbers for that act as well as identifying material such as family number, session number, and task item discussed. Thus there were approximately 1800 IBM cards of data for each family session because each session averaged 1800 acts. This method allowed for the greatest flexibility in data analysis, as it provided for sequential or process analysis as well as summary measures.

Time Estimates for Work

From records on amount of work done by a number of different coders over a period of six months, the following estimates for each operation were made.

1. *Typing.* Each family session (approximately 50 to 60 minutes of discussion) took an average of 18 hours of typing time, using the four-track transcribing system.

2. *Checking the typescript.* Each family session took one person an average of 15 hours to check.

3. *Unitizing and numbering.* No systematic records were kept. Estimates for each session, however, would be in the range of six hours per family session.

4. *Coding operations.* Each family session must be coded with nine coding operations. Including time for duplicate coding for reliability pur-

poses, *each* of the nine operations took approximately 10 hours; therefore the total coding time for one family session was approximately 90 hours.

From the time a tape recording was available the average time to complete *one* coding operation to the point at which the material was in a form for IBM card punching averaged 49 hours. The complete preparation for *all* coding operations for each family session took 129 hours.

Directions for Typing Typescripts

Format

1. Type on ditto masters.
2. Triple space copy, except for the items and the opening directions that the experimenter reads; these are single-spaced.
3. Margins: right—1 inch; left—1 inch.
4. Cover sheet. Includes case number, date, questionnaire items used, time taken for each, designation of isolate in each, a blank column on the left for "winner," total time, average time per item, and the initials of the experimenter.
5. Page numbers. Number pages consecutively through the typescript. Include on each page the case number (e.g., 17/002x, 18/002x, etc.).
6. Each time the experimenter reads a new item, begin typing that item on a new page.
7. At the top of each new item put, in parentheses, the sequential order of the item (if it is the second item given to the family, for example, this number is 2) and the number of that item in the questionnaire (this can be obtained from the cover sheet, e.g., #15), thus the numbers should look like (2-#15) or (7-#17).
8. Designations for the people in the group are the following.

Mo   (for mother)
Fa   (for father)
Son
Dau (for daughter)
EX   (for experimenter)

Symbols for Certain Incidents

1. *Laughter.* Any time laughter occurs, whether on the part of one or more people in the group, the symbol (L) should be included. If it is clear that only one person laughed put (L) by that person's designation (or in the appropriate spot in his speech). If more than one, or all, laugh put (L) by each of their designations.

Mo   (L) That's cute./
Dau and doesn't come back for months at a time/and (L) which I doubt./
Fa   (L)/
Dau (L)/
Mo   (L)/

2. *Interruptions.* Any time someone interrupts another person a symbol (I) should be included. This symbol is placed at the beginning of the speech of the person who does the interrupting, not in the speech of the person who is interrupted.

Mo   The only thing that I would disagree with is
Fa   (I) But when he first said the question/I thought . . ./

An interruption is classified as such only when

(a) There is no pause between the statement that is interrupted and the one that interrupts, *and*
(b) The interrupted statement is clearly incomplete *and*
(c) The amount of overlap between the interrupted statement and the interruption is no more than *one* act.

3. *Simultaneous speech.* Any time two or more people speak at once each of these people is given the symbol (S) to mark a simultaneous speech. If they both start at the same time, the (S) is put at the beginning of the speech; if someone interrupts and both continue talking, the (S) is put in at the beginning of the simultaneous speeches.

Mo   (S) if he went out for days and for weeks/
Fa   (S) if it was so long/that it might be days./

Simultaneous speeches are distinguished from interruptions in the following way.

(a) The speech that is broken into is completed, that is, the idea is finished, *and*
(b) part of the second speech is spoken at the same time as part of the first speech, *and*
(c) the amount of overlap is *greater than one act* in length.

4. *Pauses.* In instances when there are pauses during someone's speech or at the end of it, put in the symbol (P) to indicate a silence. A "pause" is defined as any silence in which it is felt that someone "should" be speaking.

Fa   I think you get your point across. (P)/Well, perhaps . . .

Content

The purpose of the typescript in our research is to allow us to measure many different aspects of communication—such as whether people finish sentences or not, whether they use a lot of "fillers" like "ah," "um," "I mean" in their sentences and whether they tend to stutter or repeat words and phrases. Therefore it is essential that the content be recorded accurately whether it makes sense or whether it is grammatically correct or not. To allow us to measure these things, use the following guides in typing.

1. Include every non-content verbalization. Use letters that come closest to the sound you hear.

Fa   Ummm.
Mo   Ahh.
Fa   Hmmm.
Dau   Uh, well, I mean that . . .

2. Punctuation. Use only the following punctuation.
Periods
Commas (sparingly)
Question marks (only if the sentence is clearly a question)

Do not use exclamation points, series of dots, or quotation marks. If the sentence is interrupted or trails off use no punctuation at the end.

3. In all instances when there is a sound or series of words that you cannot understand, put in a symbol (N.A.) to indicate that there was something said but it is "not ascertainable."

4. Record the words and sentences as you hear them, whether they are pronounced correctly or not, and whether they are complete or grammatically correct or not.

Procedure for Checking Typescripts

Content

1. Add every word or phrase that has been omitted by the typist.
2. Change incorrect words.
3. Fill in as much of the content labeled N.A. as can be heard.
4. Record "who-speaks-to-whom" in left-hand margin, using rules described in "Who-to-whom" Code.

Symbols

1. Cross out all (S) symbols that occur in the statement that immediately precedes a statement labeled (I).

Mo   Would you say well no,/Patsy, don't you bother? (X) I get the/
Fa   (I) Don't misunderstand the question either./
Mo   Well, I guess pressuring doesn't (X) do any/
Fa   (I) Well, I guess/we're agreed/that let him go with the parents
         until such a time/as she decides/that he shouldn't./

2. Put in any of the following symbols that have been omitted in the typing and take out any that are errors. Especially note the length of pauses.

(L)   (P)
(I)   (S)

(See typing rules for the use of these symbols.)

Additions

1. Underline the parts of statements that occur simultaneously; then link them together by a line.

Fa   I didn't answer that question tonight./ This is the way me and
         Mama answered it (S) *from last week./*
Mo   (S) *This is from last week./*
Dau But pressuring a 20 year old, don't you think/a 20 year old should
        have some kind of (S) *I mean/a 20 year old is old enough to
        know./*
Mo   (S) *No/no/ I ah* Well, if Patsy wants to come with us down to
        visit Nana or something/

2. When the second of the two simultaneous speeches is on the following page, underline the first simultaneous speech and drawn an arrow to the right-hand margin, labeled with a letter and the person who is speaking simultaneously at that point. The second simultaneous speech on the following page is also underlined and an arrow is drawn to the left-hand margin of the page, labeled with the same letter and the person with whom they are speaking simultaneously.

Dau To me it implied/that she (S) *already knew how./*

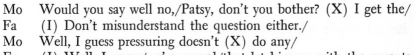

A W/Fa

Following page:

Fa   (S) *That's right.*

3. Draw a line across the page at the point the experimenter leaves the room following his reading of the discussion item and at the point the Experimenter enters the room (provided anything is said to or by him prior to the reading of the next item).

Procedure for Numbering Units

In general, units should be serially numbered from the beginning to the end of the session, with numbering going in the sequence in which acts occurred in time. Four-digit numbers are used, beginning with 0001 and possibly continuing to 9999.

Each unit is numbered at the beginning of the unit, with extra zeros omitted. In the right-hand margin every tenth serial number is written in full so that any particular act can be easily located. The first and last serial numbers on a page are written in at the bottom and top of the page.

Exceptions

1. All acts that occur while the experimenter is in the room are *not* numbered. These acts are identified by the line across the typescript at the point the experimenter comes in and leaves the room.

2. Simultaneous speeches: These speeches are put into a different sequence from the one on the typescript, depending on the following characteristics.

The simultaneous speeches are noted by an (S) symbol and by underlining the part of the speech that is actually simultaneous with another person.

Statements that are simultaneous are ordered according to their occurrence in time. The statement that is broken into is put first; numbering continues to the end of a complete sentence (defined as a "completed idea"). At the end of the completed idea the second simultaneous speech is inserted; this insertion includes only the part of the second statement that is actually underlined. If the first simultaneous speech continues beyond one completed sentence, it is then ordered after the "breaking into" statement. If the first statement does not continue beyond the completed sentence, numbering of the second simultaneous statement is continued.

Examples for Numbering Simultaneous Speeches

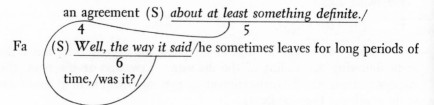

Dau   Alright,/well then we can make it specific./So that we can come to

an agreement (S) *about at least something definite./*

Fa   (S) *Well, the way it said*/he sometimes leaves for long periods of

time,/was it?//

1   2   3

Mo   But I mean/there are certain uh standard rules/that a child should

4   5

be, abide by./ That's what/I was in uh (S) *was thinking about.*/

7   8

Just those two things and nothing else,/that's true./

6   9

Fa   (S) *That's right.*/ (P) But that stressed just those two things alone./

1   2

Son   She's going to try to pick up the baby/or give her some toys or

3   4   5

something./ Attract his attention/or stop from crying./ All de-

6   7

pends/(S) *how bad uh badly upset she is,/I would say.*/

8

Fa   (S) *Isn't this/*

1   2

Mo   Well, I mean./ Uh, uh in kindergarten isn't as strict as (S)

5

school./ *That's right. And in thinking it over*/

3   4   6

Fa   (S) *You know/isn't it true, Bea,*/that five out of ten kids that go

7

to kindergarten,/half of them don't even want the idea./

Unitizing Rules

Purpose

This is a set of rules for dividing interaction into small units to which the other codes are applied. The unit is the same for all codes.

An "act" is the basic coding unit. Ideally, acts are the smallest meaningful segments into which statements can be divided. This means essentially that an act is a part of a statement that contains enough information to be coded into the other code categories, such as Focus, Affect, and Subject-Object. The basic assumption is that the simple English sentence constitutes such a basic act.

A "statement" is the complete content of one person's speech, bounded on either side by the speech of another person. Thus a statement may include one or more acts.

The "ideal" act has the following characteristics: (a) an explicit, complete subject, and (b) an explicit, complete predicate (including a verb and sometimes an object as well as modifiers).

The purpose of the following rules is to handle instances in which the above attributes are not clearly and completely present. The rules deal with the major categories of possible acts: both subject and predicate present, either subject or predicate present, and neither present categories. Rules are stated so that if Rule I applies, then Rules II and III need not be considered. Conventions for particular coding problems are also listed at the end. Units are noted on the typescript by a diagonal mark at the end of each unit.

Rules for Breaking Speeches into Units

I. *Single subject and single predicate are explicit and complete. Each set is coded as a separate act.*

> (A) Single explicit subject and predicate that together form one complete sentence (typically ended by a period).
> Examples:
> He's coming in./
> A half year doesn't make that much difference./
> You read it./
> It was the wrong thing./
> (B) Compound sentences, composed of two or more classes each with an explicit subject and predicate. Each clause is coded as a separate unit if it meets one of the following criteria (A "clause" is defined as an independent clause, not an infinitive clause.)
>
>> 1. If the clause is an independent clause (it has a complete meaning and could stand alone) and is connected to another clause by a coordinating conjunction, it is coded as a separate act.
>
> Coordinating conjunctions are: and, or, for, but, nor.
> Examples:
> He was sick/and he couldn't work./
> He had threatened him many times before/and that implies premeditation./
> He wants sympathy/and I don't like people like that./
> I was a Boy Scout/and no particular boy should be the beneficiary of one bicycle./
> Was this for subscriptions/or is this a contest?/
>
>> 2. If the clause is a dependent clause and the clause has a complete subject and predicate and a clear meaning, then it is

coded as a separate act. Dependent clauses are connected with
the rest of the sentence by subordinating conjunctions.

Subordinating conjunctions are:

that	since	if . . . then
though	because	when
inasmuch	for	after
as	however	how
before	nevertheless	therefore
what (meaning "that which")	until	whether

Examples:
Why do you think/that he shoulda kept it to himself?/
I'm licked/before I start./
I think this/if they're 19 years old/then they're old enough./
I think/that the question was put that way/because if you
    stayed home/then it would be to watch over the children./
She doesn't agree/that she should be chased out./
I married/when I was 19./

3. If the clause has a complete subject and predicate, has a clear
meaning, and is connected with another clause by an *unstated
conjunction*, then the clause is coded as a separate act. The
unstated conjunction in many instances is "that."

Examples:
Or did you think/(that) it was necessary for you to stay
    home?/
I think/(that) you should/
I think/(that) they're old enough to have a party./
Now, it depends on which way/(that) you interpret it./
I don't think/(that) it was meant that way./
If they had planned this party in advance/(then) they
    wanted to have a good time./
Why do you think/(that) you should stay home?/

II. *Either subject or predicate is complete and explicit.* (These are all
incomplete independent clauses.) These may or may not be separate acts
depending on the following rules.

(A) Subject is complete and explicit; no predicate. Code as a
fragment, that is, it is coded according to the rule in III-C. (The
content is not clear; therefore it cannot be coded.)

Examples:
  But he . . ./
  I . . ./
  . . . and I . . ./

(B) Subject is complete and explicit; incomplete predicate: Code as an act or a fragment, depending on whether the predicate is implied in the previous act. (Definition of an incomplete predicate: either a part of the verb is not stated, "I would . . ." or the object is left out, " she definitely needs . . .").

1. Complete subject, incomplete predicate occuring at any point in the statement, where the predicate is implied in the previous act. Code as a separate act.

Examples:
  Should the employees speak to the boss/or should the foreman?/
  Does the mother choose the coat/or does the daughter?/

2. Complete subject, incomplete predicate occurring at any point in the statement, where the predicate is not implied in the previous act. Code as a fragment (see rule III-C for fragments).

Examples:
  I think/it's a question of where *we thought* . . ./ (where sentence is incomplete)
  But then if it started crying again I'd . . ./ (where sentence is incomplete)

(C) No explicit subject: complete (or partial) predicate.

1. Code as separate act if
  (a) the subject is clearly implied in the context *and*
  (b) the predicate is complete or partially complete (the implied part of the predicate is clear from the context).

Examples:
  /or let him cry/and get used to it./
  You know/he'll be quiet/calm down/may go to sleep./
  You can't just leave the baby there/just dress him/and change him./
  He said/he was all right/and he was in his own community/ and didn't harm anyone./

2. Coded as part of a larger act if
  (a) the subject is not clearly implied, *and*
  (b) the predicate is incomplete and not clearly implied in the context.

III. *Neither complete explicit subject nor complete predicate.* These may or may not be coded as separate acts depending on the following rules.

(A) Elliptical sentences with clear content from the context. These are combinations of words understood to be a complete sentence when the context is taken into account: code as separate acts.

Examples:
(You raised your daughter all by yourself?/) All by myself./ And my son too./
(He's going to say,/"Look at me,/I'm a nut."/) To get pity./
(It's a question of where . . ./) Where the line comes./
(I think they should . . ./) Keep her semi-busy./

(B) Elliptical sentences with clear content from the generally accepted cultural meaning. These are combinations of words that imply a complete sentence; they are coded as a separate act.

Examples:

Good.	Remember?
What?	Right.
See?	O.K.
Yes.	No/I wouldn't fight./
No/no/I didn't mean that./	If he is a good friend/or not./
Say.	

Not elliptical sentences. These are treated as fragments. For example:

Oh
Well

(C) Combinations of words with unclear content (either from the context or the common culture). These are *fragments* and are coded as acts or not, depending on the following rules.

1. Coded as a separate act if the fragment is the complete statement (i.e., this is the only thing the person says). For example:
   But it's just . . ./

2. Coded as part of another act if the statement in which the fragment occurs has more content than just the fragment.
   Rules for inclusion of a fragment in an act.

   (a) Put the fragment with the neighboring act to which the fragment has the closest content connection.

Examples:
> He flared up very easily *and he*/you know./ Why didn't
> he give up?/
> I know/he must have looked into things *and nine times*
> *out of ten . . ./*
> But sometimes, *uh*, I said/that he didn't forget any-
> thing . . ./

(b) If there is no clear content connection between the fragment and the accompanying act, include it in the act
that follows. For example:

> So what?/*So his parents*, it's/it's inherited./

Unitizing Conventions

1. Code to minimize the number of acts when there is doubt about
utilizing.

2. *Inverted sentences.* Phrases added at the end of sentences (you know,
I guess, you might say, isn't it) are coded as separate acts. (If ordered in
the usual way they would be the subject and verb of the sentence, e.g.,
You know/that I feel . . ./)

3. *Parenthetic independent clauses.* When one independent clause (complete sentence) interrupts another independent clause they are coded as
two separate acts, as if one followed another. The clauses that interrupt
must have differences in content and must not be integrated into the sentence with conjunctions or adverbs. For example:

> Wasn't he operating [maybe I'm just dumb] under a persecution com-
> plex?/ ("Wasn't he operating under a persecution complex?" is one
> act; "Maybe I'm just dumb" is another act.)

Scoring Convention. Put brackets around the parenthetic clause to
indicate that it interrupts an act.

4. *Quotations.* All quotes are broken into separate units. Treat as a quote
all the instances in which the form is like a quote even though there aren't
any quotation marks. But if the quote has no verb, then treat the quote as
the object of the introduction.

Examples:
> My husband said/"I'm too tired to work/and I can't go on any
> longer."/
> But I do think/that many people think of funny things,/ "My life is
> useless," and everything./
> It said "school children."/

5. Non-content verbalizations are not units unless they form the complete statement. When they occur within a statement, treat them as fragments.

Examples:
Um, ah, huh, oh, uh, eh, mmm, hmm, ihh.
Laughter.

6. "I mean" and "you know" are always considered to be separate units, whether they occur at the beginning, at the end, or in the middle of a unit. If they occur in the middle of a unit they are put in brackets as are all parenthetic independent clauses.

Examples:
If they do it [you know] sometimes./
Well, I mean/do you agree now because/
I was a little hesitant/ you know./

7. Sentences in which the *subject is a clause* (having a subject and verb of its own) and the *object is a clause* (having a subject and verb of its own) and they are connected by a neutral verb (is, are, did) are separated into *two* units. Thus the fact of the connection made by the neutral verb is not taken into account; only the content of the two clauses is considered.

Examples:
The fact that he did it this way/is what I am talking about./
Why they were here/is the thing I am interested in./

8. *Repetitions and false starts.* Phrases and words that are repeated are coded as separate units only under the following circumstances.
(a) the phrase has a subject and verb explicitly stated, *and*
(b) the phrase is completed later in the statement, *and*
(c) the words that are repeated are exactly the same as the first set.

Repetitions that are units:
Well, if *that's/that's* your interpretation of strict./
It didn't/it didn't mention the home./
That's/that's/that's why I say./
Or *should she/should she* give up the practicing./

Repetitions that are not units:
And that's the way/we *try to try* to look at it./
Cause *you can't* just *you're dressing* something up as something special here/but it won't apply over there./
Well now *we went I went* through it there with Gigi down to the Y./

9. *Infinitives.* Infinitives and infinitive phrases cannot stand as units by themselves. Exceptions occur in the following instances.

(a) When an infinitive or an infinitive phrase is completely disconnected from a sentence (i.e., it does not serve as an object or a modifier) each infinitive or infinitive phrase can stand as a separate unit. For example:

> The way they mistreated the person,/the person that was bedridden./
> *To move him,/ to change sheets* and things like that./

(b) When an infinitive or infinitive phrase serves as one of many compound objects that all have the same subject and verb, then the second, third, and fourth, etc., objects can be split off and serve as separate units.

Examples:

> If she voluntarily decides to do that/*to give up* the piano/and then *to do something.*/
> That if you have something to say/it's much better to say it/and *to explode*/and *to get it out of your system*/than *to keep it in.*/

(c) When an infinitive phrase follows a comparative conjunction, the infinitive phrase is coded as a separate act. These conjunctions are usually "than," "rather," "but."

Examples:

> I'd rather work by myself/*than to have to work* with a bunch of other people./
> I'd like to have somebody around/*than to just work along.*/
> I agree/that you should be allowed to discuss/*but* not *to go beyond* in a defiant way./

10. *Gerunds.* Gerunds, along with their objects and modifiers, are coded as separate acts only if they are neither subjects nor objects of a verb.

This rule is specified further in the following instances:

(a) Gerund phrases that are completely disconnected from any other sentence or part of a sentence can stand as units by themselves.

Examples:

> Whereas *forcing* herself to practice the piano/which isn't going to get her anywhere/
> *Taking* into consideration the rest of my children/if they didn't want to get out of bed./
> That *being* more money involved in this/and there are certain things like becoming President./
> Yes/*being* in their own home/but not being with, grandpa didn't want to move in with us./

(b) When gerund phrases are used as compound objects of a verb, the second, third, fourth, etc., object phrases can be broken off into separate units. The phrases are usually connected by conjunctions that imply a comparison (but, than, rather, or, instead).

Examples:

There's quite a difference between sitting down/and *playing*/and *amusing* yourself/and *going*/and *spending* an hour in good hard practice./

I think/she's going to do it at the expense of raising her children properly/or *giving* the proper attention to her children./

You're instructing/or *working* with them./

And people think in terms of being President/or *being* the head of a school./

And I felt/that if by *letting* him come with them/it may help him over a rough edge./

Gerund phrases that are not units:

They said/should the parents have any say in *influencing* their friends./

People think in terms of *being* President./

They were talking about a fellow's *having* trouble with his girlfriend./

I can remember *going* to the movies with a girl and ahh 7th or 8th grade./

Sample Typescript

Ex   Margaret loves to play the piano but she knows that she does not have enough talent to become really good no matter how hard she practices. She has decided to stop taking lessons and to spend her spare time doing volunteer hospital work. Do you think she is wise to stop taking lessons?

Here father and daughter said, "Yes"; mother said, "No."

Dau   (L) Now I know why I had to keep taking piano lessons. (L)

Mo   (L)

Fa   (L)

07	08	09	10	11	12

Mo   No/no./ it said/she loved it/but she thinks/that she'll never be a great pianist./

                                13   14
D-4   Dau   Well I I liked it all right/(S) *but I* *didn't* like like practising.

D-4   or anything like that./
                                15
         Mo   (S) *Yeah.*/
                                16
         Fa   (L)/
                                17   18
M-O   Mo   But we discussed that (S) *last time*/so let's have your point of

                view, (Dau's name)./
                                19
         Fa   (S) *Yeah.*/
                                20
D-4   Dau   Ohh, about this?/
                                21
         Mo   Hmm mm./
                                22
         Fa   Wel-/
                                23   24   25
D-4   Dau   (I) Well you mean about about why/I feel/that she should stop?/
D-M
                                26
         Mo   Yes./
                                27   28   29
D-4   Dau   Hih well I mean/is she d- if she feels that (P)/ I just have no
D-4   30   31
D-M   reason/ I just kind of felt/that uhm that it wasn't that important
                                32
D-M   for her to take piano lessons/if she knew ho- she loved playing
                                33   34   35
D-4   the piano./ She obviously knew how to play./ I mean/it said/she
D-4   36   37   38
D-4   loved playing/so she knew how to play/and so I just felt/she
                                39   40
D-4   should sh- play without taking lessons./ And that if sh- you know/
D-4   41   42
D-4   if she felt/that it were time to get on to doing something else/and
                                43   44
D-M   hospital work is certainly ahh a valuable thing/ as well as taking
D-4   45   46
D-4   piano lessons./ So I just felt/that she should stop taking piano

lessons./
        47   48

Mo   Well I think/that I f- came around ehh to that last week./ The
                     49   50   51

reason that I said no/was that I thought/that if she love playing   750
                       52

the piano/and just because she'd never be a great pianist/is no
                     53

reason for (S) *her to have to stop.* And ahh (S) t- and to do h-/
         54

Dau (S) *Well that's right./*
                        55

Dau (I) But she can love taking without taking lessons./
          56   57   58

Mo   W- well you see/that's it./ That I just assumed in that quick
                            61   62

(S) *thing ahh/* that she was stopping/because she'd never be
                   63   64

great/and ahh if she enjoyed taking lessons/and enjoyed playing/ 761
               65   66

never being great isn't that important in my mind./ And I think/ 765
          67   68   766

ahm we agreed on that,/didn't we?/
         59   60

Dau (S) *Yeah,/right./*
            69   70

Fa   Well we agreed/that ahh it was all right for her to stop (S) *last* 770
                             72   73   with Mo

*time/*and ahh ahh turn to something else/but certainly ahh ahh
                                         74

the fact that she wasn't going to be a talented pianist/was not the
                          75

reason for stopping/but the reason for stopping was/that uhh
               76   78

(S) *she was playing the piano./* She'd had enough/and she
         79   with Dau   80

wanted to go on to something else/ and it wasn't ehh giving up
                         81   82

playing the piano/because she did play the piano/and could go 786
                        83

on playing it/ (S) *but she didn't want to use her time./*
                           → with Dau

71
Mo   (S) <u>*Hmm mm.*</u>/
                     77
D-4   Dau   (S) <u>*She'd had enough.*</u>/
                                 84   85   86
D-4   Dau   (S) <u>*See this doesn't*</u>/ <u>*well actually*</u> I mean now/this doesn't give
                                                                                87
D-4   any information (S) <u>*at all.*</u>/ *This it implies that*/
                        88   89   90
M-D   Mo   (S) <u>*No,*</u>/*it implies*/*that she wanted to keep on hmm hmm*/
                        91   92   94
D-4   Dau   (I) Well no/it (S) *implied that* to you./ To me it implied/that
                                            95   98
D-M   she (S) *already knew* how/but it implies (S) <u>*it only*</u> implies/ by
                                    99
D-M   the way you read it./
                            93
        Fa   (S) <u>*Yeah*</u>/
                             96
M-4   Mo   (S) <u>*Hmm mm*.*</u>//   (* Yes)
                             97
        Fa   (S) <u>*Yeah.*</u>/
                800
        Fa   (S) Yeah
                01
        Mo   That's right./
                02
        Fa   Uh huh/
                                    03   04
D-4   Dau   Because this this gives less information/ I think/then (L) the
                                05
                other one (S) does./
                                06   07   08
F-4   Fa   (S) <u>*Yeah*</u>/ (S) <u>*I'd accept the-*</u> this's a good point/that you don't
                                                                09
F-D   give up ahh ahh/simply because ss- somehow or other the uhh
F-D   11
F-D   idea got across to you/that you'll never amount to anything./
                            10
        Mo   (S) <u>*Yeah.*</u>/
                     12   13   14   15
D-4   Dau   I mean/you might/you know might/you might/

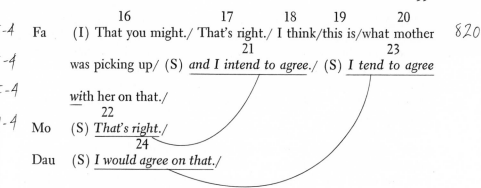

Code: Acknowledgment

Purpose

The purpose of this code is to measure the degree to which and the ways in which speakers "acknowledge" what has gone before them in the discussion. It is set up in stimulus-response form. Each statement is coded for its stimulus qualities, i.e., for the kind of expectation implied in the statement. Each statement is also coded for its response qualities, i.e., for the type and degree of acknowledgment of the immediately preceding stimulus statement. These two codes are independently coded. (The stimulus for this code was provided by J. Ruesch, *Disturbed Communication*. New York: Norton, 1957.)

We are particularly interested in the degree of acknowledgment, that is, in the extent to which the speaker takes into account the full meaning and intent of the previous speaker's comment. Therefore the different types of response are viewed as falling along a continum of degree of acknowledgment.

(1) The fullest type of acknowledgment involves an explicit recognition of both the specific *content* and *intent* of the previous speaker's statement. For example, a direct question is responded to by a direct answer or a demand for agreement is responded to with an explicit agreement or disagreement. This degree of acknowledgment is represented in our Category 1 of the Response code.

(2) A moderate degree of acknowledgment is involved when the specific *content* and/or *intent* is responded to. For example, if one speaker talks about whether the girl should be allowed to pick out her own coat the second speaker is acknowledging this content when he continues to talk about whether she should pick out the coat, even though he may not respond to the first speaker's intent. This is represented in Category 2 of the Response code.

(3) A lower degree of acknowledgement is involved when the second speaker recognizes in his statement that the previous speaker has said "something," but he does not respond explicitly to the particular *intent* or *content*. For example, the second speaker may note by "mmm" that he has heard what was said, or may respond to an interruption by saying "I'm still talking." This is represented in our Category 3 (Recognition) of the Response code.

(4) Finally, there is a category of nonacknowledgment in which the second speaker seems to be paying no attention to what has immediately preceded him, neither to the content nor to the intent of the speaker. This does not mean that his own statement is fragmented; it may be perfectly coherent and completed, but it is simply not connected to what has immediately preceded it. This is Category 4 of the Response code.

Stimulus Code

Purpose

In this part of the code each statement is coded according to the kind of expectation the statement sets up for the next speaker. "Expectation" refers to the limits set on possible responses by the content of the stimulus statement and by the grammatical form.

Summary of Acknowledgment: Stimulus Categories

1	Inductions or direct commands
2	Questions
3	Affirmations
4	Elliptical affirmations
5	Fragments
0	Not ascertainable

Procedures

The unit that is coded is the full statement, that is, a complete speech bounded on either side by the speeches of someone else. When this statement is composed of several acts, each act is given the same code number.

If more than one stimulus *type* occurs in a statement, code the one that occurs last (excluding fragments and elliptical affirmations). Thus in a long speech if the first few acts comprise a question and the last few acts form an affirmative statement, the affirmative statement takes priority.

Examples:

Son   Did he have a right reason?/ At six years old they don't know/ what they're doing./

The last stimulus type is the second sentence, coded as 3.

Mo   Wait a minute./ They think as a ss/

The last stimulus type is the "Wait a minute," coded as 1 (Induction).

In coding statements as stimuli follow the sequential ordering of acts (i.e., the way the acts are numbered), not the order in which acts may be typed on the typescript. This rule allows simultaneous speeches and interruptions to be considered in the order in which they actually occurred. For example:

                    02   06

Mo   Instinct (S) Stevie last year how old are they./ Six years old/Stevie
           08
      (S) all of a sudden from a quiet little boy went around/
      03

Fa   (S) aw no/
      04

Son   (S) Instinct/
      05

Fa   (S) aw no./
      07

Son   (S) Yes./

Act 02 is one statement; Acts 03, 04, 05 are each separate statements; Act 06 is one statement; Act 07 is one statement; Act 08 is one statement.

Categories: Acknowledgment, Stimulus

1. *Inductions:* Included here are:

(a) All statements that explicitly demand, ask for, or request changes in opinions about the task item or that request that someone take a stand on the item; it does not include statements of the fact of the agreement or disagreement.

Examples:
Will you agree on that?/
So you agree?/

(b) Direct commands of people in the situation. It does not include inductions that could not actually be carried out in the room. (e.g., Look at Castro).

Examples:
Talk into the microphone/so they can hear you./
No,/wait a minute./
Well, now look./

2. *Questions.* Included here are both direct questions of people in the group or of the group as a whole (with the exception of the questions that fall into Category 1) as well as rhetorical questions that may or may not demand an answer. This is a broad category in which *any* question, regardless of content, is included.

Examples:
Did you hear the question right?/
If everyone is fighting with each other/how can you do the job?/
How capable is the mother of the children?/

3. *Affirmative statements.* This category includes statements that are affirmative in nature; thus it excludes fragments, inductions, and questions. It includes statements that might be fragmentary but that are clear in context, i.e., combinations of words understood to be a complete sentence when the context is taken into account. (See III-A of the Unitizing Rules.) It does not include combinations of words that imply a complete sentence without context. (See III-B of the Unitizing Rules.) Ambiguous "you" statements are also included here.

Examples:
It's for the troop itself./
It's his own business./
Uh, you don't think/
Nursing homes take better care of an elderly person./
You can't answer yes or no./ (Ambiguous "you")
(You raised your daughter all by yourself?/) All by myself./
And my son too./ (Clear in context)

4. *Elliptical affirmative statements.* Affirmative statements that have no explicit content, but that are complete units and are elliptical sentences according to the Unitizing Rules, i.e., combinations of words that are clear without context and that imply a complete sentence (See III-B of the Unitizing Rules). By convention also included in this category are "That's right" and "I agree."

Only the following are included in this category:

Yes	Good	Remember
No	All right	Right
Sure	O.K.	What
Well no	Uh huh (i.e., yes)	Naturally
See	Yes but	Positively
Say	Heavens no	Of course
Maybe	That's a point	

5. *Fragments.* Included here are all statements that are fragments according to III-C of the Unitizing Rules, i.e., combinations of words with unclear content either from the context or the common culture.
Examples:

Ah, they/	This segregation business/
(L)/	Well/
Mmm/	

0. *Not ascertainable.* This code is used *only* for instances in which there is positive evidence that someone has spoken and positive evidence that the content is not ascertainable or noncodable. Thus the only statements coded in this category are of the following type:

Examples:
Son   (N.A.)
Mo   Coughs   (N.A.)
Fa   Sighs

Response Code

Purpose

The purpose of this code is to classify each statement in terms of the degree to which it acknowledges the intent and the content of the immediately preceding speaker.

Specific definitions of categories and examples vary according to the nature of the stimulus being responded to; in coding, these specific definitions should be referred to. The following summary of the code is simply for the purpose of showing the similarities in types of response.

Summary of Acknowledgment: Response Categories

1	Complete acknowledgment
2	Partial acknowledgment
3	Recognition
4	Nonacknowledgment
5	Fragments
6	Induction[a]
7	Question[a]
8	Affirmation (both 3 and 4)[a]
0	Not ascertainable

[a] These are responses only to Stimuli 4 and 5.

Procedures

The unit that is coded is the *full statement;* when this statement is composed of several acts each act is given the same code number.

Priority rule. When full statements could be coded into more than one response category, the category implying *more* acknowledgment takes priority.

Context for responses. The context to which the response can be referred is *only* the immediately preceding stimulus statement. Follow the numerical order of acts, not the order in which the acts are typed on the page.

Examples:

		Stimulus and Response Code Numbers
S:	But when they're 6 years old/ they're when they're 6 years olds/ there are no facts./	S-3
R:	Please, there are no facts./	S-3; R-3
S:	They're just, well they don't know anything/ and they're acting out of instinct/	S-3; R-4
R:	Little Howard he/	S-4; R-5

The meaning of specific words and phrases may be clear if the larger context is used (e.g., the rest of the page); this meaning *can* be used in coding stimuli and responses. The rule is the same as the "clear in context" elliptical sentences rule described in the Unitizing Rules. (See III-A of the Unitizing Rules.)

Coding responses when they are simultaneous with the stimulus speech. We assume that when a person's speech is broken into by another speaker, the first person *could* acknowledge the "breaking in" speaker if he wanted to. Because of this assumption, we use as context for the response code only the immediately preceding statement.

Examples:

		Stimulus and Response Code Numbers
	1	
Son	Instinct. Stevie (S) last year. How old are they?/	S-2
	2	
Fa	(S) Aw no/	S-4; R-4
	3	
Son	(S) Instinct/	S-5; R-5
	4	
Fa	(S) Aw no/	S-4; R-8
	5	
Mo	Six years old./	S-3; R-8

In the above, the mother's speech cannot be referred back to the son's first speech and coded as an answer to a question.

"That" and "it." In obtaining the meaning of "that" and "it," go back as far as necessary to get the meaning, as long as clear content can be pointed to to which the "that" refers.

Instances when "that" referent is clear:

S: I think/that this doesn't mean/that a son shouldn't help his mother./

R: No/I didn't say that./
   ("That" stands for all of the content in the previous sentence; thus both the intent (the "no") and the content ("that") is acknowledged.)

S: No/I don't say that./

R: In fact you know very well/ I don't feel *that way* about it./
   ("That" gets its meaning through the "that" in the stimulus statement to the previous statement.)

Instances when "that" referent is not clear:

S: Well you have to do it in good taste/and if the situation warrants not telling him/because he's flighty and/

R: Well if somebody's going to come all apart, why/

R: Well, *that* is the reason./
   ("That" does not clearly refer to any previous content.)

The first statement following the reading of the task item is coded as a Response in Category 0.

Categories: Response to Inductions

1. *Agreement/Disagreement response.* All explicit agreements and disagreements are included here, with or without specifications of the area of agreement. Instances in which commands are followed or not followed are included here.

   Examples:
   S: Do you agree?/
   R: Yes./

   S: Talk into the microphone./
   R: No/he doesn't have to./

2. *Expands, limits, repeats, clarifies the induction.* These are responses that follow directly from the attempted influence but do not agree or disagree. They acknowledge either the content or the intent of the previous speaker's command.

Examples:

    S: Raise your hand./
    R: We didn't disagree on it./We didn't agree
        on it./   (Acknowledges intent.)

    S: You have to agree/that she should pick out the coat herself./
    R: I agree on what?/   (Acknowledges content.)

3. *Recognizes the induction.* The response indicates simply that the request for change has been heard but does not agree or clarify. For example:

    S: So you agree?/
    R: Well, I think/maybe we should consider the question again
        the way/it was put./

4. *Nonacknowledgment of the previous statements.*
    Examples:

    S: You have to agree./
    R: Is that a one-way mirror?/

    S: Now wait a minute./
    R: I guess not. But still./

5. *Fragment.* Response to induction is a fragment (defined according to the Unitizing Rules). For example:

    S: Do you change your mind?/
    R: Well./

Categories: Response to Questions

1. *Answered, with complete acknowledgment of question.* The response to the question includes an explicit acknowledgment of the previous speaker's position in the discussion or the intent of his question as well as the acknowledgment of the content of his question. Usually these are "yes" or "no" answers along with content clearly related to the question.
    Examples:

    S: Well, are we all agreed?/
    R: Yeah,/we're agreed./

    S: Did you hear the question right?/
    R: Yes,/I heard the question./

2. *Answered, with partial acknowledgment of a question.* The response is a less explicit acknowledgment of the intent *and* the content of the question. Answers that are not clearly referrable to the question are coded in 3. This category includes acknowledgment that the question

is a question although it is not answered, or instances in which the question is answered appropriately with a simple "yes" or "no."

Examples:

S: What do you do about it?/
R: It depends on/what we decide to do./

S: Why should he want to go see friends of his parents all the time/ and not go see people in his own age group?/
R: I think/he's better off with people and with his own./

3. *Question is recognized, but not answered.* Includes instances in which the responder does not recognize the fact that a question has been asked but does continue to talk about similar content. This also includes recognition responses — sounds and phrases that indicate the question has been heard are included here.

Examples:

S: Yes, but under the circumstances, huh?/
R: Mmm/

S: It gives them a chance to get themselves in order/and just as they're supposed to./ If they have any business to take care of/straighten it out?/
R: Would you give that same answer in all situations?/

S: Does that mean/that if your mother was in the house/you would neglect the children?/
R: I'm still talking./

4. *Question is not acknowledged and not answered.*

Examples:

S: Alright,/when you say 7 or 8 hours/supposing/it was from 8 o'clock till 5 or 6 o'clock every morning?/
R: No or yes./

S: That's his own fault./ Right?/
R: I always felt,/ and well jeez, if I don't./

S: We'll have none of that,/all right?/
R: Get you going on that wallpaper./

5. *Question is followed by a fragment.* (Fragments are defined in the Unitizing Rules.) The revelance of the response to the question is thus not ascertainable.

Examples:

S: If everyone is fighting with each other/how can you do the job?/
R: Oh, if they want the/

S: Why did you say it?/
R: (L)/

Categories: Response to Affirmative Statements

1. *Complete acknowledgment* of the previous speaker's position in the
    discussion on the intent of his statement as well as acknowledgement of
    the content of the previous statement. This can be in the form of
    questioning the intent and content. Included also are responses that
    explicitly agree or disagree that are further clarified by content. An-
    other kind of response to intent is "giving in" on the item disagree-
    ment, or responding to this "giving in" even though the response does
    not label the fact of the "giving in." [1]

    Examples:
    S: I think/the girl should pick out her own coat./ ("giving in")
    R: All right./ Raise your hand./

    S: It's for the troop itself./
    R: Well then I guess/I agree with that./ I think/it'd be better,/I've
         changed my mind./

---

[1] Note regarding Categories 1 and 2:

(a) Ways of responding to the *intent* of the previous speaker. In general, Category 1
demands response to intent, *and* content; Category 2 demands response to intent *or*
content. The following types of response are used as indicators of a response to the
intent of the speaker.

<u>Yes</u>,/I think/that she should . . ./
<u>No</u>,/the boy should stay home . . ./
<u>I disagree</u>/that . . ./
   <u>I agree</u>/that . . ./
   <u>But, I</u> think . . ./
   That's right + content.

These indicators usually appear at the beginning of a statement although they may be
used if they appear elsewhere and if they clearly refer to the other person and not to
one's own content.

(b) When there is explicit agreement or disagreement along with relevant content,
this is coded in Category 1.

S: Well, those were the circumstances/that were given./
R: Under those circumstances I agree/he should do everything for his mother./

When there is explicit agreement or disagreement, without explicit relevant content,
this is coded in Category 2.

S: So I put a big No/and I'm not changing./
R: I agree with you./
Also: I agree with that./
        I agree./

S: I hear so many people/that push their sons/and it don't get them anywhere./

R: Yeah,/but it depends on/if they're pushing them in on his own decisions./

S: I don't believe/she'd have any trouble ah inviting young men to the house/and having a chance to be married./

R: Okay,/ I agree./ I agree/that she should move out./

S: I'd move out./ Possibly I'd say so./

R: You mean/just because you're going to be 23/you're just going to move?/

S: Well then he obviously is ashamed/of what he's doing/if he doesn't want to tell his parents./

R: Not necessarily./ He might be stubborn like me./

2. *Acknowledges by completing, expanding, limiting, clarifying, questioning, agreeing, disagreeing with the affirmative statement.* Included here are all instances in which the content of the stimulus is taken into account and the content is in some way changed. Also included are instances in which intent is acknowledged but content is not. Instances in which the responder completes the speaker's sentence in a way that makes sense are also included.

Examples:

S: Well, nobody's pushing you./

R: No,/but still, I mean the idea is with . . ./

S: He did,/he said/use your own judgment/and think about it/ as though you were the one involved./

R: Well, if I was the one involved,/I wouldn't/

S: If once they stop the lessons,/they don't usually knock themselves out learning a great deal more./

R: Yah,/that's right./

S: Maybe it went back to/when I was younger./I always wanted a bicycle./

R: Like Richie wanted a bicycle./

S: If I have a child/and he's 20 years old/I'll think of him as a big boy./

R: That goes out for and he goes out for several days/and comes back without . . ./

S: I found out/that the more pressure you put on them,/ the less they're going to do./

R: So you didn't get any results without it./

S: If it's a matter of hours./

R: If it's a matter of hours/he has a right to keep it to himself./

S: Nursing homes take better care of an elderly person./

R: Do you know this for a fact?/

3. *Recognition of an affirmative statement.* Five types of response are included here.

(a) The response is a simple agreement or disagreement without clarification or expansion.

Examples:

S: It's his own business./

R: Oh, no./

S: Like say/Nanny wants a washing machine brought down the cellar, something like that./

R: O.k.,/o.k./

S: Well it had something to do with it/and I think/ it's a combination question./

R: Ya./

(b) Includes recognition responses that are sounds (Mmm), etc., as well as fragmentary phrases that indicate the previous statement has been heard.

Examples:

Mmm   But
Oh   Then
Oh dear.   Umm

S: Your daddy was a Boy Scout./

R: Mmmm./

(c) Includes instances in which there is a clear response to intent (through a "no" or "yes") but in which the content is clearly irrelevant to previous content. These are usually the statements in which the responder says "yes" in order to be able to break into the conversation.

Examples:

S: In fact you know very well/I don't feel that way about it./

R: Yeah,/but under the circumstances if he's giving them./

S: He just got into a state./

R: Now wait a minute/ Now wait a minute./ No/no/no/

(d) Includes instances in which there is *no* clear content connection with the previous statement but the responder *is* clearly talking about the same topic and not changing the subject.

Examples:

S: Yeah,/but Johnny, even when you were 20 and 22./

R: Well, if a person was 40 years old/and he was making the wrong decision/and you could help him/you should help him./

S: All he possibly can for his mother./

R: His mother wants him to do work in their own house./

(e) Includes instances in which the responder repeats the whole statement of the previous speaker.

Examples:

S: If it's a matter of hours./

R: If it's a matter of hours./

4. *Nonrecognition of an Affirmative statement.* These are responses that clearly do not recognize or respond to the intent *or* the content of the previous statement. It includes instances in which one person finishes the other's sentence with irrelevant content. For example:

S: (I) No,/no,/no,/the situation was/

R: (I) All he possibly can for his mother./

Includes instances in which the second person completely changes the subject of the first person's speech.

Examples:

S: Well, you have a point there./

R: Very often. If if they said/well a my son ah [you know] disagreed talks back to me once in a while,/that's natural./

S: And I figured/that was the reason./

R: Goes out for long walks./ And then he comes back/his parents want to know/where he's been./

5. *Fragment.* Response to the statement is a fragment (defined according to the Unitizing Rules) and thus the connection with the stimulus statement is not ascertainable.

Examples:

S: I, you haven't answered the question yet./

R: I'll Oh./

S: You don't have to,/we don't have to come to an agreement./

R: I mean ah./

S: Because that's knowing Leslie./

R: (L)/

Categories: Response to Elliptical Affirmative Statements

Since these stimuli clearly have no content that can be carried over or responded to and since the intent that they carry is so general, we are assuming only that these stimuli can be completely acknowledged (as in Category 1) or completely not acknowledged (as in Category 4); there is no possibility of degrees of acknowledgment between these types. All other responses that fall neither in 1 or 4 are coded as if they were responses to fragments.

1. *Complete acknowledgment.* This type of response is comparable to Category 1 of the other responses in that both the intent of the stimulus and the content of the stimulus are being responded to. In most instances this seems to be responses in the form of a question, asking about the motivation of the "yes" stimulus. The content or intent of the statement preceding the "yes" stimulus is not used to make a judgment about the type of response.
   Examples:
       S: Yeah./
       R: Does that mean/you agree?/

       S: I agree./
       R: Do you?/

       S: Yeah./
       R: Do you agree to that?/ That they should give up their money/ or not?/

       S: It's tomorrow./
       S: Tomorrow./
       R: That's right./

2. Not present for this stimulus type.
3. Not present for this stimulus type.
4. *Nonacknowledgment.* This nonacknowledgment category is narrow and explicit. It includes only instances which have *all* of the following characteristics:

   (a) The Stimulus 4 statement ("yes," etc.) is labeled in the typescript as being simultaneous either with the preceding or following statement.

   (b) The person who spoke preceding the stimulus is the same person who follows the stimulus.

   (c) The third speech is a continuation of the same sentence, without a break in the content or a comment on the intervening "yes."

Thus what is included here is only a response in which a speaker clearly talks *past* a Stimulus 4 without acknowledging it.

Examples:

S: He was picked up/(S) *so he wouldn't make a noise/*
R: (S) *Naw/*
R: So the result is/he opened his mouth/and made more noise./
(Response type 4)

S: Why should there be (S) *embarrassment/*
R: (S) *Yes/*
R: If the girl was engaged once before./ (Response type 4)

S: If the doctor says/there's nothing wrong (S) *with them/*
R: (S) *Yeah/*
R: And if the mother's taking the proper care of the child./
(Response type 4)

All responses to Stimulus 4's that do not fall into 1 or 4 are coded as if they are responses to fragments. The assumption here is that these stimuli do not set up, in themselves, requests for specific responses; therefore it is difficult to make a judgment about degree of acknowledgment. These types of response are coded according to their stimulus quality, as defined in the Stimulus Code.

5. *Response is a fragment.*
6. *Response is an induction.*
7. *Response is a question.*
8. *Response is an affirmative statement* (of either 3 or 4 quality.)
0. *Response is N.A.*

Categories: Response to Fragments or N.A. Stimuli

Since fragments contain so little information that "acknowledgment" cannot be judged (although it is true that in the family's culture fragments may have meaning or intent that can be acknowledged) we classify responses to fragments with the same code as Stimuli. Definitions of these categories are the same as in the Stimulus Code.

5. Fragment.
6. Induction.
7. Question.
8. Affirmative statement (of either 3 or 4 quality).
0. N.A.

Coding Conventions

1. "No" and "Yes" as response.
   (a) Simple "yes" and "no" responses. These are instances in which the "no" or "yes" comprise the full statement.

(1) If it is in response to an induction stimulus (1), it is coded as a 1 response.

(2) If it is in response to an affirmative stimulus (3), it is coded as a 3 response.

(3) If it is in response to a question stimulus (2), it may be coded as a 2 (if the "yes" is an appropriate answer) or a 3 or 4 (if the "yes" is inappropriate).

(4) If it is in response to an elliptical affirmative stimulus (4), it is an 8 response.

2. Instances in which the degree of acknowledgment *changes* within one response. When these changes occur, the procedure for deciding on a response category is the following.

Look at the first act and ask, "What is its degree of acknowledgment"? Keep this code category in mind as you go on to each successive act. For each of these successive acts, ask, "Does the degree of acknowledgment of the stimulus change in this act"? Then, code the whole statement into the category that implies the greatest degree of acknowledgment. In other words the degree of acknowledgment can never be lower than the first act but it can be made higher if later acts show more acknowledgment. This rule does not take into account the instances in which the person begins his speech by acknowledging and then goes on to change the subject.

Examples:

"Yes, but . . ." statements, in response to an affirmative stimulus, in which the remainder of the content is completely irrelevant to the stimulus would be classified as 3 because "Yes" by itself is a 3.

"Uh huh. Don't play with the microphone." would be 3 because sounds in response to the previous statement are 3 even though the remainder of the statement is irrelevant.

3. Fragmentary responses are those that do not have enough content to be coded into another response category. In some instances these may include what, in the unitizing rules, would be called a full unit. For example:

S: What is best for the child?/
R: Well, she should/
R: Suppose the child/

Both responses are fragments and coded as 5.

Code: Affect

Purpose

This code is designed to classify each act according to the explicit affective content of the words used. The point of view used to make a judgment about affect is the point of view of the meaning of the words in the common culture, not the affective meaning implied by the context of the interaction or the tone of voice used. For this reason each act is coded as if it were an isolated element and the generally accepted affective meaning of the words is given to the act. For example, when the verb "to like" is used in a sentence this is coded as positive affect, no matter in what context it occurs or what tone of voice is used.

This is an expanded and revised form of the "affect" dimension found in the code developed by T. M. Mills, *Group Transformation*. Englewood Cliffs, N. J.: Prentice-Hall, 1964.

Summary of Affect Categories

1	Positive affect in persons' relationships (moving toward)
2	Positive states of people
3	Positive qualities in events, situations
4	Neutral affect in persons, states, or things
5	Negative qualities in events, situations
6	Negative states of people
7	Negative affect in persons's relationships (moving away/against)

Procedures

In the categories are two major dimensions. One of these has to do with whether an *interpersonal relationship* is explicit or implied in the act or, in contrast, whether no interpersonal relationship is implied. (The contrast between "He confided in her" and "He knew the answer" exemplifies what we mean by "interpersonal relationship.")

The second dimension in the category system has to do with the *quality of the affect*—whether the affect implied in the act is positive, neutral or negative. ("He like her," "He mentioned it," and "He disliked her," are examples of the three kinds of affective states.)

No inference about the meaning of a unit may be made from one act to another. Each act is generally coded out of its interaction context.

Specific coding conventions are listed at the end of the code.

Categories

1. *Positive affect in persons' relationships (Moving toward).* Expressed or clearly implied in the act is an "interpersonal" relationship, involving coming closer to another person or persons. This "coming closer" can be by giving or receiving, liking, becoming like, being with another person or persons.

   The "interpersonal" aspect of the act may occur in either of two ways.

(a) The interrelationship is explicit in the act.

Examples:
  He met a friend./
  I sit next to Marion./

(b) The verb used in the act is one that normally requires an interpersonal relationship in order for it to have meaning.

Examples:
  You agree with me./
  You need to confide./

Examples of verbs that imply moving toward people:

to conform	to sit next to someone	to join
to stay home	to like someone	to forgive
to understand someone	to be with	to sympathize
to teach someone	to trust someone	to be close
to be taught	to care for someone	to explain
to agree	to confide	to convince
to want sympathy	to feel sorry for	to discuss
to want someone	to give in	to tell

  You agree on that./
  He wants sympathy./
  I tell a problem to someone else./
  I can see your point./
  If they all pool their resources./
  The Boy Scouts are a group./
  He's willing to go along with his parents./
  I wouldn't hold him back from going./
  He wants you to pick him up./
  He tells of his own free will./

2. *Positive states of people.* Included here are all acts in which people are described as being in a state of gratification or pleasure but which have no "interpersonal" component. For an act to fall in this category, it must have both characteristics:

(a) The relationship between the pleasure and the person must be explicit in the act; *there must be a person or persons actually* mentioned.

Examples:
  I find it better./
  It would give them a chance of winning./

(b) The state of pleasure or self-gratification is evident in the words (usually the verbs) used; the judgment about "pleasure" is made from the point of view of the common culture (i.e., from the point of view of most people in our society.)

Examples:

    You can go places./
    He will benefit from it./

Examples of verbs that imply positive states of people:

to understand an idea	to have initiative	to hope
to play the piano	to win	to express oneself
to be: nice, better, good	to benefit	to be capable
	to succeed	to clarify
to like an object	to strive	to be sensitive
to enjoy an object	to try	to learn
to deserve		to have responsibility

Examples of statements that imply positive states of people:

    A lot of boys could enjoy a TV set./
    Richie liked a bicycle./
    It would give them a chance of winning/
    You can go places./
    He deserves the most./
    I find it better./
    They do get out on their own./
    She's going to try to do something./

3. *Positive qualities.* Included here are all acts that refer neither to an interpersonal relationship nor explicitly to the state of a person (i.e., no person is mentioned in the act and no interpersonal relationship is implied). The act is coded as a positive quality because the words, usually adjectives and adverbs, refer to states, judgments, or situations that are generally seen as valued, pleasurable, or gratifying from the point of view of the common culture.

Examples:

That is cute./	All right./
It would be better./	That's right./
That is good./	That's true./
It isn't crying./	It's a good way./
That's the important thing./	That is understandable./
Do not forget./	

Also, by convention, the elliptical sentences that stand for agreement are coded in this category.

Examples:

Yes/	Right?/
O.K./	Naturally./
All right./	Definitely./

4. *Neutral.* Included in this category are all acts that have no implication of a state or relationship of pleasure or displeasure. These tend to be descriptive statements, without qualifying evaluative adjectives or adverbs, of activities or situations that lend themselves to being either positive or negative but are neutral unless there is further information within the act. Also included are all elliptical statements that are clear without looking at their context and that have no positive or negative connotations.

Examples of verbs that have netural qualities:

to realize	to know
to work	to think
to go out	to make
to sell	to cook
to go to school	to sit
to do	to watch
to mention	to interpret
to wonder	to be in an occupation
to tell (with no personal object)	to have the final say
to talk (with no personal object)	to listen
to control (with no personal object)	

Examples of statements that have neutral qualities:

What can you say?/	They would know/what to do./
I feel/	Todd doesn't know about that./
and express their opinion./	They remember, just like a dog./
They didn't phrase the question that way./	If they had said/
	That's a natural thing./
If they do it sometime./	"Harshly" means a beating./
I think/they should./	Authority governs the home./
Now he's 24./	Probably./

5. *Negative qualities.* Included here are all acts that have no reference to an interpersonal relationship or to the state of a person (i.e., no person is mentioned in the act and no interpersonal relationship is implied). The act is coded as a negative quality because of the words, usually adjectives and adverbs, used. Negative quality is judged from the point of view of the common culture; it includes states and situations that are generally seen as bad, dissatisfying, and unpleasurable.

Examples:
It is a sign of weakness./
It is doubtful./
That's a confusing question./

That is wrong./
It's sort of a mad noise./
That's a very poor start./
Too much of those is bad and wrong./

Included, by convention, are also all elliptical sentences that stand for disagreements. For example:
No./

6. *Negative states of people.* Included here are all acts in which people are described as being in a state of displeasure or dissatisfaction, but which have no "interpersonal" component. For an act to fall into this category, then, it must have both characteristics:

(a) There must be a *person or persons actually mentioned in the act*, that is, the relationship between the person and the displeasure must be clear.

Examples:
The only thing that confused me./
I was a little hesitant./
He had a problem./
We don't have to come to an agreement./

(b) The state of displeasure or dissatisfaction is evident in the words (usually verbs) used; the judgment about the displeasure is made from the point of view of the common culture.

Examples:
Otherwise they'll lose their own personality./
He was unable to finish the work./
I was in doubt on that one./
I hesitated too./
They haven't turned out too good./
She was upset./
She denied taking the money./
You haven't answered the question yet./

7. *Negative affect in persons' relationships (Moving away/against).* Expressed or implied in the act is an interpersonal relationship, involving moving away from or against another person. Included are things like attacking someone, punishing someone, leaving someone, or being attacked, punished or deserted. The interpersonal aspect of the act may occur in two ways:

(a) The interrelationship is explicit in the act.

Examples:
I don't like people like that./
They didn't explain it to us./

(b) The verb used in the act normally requires or implies interpersonal relationship in order for it to have meaning.

Examples:

I don't agree./

He should have kept it to himself./

Examples of verbs that imply moving against/away:

to be different	to take away from someone
to keep things to yourself	to pressure someone
to go away from home	to scare
to talk back	to force or be forced
to hurt someone	to rebel
to disagree	to compete
to have a problem with a	to dislike
person	to tease

Examples of statements that imply moving against/away:

I should probably have disagreed with that./

of driving them away from home./

It makes them lose respect for their parents./

He has a problem between his job and his girl./

You got punished harshly./

It seems to me like a terrible thing to send your mother to a nursing home./

You're going to have trouble convincing me on that./

Does he have a right to keep it to himself?/

You wouldn't expect me to stay./

0. *Not ascertainable.* All acts that cannot be coded in 1–7 are included here; these are generally fragments and acts without verbs. Also included are acts with *parts* of verbs that cannot be completely understood in themselves. Also all elliptical statements that are clear only when context is taken into account are included here. In this code context cannot be used.

Examples:

No only my mother, mama's mother./

and not days./

or not./

not me./

Conventions for use with the Affect Code

1. Context. No inference about the meaning of a unit can be made from one unit to another. This rule includes the inference about the

meaning of "it" and "that" as well as the meaning of all units that are elliptical sentences unclear without context.

Examples:

I'm not certain whether he did it/ or not./   4/0

That is it./   4

She was not./   4

Should he help his mother/or not?/   1/0

You could be a (concert pianist.)/   4

Exceptions to the inference rule:

(a) Subjects of sentences can be inferred from context when the verb is clearly a personal one (that is, one that doesn't make sense unless some person is involved.). In this instance a general "you" can be inferred so that it is possible to code these acts into 1, 2, 5, or 6.

Examples:

and rob a bank/   6

misconstrued it/   6

(b) Subjects can be inferred from context when there is a series of verbs, all of which have the same subject but which fall in separate acts. For example:

He came in/sat down/and fell over dead./

(The "he" as the subject can be inferred in the second and third act.)

(c) Subjects can be inferred when the act is a command.

Examples:

(You) Try to remember./

(You) Finish your work./

2. Passive voice. All passive voice statements should be changed to the active voice before making the coding judgment. For example:

She was hit by the train./ (Becomes: The train hit her./)

3. Acts that include (a) a fragment and a true unit, or (b) two true units that have been misunitized. The decision as to which part of the act to code for affect is based on the general rule to add positive (+) and negative (−) affect in preference to neutral (0) codes. Thus, when there is a choice, code the + or − aspect over the 0; if the choice is between + and −, code the one that comes first in the act.

4. Priority rule for coding "within act" conflicts. When one act contains components that would call for coding the act into two or more very different categories (for example, coding it in both "moving away"

and "moving toward" categories), the section or aspect of the act that carries the major meaning of the act is given priority.

Examples:

Mother told us to get out of the house./
    (The "told us" part is 1 while the "get out" part is 7; in this instance the "get out" part is judged more important and given priority.)   7

Call the cops./
    ("Call" is seen as "moving toward" and therefore is given priority.)   1

5. Commands. The fact that a unit is a directive toward someone else is not taken into account in the code; the requirement that someone act or the force that might be implied in the command form is not used to code. Only the words themselves are used as a basis for judgment. There is one exception, however; the *"you"* that is the implied subject *can* be inferred.

Examples:

(You) Try to remember./ 2 ("Try" is positive.)
(You) Finish your work./ 4 ("Finish" is neutral.)
(You) Listen./ 4 ("Listen" is neutral.)

6. "Let's," "we'll" statements. Although the "let's" and "we'll" might imply "being together" and therefore Category 1, do not use this interpretation in coding these statements. Instead, treat them as if they were an "I."

Examples:

Let's use a different angle./ 4
Let's put it that way./   4
Let's go fishing./   2
Let's find it soon./   4

7. "Should," "ought," "have to" statements. In some statements, when the context is taken into account, these statements might be interpreted as "moving against" since they carry the meaning "to be forced" or "to force." We are *not* taking the "to force" connotation into account in coding the act. Instead, the act is coded as it would be if the "should" were completely neutral.

Examples:

He doesn't have to explain./ (He does not explain.)   7
If he had to do it exclusively for his mother./ (He did do it exclusively for his mother.)   1
He should./   4

They have to realize their limitations./   6
They should call the cops./   1

8. "Can," "cannot" statements. In coding these statements, first take out the "can" or "cannot" and make a judgment about whether the act is basically positive or negative. Then classify the act according to the table below; e.g., if the act is basically positive and the verb includes "cannot" then the act should be coded as a negative affect act.

	Can	Cannot
Positive Affect	+	−
Neutral Affect	0	0
Negative Affect	−	+

Examples:

He cannot be a nuclear physicist./   4
He can be a nuclear physicist./   4
You can get your feet off the ground./   2
You cannot get your feet off the ground./   6
You cannot fail the test./   2
You can fail the test./   6

9. Occupational roles are always classified into Category 4 (neutral) unless the statement includes an additional evaluation, usually in the form of an adjective.

Examples:

You'll be a nuclear physicist./   4
You'll be the best nuclear physicist./   2

10. Qualifications implied by "if," "maybe," "supposing" and "might" are not used in making the affect judgment. Code the act as if the "if" were not there.

Examples:

If he's a good friend of yours./   1
What if you don't want to./   4
Maybe the guy don't even know./   4
If I wanted a car./   2
But the son he needs the money./   2
She might feel different./   6

11. Negations. All negatives of positive and negative verbs automatically put the act in the opposite affect category, i.e., if a positive verb is negated, the act becomes negative.

Examples:

I don't care./   6
He no look good./   6
You don't want to give everything./   6

You're probably not wrong./   2
Is she not bad?/   2

Negations of neutral verbs can be positive, negative, or neutral, depending on the affective meaning of the negated verb.
Examples:

I am not saying./   6
I don't know./   6
He didn't sit down./   4

12. Questions. In coding questions ignore the doubt suggested by the form of the question. Code as if questions were in the form of a declarative statement.
Examples:

Is that a good thing?/ (That is a good thing.)   3
Why did you pick that?/ (You picked that.)   4
Do you agree? (You agree.)   1
Don't you agree? (You do not agree.)   7

13. To want. "To want people" is interpersonal; "to want an object" may be positive, negative, or neutral, depending on the quality of the object.

To want a person: Code 1 or 7

Examples:

He wants his mother./   1
The parents want the child to look well./ 1
I want you to wash the dishes./   1
He doesn't want his mother./   7

To want an inanimate object: Code 2, 4 or 6, depending on the quality of the object.

Examples:

I want a new winter coat./   2
He doesn't want to go to school./   4

14. To need. "To need" is generally negative, implying that someone is deprived of something that he should have. Thus these acts will be either 6 or 7, depending on the nature of the object.
Examples:

He needs it./   6
I need a new winter coat./   6
I need money./   6
He needs his mother./   7

15. Too. When "too" as a modifier clearly implies criticism, the statement can be coded as negative.

Examples:
> She was gone for too long a time./   6
> You talk too much./   6

16. Conformity.   Acts that include verbs implying "to conform," such as "to be like," "to be different from," "to be an individual," etc., can be coded as "moving toward" or "moving away" or as neutral, depending upon the remainder of the act.

(a) Acts that imply "to conform" and that explicitly include a specific person or group to whom the person is conforming are coded as 1 or 7.

Examples:
> He should be like the rest of the kids./   1
> The kid wouldn't be dressed in conformance
>   with the other kids./   7

(b) Acts that imply "to conform" but do not explicitly mention the person or groups being conformed to are coded as 4.

Examples:
> Oh, he's an individual./   4
> He should be like the rest./ 4

17. Remember/Forget.   The following conventions are used for these verbs.

4 To remember
4 Not to forget
6 To forget
6 Not to remember

Examples:
> I wouldn't even remember./   6
> He remembered the meeting./   4
> He forgot the meeting./   6
> He didn't forget the meeting./ 4

18. To agree.   To agree can be either 1 or 2, depending on what the object of the agreement is.

Person as subject, no objects: Category 1

Examples:
> I agree./
> You agree./

Person as subject, person as object: Category 1

Examples:
> I agree with you./
> We agree with you./

Person as subject, impersonal object: Category 2

Examples:
    We agree with that./
    I agree with that statement./

19. One-word statements.   One-word statements that are elliptical state-
    ments clear without context *can* be coded for affect.

    Examples:
        Simon Legree./   6
        Love./   2

20. Category 4 versus Category 0.   In order for a unit to be classified as
    a 4, there has to be a verb *or* part of a verb in the act. Without a verb
    the act is 0.

    Examples:
        But the two./   0
        Or something./   0
        Rather than mother./   0
        Or he wouldn't./   4
        Could be./   4

21. To let.   When "to let" stands for "to permit," it can be coded as a 1
    or a 7, where the personal subject is understood.

    Examples:
        Let him go./   1
        Let him do it./   1
        Let him stay out late./ 1
        Let him stay home./   1
        Don't let him go./   7
        Let him move away./   7

22. May.   When "may" is used as a request to someone it is *not* assumed
    to be a "moving toward" statement. Instead, the "may" aspect is
    ignored, the sentence is turned into the declarative form, and the re-
    mainder of the verb is used to make a judgment about affect.

    Examples:
        May I talk to you?/   1
        May I leave you?/   7
        May I sit down?/   4
        May I?/   4

23. Direct address.   The fact that a person is addressed directly by an-
    other is not enough to make that act a "moving toward" act. Only if

the word that is used for the direct address is a positive word in itself is the act coded for its positive affect.

Examples:

Mom, look at this./	4
Don't you, honey?/	2
Dad, be quiet./	7
Dad, listen./	4

24. Quotation of an affect-laden word. If the quote is a single word (not a unit in itself), it is treated as if it were a neutral object. It is not given affective weight.

Examples:

It said, "pressure."/	4
It is pressure./	5
It said, "an argument."/	4
It is an argument./	5

25. To keep a secret. This verb, and its variants, is basically a *negative* verb since it is given the "moving away" connotation. It may be coded as a 5 or 7, depending on the subject and object of the sentence.

Person as subject: 7

Examples:

She's been keeping it a secret./
You're keeping it a secret./

Impersonal subject: 5

Examples:

It's a big secret./
It's going to be a secret./

26. Negations. Negated verbs that imply a positive affect should be coded as negatives. These are usually in the question form.

Examples:

Why doesn't he go visit her?/ Change to: He doesn't go
visit her./)   7
Why not tell him about it?/ (Change to: Do not tell him
about it./)   7

27. To say. "To say" with a personal object is 1; "to say" with an impersonal object is 4.

Examples:

He'd say to you./	1
What can you say?/	4

28. To have the final say.   By convention this coded as 4.

29. To obey; to respect.   Each of these verbs is assumed to be positive but not necessarily interpersonal.

    Examples:
He obeys./	2
He obeys him./	1
He respects the rules./	2
He respects her./	1

Code: Breaking-into-Speeches

Purpose

In this code we record who interrupts another's statement and whether the interruption is attempted or completed. The fact of the interruption is noted on the typescript by an (I) or an (S) at the beginning of the statement. Specific definitions of attempted interruptions (S) and completed interruptions (I) are presented in the Interruption Code.

Although these two codes, Breaking-in and interruptions, handle the same phenomena, the rules for recording of code numbers is different. Breaking-in codes are recorded into the act of the person who interrupts. Interruption codes are recorded into the act of the person being interrupted.

Summary of Breaking-in Categories

1	Interrupting act
2	Simultaneous act
0	All other acts

Procedures

The unit to be coded is the act that interrupts. If an (I) and a (S) occur in the same act, the (I) takes priority.

Categories

1. Interrupting act.   Any act with an (I) in it.
   Example:
   Fa   Well, in my opinion/
   Son   (I) But, I said/
         (Son's act is coded 1)

2. Simultaneous act.   Any act in the *second* of two paired simultaneous speeches that has either an (S) in it *or* that is underlined because it is simultaneous with the first act(s).

Example:

Son   All depends/(S) *how bad uh badly upset she is/I would say./*
Fa   (S) *Isn't this?/*
       (Father's statement is coded 2)

Examples of Coding Procedures

                                    01
(a)   Son   And that was my answer for ah (S) *avoiding it./*
                     02
       Mo   (S) *Mmmm./*
              Act 02, the second of two paired simultaneous speeches, is
              coded 2.

                      01
(b)   Fa   But that's what I/
                     02   03
       Mo   (I) Why you know/I couldn't agree with you./
              Act 02 is coded 1.

                   01   02
(c)   Mo   (S) *I would/I would talk to her./*
                      03   04   05
       Fa   (S) *I would/ah it it says/it's an* elderly person./
              Acts 03, 04, 05 are coded 2; acts that are partly simultaneous
              are coded as simultaneous acts.

                   07   08
(d)   Mo   (S) *I tried to/it's I tri I tried* to separate./
                           09   10
       Fa   (S) *You wouldn't allow him to meet them/if you could./*
              Acts 09, 10 are coded 2. Intervening non-simultaneous speech
              is not taken into account in tihs code (as in 08 above.)

                    80   81
(e)   Son   But hu like uh I like to be a football player/but I doubt/I'd
                            82
              ever (S) *make a football player./*
                                   83
       Mo   (S) *Well that is is* (S) *rather an impossible thing./*
                            84
       Fa   (S) *Yeah./*
                            85
       Fa   (S) *How about baseball/*
              Acts 83, 84, 85 are coded 2.

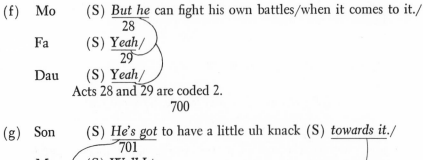

(f) Mo   (S) *But he* can fight his own battles/when it comes to it./

Fa   (S) *Yeah/*

Dau   (S) *Yeah/*

Acts 28 and 29 are coded 2.

(g) Son   (S) *He's got* to have a little uh knack (S) *towards it./*

Mo   (S) *Well I/*

Fa   (S) *He's going to* have the a talent/

Acts 701 and 702 are coded 2.

Code: Focus of the Act

Purpose

By the term "focus" is meant that part or aspect of the situation to which the act refers. This code therefore, is centered on the content of the interaction rather than on the style of interaction. Four main foci are distinguished.

I.   Agreement/disagreement/consensus.   An important feature of the situation in which the experimental families find themselves is that there is a disagreement among them and a requirement that they try to arrive at a consensus.

II.   Rules/procedures/context.   The rules and procedures of the experimental situation may be topics or objects of comments or questions. These acts are concerned primarily with what the family is supposed to be doing and how they are expected to go about it. Also included in this category are statements about the physical setting and objects in the room.

III.   Persons/states or opinions.   Individuals in the groups may be the direct focus of an act, with reference being made either to some quality they have or to their opinion.

IV.   Content.   All other acts that have a clear substantive meaning are coded here. Three sub-categories distinguish among acts that refer to the questionnaire item itself, to personal experiences, or to other extensions of item content either through interpretation or valuation.

V.   Not ascertainable.   Fragments, statements with unclear meaning in which judgments about focus are not possible.

Summary of Focus Code Categories

1	State of agreement
2	Rules, procedures, context
3	Person's states (in the group)
4	Other persons' opinions (in the group)
5	One's own opinion
6	Item content
7	Personal experience
8	Opinion and evaluation of item
9	Not ascertainable (NA)

Procedures

Priority rule for coding. In instances when two categories are equally applicable, select a category in the order in which they are listed: Agreement, Rules, Persons, and finally, Content. Use the same priority rule within these categories.

Context. Code each act independently according to the main focus of that act. When a single act is not codable (i.e., does not contain enough content to make a judgment about the focus), use the full sentence as context and code that act into the category representing the major focus of the sentence.

Examples:

Mo   But that's because (3)/I was a little hesitant(3)./

Fa   That's one thing (2)/they didn't explain to us (2)/Yes (2)/ he did (2)./

Code Categories

1. *State of agreement.* The explicit focus of the act is the *state of agreement* or disagreement that exists in the group or between any of its members. The words *"agree"* or *"disagree"* in some form, or a close synonym (e.g., concede, to be unanimous), must be used explicitly in the act.

   Examples:

I agree with you./	Do we agree?/
Then we all agree on that./	We can't convince you./
We concede./	So that's the agreement./
We were two against one./	

2. *Rules, procedures, context.* Questions, comments, statements about rules, or procedures, or other social-psychological and physical aspects of the experimental situation. This includes:

   (a) References to the group's relationship to the experimenter.

(b) Statements about the item (or the questionnaire) when it is considered to be an object in the situation; this includes *only* those acts that comment on or evaluate the item but contain no content from the item.

(c) Commands to other group members that make use of the implicit rules or attempt to change rules.

(d) Comments on physical characteristics of the experimental situation.

(e) Suppositions about the group in the room that serve to alter the rules.

(f) Comments on present actions of the group members.

Examples:

> What's the next one?/
> Does she come in/when we tell her?/
> Is it alright/if I change my mind?/
> Ask him/if we're going home/
> It's gotta be two against one./
> (I don't know)/if we're discussing these in enough detail./
> But we have to pick one or the other./
> This is a nice ashtray./
> I sort of took the question./
> Suppose/ that we're a jury./
> Where are you going?/

3. *Persons' states.* References to or comments about attributes, qualities, or states of *persons in the group* (except for states of agreement coded as "1"). The "states" referred to in this category are states of people that occur while they are in the group meeting, not past or future states. It also includes acts that describe actions of people in the group, the predominant meaning of which has to do with the state of one person.

Examples:

> You are very hard-hearted./
> We are getting all emotional about it./
> Maybe I'm just dumb./
> I'm licked/before I start./
> You're stubborn./
> I must have been crazy/when I answered that./

4. Explicit comments on, references to, and questions about *other's opinions* or the opinion of the group as a whole. Included are:

(a) Comments, questions about the reasons for the other selecting an opinion.

(b) Evaluations and judgments about the quality of the other's opinion.

(c) Phrases that are responses *to* another's opinion: Yes, no, o.k., all right; "see," when it forms the complete statement or when it forms the first act in a statement.

(d) Acts in which the "you" is *ambiguous* as well as those in which the "you" clearly refers to the other person's opinion.

(e) Acts containing "you know."

(f) Acts that comment on, question, or evaluate the action of another person while in the group situation. In some of these instances "you" may be implied and not actually stated.

Examples:

I see your point./
But you're right in a way./
Why did you pick that?/
That was quite a swing (in opinion)/
What do you know/(if he's a good friend)/(or not.)/
Yes./
All right/(That's what the doctor wanted to know.)/
(I think)/you know/(that he should.)/
So why bring it up?/
See?/
That's right./

5. Explicit comments on, references to, and questions about *one's own opinion.* This includes all instances in which an opinion is labeled as belonging to oneself by an introduction like "I think," "I feel." Includes acts that comment on, question, or evaluate one's own actions that occur in the group situation.

Examples:

I mean/(that . . .)
I feel/(that . . .)
I'm not sure about this/
I can see the point./
I don't know why/I said that./
I remember/(what you said.)/

6. *Item content.* This includes repetition of the content of the item being discussed. The item content referred to must be stated in a way that is correct or in the form of an accurate paraphrase. If, *within* the same act, there is an added evaluation, a changed meaning, or the words are labeled as an opinion, then the act becomes an "8." All acts coded into this category must be explicitly labeled by the speaker or by

the previous speaker as referring to the content of the item. Included are:

(a) Answers to explicit questions about the item content, when the answer is clearly correct.

(b) Explicit questions about the item content.

(c) Explicit references to the item content; "explicit" means that the speaker identifies the content as having been in the item.

(d) Direct quotations from the item explicitly labeled. (Instances of 6(d) take priority over Category 2.)

Examples:

This is talking about saving up for a college education./
How old is he?/
(The question said)/if your 19-year-old daughter has a party/should the parents go out/or should they stay home?/
(It turned around and said)/"do you think/he should?"/

7. *Personal experience.* Reference to experiences or incidents in one's own life, in the lives of others in the group, or in the lives of other real people whom group members know. This category includes real, conditional, and hypothetical experiences. Discussion of "past" rules and procedures goes into this category.

Examples:

If I had a party/and I asked you to leave/
I've come across this problem in my family./
My mother said/when you're old enough to buy your own loafers/ you buy them./
I'll be old and grey and dead/and I won't go anywhere./
I might say "yes."/

8. *Opinion and evaluation.* Includes all acts that contain relevant content about the item being discussed but that go beyond the information contained in the item itself. Ideal acts are opinions, interpretations, and evaluations. "Interpretations" includes instances in which the speaker may think that he is reporting the item accurately but has added information, distorted, or in some way altered the meaning of the item. Statements of fact about the external world are also included as are analogies and hypothetical examples that are not personal.

Examples:

(It meant)/why should they have to go out./
(I think)/this is a better way for a group (in item) to function./
But they see TV all the time./
(Suppose)/that he hadn't killed his boss./
If they're 19 years old/they're old enough to have a party./
But this particular fella has a problem between his job and his girl./

9. *Not ascertainable.* This code is used for all fragments and for all other units in which the focus is not clear.

Examples:
In this boy's case . . ./
Oh, not be/
The question said . . ./
Oh./
Well, well . . ./

Coding Conventions

1. Yes, no, o.k., all right, that's right. These responses are coded in several categories, depending on whether they occur in statements with other words or whether they stand alone.

(a) When they constitute the complete statement they are automatically coded into Category 4 (comments on other's opinions).

Examples:

Fa   Do you agree now because/
Mo   No/   (4)

Mo   He see?/
Fa   Yes./   (4)

(b) When they stand at the beginning of a statement they are automatically coded into Category 4.

Examples:

Fa   Do you really?/
Mo   Yes./   (4)
Fa   All right (4)/ That's what the doctor wanted to know./

(c) When they stand elsewhere in the sentence they are coded according to the major focus of the whole sentence (as described in the context rule).

Examples:

Fa   That's one thing (2)/they didn't explain to us (2)/
     Yes (2)/he did (2)./
Dau   That's (5)/what I mean (5)/ya (5)./

Code: Interaction Process Analysis

Purpose

Interaction Process Analysis categories are used as described in Bales' original work, with a few exceptions. (See R. F. Bales, *Interaction Process Analysis*, Cambridge, Addison-Wesley, 1950.) These exceptions are described under Procedures.

Summary of IPA Categories

01	Shows solidarity
02	Tension release
03	Agreement
04	Gives suggestion
05	Gives opinion
06	Gives orientation
07	Asks for orientation
08	Asks for opinion
09	Asks for suggestion
10	Disagreement
11	Shows tension
12	Antagonism
0	Not ascertainable

Procedures

First, the unit to be coded is the same as described in our Unitizing Rules, i.e., an "act" is the basic coding unit. Ideally, acts are the smallest meaningful segment into which statements can be divided. (See page 343, the Unitizing Rules.) This unit differs slightly from the IPA unit although the basic unit for each is the simple sentence. The context that can be used to code each of these small units is defined below.

Second, the code is applied to typed transcripts coded while the coder is listening to the taped session. The purpose of this method is to allow for accurate coding of each act while, at the same time, providing data on tone of voice necessary to make an accurate coding judgment, especially for categories 1–3 and 10–12. (See N. Waxler and E. Mishler, "Scoring and reliability problems in Interaction Process Analysis," *Sociometry*, March 1966.)

Third, the context to be used in categorizing each act is the same as that defined by Bales. (This might be more accurately defined as the degree of inference used in making the judgment.)

1. The immediate last-mentioned, or next-anticipated social act takes precedence over the more general social context in making an inference about the intent of the speaker.

2. The reactive or anticipatory characteristics of the act take precedence over its symptomatic significance.

3. The meaning of the act for the other person takes precedence over the imputed, perhaps unconscious, meaning for the actor.

One addition is made to the context rule in our use of the categories. That is, in general, the complete sentence (which is usually composed of more than one unit) should be coded into the same category. Only if there is a very clear switch within the sentence, with content or affect definitely changing, should the category change within the sentence. For example:

Dau   That wasn't the way (10)/the question was put. (10)/
Fa   Sure (10)/ya (10)/that's the way (10)/that it was. (10)/

Mo   I agree (03)/that she should have a period of adjustment to herself (03)/and my theory was that (06)/the way when I read it (06)/ think must have felt (06)/that she was excluding everybody (06) . . ./

Priority rule. Favor the category more distant from the middle of the list, i.e., the "expressive" categories. This priority rule applies to the judgment about the series of units within a statement as well as the judgment about each unit.

Categories

01   *Shows solidarity.* Acts in this category serve to raise others' status, give help, or reward. The focus here is the relationship to the other person, rather than the focus on the idea or agreement. Included are:

showing solidarity, affection, sympathy; confiding; raising other's status; complimenting; approving; giving help; assisting; sharing; loaning; nurturing; rewarding; mediating; pacifying.

This includes the stronger end of the two-point scale of showing solidarity. A less supportive statement would be classified into Category 3.

Examples:
You have a right to disagree./
No/you don't have to agree./
The way you see it is right/and the way we see it is right./
You have a point there./
You can have your own opinion./

02   *Tension release.* Spontaneous expression of affect, functioning to release tension. Many of the acts in this category are nonverbal, such as laughter.

(a) Spontaneous relief: satisfaction, gratification, pleasure.
(b) Joking: amusement, friendly jokes. If the element of negative affect is greater than positive affect, the act is coded in 11 or 12.
(c) Laughter: scored in the same way as joking.

This includes most of the acts that indicate *personal* tension or anxiety in the situation (in contrast to interpersonal tension) with the indication that this tension is being released. Also included are acts having to do with the relationships between people in the group at the *present* time that indicate some kind of positive affect. These usually have to do with group procedure.

Examples:
    Wait a minute./ (in a nonhostile tone of voice.)
    That wasn't so bad./

03 *Agreement.*   This includes statements of agreement around an issue or passive acceptance, understanding, concurrence, compliance. The focus is on the content of the discussion in contrast to the relationship with the person. Examples are

(a) Passive, humble response to solidarity and support.
(b) Agreement to suggestions, opinions.
(c) Positive responses to facts; showing comprehension.

Besides direct statements of agreement, this category can contain

(1) The less supportive statements that clearly show solidarity but are not strong enough to go into Category 1 (using tone of voice *and* content as cues).

(2) Statements about the state of agreement. These may include statements showing past agreement or statements describing what the condition of agreement is at the present time.

Examples:
    You and I agreed./
    I agreed at the beginning./
    Yes./
    All right/ I'll agree with you./
    Well, that's true./
    Mmmm/ (when it implies "go on.")
    Well, o.k.,/o.k./
    Yes,/I was wrong./

04 *Gives suggestion.*   This includes processes of cooperation, giving direction that imply autonomy for others. The focus is largely on the group procedures.

(a) Cooperative action: suggestions to attain a goal, procedures to solve problems, requests to carry out procedures.

(b) Suggestions about desired actions of others: persuasion, suppositions about procedures.

This category is limited to suggestions about the group procedure at the present time, about how to discuss, what is appropriate, suppositions about procedures.

Examples:
    You should talk English./

Get the next one (item)/
Suppose/that we're the judges./
Wait till we get through./

05 *Gives opinion.* This includes opinions that are stated in the present tense (not the past tense) and suppositions and hypothetical examples about the item.

(a) Opinions: these can be about the task, oneself, others, the group, or the external world.

(b) Suppositions and hypothetical examples: these are included when they function to bring out opinions of oneself or others.

(c) Any sentence that includes "I think" or "I feel" is automatically categorized as an opinion; this generally includes the whole sentence, not just the act in which the "I think" occurs. The exception to this is when the affective meaning clearly changes in the middle of the sentence.

(d) Instances in which "I think" is not present in the sentence but it could be inserted without changing the meaning or the intent of the speaker are coded as opinions.

(e) Hypothetical personal experiences are included here.

Examples:

(I think) once in a while he can talk back./
(I think) it's a sign of weakness./
I firmly believe/that I owe it to my parents./
I don't think/they can change you./
Maybe we got off the track because . . ./
You'd like to be a successful singer/and you just can't be./
Well I figure the chairman's . . ./
Once in a while he can talk back./

06 *Gives orientation.* This includes giving nonevaluative information, and clarification or repetition of information.

(a) Opinions in the past tense: this includes restatements of opinions.

(b) Clarifications of past events or statements, including the content of the item.

(c) Noninferential reports about oneself or others or the external world; although these reports may not actually be "fact," they are stated in such a way as to be testable and are not labeled as opinion. This includes statements about the world that, if they had an "I think" attached to them, would not ordinarily result in an argument.

Examples:

There are two points/that I would like to make./
I see a lot of kids/and they answer back./

I always help Mommie./
What I thought is/if you went out to get a job/and . . ./
But the question is such that/should he help his parents/
I've worked in a nursing home./
I thought/that she should pick out the coat./
I said/it was a matter of opinion./
There is the fact/that the Boy Scouts are a group./
Nowadays a great many boys do have bicycles./

07 *Asks for orientation.* This is the question form of Category 6. It
includes asking for nonevaluative information, clarification, repetition.
(See Category 6 for more complete definition.)
Examples:
Didn't you ever talk back to me?/
Would you repeat that?/
Was it long walks (in the item)/or was it a long time in days?/
What did you say on that one?/
Do Boy Scouts work in groups?/

08 *Asks for opinion.* This is the question form of Category 5. Includes
asking for present opinions and asking for hypothetical examples about
the item to serve to analyze or diagnose the case. (See Category 5 for
more complete definition.)
Examples:
If everyone is fighting/how can you do the job?/
What do you say?/
You think it right to tell him right away?/
So do you agree with me?/
What should our policy be?/
Don't you think/the parents have a right to know?/
How capable is the mother of the children?/

09 *Asks for suggestion.* This is the question form of Category 4. In-
cludes asking for cooperation, direction, whether these are explicit or
implicit. The focus is largely on group procedure. (See Category 4 for
more complete definition.)
Examples:
You do the next one?/
Do you want me to say/what I thought?/
Should we all raise our hands?/
Can I say first/why I disagree?/

10 *Disagrees.* Includes actual disagreements, passive rejection, withholding of resources. It may include nonverbal interaction that is inter-

preted as coldness, hesitance, disbelief, amazement. This category includes the most mild expressions of negative affect. In general three types of act are included in this category.

(a) Statements about the fact of a disagreement, whether this is in the present or in the past (as in Category 3). For example:

> You and I disagreed./
> I disagree with you./

(b) Statements that have a hostile or aggressive tone or meaning, but that are not strong enough to go into the more extreme Category 12.

(c) Statements that function as disagreements with the opinion or argument of another person, but that are not labeled explicitly as disagreements.

Examples:

> You're wrong./
> But this is something different./
> You don't want to go to your mother/and leave your wife home./
> That's kinda stretching it./
> No/that isn't the only thing./
> That wasn't the way/the question was put/

11 *Shows tension.* This category includes acts that indicate *personal tension* or anxiety in the situation; non-content as well as content cues are used.

Examples:

> Laughter
> Stuttering
> Oh, this is terrible./

12 *Antagonism.* Included are two types of act.

(a) Statements that have a hostile or aggressive tone or meaning stronger than those in Category 10. Included are sarcasm, shouting, etc.

(b) Statements that, from content and context, are antagonistic; examples are baiting, daring, attacking, insulting.

Examples:

> And you'll cry your heart out (sarcastically)/
> That's as much of an agreement/as you're gonna get out of me./
> That's an old-fashioned idea./
> I'm still talking/

0 *Not ascertainable.* Included here are all acts that are fragmentary and for which no judgment can be accurately made.

Code: Interruptions, Attempted and Completed

Purpose

This code is designed to measure whether an attempt is made to interrupt another person's statement. Sometimes when the second person starts talking while the first person is still talking, the first person stops, leaving his idea incomplete. This is a full or *completed* interruption, noted by an (I) at the beginning of the interrupting act. Sometimes, however, the first person continues talking until he completes his idea even though the second person has broken in. This is an *attempted* or incomplete interruption; it is noted in our typescript as a simultaneous speech by the symbol (S).

Specific differences between interruptions (I) and simultaneous speeches (S):

    (1) Interruptions (I). These are instances in which
        (a) The idea of the interrupted statement is clearly incomplete.
        (b) There is no pause between the interrupted statement and the interruption.
        (c) The amount of overlap between the interrupted statement and the interruption is no more than *one* act.

    (2) Simultaneous (S). These are instances in which
        (a) The idea broken into is completed.
        (b) The amount of overlap is greater than one act in length.

In this code we wish to count separately both of these types of interruptions, attempted and completed. We also wish to record who the "interrupter" is.

Summary of Interruption Categories

Simultaneous Speech		Interruptions	
1	Speaker following (S) is Father	4	Interrupter is Father
2	Speaker following (S) is Mother	5	Interrupter is Mother
3	Speaker following (S) is Child	6	Interrupter is Child
	0 All other acts		

Procedures

We record the acts that are interrupted and who does the interrupting. Types of interruption are separated into *complete* (noted by an I) and *attempted* (noted by an S). The act(s) that are interrupted are coded, with the code category itself indicating who did the interrupting.

Categories

Simultaneous speech. If the symbol (S) appears anywhere in a statement *except* at the beginning of the statement, this means that the following speaker began speaking at this point but the first person continued talking. Code all the acts that are partially or totally underlined in the first person's speech, using the same code number for each. Also note who the following speaker was, i.e., who did the interrupting.

1 Speaker following an (S) is father.
2 Speaker following an (S) is mother.
3 Speaker following an (S) is child.

The code numbers are recorded into the acts of the person who is interrupted, *not* into the acts of the person who did the interrupting.

Examples:

Son All depends/(S) *how bad uh badly upset she is/I would say./*
Fa (S) *Isn't this?/*
 (Italicized portion of son's statement is coded as 1.)

Fa No/no/the question says/(S) *should the doctor tell her./*
Dau (S) *Or should you delay it?/* Yes./
 (Italicized portion of father's statement is coded as 3.)

Interruptions. If the symbol (I) appears at the beginning of a speaker's statement, this means he has interrupted the previous speaker. The previous speaker's *last* act is coded as interrupted, with the codes indicating who the interrupter, or following speaker, is.

4 Interrupter is father.
5 Interrupter is mother.
6 Interrupter is child.

Examples:

Dau Well, that, that doesn't/
Fa (I) I still say/you should tell him./
 (Daughter's act is coded 4.)

Fa That's right./ I I think/that he should be told./
Dau (I) You have the right to know/you're dying./
 (Father's last act is coded 6.)

0 All acts without attempted or complete interruptions.

Code: Metacommunications

Purpose

A metacommunication is defined as a communication that gives *explicit* instructions about how a message is to be interpreted, or how the context of the situation is to be interpreted. It is a communication *about* the situation or a communication *about* a communication. While all communications have a metacommunicative aspect, our coding system includes three specific types of metacommunications.

1. Metacommunications about communications: statements that tell how previous communications should be interpreted and statements that tell how messages in the future should be interpreted (e.g., Don't take this seriously; What I meant to say was let her pick out the coat.)

2. Metacommunications about the procedures and the context of the situation: these are communications that comment on, and thus further specify, the situation in which the group finds itself. In general these metacommunications are centered on comments about the rules of procedures (e.g., We've got to come to an agreement.)

3. Metacommunications about roles: messages that place the speaker or someone else in the group in a particular role or quality category and then interpret that person's communication in terms of the role or quality category (e.g., I'm a little bit of a psychiatrist myself so I said she should make up her own mind.)

Summary of Metacommunication Categories

1	Points out incongruities in statements
2	Qualify others' statements
3	Qualify one's own statements
4	Disqualify others' statements
5	Disqualify one's own statements
6	Metacommunications about rules
7	Metacommunications about roles, qualities
0	No metacommunication present

Procedures

In order to be classified in this code the above types of metacommunication must be *explicit*, that is, no inferred words, motives, or interpretations can be used to judge that a metacommunication is present. In order to be coded as a metacommunication there must be two sets of words present.

1. A clear, unambiguous reference to the object of the metacomment.

2. An explicit instruction about how the content of a message is interpreted.

The following table summarizes the characteristics that must be present for a sentence to be coded as a metacommunication.

	Object (Targets) of Metacommunications		
	Messages (Own or Other; Past or Present)	Rules	Roles (Own or Other)
Concrete mention of object of metacomment	What you/I said . . .	What they said . . .	What you/ I are . . .
Modifying comments that give instructions about the object: can be verbs, adverbs, clauses that:	Evaluate Question Modify Stress Qualify	Evaluate Question Modify Stress Qualify	Evaluate Question Modify Stress Qualify

General cues for distinguishing a metacommunication from a nonmetacommunication are the following.

1. Distinguishing the target, or object, of the metacommunication. We code only the metacommunications in which the comment is clearly referred to one's own communication, the communication of someone else in the group, the communication of the experimenter, or the role or quality of some specific person in the family. Thus a personal subject or object must be present in the act as the subject or object of the metacommunication. Personal subjects/objects are: I, you, we, they, us, them, etc.

Examples:

What *you* just said is right./
They told us/*we* have to come to an agreement./
I said/he should tell his parents./
You're prejudiced/and that's why you feel that way./

A substitute for the personal subject or object is "that" or "it." When "that" or "it" can be clearly replaced by "what you said" and the same meaning retained, then the personal subject or object need *not* be explicit. For example, "That's right" may be coded as a metacommunication since it translates into "What *you* said is right."

2. Modifying comments that give instructions about the communication. In general the "instructions" that are included in the metacommunication are in the form of an evaluating verb, adverb, or clause that tells the hearer how to evaluate a past or present communication. Examples of these words are: true, strongly, still, funny, etc. Some verbs in themselves, however, carry instructions about interpretation.

Verbs that have metacommunicative function, without modifiers:

mean that . . .   am convinced that . . .   deny that . . .
believe that . . .   doubt that . . .   explain . . .
                         admit that . . .

(Each of these verbs tells the hearer how to interpret what is to come.)
Verbs that require modifiers before they have metacommunicative function:

think that . . .   understand . . .   guess . . .
feel that . . .   assume that . . .   conclude that . . .
                         interpret . . .

Modifiers strong enough to be coded as metacommunications:

really   certainly   funny
strongly   truly   still

Modifiers not strong enough to code as metacommunications:

actually   just
do (think) (feel)   personally

Using the above general definition and the two major requirements for the presence of a metacommunication, the following sentences are examples of codable metacommunications.

Well, I *mean*/that wasn't the problem./
I *said*,/I said/we've discussed that before./
I *still don't think*/he should./
You certainly don't believe/that that is right./
We have to come to a final decision./
Since I'm a mother/I think/she should./

Nonmetacommunications:

I actually think/that she should./
Let's come to a decision./
What do you think about the idea/I just explained?/
He (the boy in the item) is 20 years old./

Code only the part of the statement that actually includes the metacommunication, even though the full statement is used as context. In most instances this means that for each metacommunication only *one* act is coded. In the following examples only the underlined acts are given code numbers.

That's the truth./ He should tell his parents./
What do you mean by emotional?/ You need to define your terms./
You just said/I had to agree with you./*And now you say*/I have a right
  to my own opinion./

I'm not sure about this/but I think/it's wrong./
I'd say/*that you're prejudiced*/and that's why/you feel that way./

Priority goes in the order of the categories, with Category 1 taking precedence over all others, Category 2 over all except 1, and so on.

The total preceding interaction is the context to be used for general understanding of the content. However, references for "that" and "it" and "you said," and so on, can be made *only* to the immediately preceding statement; reference back beyond this statement is not allowed.

Code Categories:

Communications about communications. Categories 1–5 are of this type. These are explicit references to communications that have gone before or that are to come. The communication that is being referred to must be explicit and clear (either through repetition of the content or reference through a "that" or "it"), the source of the communication must be someone in the family, and some extra evaluative message must be added that tells how to interpret the communication.

1. *Communications that point out incongruities in communications.* All types of communication incongruities are included here: between people or within one person, in the present or between past and present, between or within affects or words. In order to be coded into this category the fact of the incongruous communication must be made explicit; i.e., the speaker must state or explain *both* sides of the incongruous message, not simply allude to or imply it. This category occurs rarely.

    Examples:
    You just said/I had to agree with you/and now you say/I have a right to my own opinion./
    You don't want to look at his background/and again you do;/you don't want to look at the bad part,/you only want to look at the good part./
    First Mother tells me to take her side/and then you tell me to take your side./

    These are *not* metacommunications in category 1:
    But you just said/I had a right to my own opinion./
    He sounds/as if he might say no./
    I thought/you felt just the opposite./

Communications that qualify communications. Included here are two types of metacommunication that point out how a past or present communication should be interpreted. "Pointing out" can be in the form of

emphasis or stress   questioning
evaluation   modifying
defining

The only type of qualification not included in this category is the disqualifying type, where the modifiers serve to minimize or make a communication weaker. Subcategories in this general type refer to whether one's *own* past (or present) communication is being qualified or whether the qualification is of the communication of *someone else*.

2. *Qualify others' statements.* This category includes metacommunications that are comments on the past communication of another person in the family; the content of these past communications must either be stated in the metacommunicative statement or must be represented by a "that" or an "it" that clearly stands for the past communication. In addition to the presence of the communication being commented on, there must also be an additional set of qualifying words that tell how the previous communication has been taken or interpreted. These may be words that evaluate, question, modify, emphasize or otherwise qualify the communication.

Examples:

Fa   That's ah
Son of course I think/the ideal thing was well it might be going a little strong for the *I can see his point.*/

Son Well what do you mean by a little bit?/
Fa   Now supposing she started askin you about your trip./ You would would you like ah *you say*/you wouldn't mind talking about her trip./   (Emphasizes)

Mo   And of course there's always times/where there's always times/ where the child is too big/and you just can't fight them./
Fa   Yeah/*that's true enough*/   (Evaluates)

Son What is the answer?/
Fa   So *what you're saying to us is*/that if you have a fifteen year old boy/you're going to say to him/Sam, go to bed./
                                               (Emphasizes)

Mo   Because none of the children are there aren't two children/
Fa   *You mean*/because the child just sheds some tears/ipso facto there's something wrong?/   (Clarifies)

Mo   David, why not leave it,/it depends on the child./
Son No,/What do you *what does that mean?*/
                                               (Questions)

Statements that are not coded in Category 2:

Fa   Is 10 o'clock ridiculous?/

Son   This is the American home, naturally. Ten o'clock?/

Fa   Is that ridiculous?/

Son   No,/*it's not ridiculous.*/It's just borderline./

> ("It" does not refer to a
> communication.)

Son   You think/we all and three people. Multiply it out./

Fa   You're looking at it on a percentage basis./

> ("It" does not refer to a
> communication.)

Mo   Than if the kid still picks on him/then go down/and see the teacher/and see/if they can't rectify the thing./

Son   That's the same idea/I had./

> (No evaluation)

3. *Qualify own statements.* Comments on past or present communications of oneself. As in Category 2, both of the following aspects must be present.

(a) Content of the communication being commented on must be explicit or clearly represented by an "it" or "that."

(b) A set of qualifying words that tell how the communication is to be taken must be present; these words may evaluate, question, modify, emphasize or otherwise qualify.

Examples:

Fa   *I tell you one thing about kids.*/They can call you yellow and everything/if you fight back/   (Emphasizes)

Fa   But you're agreeing with us now./ You'll let him talk back./ Well *we say we say* that about talking back./ We don't mean calling you names or sassy or something like that./

> (Emphasizes)

Fa   If he picks on you again/belt him back./

Mo   Well that's/*what I say.*/You try to rectify the thing first,/you know./   (Clarifies)

Mo   And then I would say yes or no./*I mean*/a 11 year old boy when he's got to express himself . . ./

> (Clarifies)

Statements that are not coded in Category 3:

Fa   I could say/that you were reluctant to get out of bed to resume your studies./   (Conditional "says" are not included.)

Fa   I'm trying to get your mind on the rail, on the cartrack./
                                             (No reference to a com-
                                                munication.)

Fa   You let it cry up?/
Mo   Yes./
Fa   My answer is the same./ Let it cry out./(No evaluative state-
         ment)

Fa   My question my answer on that question was/that he came
         home crying/and somebody hit him./ Didn't say/why he
         hit him./ So I said No./This was wrong for the mother to
         go out/and hit him back./   ("I said" refers to an-
                                             swering the question-
                                             naire.)

Son   Well seeing as I'm the one/that disagreed with personally/
         an I'm the type of a person/that doesn't like to talk to
         em about myself to strange people./ An that was my answer
         for avoiding it./   (No qualifying words.)

Communications that disqualify messages. These are messages that
explicitly ask the hearer to disregard, take less seriously, deny the legitimacy
of, or subtract from the importance of a communication that has already
occurred or one that is about to occur. These metacommunications must
have the same general characteristics as those in Categories 2 and 3.

1. The communication that is being disqualified must be stated or
clearly referred to with a "that" or an "it."

2. An extra evaluating word (or words) must be included telling how
the hearer is to interpret the communication; in this instance, the evaluating words serve to disqualify, or to say "don't take this seriously."

This kind of metacommunication can be attached to one's own statement
or it can be applied to a message from someone else in the group.

4. *Disqualify others' communications.* Usually the metacommunication
here refers to a communication that the other person has already given.
It must be labeled as belonging to that other person (with a personal
pronoun or a "that" clearly referring to the previous communication)
and must also carry some meaning that intends to weaken this previous
statement.

Examples:
   Mo   I would give the boy a chance to explain/and tell/why he
            wants to go./
   Son   But that isn't/*what you said.*/

Fa	All of us get terribly frightened./
Mo	Irwin *you're all wrong on that/*

Son	Didn't you ever hear of the old saying, sink or swim?/
Mo	*That has nothing to do with it./*

Fa	*You didn't really mean that./*

Fa	Eight o'clock fifteen year old boy./
Son	*Why that's ridiculous./*

Statements that are not coded in Category 4:

Fa	They just want to hear your your your your thoughts or your your feelings./
Mo	*It's just your opinion./* (Disqualifying not strong enough.)

Son	That's the same idea/I had./
Fa	What idea?/
Son	The same thing she said./ I just couldn't express it./
Fa	*Well that's no good./* Cuz they'll think you're a sissy./ (Referrent of "that" is unclear.)

Son	Perhaps the parents were having a business visitor coming./
Fa	Again, you're giving us extenuating circum there./ (Not clearly a disqualification.)

5. *Disqualify own communications.* The metacommunications in this category include those that give instructions about how one's own past communications are to be interpreted or how one's own immediately following communication is to be taken. As in Category 4, the communication being disqualified must be labeled (with a personal pronoun or a "that" clearly referring to the previous communication) and the statement must carry some meaning that intends to weaken this previous statement.

Examples:

Fa	Larry's little boy he stands up for himself./ *I don't believe/* that he runs home/and tells his mother./ (Disqualifies the communication that follows.)

Fa	I'll agree with him a hundred percent/uh some have it/and some don't/*but I still don't think*/they'd strive for something/they really wanted without getting it/ (Disqualifies the communication that follows.)

Mo   We're talking of four and a half./
Son   Well I'm not *I'm not qualified* to talk on this problem./
      Because at least sixteen I remember/because that was only
      nine years ago./
      (Disqualifies own future communication about problem.)

Son   Well *I don't feel qualified* to talk about four and a half year
      olds./
      (Disqualifies own statement.)

Fa   He should rebel./
Son   *I didn't say that.*/No/
      (Disqualifies own following statement, represented by
      that.)

Fa   *I don't mean* to put the pressure on him./

      (Disqualifies following phrase.)

Fa   It's a small detail./*And maybe I'm wrong,*/maybe the kiddo
      shouldn't have had his own uh/
      (Disqualifies the following phrase.)

Statements that are not coded in Category 5:
Son   Like you said,/but that isn't/what the question said,/you
      know./
Mo   *Oh I answered wrong,*/didn't I?/
      (Reference is to the answer on questionnaire.)

Fa   You were belonging to clubs/and I had to say to you,/ David,
      go to bed./ *That's for the birds.*/
      (Comments on past behavior, not communication.)

Mo   (Long discussion of how she sees the item.)
Fa   Oh then I'm wrong on the interpreting./*I interpret it the
      wrong way.*/
      (Reference is to the item, not a communication.)

Metacommunications about rules and procedures.   These are communications that comment on and thus further specify the situation in which
the group finds itself. Although it is possible for the group members to
comment on the physical context (the room, the furniture, etc.) and to
comment on each other and the experimenter as physical objects, our code
is limited to comments about the rules of procedure. Although these are
not directly comments on communications, as are all of the other metacommunication categories, they are indirect comments on communications

since the rules of procedure have originally been explained or implied by the experimental instructions. The reason for assuming that these comments on rules and procedures have metacommunicative quality is that an explicit comment on a rule tells the whole group how to interpret what they do or say in the remainder of the meeting or what has gone before. Thus these comments give instructions about communication as do the other coded metacommunications.

6. *Metacommunications that point out existing rules or suggest changes in rules.* These are statements that make explicit one of the following characteristics of the situation.

(a) The experimenter's instructions about how the group is to proceed.
(b) The expectations about procedure that one would commonly have for this kind of group discussion (e.g., no one is supposed to leave the room, even though this rule is not made explicit by the experimenter).
(c) The fact that suggestions may be made about new rules of procedures.

In order to be coded, a statement must make explicit what the rule is that is being commented on. Thus an act that *carries out* a rule but that does not include a statement *of* the rule is *not* coded (e.g., Listen; Raise your hand; Wait a minute). The most common statement coded here is one that states the rule and labels it as a rule by saying "we ought to" or "we should" do something; a sense of compulsion is a cue to the statements coded in this category.

Examples:

Son   Well if there was no conflict/why would they ask?/
Fa   *They just want to hear your thoughts or your feelings./*
      (Explicit statement of the rule given by experimenter.)

Fa   You've already created a trip./Now you've got a business trip./
Mo   *We can't bring those things in, David./ You can't create things./*
      (Statement of an explicit rule.)

Fa   *We're supposed to think it out./*
      (Statement of an explicit rule.)

Son   *If you don't say anything/*the faster we get out of here./
      (Suggestion for change in implied rule.)

Mo   *Well I shall have to throw the question out./*I can't agree with you/or disagree because . . ./
      (Suggests change in rules.)

Fa   *It (the item) had to be answered with an explanation./*
                (Statement of the rule of procedure about giving reasons
                for answers.)
Statements that are not coded in Category 6:
Son   I have to put some sound effects in this thing (the micro-
        phone.)/
                (Does not state rule given to or implied in situation.)

Mo   Well don't you think/we've given this enough thought?/
                (No statement of "giving thought" as a rule.)

Son   That was the only way given to me to express my feelings of
        not wanting to talk to the woman./
                (Does not directly express the rule about having to choose
                one questionnaire answer.)

Fa   I think/we'll agree to disagree on this one/because too much
        of an age difference in . . ./
                (No statement about rule or change in rule.)

Son   Do you want me to raise my hand?/
                (Carries out a rule but doesn't state it.)

Mo   They were worded in such a way/that you couldn't say yes or
        no./
                (Doesn't suggest a change in rules.)

7. *Metacommunications about roles.* These are messages that place the
speaker or another group member in a role or quality category and then
go on to use that role/quality membership as a means of qualifying a
communication. These kinds of message must have *all* of the following
characteristics in order to be coded:

(a) The placement of the speaker or someone else in the group in a
social role or a *quality* category. (By social role we mean only sex role,
occupational role, generational role and age role.)

    I can't concentrate . . ./
    You're prejudiced . . ./
    As a mother . . ./
    Since I'm a foreman . . ./

(b) A connective word that clearly shows that the quality or role of
the person is being used to qualify or modify the communication.

    I can't concentrate/*so* I said . . ./
    You're prejudiced/*therefore* you . . ./
    As a mother *I think* . . ./

(c) A statement of a communication that is being qualified by the role or quality of the person. This communication must be stated explicitly or represented by an "it" or "that" that is clear in reference.

I can't concentrate/so I said *that.*/
You're prejudiced/therefore *you felt/that he shouldn't go.*/

Examples:

Son   *Personally I'm the type of person/that doesn't like to talk to em about myself to strange people/*and that was my answer for avoiding it./

Son   Well it looks/*like I'm the stubborn one here/and I just picked that one/because I like to work by myself.*/

Statements that are not coded in Category 7:

Fa   I'm glad/that we're both in agreement./
       ("Glad" is not a stable quality of a person.)

Fa   Of course you want to understand/that my feelings are from somebody/that has sort of more or less been on their own/ since they were ten./
       (There is no specific communication that the quality "being on one's own" serves to modify.)

Mo   I just put myself in the spot of the person/and had that disease./
       (No specific communication modified by this quality.)

Mo   Oh I don't I I I still don't think/that I know/
Son   Well maybe you're looking at it as a female./
       (Reference of "it" is not clear.)

Son   I think as a boy./
       (Communication being qualified by the role "boy" is incomplete.)

Fa   You see/right away you're becoming a pessimist./
       (No explicit communication present that is qualified by quality "pessimist".)

Coding Conventions for Metacommunications:

1. Conventions for the use of Categories 2, 3, 4 and 5.

(a) In order for a qualification or disqualification of a communication to be included as a metacommunication in 2, 3, 4, or 5, both of the following characteristics must be present in the statement.

(1) Presence of a personal subject or object, pointing out whose communication is being commented on; or, presence of "that" or "it" which clearly refers to the preceding act and which stands for "what you just said."

Examples:

That's different./ ("What you just said" is different.)
I just said/he should/
You were stupid to say *that*./
I mean/she should./
That's right./ ("What you just said" is right.)

(2) Presence of a set of words that give instructions about how the communication should be or should have been taken; these are the qualifying or disqualifying words, further specified under the categories.

(b) Incomplete statements. In order for a metacommunication to be coded, the content of the communication that is being qualified must be complete.

Codable:

I *mean*/she should buy her own coat./
What I said was/that the girl should buy her own coat./
I'm not sure about that./
That was a foolish thing to say./

Not codable because the communication being referred to is not complete or is unclear:

I mean/
What I said was/
What I meant to say uh ah umm well go ahead ah/

(c) Emphasis through repetition. Simple repetition of an idea or statement is not enough to be classified as a qualifying metacommunication. Instead, the words "I said" or "you said" must also be added as a label.

Codable:

Mo   Give her a chance./
Fa   I *said*/give her a chance./

Not codable:

Mo   Give her a chance./
Fa   Give her a chance./yes./

(d) Hypothetical, conditional, or future verbs. When the verb in the statement refers to a communication that has not in reality occurred and does not follow, then it can not be given metacommunicative meaning. Thus all phrases like "I would say" or "I might say" or "I will say" are not coded. Verbs in the present or past form, however, can be coded. "I said" and "I say", when followed by the communication being referred to, serve the function of emphasis of what follows.

Codable:
> *But you just said*/she should pick up the baby./
> *I say*/give her a chance./

Not codable:
> *I might say*/that she should pick up the baby./
> *I will say under these circumstances*/it is all right./

(e) References to the item or the questionnaire procedure: When the person's answer on the questionnaire is referred to *as if* it were a communication it is not coded. Thus statements like "I said she should stay home," when it really means "I answered the question with 'she should stay home'" are not interpreted as past communications and therefore are not coded.

(f) Statements of belief or opinion are not metacommunications. Only if there is an object clause introduced by "that" or its equivalent is there a possibility of coding it since in this instance the phrase following "that" is the communication that is being qualified.

Codable:
> *I believe*/that they should be punished physically./
> *I don't believe*/that democracy is good./

Not codable:
> I don't believe in punishing them physically./
> I don't believe in democracy./

2. Conventions for Category 2.

(a) "To think" is not interpreted as a verb of emphasis unless there is an emphasizing adverb. Thus "Do you think that she could," is not coded as a metacommunication unless in the form "Do you strongly think that she could?"

(b) Ambiguous "you": Include in Category 2 only those statements that clearly refer to someone in the family. If "you" has an ambiguous referrent it should not be used as evidence for a metacommunication.

(c) Statements in the following form are not coded in Category 2 because the reference is not clearly to a communication.

You're right./	All right./
You're in agreement./	Right./

3. Conventions for Category 3.

(a) "To think" is not interpreted as a verb of emphasis unless there is an emphasizing adverb. Thus "I think that she should" is not coded as a metacommunication unless in the form "I strongly think that she should."

(b) Statements that refer to the communication of the group as a whole are included in this category if they meet the other criteria for metacommunications. The pronouns "we" and "us" are the cues for these statements. For example:

Fa   Well *we say that* about talking back./
Mo   *We meant*/they go/and do all kinds of things/rather than go to bed./

4. Conventions for Category 4.

(a) Ambiguous "you": include in Category 4 only those statements that clearly refer to someone in the family. If "you" has an ambiguous referrent it should not be coded.

5. Conventions for Category 5.

(a) Statements that refer to the communications of the group as a whole are included in this category if they meet the other criteria for metacommunications. The pronouns "we" and "us" are cues for these statements. For example:

Mo   *Perhaps we were wrong in saying*/that the girl should pick out her own coat./

6. Conventions for Category 7.

(a) If there is no clear connective word or phrase present do not assume it. The role/quality must be clearly related by the speaker to the communication.

Code: Negation/Retraction

Purpose

These are two independent codes designed to measure the use of certain kinds of grammatical construction. We assume, as Weintraub does, that the choice of certain words and modes of speaking may indicate the individual's preference for a specific defense mechanism. Here the assumption is that negatives, when commonly used, may indicate denial or negation, whereas retractors (although, however, nevertheless) may indicate undoing.

This is a revised form of the code developed by W. Weintraub and H. Aronson, "The application of verbal behavior analysis to the study of psychological defense mechanisms: methodology and preliminary report," *J. Nerv. Ment. Dis.*, *134*, February 1962, 169–181.

Summary of Negation/Retraction Categories

	Negation		Retraction
1	Negator present	1	, Retractor present
0	Negator absent	0	Retractor absent

Procedures

Each code, negation and retraction, is coded independently. Each code is a presence-absence one and the single act is the context used for coding.

Categories

Negation

1. Presence of a negator. The *only* indicators of negation are:

   Not   Never
   No   None
   Nothing   Neither . . . nor

   These are coded in Category 1, according to the following rules:

   (a) When used to negate a verb.
   (b) If, when rephrased, it would negate a verb: i.e., "Never mind the trips," could become "don't mind the trips,"
   (c) The negator must be explicitly stated, not implied.
   (d) "No" in response to a *question* is not considered to be a negator.
   (e) A verb that implies some kind of negation in its content is *not* coded as a negator, e.g., disagree, disapprove.

   Examples:
   You *don't want* to give everything./
   I *won't go* anywhere./
   They gotta give some money, but *not* all of them./
   Well, *never mind* the trips./
   He got *no* money./He got *no* job./
   I *don't* understand that./
   She *can't* help the mother./

0. Absence of negator.

Code: Pauses

Purpose

The purpose of this code is to record the fact of silences in the interaction in the sequential position in which the silences occur. Silences are noted on the typescript by the typist, with a symbol (P). A silence is defined as a period of time in which the average participant might feel that someone *should* be speaking.

Summary of Pauses Categories

1	Presence of pause (P)
0	No pause (P̄)

Procedures

Pauses are noted on the typescript with a symbol (P). If there is doubt as to which act the (P) should be recorded for, code it into the act that precedes the (P) rather than for the act that follows.

Categories

1. Presence of a (P)

    Examples:

    Fa   Because I don't think/Michael would talk about himself. (P)/
           (The second act is coded 1)

    Mo   Ask her a few questions. (P)/That's/what I would do./
           (The first act is coded 1)

0. All acts without a (P)

Code: Subject/Object

Purpose

This code serves to classify subjects and objects in each act into internal and external cells, depending on whether they refer explicitly to someone in the group or to someone or something outside of the group. Since it is possible that the subject and the object of the act fall into different cells, a separate coding judgment is made for the subject and the object of the act, although the category systems themselves are the same. Within the internal and external categories is a series of subcategories that further specify the nature of the subject or object.

Summary of Subject/Object Categories

	Subject of the Act		Object of the Act	
	1	I	1	me
Internal	2	you	2	you
to the	3	you (ambiguous)	3	you (ambiguous)
Group	4	you and I; we	4	you and I/me; us
	5	impersonal subjects	5	impersonal objects

Summary of *Subject/Object Categories* (Continued)

	Subject of the Act		Object of the Act	
	6	experimenter	6	experimenter
External	7	persons in items	7	persons in item
to the	8	other persons	8	other persons
Group	9	absent family members	9	absent family members
	11	impersonal subjects	11	impersonal objects
	0	no subject; not ascertained	0	no object; not ascertained

Procedures

Coding is done directly from the typescript. The context to be used is the single act. In order to be coded in a subject and an object category the subject and object must be explicitly included in the act, not inferred from the content.

General procedures for selecting subjects and objects

1. Simple sentences with one clear subject and one clear object provide the best examples of the coding procedure. (In the following examples subjects and objects are underlined.)

   Everyone has a *TV set* in their house./
   They're working toward *something*./
   It's an *organization*./
   I agree with *you*./
   You can't go on a *trip*./
   He won't pay *you*./

2. When sentences have fragments or several clauses, all of which have been included in one act, a judgment is made about which aspect of the act is most important in order to code it into the proper cell. (This includes acts with false starts, etc.)

   (a) Fragments in combination with a complete sentence: ignore the fragment when classifying the subjects and objects in the statement. (Subjects and objects are underlined.)

   Examples:
   And *I* think it's more/
   But he a, *that's* not *it*./

   Yes, that the parents/ (Only the "yes" is coded.)
   Stay up all night yes well/ (Only the "yes" is coded.)

   One exception to this rule is the following. When the fragment is clearly an integral part of the unit but the idea has been cut off (usually by an interruption) then all of the unit, including the fragment, can be coded. For example:

I think *that he*/(Here the "he" is coded as if it were an object.)

3. *Priority rules.* For both subjects and objects, if there is doubt about what word is the subject or what word is the object, or there is doubt about which category the word belongs in, then

  (a) give priority to the internal over the external categories.
  (b) give priority to both internal and external over Category 0.
  (c) give priority to *people* as subjects or objects over *things or states* as subjects or objects.

Where there is a choice between classifying a one-word act as a subject or an object, subjects get priority.

Examples:
  Fa   Who disagree?/
  Dau   Me./ (I disagreed.)

Categories: Subject of the Act

Internal Subjects

1. *I or its substitute, proper names.*

  Examples:
    I agree with you./
    I mean it./
    Pat, don't get mad./ (Talking to himself.)

2. *You.* Referring clearly to persons in the room, including both singular and plural forms, and substitutes for *you*, such as "he," "mother," etc., that clearly refer to one other person in the room. (When in doubt, code in 3.)

  Examples:
    You can't go on a trip./
    You two agree./
    Well, if *Dad* says . . ./
    Who's the one/that's disagreeing?/

3. *You* (ambiguous). Not referring clearly to persons in the room, includes the use of *you* that is synonymous with "*one*."

  Examples:
    You helps just the same./
    You see the son without a job./
    You have to have everyone together./

4. *You and I* or *We*. When reference is clearly to the self and one or more other persons in the group; can be substituted for by "both," "family," "group." These may include past, present, or future references. Also included are ambiguous "we" statements in which it is unclear whether "we" refers to "family."

   Examples:
   You and I agree./
   Both of us agree on a compromise./
   The way *we* see it/is right, too./
   When can *we* go home?/
   We used to go to the beach./
   We've had two world wars./

5. *Impersonal subjects*. Anything *in the room* that is not a person; this may be clothing, ideas, opinions, problems, parts of the body, appearances, etc.

   Examples:
   That's a nice sweater./
   Your idea is all wrong./
   It's birch./
   This is terrible./
   That is true./
   That is so./

   External subjects

6. *Experimenter(s)*:

   Examples:
   They listen/when we talk./
   When does *he* come back?/
   They see from over there?/

7. *Persons explicitly mentioned in the task item*. Not generalized people, only those explicitly mentioned.

   Examples:
   The *Boy Scouts* are working toward something./
   How old is *he*?/
   Suppose/that *he* hadn't killed./
   The *chairman* got the other people to work for him./

8. *Other persons*.

   Examples:
   Everyone has a TV set./
   They just stare at the picture./
   If *he's* your friend./

9. *Absent family member.*   Does *not* include hypothetical family members.

Examples:

    My *mother* said/when you're . . ./
    Was (*brother*) here last week?/
    Your *parents* would have forbidden you./

11. *Impersonal subjects.*   Including the *task* given to the group.

Examples:

    It's an organization./
    This is talking about saving for college./
    His *job* is good./
    The *question* said/

0. *No subject or not ascertainable.*   This includes instances in which the subject may be implied but it is not actually stated, and instances in which there is no subject because the act is fragmentary.

Examples:

    (I) guess/ there are some people/who can do that./ (First act is 0.)
    (I would) Make sure/the kids don't get into trouble./ (First act is 0.)
    Yes./
    Not necessarily./
    Now would./
    Oh, but./
    Umm./

Categories: Object of the Act

General procedures for coding objects.

1. When the direct object is inanimate and the indirect object is animate, the indirect object takes precedence in making the object judgment.

Examples:

    You buy *me* a car./
    You'd give *me* the money./
    The *Boy Scouts* might give *her* the TV./

2. Selection of objects.

(a) Auxiliary verbs and parts of compound verbs are *not* coded as objects. For example:

    They might feel/as though they were being held back./
      ("Feel" is not an object.)

(b) Adverbs may or may not be coded as objects, depending on the following characteristics.

Adverbs that denote *"where"* may be objects if there is no clear direct or indirect object.

Examples:

He went *out.*/
Where are you going?/

Adverbs that denote "how" and "when" are *not* coded as objects.

Examples:

Thinking *ahead*/I felt/that he . . ./
Answer *quickly.*/
How do you feel?/
They came *earlier.*/

3. Our definition of an object is similar to but not identical with the usual grammatical definition. We include in the "object" code direct objects, indirect objects, objects of prepositional phrases, and sometimes adjectives. These are usually things or people that are *acted on* or modifiers of the subject that are classified as impersonal.

Examples:

Stop the *train.*/
Give it to *me.*/
That is *ridiculous.*/

Categories: Internal objects

1. *Me* or its substitutes, such as I.

Examples:

You'd give *me* the money./
(that's the way)/it sounded to *me.*/

2. *You.* When the reference to someone in the group is explicit; this may be both a plural and a singular form of you.

Examples:

I agree with *you.*/
I'll agree with *youse.*/
He can see *you.*/
They hear *you* talking./

3. *You* (ambiguous.) When the reference is not clearly to a "you" inside the group.

Examples:

He can pay *you* back./
If he doesn't talk back to *you.*/

4. *You and I or Us.* Reference to the self and one or more other persons

in the group. Also included are ambiguous "us" statements in which it is unclear whether "us" refers to the family or not.

Examples:

Do you agree with *us?*/
They listen to *us.*/

5. *Impersonal objects.* Objects present *in the room,* such as clothing, ideas, opinions, parts of the body, problems, appearances. Impersonal objects in the form of pronouns (usually "it" and "that") can be coded as internal only when they refer to ideas, opinions, or statements that have been mentioned previously in the discussion. If the phrase "my opinion," "your idea," or "his statement" can be clearly substituted for "it" or "that," the pronoun is coded as Category 5.

Examples:

Then everybody knows *your problems.*/
That's a nice *sweater.*/
Why do you pick *that?*/
That's your *opinion.*/
Hold up *your hand.*/
Do you feel *that* way?/   (Where "that" could be substituted with "the way I just said.")
It is a good reason./   (Where "it" stands for "your reason.")
That is *right.*/
That is *so.*/
We haven't come to an *agreement.*/

Categories: External objects

6. *Experimenter(s).*
Examples:
You can't see *him.*/
Call *him.*/

7. *People explicitly mentioned in the task item.*
Examples:
You see the *son* without a job./
He doesn't have to tell his *parents.*/
This woman has three *children.*/

8. *Other persons.*
Examples:
I don't talk to *people.*/
The Boy Scouts might give *her* a TV./

9. *Absent family members.*

Examples:
 I told (*brother*) that last week./
 I trusted my *children*./

11. *Impersonal objects.* Including group members' possessions that are not actually present in the room. This also includes qualities of people and things not present in the room. Impersonal objects mentioned in the item are external, and are coded as 11, even when they have been mentioned previously in the discussion.
 Examples:
 Everyone has a *TV set*./
 They're working toward *something*./
 You can't go on a *trip*./
 When can we go *home*?/

0. *No object* or *not ascertainable.* Instances in which there is no object either because it is implied but not explicit or because the act is fragmentary.
 Examples:
 Yes./   I think./
 Why?/   Mmmm./
 I don't agree./   Well, it is./
 I'm licked./

Coding Conventions

1. All statements in the passive voice should be changed to the active voice before being coded. For example:
 "You would have been forbidden by your parents to see someone like that."/ Change to: "Your *parents* would have forbidden *you* to see someone like that."

2. Interrupted sentences. Put interrupted statements together in order to use all possible information to make the subject/object judgment. Each part of the interrupted statement then is given the same subject-object code.

3. Questions. Reverse the order of all questions before coding the subject/object.
 Examples:
 Are we agreed?/   We are agreed./
 What do you mean?/   You mean what./
 Why did I say that?/ I said that./

4. Category 7. This is a category that should be kept as small and specific as possible. All the people in this category must have been specifically

mentioned in the task item. The use of their names, their designation ("he," etc.), pronouns standing for their names, or their characteristics ("husband") can also be included here. If the designation is altered ("boyfriend" rather than "husband") or if it is generalized ("children" rather than "child") then it is coded into Category 8. If the person in the item is *specified* (that is, "children" is changed to "the child"), then it can still remain in No. 7.

5. Rule for discriminating between categories 5 and 11. This rule applies to both Subject and Object codes;

Category 5. This includes

(a) Subjects and objects that are explicitly defined as present in the room. Specifically, these are:

Subjects or objects that are located in the room.
    the walls
    the table
    the microphone

Subjects or objects that are explicitly mentioned *in the act* as belonging to a member of the family.
    your opinion
    his idea
    your hand

Subjects or objects that are explicitly designated *in the act* as having been said previously in the discussion.

Examples:
    What *you* said before/
    didn't *you* just say/that it was o.k./

(b) Subjects and objects that are not explicitly related, in the act, to what has occurred or belongs in the room, can also be coded in Category 5, depending on the following rules:

Impersonal subjects and objects can be referred for context to the immediately preceding statement. If it is clear that the subject or object refers to the *fact* of the preceding statement (as an idea or opinion), the subject or object is coded as Category 5.

Examples:

Fa	His parents aren't entitled to know./	
Mo	That's true./	("What you just said" is true./)

Dau	I was under the impression that he/	
Fa	That's kind of stretching it./	("What you just said" is kind of stretching it./)

Code: *Tension*

Purpose

These are five codes designed to measure the degree of tension expressed in the situation. The basic assumption is that any deviation from or disruption of a continuous and connected statement is a mark of tension. The specific codes focus on different types of disruption. All of these are coded directly from the typescript. Some of the summary indices are appropriate for describing an individual's tension and some will describe group tensions.[1]

These measures are similar to those developed by George Mahl, "Disturbances and silences in the patient's speech in psychotherapy," *J. Abnorm. Soc. Psych.*, 53, July, 1956, 1–15.

Summary of Tension Categories

A. Incomplete sentences
    1 Incomplete sentence
    0 No incomplete sentence
B. Repetitions
    1 Repetition
    0 No repetition
C. Fragments
    1 Fragment
    0 No fragment
D. Laughter
    1 Laughter
    0 No laughter
E. Number of Tension Indicators in act
    0 No tension indicators
    1 1 tension indicator
    2 2 tension indicators
    3 3 tension indicators
    4 4 tension indicators

Procedures

1. Each type of tension indicated is coded in a separate card column. The code is a presence/absence one in which, for each act, a separate judgment can be made as to the presence or absence of any specific indicator.

2. Each individual indicator must occur within one act in order to be coded. (The one exception to this is stated in the Repetition code.)

---

[1] The Tension code is referred to in the text as a code for Speech Disruptions. The code category labeled Fragments here is called Incomplete Phrases in the text.

3. Identical words or sets of words may *not* be used as indicators for more than one category. However, the complete act can be given more than one code, so long as different words are used as indicators of tension.

4. *Priority rule.* If the exact same set of words can be coded as an incomplete sentence, a repetition, and a fragment, the following order of priority is used to determine which *one* code is to be used:

(1)   Incomplete sentence.
(2)   Repetition.
(3)   Fragment.

This priority rule applies only to instances when the same set of words is being considered; it does not apply to the whole act.

Categories

Incomplete sentence

1. *Incomplete sentence.* All instances in which the idea has not been completed but the sentence has *not* been interrupted (is not followed by an I) are classified as an incomplete sentence. These only occur at the *ends* of statements. Essentially these are statements that "run down" and are not finished by the speaker. Elliptical sentences such as "yes," "no" are *not* considered to be incomplete.

Examples:

Mo   Because they've already said/*that half of them want*/
Fa   Yes./

Fa   Well, Lew doesn't agree with me *because*/
Mo   No/you don't have/you've got your own opinion./

Mo   I think/he should do his uh clean up his own first/where he's living and *uh*/
Fa   You just answered the question/as it's presented./

Mo   *Oh*/
Fa   Yes./

0.   No incomplete sentence

Repetition

1. *Repetitions.* These include exact repetitions of words, phrases, or complete sentences, defined according to the following rules.

(a) Repetitions that occur within one act: the repeated words must be exactly the same as the first but there may be other words included between them. For example:

Well I I feel that . . ./
He sat *next to* uh *next to* her./

(b) Repetitions that occur across acts are coded only if the entire content of the act is repeated in the exact form of the original and there are no other words or phrases interspersed. For example:

No/No/No/No/
I didn't/I *didn't*/

(c) Instances in which one person repeats another person are *not* coded as repetitions.

(b) Instances in which noncontent verbalizations are repeated in one unit *with* other words intervening, are *not* coded as repetitions. For example:

you've *uh* got *uh* your own *uh* opinion./

(e) Repeated adjectives or adverbs when used for emphasis are *not* coded as repetitions. For example:

He was *very very* good./
It was a *red red* rose./

0. No repetitions.

Fragment

1. *Fragments.* This category codes for the presence of one or more fragments in an act. (The definition of a "fragment" is the same as in Section III-C of the Unitizing Rules.) In general a fragment may be a single word or a combination of words with content that is unclear from the context or the common culture. A fragment may be included in with another complete act or it may be the full statement. Stuttering is included here. Specific rules for use of Category 1 are the following.

(a) Fragments with unclear content; either unclear from the context or unclear in the common culture:

Examples:
So his parents, it's it's inherited./
Uh *just for one person.*/
And there would be, one boy would of course win it./
Or they could try/*have* uh put all their subscriptions together./
Well, I went to the store.

(b) *Noncontent verbalizations* that are included within an act are coded as fragments; noncontent verbalizations are defined as sounds that may carry implied meaning but are not words. A noncontent verbalization that forms the complete statement is *not* coded as a fragment.

Examples:
She *uh* really doesn't want to play the piano./
Uh just for one person./
They could *uh* have something that was *uh*/

(c) "False starts," are coded as fragments, when they are all in one unit. For example:

That uh, well he would just have to./

(d) If an act is an elliptical sentence according to the Unitizing Rules, and thus is clear in context, it is *not* a fragment. (See Section III-A and B of the Unitizing Rules.)

Examples:
Right./
Yes./

Son You're making the child uh/
Mo *Belligerent.*/

0. No fragments.

Laughter

1. *Laughter.* Each individual who laughs is coded as such; the indicator for laughter is an (L) on the typescript, next to the name of the person who laughs. For example:

Mo That's cute. (L)/

0. No laughter.

Number of tension indicators in an act. For each act, code here the *number* of the above four codes in which positive evidence of tension is present.

0 No tension indicators in the act.
1 1 tension indicator in the act.
2 2 tension indicators in the act.
3 3 tension indicators in the act.
4 4 tension indicators in the act.

Code: Who Speaks to Whom

Purpose

The purpose of these two codes is to record who is speaking and to whom that person is speaking. Who speaks to whom is recorded originally on the fourth track of the tape on which the family session is recorded; this is done by the observer watching the session.

The basic data used for the observer's judgment of to whom a statement is directed are the eye movements of the speaker. We assume that a statement is directed toward the person at whom the speaker is looking as he talks. If within his speech, he looks at a second person then the target of the speech is changed accordingly.

This who-to-whom is transferred from the tape to the typescript during the checking operation, and the data on the target of a statement are coordinated with the content of the statement; the initials of the speakers are recorded in the margin next to the typed speech.

Summary of Who-to-Whom Categories

Who Speaks		To Whom	
1	Father	1	Father
2	Mother	2	Mother
3	Child	3	Child
0	N.A.	4	Neither
		5	Both
		0	N.A.

Procedures

The following rules are for use in transferring the who-to-whom information from the typescript to the code sheet. Each act is coded once according to who spoke and once according to whom the speech was directed.

1. In instances in which the "to whom" person changes within one statement (i.e., there are several "to whom" notations in the margin next to one person's speech) we want to record the fact that this change occurred. Record the changed target of the speech into the act that is closest in space to the "to whom" notation. This amounts to the assignment of the "to whom" category to the first act in the nearest line of type.

2. In instances when there are *two* "to whom" notations and only one act into which they can be recorded, change the "to whom" to "Both" Category 5.

3. In instances when there are *two* "to whom" notations and only one act into which they can be recorded and one of the "to whom" is "Neither" the *person* who is spoken to takes priority.

4. If the "who" designation of the observer does not agree with the designation of the person speaking typed on the typescript, the typed speaker takes precedence and should be coded into the "who" category.

5. "Neither" category. This category includes only the instances in which there is positive evidence that the person is speaking to no one, i.e., "neither" must be recorded on the typescript. All instances in which no "to whom" person is recorded are scored into the N.A. category.

Code Categories

Who speaks.

1 Father
2 Mother
3 Child (son *or* daughter)
0 N.A.

To whom.

1 Father
2 Mother
3 Child (son *or* daughter)
4 Neither
5 Both
0 N.A.

References

Bales, R. F. *Interaction Process Analysis*. Cambridge: Addison-Wesley, 1951.

Bales, R. F., Strodbeck, F. L., Mills, T. M., and Roseborough M. E. Channels of communication in small groups. *Amer. Sociological Rev.* (1951), *16*, 843.

Bateson, G., and Ruesch, J. *Communication, the Social Matrix of Psychiatry*. New York: Norton, 1951.

Bateson, G., Jackson D. D., Haley, J., and Weakland J. Toward a theory of schizophrenia. *Behavioral Science* (1956), *1*, 251–264.

Baxter, J. C., Arthur, S., Flood, C. G., and Hedgepeth, B. Conflict patterns in the families of schizophrenics. *J. nerv. ment. Dis.* (1962), *135*, 419–424.

Bell, R. Q. Retrospective and prospective views of early personality development. *Merrill-Palmer Quart. Behav. Develpm.* (1950-60), *6*, 131–144.

Bell, R. Q. A reinterpretation of the direction of effects in studies of socialization. *Psych. Rev.*, forthcoming.

Blalock, H. M., Jr. *Casual Inferences in Non-Experimental Research*. Chapel Hill: University of North Carolina Press, 1961.

Blau, P. M. *Exchange and Power in Social Life*. New York: Wiley, 1964.

Blau, P. Structural effect. *Amer. Sociological Rev.* (1960), *25*, 178–193.

Bleuler, E. *Dementia Praecox or the Group of Schizophrenics*. New York: International Universities Press, 1950.

Blumenthal, M. D. Mental illness in parents of phenylketonuric children. *J. psychiat. Res.* (1967), *5*, 59–74.

Bowen, M., Dysinger, R. H., and Basamania, B. Role of the father in families with a schizophrenic patient. *Amer. J. Psychiat.* (1959), *115*, 1017–1020.

Brodey, W. Some family operations and schizophrenia. *Arch. gen. Psychiat.* (1959), *1*, 379–402.

Caputo, D. V. The parents of the schizophrenic. *Family Process* (1963), *2*, 339–356.

Cheek, F. E. The 'schizophrenogenic mother' in word and deed. *Family Process* (1964a), *3*, 155–177.

Cheek, F. E. A serendipitous finding: sex roles and schizophrenia. *J. abnorm. soc. Psychol.* (1964b), *69*, 392–400.

Cohen, J. A coefficient of agreement for nominal scales. *J. educ. psychol. Measmt.* (1960), *20*, 37–46.

Coleman, J. S. *The Adolescent Society*. New York: Free Press of Glencoe, 1961.

Davis, J., Spaeth, J. L., and Huson, C. Analysing effects of group composition. *Amer. Sociological Rev.* (1961), *26*, 215–225.

Farina, A. Patterns of role dominance and conflict in parents of schizophrenic patients. *J. abnorm. soc. Psychol.* (1960), *61*, 31–38.

Fiske, D., and Maddi, S. *Functions of Varied Experience.* Homewood, Ill.: Dorsey, 1961.

Fleck, S., Lidz, T., and Cornelison, A. Comparison of parent-child relationships of male and female schizophrenic patients. *Arch. gen. Psychiat.* (1963), *8*, 1–7.

Fromm-Reichman, F. Notes on the development of treatment of schizophrenics by psychoanalytic psychotherapy. *Psychiatry* (1948), *11*, 263–273.

Gibbs, J. Norms: The problem of definition and classification. *Amer. J. Sociology* (1965), *70*, 586–594.

Goldfarb, W. *Childhood Schizophrenia.* Cambridge: Harvard University Press and the Commonwealth Fund, 1961.

Goldman-Eisler, F. Speech production and the predictability of words in context. *Quart. J. exper. Psychol.* (1958), *10*, 96–106.

Gottschalk, L. A., Gleser, G. C., and Hambidge, G., Jr. Verbal behavior analysis. *Arch. Neurol. Psychiat.* (1957), *77*, 300–311.

G.A.P. Report: Some observations on controls in psychiatric research, R42, New York: Group for the Advancement of Psychiatry, 1959.

Haley, J. The family of the schizophrenic: a model system. *J. nerv. ment. Dis.* (1959), *129*, 357–374.

Heinicke, C., and Bales, R. F. Developmental trends in the structure of small groups. *Sociometry* (1953), *16*, 7–38.

Kantor, R. E., and Herron, W. G. *Reactive and Process Schizophrenia.* Palo Alto: Science and Behavior Books, 1966.

Kendall, P., and Lazarsfeld, P. Problems of survey analysis. In Robert K. Merton and Paul Lazarsfeld, *Continuities in Social Research: Studies in the Scope and Method of 'The American Soldier'.* Glencoe: Free Press, 1950, pp. 195-196.

Kish, L. Statistical problems in research design. *Amer. Sociological Rev.* (1959), *24*, 328–338.

Laing, R. D. *The Divided Self.* London: Tavistock, 1960.

Lazarsfeld, P. F., and Menzel, H. On the relation between individuals and collective properties. In Amitai Etzioni (ed.), *Complex Organizations.* New York: Holt Rinehart and Winston, 1961.

Lazarsfeld, P. F., and Rosenberg, M. *The Language of Social Research.* Glencoe: Free Press, 1955.

Leik, R. K. Instrumentality and emotionality in family interaction. *Sociometry* (1963), *26*, 131–145.

Lennard, H. L., Beaulieu, M. R., and Embrey, N. G. Interaction in families with a schizophrenic child. *Arch. gen. Psychiat.* (1965), *12*, 166–184.

Lerner, P. M. Resolution of intrafamilial role conflict in families of schizophrenic patients. I: Thought disturbance. *J. nerv. ment. Dis.* (1965), *141*, 342–351.

Lidz, T., Cornelison, A. R., Fleck, S., and Terry, D. The intrafamilial environment of the schizophrenic patient: I. The father. *Psychiatry* (1957a), *20*, 329–342.

Lidz, T., and Fleck, S. Family studies and a theory of schizophrenia. In T. Lidz, S. Fleck, and A. Cornelison, *Schizophrenia and the Family.* New York: International Universities Press, 1965, pp. 362–376.

Lidz, T., Fleck, S., Alanen, Y. O., and Cornelison, A. R. Schizophrenic patients and their siblings. *Marital Psychiatry* (1963), *26*, 1–18.

Lidz, T., Fleck, S., Cornelison, A. R., and Terry D. The intrafamilial environment of the schizophrenic patient: II. Marital schism and marital skew. *Amer. J. Psychiat.* (1957b), *114*, 241–248.

Lu, Y. Mother-child role relations in schizophrenia: a comparison of schizophrenic patients with non-schizophrenic siblings. *Psychiatry* (1961), *24*, 133–141.

Lu, Y. Contradictory parental expectations in schizophrenia. *Arch. gen. Psychiat.* (1962), *6*, 219–234.

Maher, B. A. *Principles of Psychopathology.* New York: McGraw Hill, 1966.

Mahl, G. F. Disturbances and silences in the patient's speech in psychotherapy, *J. abnorm. soc. Psychol.* (1956), *53*, 1–15.

Mednick, S. A. A longitudinal study of children with a high risk for schizophrenia: first three-year follow-up. In *The Origins of Schizophrenia,* Proceedings of the First Rochester International Conference on Schizophrenia. Amsterdam: Excerpta Medica Foundation, 1967.

Mills, T. M. *Group Transformation.* Englewood Cliffs: Prentice-Hall, 1964.

Mishler, E. G. Families and schizophrenia: an experimental study. *Mental Hygiene* (1966), *50*, 552–556.

Mishler, E. G., and Scotch, N. A. Sociocultural factors in the epidemiology of schizophrenia. *Psychiatry* (1963), *26*, 315–353. Reprinted in *Int. J. Psychiatry* (1965), *1*, 258–295.

Mishler, E. G., and Waxler, N. E. Family interaction patterns and schizophrenia: a review of current theories. *Merrill-Palmer Quart.* (1965), *11*, 269–315. Reprinted in *Int. J. Psychiat.* (1966), *2*, 375–413.

Mishler, E. G., and Waxler, N. E. Family interaction and schizophrenia: an approach to the experimental study of family interaction and schizophrenia. *Arch. gen. Psychiat.* (1966), *15*, 64–74.

Mishler, E. G., and Waxler, N. E. Family interaction patterns and schizophrenia: a multi-level analysis. In *The Origins of Schizophrenia,* Proceedings of the First Rochester International Conference on Schizophrenia. Amsterdam: Excerpta Medica Foundation, 1967a.

Mishler, E. G., and Waxler, N. E. Family interaction and schizophrenia: alternative frameworks of interpretation. Paper presented to the Conference on the Transmission of Schizophrenia sponsored by the Foundations' Fund for Research in Psychiatry, Dorado, Puerto Rico, June 26-30, 1967b.

Mishler, E. G., and Waxler, N. E. (ed.) *Family Processes and Schizophrenia: Theory and Selected Experimental Studies.* New York: Science House, 1968.

Morris, G. O., and Wynne, L. C. Schizophrenic offspring and parental styles of communication: a predictive study using excerpts of family therapy recordings. *Psychiatry* (1965), *28*, 19–44.

Parsons, T., and Bales, R. F. *Family, Socialization and Interaction Process.* Glencoe: Free Press, 1955.

Payne, R. W. An object classification test as a measure of overinclusive thinking in schizophrenic patients. *Brit. J. soc. clin. Psychol.* (1962), *1*, 213–221.

Payne, R. W., and Friedlander, D. A. A short battery of simple tests for measuring overinclusive thinking. *J. ment. Sci.* (1962), *108*, 362–367.

Phillips, L. Case history data and prognosis in schizophrenia. *J. nerv. ment. Dis.* (1953), *117*, 515–525.

Reiss, D. Individual thinking and family interaction. *Arch. gen. Psychiat.* (1967), 80–93.

Riley, M. W. *Sociological Research, Vol. 1: A Case Approach.* New York: Harcourt, Brace and World, 1963.

Robinson, W. S. Ecological correlations and behavior of individuals. *Amer. Sociological Rev.* (1950), *15*, 351–357.

Rosenthal, R. *Experimental Effects in Behavioral Research.* New York: Appleton-Century Crofts, 1966.

Ruesch, J. *Disturbed Communication.* New York: Norton, 1957.

Schaffer, H. R. The too-cohesive family: A form of group pathology. *Int. J. soc. Psychiat.* (1964), *10*, 266–275.

Sherif, M. Group influences on the formation of norms and attitudes. In Eleanor E. Maccoby, Theodore M. Newcomb, and Eugene L. Hartley (eds.), *Readings in Social Psychology,* 3rd ed. New York: Holt, Rinehart and Winston, 1958.

Siegel, S. *Non-parametric Statistics.* New York: McGraw-Hill, 1956.

Sharan (Singer), S. N. Family interaction with schizophrenics and their siblings. *J. abnorm. Psychol.* (1966), *71*, 345–353.

Singer (Sharan), S. N. Family interaction with schizophrenic and nonschizophrenic siblings. Unpublished dissertation, Graduate School of Education, Yeshiva University, 1965.

Singer, M. T., and Wynne, L. C. Thought disorder and family relations of schizophrenics: III. Methodology using projective techniques. *Arch. gen Psychiat.* (1965), *12*, 187–200.

Singer, M. T., and Wynne, L. C. Thought disorder and family relations of schizophrenics: IV. Results and implications. *Arch. gen. Psychiat.* (1965), *12*, 201–212.

Slater, P. E. Role differentiation in small groups. *Amer. Sociological Rev.* (1955), *20*, 300–310.

Stabenau, J. R., Tupin, J., Werner, M., and Pollin, W. A comparative study of families of schizophrenics, delinquents, and normals. *Psychiatry* (1965), *28*, 45–49.

Strodtbeck, F. Husband-wife interaction over revealed differences. *Amer. Sociological Rev.* (1951), *16*, 468–473.

Venables, P. H. Input dysfunction in schizophrenia. In Brendan A. Maher (ed.), *Progress in Experimental Personality Research, Vol. 1.* New York: Academic, 1964.

Waxler, N. E., and Mishler, E. G. Scoring and reliability problems in interaction process analysis: a methodological note. *Sociometry* (1966), *29*, 28–40.

Webster's New Collegiate Dictionary, 2nd ed. Springfield: Merriam, 1956.

Weintraub, W., and Aronson, H. The application of verbal behavior analysis to the study of psychological defense mechanisms. *J. nerv. ment. Dis.* (1962), *134*, 169–181.

Wynne, L. C., Ryckoff, I., Day, J. and Hirsch, S. Pseudomutuality in the family relations of schizophrenics. *Psychiatry* (1958), *21*, 205–220.

Wynne, L. C., and Singer, M. T. Thought disorder and family relations of schizophrenics, I. A research strategy. *Arch. gen. Psychiat.* (1963), *9*, 191–198.

Zelditch, M. Jr. Role differentiation in the nuclear family: A comparative study. In Talcott Parsons and Robert F. Bales (eds.), *Family, Socialization and Interaction Process.* Glencoe: Free Press, 1955.

Zuk, G. Boszormenyi-Nagy, I., Heiman, E. Some dynamics of laughter during family therapy, *Family Process* (1963), *2*, 302–314.

Zuk, G. On silence and babbling in family psychotherapy with schizophrenics. *Confin. Psychiat.* (1965), *8*, 49–56.

Index